# The Falklands Military Machine

## Captain Derek Oakley, MBE, RM

Guild Publishing
London

# The Falklands Military Machine

### Captain Derek Oakley, MBE, RM

**In the Spellmount Military list:**

*The Territorial Battalions – A pictorial history*
*The Yeomanry Regiments – A pictorial history*
*Over the Rhine – The Last Days of War in Europe*
*History of the Cambridge University OTC*
*Yeoman Service*
*The Fighting Troops of the Austro-Hungarian Army*
*Sea of Memories*
*Intelligence Officer in the Peninsula*
*The Scottish Regiments – A pictorial history*
*The Royal Marines – A pictorial history*
*The Royal Tank Regiment – A pictorial history*
*The Irish Regiments – A pictorial history*
*British Sieges of the Peninsular War*
*Victoria's Victories*
*Heaven and Hell – German paratroop war diary*
*Rorke's Drift*
*Came the Dawn – 50 Years an army officer*
*Marlborough – as military commander*
*Kitchener's Army*

**In the Military Machine list:**

*Napoleon's Military Machine*
*Wellington's Military Machine*
*Falklands Military Machine*

**In the Nautical list:**

*Sea of Memories*
*Evolution of Engineering in the Royal Navy Vol 1
1827-1939*

**In the Aviation list:**

*Diary of a Bomb Aimer*

**Falklands Military Machine**

This edition published in 1989 by
Book Club Associates
by arrangement with
Spellmount Ltd
12 Dene Way, Speldhurst,
Tunbridge Wells, Kent TN3 0NX

CN 4907

© Ravelin Limited 1989

Design by Ravelin Ltd, Braceborough, Lincs.
Figure artworks by Richard Scollins.
Cartography by Transmedia Graphics, Binstall, Leics.
Typesetting by Vitaset, Paddock Wood, Kent.
Printed in Great Britain by W.S. Cowell Ltd, Ipswich, Suffolk.

# The Falklands Military Machine

## Captain Derek Oakley, MBE, RM

# Introduction

With a total population of 1,800 spread over 4,700 square miles of inhospitable country, little known to the people of Great Britain before 1982, the Falkland Islands seem an unlikely place for a nation to go to war. With the demise of the British Empire in the post World War 2 era, the granting of independence to colonies, protectorates and other dependencies, there were few directly administered territories left to Great Britain. It was therefore the protective instinct, a throw back to the pioneering colonial spirit that kindled and burnt within the heart of the country when the Argentinians blatantly contravened international law and invaded the Falklands.

The limited strategic and commercial value of these islands cannot be denied, but they were a British possession. They lie 400 miles from the South American mainland on an ocean trading route of yore, one still widely used for traffic between the maritime nations of the area. It is a region where British influence has waned through the years, although Argentina boasts the largest ex-patriot British population of any country in South America.

To set this small dependency into perspective, we must first look at its geographical features. Over 1,000 of the population lived in the capital, Port Stanley, while the remainder were spread across the almost equally sized islands of East and West Falklands. More than a hundred other small islands comprise the group and the loftiest peak is Mount Usborne at 2,312 feet above sea level. The islands are chiefly moorland, a mixture of peat bog and scree over which nearly three quarters of a million sheep graze. It is rolling countryside, somewhat reminiscent of Dartmoor with rocky crags topping the many peaks. There are virtually no trees, just a few scrubby bushes, and the wind and snow swept hills are bleak and forbidding.

There is little of value in the mineral deposits on the islands, but the accumulation of blocks of quartzite, irregular in form, but having a tendency to long runs and sharp points, make it a difficult terrain to negotiate. The stone runs appear as though they are gently sliding down into the valleys.

The coastline is long, rambling and until recently mostly uncharted. It is inundated with bays and creeks, inhabited by penguins and sea birds. Indeed the ornithological life is one of its main attractions with sea fishing providing a living for some. Those who live out on 'camp', as the countryside beyond Port Stanley is called, are farmers or kelpers, named after the 'kelp' or seaweed, in touch with their fellows only by radio and the occasional visit. Roads are almost non existent, the one exception being an unsurfaced track between Stanley and the second largest community, Goose Green and the nearby Darwin of 100 people, on the west coast of East Falklands. They are a hardy, taciturn race, almost totally of British stock, regarding themselves as purely English, this being their only language.

Those living on West Falklands, which takes the full brunt of the cold, predominantly westerly winds of the region, were even more isolated, the settlements grouping themselves mainly around Fox Bay and Port Howard. The mean temperature at the height of summer is only 50°F, although 77° was once recorded. In the winter, when this campaign was fought, the mean day temperature was barely four degrees above freezing and mostly below that, particularly at night. It needs a tough, dedicated person to survive in these conditions, let alone make a living. The climate during the southern winter is generally damp, with rain, although not often heavy, falling on an average of 250 days a year. The freezing temperatures and lack of shelter afford little chance of drying out once you are exposed.

Wild life abounds around the coast with three types of penguins breeding there migrating to the mainland, 400 miles away, in the winter. Upland geese, which can be edible, outnumber the sheep while grebes, gulls and other sea birds offer the ornithologist an uninhibited treasure trove.

The other islands that are part of our story are South Georgia and South Thule. The former is about 800 miles east of the Falklands and virtually uninhabited since the closure of the whaling stations at Grytviken and Leith in the 1950s. It is about 100 miles long and 18 miles at its widest with many bleak mountainous peaks rising over 7,000 feet, the highest being Mount Paget at 9,925 feet. Although 800 miles north of the Antarctic Circle the islands are covered with over 150 glaciers running down to the hundreds of bays and inlets and the weather generally far worse than the Falklands. In 1982 the British Antarctic Survey Team of 30 were based at Grytviken and two freelance photographers, Cindy Buxton and Annie Price, were filming near Leith. They were the only human inhabitants of South Georgia which was administered by Governor Rex Hunt at Stanley.

Southern Thule is an inhospitable islet a further 500 miles south east of South Georgia where there was a small scientific and meteorological base which had been occupied by the Argentinians since 1976.

The Falklands were first discovered by the Arctic explorer John Davis on 14 August 1592, and two years later Sir John Hawkins, an English adventurer also sighted them. Sailing these southern oceans Willem Schouten was the first to round and name Cape Horn in 1616. The Southern Atlantic also became a favourite with the Spanish and Dutch fleets when buccaneering was at its height and rich prizes could be gleaned from the trading routes. However it was more than 70 years later that the first recorded landing was made on the islands by a privateer John Strong on 27 January

1690. He is thought to have named the passage between the two main islands after Lucius Cary, Viscount Falkland who had been killed at the battle of Newbury, but it was more likely that he named it after Anthony Carey, the 5th Viscount Falkland who became First Lord of the Admiralty in 1693.

It was not until 1748 when Commodore Anson returned from a round the world voyage that he suggested that a 'convenient station' might be sought in the region to make us 'masters of those seas'. In fact he had never sighted the Falklands. At this time the trade war between the maritime nations of England, Spain, Portugal and France was at its height and many clashes occurred off the coast of South America. On Anson's recommendation the Admiralty sent an expedition under Commodore Byron who raised the Union Flag on Saunders Island on 23 January 1765, claiming sovereignty in the name of King George III, little knowing that the French had landed Canadian settlers at Port Louis on the eastern side of the islands a year earlier. The first British garrison arrived twelve months later and the Royal Marines started their long asso-

*The memorial on Darwin Hill to those men of 2 Para who lost their lives in the battle for Goose Green. It shows the typical bleak and featureless terrain over which much of the campaign was fought. Coupled with the Antarctic winter weather it was a cold, wet and uncomfortable war.*

ciation with the islands, when 25 of them erected a wooden block house at Port Egmont on West Falkland. In 1766 the French, who had also claimed sovereignty, formally handed over the islands to the Spanish and they sent a garrison to Port Louis, now named Soledad, on 1 April 1767 giving them the name 'La Islas Malvinas'.

A strong Spanish force of five sloops forced the British garrison to surrender their settlement on West Falkland in June 1770, but a favourable agreement was later reached. The British government took this as an affront and although they mobilized the fleet, they decided because of a lack of French support, to abandon the islands completely in 1774, but not before the *Endeavour* had fixed a lead plaque stating clearly the claim to sovereignty. The Spanish remained at Port Louis until 1816 when the Plate

colonists broke away from Spain and formed their own independent countries in South America. The Spanish then abandoned their settlement.

Various visits were made to the islands in the next two decades, the French and Americans squabbling over trading rights. In 1829 Louis Vernet set up a new colony at Soledad in the name of Buenos Aires, but the settlement suffered at the hands of the Americans. On 20 December 1832 Captain Richard Onslow in the sloop *Clio* arrived at Port Egmont 'exercising the rights of sovereignty', but did not formally take possession until 3 January 1833 when the outnumbered Argentine garrison surrendered.

It was in January 1834 that the frigate *Tyne* landed a small party of seamen and marines to govern and rebuild the colony. From that day onwards the British maintained a continuous presence in the islands, slowly developing the limited potential of the settlement. In 1843 Letters Patent established the colony and Lieutenant Richard Moody of the Royal Engineers was appointed the first Governor and Commander-in-Chief. In July 1845 he moved the capital to its present site at Port Stanley, but the growth of the settlement was slow. Three years later sheep farming was introduced to the colony and in 1866 the Falklands Islands Company was established.

Port Stanley became the only service station on the trading route round Cape Horn from Montevideo to Valparaiso, and the increase in steam ships enhanced its importance, but the British government did not take advantage of this when it failed to set up a coaling station. Argentina made more overtures in 1864 even adding Islas Malvinas to their maps claiming the islands were essentially a part of Patagonia with which they are connected by a submarine plateau and therefore by rights Argentinian. The British government rebuked the claim politely but firmly, saying that negotiations would not be re-opened.

Whilst not resorting to force, the Argentinians continued grumbling. In 1879 the small Royal Marine garrison was withdrawn as an economy measure, and the civil administration was elevated to full colony status on 29 February 1892 by an Order-in-Council. Meanwhile relations between Chile and Argentina were strained over territorial claims to the southern tip of the mainland nearly resulting in war until they surprisingly agreed to British arbitration in December 1902. Chile was given access to both the Atlantic and Pacific Oceans in the Beagle Channel, while Argentina was awarded most of Patagonia including the eastern half of Tierra del Fuego. However the islands to the south were given to Chile, and continued to be a subject of contention for many years.

In 1910 the first permanent radio link between the Falklands and the mainland was established, the signals just reaching Punta Arenas in Southern Chile, 400 miles away, where there was a cable link to London. In 1914 at the outbreak of the First World War, a Royal Marines garrison was once more established, being landed from the battleship *Canopus* and fuel storage tanks were built. A new

*Vice Admiral Graf von Spee's fleet shelter in Valparaiso after their successful victory over the British fleet at the Battle of Coronel on 1 November 1914. Five weeks later, after First Lord of the Admiralty Winston Churchill despatched two powerful battle cruisers, the British soundly defeated von Spee at the Battle of the Falklands.*

**EAST FALKLAND**

*Fanning Head*

Douglas

Port San Carlos

San Carlos

*San Carlos Water*

Port Salvador

Teal Inlet

*Grantham Sound*

*Berkeley Sound*

Estancia House

Camilla Creek House

**STANLEY**

*Port William*

Bluff Cove

Airport

Darwin

Fitzroy

Goose Green

*ia*

*Choiseul Sound*

Lively Island

N

100

wireless station was set up and a cable link laid to Uruguay. Two 6-inch guns from the old cruiser *Lancaster* were set up on Sapper Hill, these still being in place in 1982, though long unserviceable. The great sea Battle of the Falklands took place on 8 December 1914 and it is interesting to note that Admiral Sturdee flew his flag in the battleship *Invincible*, a forebear of the aircraft carrier that was to play such an important part in the same waters 68 years later.

It was a quiet period between the wars, when relations between Great Britain and Argentina were generally good. Trade was brisk between the two countries, but the growing dominance of American influence south of the equator was affecting Argentina's prosperity. A military coup in 1930 engendered a wave of nationalism and her economy boomed for a time. Although there were still rumblings about sovereignty, it was not until 1933 when Britain issued a centenary set of commemorative stamps for the Falklands Islands that contention once again rose.

In retaliation the Argentines issued their own Malvinas stamp and refused visas to those born in the Falklands. Although they did not take their case to the League of Nations, they touched on the subject at international meetings when they felt it appropriate. They even laid claim to South Georgia and other Antarctic territories.

Having witnessed the first major engagement of World War 1, the area also saw the first major naval battle of World War 2 when the German pocket Battleship *Graf Spee* was forced into Montevideo where she was scuttled at the mouth of the River Plate. The British ships *Ajax*, *Achilles* and *Exeter* had refuelled and repaired in Stanley before the battle, and the base was subsequently commissioned as HMS *Pursuivant* on 5 March 1941.

Argentine, whilst maintaining strict neutrality, sympathised with the Axis cause. A coup in 1943, whilst most

*The German pocket battleship* Admiral Graf Spee *lies scuttled in the estuary of the River Plate after being cornered by the small British force of* Ajax, Achilles *and* Exeter. *Both sides suffered severe damage in the action in this engagement in the South Atlantic on 13 December 1939, the first naval battle of World War 2.*

British attention was focussed elsewhere, brought a strong Junta to power whose ambitions to expand were more forthright than their predecessors. They turned their eyes southwards and eastwards into Antarctica, encapsulating the Falklands on the way. They sent survey parties proclaiming sovereignty to occasional British bases, until Britain was forced to set up the Falklands Islands Dependencies Survey in 1944, establishing more permanent bases on Grahamland.

The upsurge in national socialism within Argentina was fuelled by the dictator-like qualities of Juan Peron from 1945 onwards. He became obsessed in his desire to challenge disputed territory in the area and once again the Falklands came into the limelight. The growth of Pan-American influence in South America did nothing to stop Peron's march. In 1959 the Antarctic Treaty demilitarised the disputed area and Britain withdrew its main interests to the Falklands, South Georgia and the Sandwich Islands. This again fired the Argentine press into action, demanding the return of the islands. Children at school, some who were to be fighting in 1982, were taught that the Falklands belonged to them. In 1948 the Organisation of American States was formed at which the Argentine delegate reitterated his country's claim. At the same time *Pursuivant* was closed and the wireless station turned over to the Falklands civil administration. This was a move which provoked violent demonstrations in the streets of Buenos Aires. An Argentine Naval Task Force was assembled and only the intervention of the British Foreign Secretary, Ernest Bevin, defused a potentially dangerous situation, when he proposed limitations on the number of ships deployed south of the 60° south latitude. This was surprisingly agreed to.

In view of the unsettled situation it was decided to send HM Ships annually to visit the Falklands and from 1953 their Royal Marines detachments were landed regularly to visit as many outlying areas of 'camp' as possible, thus reassuring the population of Britain's good intent. One isolated violation occurred in September 1964 when an Argentine pilot landed on Stanley racecourse, planted an Argentinian flag, delivered a message and promptly took off again.

Subsequently the ice patrol ship *Protector* landed her detachment annually until in 1965 Naval Party 8901 was formed and remained as the garrison till they were overrun on 2 April 1982.

There was yet another intervention on 28 September 1966 when an extremist group of Argentine nationalists hijacked an air liner and landed at Port Stanley to try to capture the islands, even taking some hostages. The incident was brought

*The Falklands Islands lie about 400 miles from the Argentine coast, which meant that fighter aircraft operating from bases on the mainland had to fly at the limit of their range unless air-to-air refuelling was available. The British declared a 200 miles Total Exclusion Zone on 30 April and long range bombing attacks on Stanley airfield by RAF Vulcans and Sea Harriers of the Task Force began the following day.*

my foundered.

The confrontation with Chile which all but escalated into open war in 1978, along with their continued claims to the Falklands, kept the Argentine people's eyes off their internal economic collapse. The national debt was astronomical with so much foreign spending. She continued to re-arm, buying the Exocet missile and two corvettes from France and fighter bombers from Israel and France.

General Videla resigned in December 1981, General Galtieri, who was already Commander-in-Chief of the army, taking his place. From the outset Galtieri's passion was the Malvinas, and speculation about a possible invasion was rife in the Argentine press in the early days of 1982.

In February Argentina once again raised the matter in the United Nations, demanding monthly meetings between themselves and Great Britain over the Falklands. The British played down the issue but agreed to keep talking and both sides felt reassured at developments. It seemed a strange time for the British to announce that this would be *Endurance*'s final deployment to Antarctica. The Royal Marines' garrison and the British Antarctic Survey Team in South Georgia and other territories felt isolated and abandoned. But Captain Nick Barker of *Endurance* had visited Argentina twice in the early months of 1982, once for a goodwill visit to the naval base at Ushuaia where the ship had a cool reception, and in February to Mar del Plata which had been warmer, but where he had been able to feel the political temperature at first hand. He sent warnings to the British government, but these were interpreted as an effort to save his ship from being withdrawn. Even the Joint Intelligence Committee briefings given regularly to the British Prime Minister gave little indication that anything untoward was happening. When the Argentine scrap metal merchants landed at Leith in South Georgia on 19 March *Endurance* was paying her farewell visit to Port Stanley. Ironically she was not to reach the UK until much later that year . . . and indeed return again to the South Atlantic in the following years.

to a close when Royal Marines surrounded the plane and the whole incident passed off without bloodshed or a shot being fired. The hijackers were returned to Argentina where they were imprisoned after trial.

From then on relations between Britain and Argentina improved. It was quite clear that the Islanders wished to remain part of the British Commonwealth, the disputed passport issue was withdrawn, and regular air and sea services were resumed to the mainland. In 1973 Peron returned from a 20 year exile to become President once more and nationalistic feeling was again stirred up. In turn there was a demand for the return of the Falklands to Argentina and the case was taken to the United Nations. On Peron's death in 1974 the Argentine press took up the Falklands issue again demanding immediate action by the government and the following year Britain responded by saying that any attack on the islands would be met with force.

In 1975 Lord Shackleton who had led an economic enquiry into the future of the whole area announced his findings, but the report was quickly repudiated by Argentina who broke off diplomatic relations with Britain. *Endurance* had been on her final Antarctic deployment in 1974, but this was rescinded in the light of the strained relations. Yet again the Argentine armed forces seized power in 1976, the powerful Junta under General Videla inheriting an economically unstable country. It imprisoned its opponents unmercifully and the United States protested at the United Nations about inhumanity when some 8,000 people who opposed the regime were either locked up or just 'disappeared'. Meanwhile Argentina was still disputing territorial regions in the south with Chile and a Court of Arbitration was set up, agreed by both nations, which pronounced judgment in favour of Chile in 1977. This angered the Argentinians and the country started a programme of re-armament, plundering the nation's dwindling resources, so that the econo-

# British Diplomacy

When he ordered the Argentine invasion of the Falklands, General Galtieri was confident that his gamble could not fail. He had only been in power a short time and needed a successful bold step which would not only satisfy the Junta, but also take the minds of the Argentinians off their internal economic troubles. Whilst he expected a mild reaction in the United Nations, he did not think that Britain would take military action so far from home and reckoned the UN would admonish him but take no further action, perhaps being glad to be rid of an age-old problem. Furthermore, he thought that the USA would remain neutral as she did not wish to involve herself in controversy over South American affairs, particularly where a state was trying to stem Communism. His foreign minister Dr Costa Mendez had been patiently wooing the United States for many months. By default Galtieri considered he would be able to take possession of the Malvinas in an almost bloodless coup, and the whole matter would soon be forgotten.

What he misjudged was Mrs Margaret

*General Leopoldo Galtieri, head of the military junta in Argentina since December 1981, flanked by two of his predecessors, General Videla (left), who resigned in March 1981 and General Viola (right) who took over for nine months.*

Thatcher, the British Prime Minister's stubborn determination to re-possess the islands by any means. When the First Sea Lord, Admiral Sir Henry Leach offered her the military wherewithal, her resolve was further strengthened. Her first aim was to ensure that she showed to the world that Britain meant business by despatching a strong Task force, and her second was to gain international support for her actions, particularly from the United States and UN. She had already stressed that Britain was the aggrieved nation and that her duty was to defend and preserve British sovereignty in a territory however small.

Even before the Argentinian's landed on 2 April Mrs Thatcher had urged President Reagan to press General Galticri to withdraw his invasion fleet, which he did using the words 'my friend Margaret Thatcher'. On Saturday 3 April, the day that Britin held an emergency parliamentary debate, both Sir Nicholas Henderson, Britain's Ambassador to the USA, and Sir Anthony Parsons, the Representative in the UN, were hard at work. The latter had called for a Security Council meeting condemning Argentine action and was supported by the necessary 10 votes, only Panama voting against, while Russia, whose adverse vote would have vetoed the motion, and Spain, who was negotiating joining the Common Market, along with China and Poland abstained. The Americans, who could no doubt see a similarity with the Suez crisis of 1956,

when they remained neutral, voted in favour of Britain. From that moment both sides used the USA for their prime negotiations.

The Security Council passed Resolution 502, though curiously not condemning Argentine aggression, and called on her to withdraw her forces from the Falklands, meanwhile urging both sides to seek a diplomatic solution. Argentina chose to ignore the call. Britain's triumph in the UN allowed her the right to use force in 'self defence if an armed attack occurs' to remove the Argentines. It also gave her an important bargaining point. In London the well respected British Foreign Secretary, Lord Carrington insisted that the Prime Minister accepted his resignation. Although he felt that much of the criticism levelled at the Foreign Office was ill-founded, he wrote '*The fact remains that the invasion of the Falkland Islands has been a humiliating affront to this country.*' John Nott, the Defence Secretary also offered his resignation but this was not accepted.

On 7 April President Reagan offered his Secretary of State, General Al Haig, who had recently retired as the military head of NATO and was sympathetic to the British cause, as a mediator. The following day Haig flew to London, where Mrs Thatcher unequivocally gave her views that there could be no solution unless the Argentines withdrew their forces. This was the message he took to Buenos Aires on 10 April, where he received an equally frosty and uncompromising welcome from General Galtieri. Haig lacked Dr Henry Kissenger's diplomatic skills and returned to London on 13th before flying to Washington to report to his government. His only bargaining points were for both sides to withdraw while a temporary administration was set up to negotiate the question of sovereignty. A final trip to Buenos Aires and back completing 35,000 miles in 12 days, again bore no fruit, but both sides were fully aware of the other's intransigent resolve.

Meanwhile both the British Task Force and Amphibious Force had sailed amidst much euphoria and publicity. In Brussels the European Community's Council of Ministers had announced economic sanctions against Argentina on 9 April. Britain broke off diplomatic relations and imposed her own trade sanctions. Just over a fortnight later

*The US Secretary of State, General Al Haig, who shuttled between Washington, London and Buenos Aires on peace missions, meets General Galtieri and Dr Costa Mendez.*

## Senior Personalities

*Prime Minister:
  **Mrs Margaret Thatcher**
*Home Secretary and Deputy Prime Minister:
  **William Whitelaw**
*Foreign Secretary:
  **Lord Carrington** (*resigned*)
  **Francis Pym**
Foreign Affairs Spokesman in House of Commons:
  **Humphrey Atkins** (*resigned*) –
  **Cranley Onslow**
Minister of State to the Foreign Office:
  **Richard Luce** (*resigned*)
Permanent Under Secretary of State to Foreign Office:
  **Sir Anthony Acland** (*recently Chairman of the Joint Intelligence Committee*)
*Secretary of State for Defence:
  **John Nott**
Permanent Under Secretary of State to Ministry of Defence:
  **Sir Frank Cooper**
Chancellor of the Exchequer:
  **Sir Geoffrey Howe**
Secretary to the Cabinet:
  **Sir Robert Armstrong**
*Paymaster General and Chairman of the Conservative Party:
  **Cecil Parkinson**
*Chief of the Defence Staff:
  **Admiral of the Fleet Sir Terence Lewin**

British Ambassador to the United Nations:
  Sir Anthony Parsons
British Ambassador to the United States of America:
  Sir Nicholas Henderson

*members of the 'War Cabinet'*

Note: **Sir Michael Palliser**, until recently Permanent Under Secretary of State to the Foreign Office was also called upon as an adviser, as was **Sir Ian Sinclair**, the Foreign Office legal adviser.

Argentina secured support at a meeting of the Organisation of American States, which recognised her sovereignty over the Malvinas and condemned Britain's retaliatory action. However, much of this support was no more than lip service while the USA, Chile, Colombia (who later changed her mind) and Costa Rica all abstained. It is significant that Chile, a long time adversary of Argentina remained friendly to Britain, and no doubt provided facilities and intelligence as the war escalated.

*Foreign Secretary Lord Carrington resigned from office saying that the Argentine invasion had been a humiliating affront to the country.*

Haig's failure to secure peace and his outward display of neutrality slowly turned to outright support for the British cause. It had taken nearly a month for America to declare her hand. Indeed her considerable involvement in allowing the use of Wideawake airport on Ascension had been played down in the early stages, although American tankers and support ships were busy topping up supplies there.

Further diplomatic moves were in hand on 1 May when General Haig and President Belaunde of Peru suggested a peace plan to the United Nations Secretary, General Javir Pérez de Cuellar, and that he might be the mediator. This coincided with the sinking of the *General Belgrano*, then the *Sheffield* and Galtieri quickly rejected any further moves. However, after a meeting with the new British Foreign Secretary Francis Pym, de Cuellar persisted and produced a six-point peace plan on 7 May and this was discussed seriously for more than a week. At one time it appeared that the Argentinians might be giving ground on sovereignty, and Sir Nicholas Henderson and Sir Anthony Parsons flew back for meetings with Mrs Thatcher on 14 May, returning to New York with an outline agreement on 17th. Argentina's flat refusal ended all hopes of a diplomatic settlement and four days later the British landed on the Falklands.

# British Political Command and Control

The Falkland Islands had their own constitution with Mr Rex Hunt as Governor and Commander-in-Chief, a Foreign Office appointment. He administered his authority through an Executive Council which consisted of two members nominated by the Governor, two elected members, the Chief Secretary and Financial Secretary. In addition there was a Legislative Council which had an additional six elected members. These two councils were responsible for the day to day running of the territory. Rex Hunt, a former RAF fighter pilot, but with 34 years service in the Overseas Civil Service, was a very experienced diplomat, having previous appointments in Malaya, Borneo, Indonesia, Vietnam and Uganda. He had arrived in the Falklands as Governor in February 1979.

The British Government was responsible for the external relations and defence of the Islands, through the Foreign and Commonwealth Secretary, Lord Carrington. As such they provided limited military support in the form of Naval Party 8901 of about 40 Royal Marines, who served in the Islands on a one-year tour, while HM Ships visited occasionally, especially HMS *Endurance* the arctic ice-patrol ship. Some of the essential services were run by local people, but many were sent out under contract by the Ministry of Overseas Development.

In April 1982 the British political team was headed by the Prime Minister, Margaret Thatcher, with Lord Carrington as her Foreign Secretary and John Nott as Defence Minister. Lord Carrington was a senior party member with an impeccable background in foreign affairs. He had been the natural choice when Margaret Thatcher formed her government in May 1979. A hereditary peer, Lord Carrington did not have a seat in the House of Commons, and initially his spokesman in the lower House was Sir Humphrey Atkins, who was acting Foreign Secretary during Lord Carrington's visit to Israel in late March. The junior Foreign Office minister was Richard Luce, who had recently taken over from Nicholas Ridley. Although Luce was an expert on Africa, he had recently turned his attention to the Americas and had, indeed, visited the Falklands.

As the crisis developed after the Argentine scrap metal merchants incident in South Georgia, conflicting and confusing statements were being made by ministers in London. Nott seemingly dismissed the threat in the South Atlantic during a debate in the House on Trident on 29 March, when former Navy Minister Keith Speed asked why £3 million could not be spent on refitting *Endurance*. The reply that the issues of Trident 'are too important to be diverted into a discussion on *Endurance*' did not please Speed who had resigned after Nott's damaging cuts in the 1981 Defence Review. Sir Humphrey Atkin's statements to the House after the invasion of the Falklands also appeared misleading and confusing.

In Britain the cabinet had overall responsibility for all decision making, acting on the advice of cabinet committees. The one concerned with the Falklands affair was the Defence and Overseas Policy Committee, which was chaired by the Prime Minister and included the Foreign Secretary, Lord Carrington, the Chancellor of the Exchequer, Geoffrey Howe and the Defence Secretary, John Nott. The Chiefs of Staff attended when ordered. At the time of the crisis the Chief of the Defence Staff was Admiral of the Fleet Sir Terence Lewin, the First Sea Lord, Admiral Sir Henry Leach, the Chief of the General Staff, General Sir Edwin Bramall and the Chief of the Air Staff, Air Chief Marshal Sir Michael Beetham. Sir Robert Armstrong, the Cabinet Secretary serviced this committee.

Immediately after the Falklands invasion Lord Carrington, Sir Humphrey Atkins and Richard Luce resigned, but John Nott's offer of resignation was rejected. Into their places came Francis Pym as Foreign Secretary and Cranley Onslow as Minister of State for Foreign Affairs. Sir Anthony Acland had, until recently, been Chairman of the Joint Intelligence Committee and was now Head of the

*John Nott, Secretary of State for Defence, offered his resignation after the Argentinians invaded the Falklands, but this was not accepted by the Prime Minister.*

*The Prime Minister, Mrs Margaret Thatcher, whose strong determination and firm resolve was one of the major factors in winning the war.*

Diplomatic Service and the senior civil servant in the Foreign Office. As the situation worsened, the decision making fell into the hands of the 'war cabinet', although major decisions, like the sending of the Task Force, still had to be agreed by the full cabinet.

The 'war cabinet' consisted of the Prime Minister, the Deputy Prime Minister and Home Secretary William Whitelaw, the Foreign and Defence

## The Defence Council

Secretary of State for Defence:
**Rt Hon John Nott MP**
Minister of State for Defence Procurement:
**The Viscount Trenchard MC**
Minister of State for the Armed Forces:
**Peter Blaker MP**
Parliamentary Under Secretary of State for Defence (Armed Forces):
**Jerry Wiggin MP**
Parliamentary Under Secretary of State for Defence (Defence Procurement):
**Geoffrey Pattie MP**
Chief of the Defence Staff:
**Admiral of the Fleet Sir Terence Lewin GCB, MVO, DSC**
Chief of Naval Staff and First Sea Lord:
**Admiral Sir Henry Leach GCB, ADC**
Chief of the General Staff:
**General Sir Edwin Bramall GCB, OBE, MC, ADC**
Chief of the Air Staff:
**Air Chief Marshal Sir Michael Beetham GCB, CBE, DFC, AFC, ADC**
Vice Chief of the Defence Staff (Personnel and Logistics):
**Air Chief Marshal Sir David Evans GCB, CBE**
Permanent Under Secretary of State:
**Sir Frank Cooper GCB, CMG**
Chief Scientific Adviser:
**Professor Sir Ronald Mason FRS**
Chief of Defence Procurement:
**Sir Clifford Cornford KCB**

Secretaries and the Paymaster General, who was also Chairman of the Conservative Party, Cecil Parkinson. It should be noted that the Chancellor of the Exchequer was not a member of this small committee at a time when financial considerations could be vitally important. All Service matters were presented by the Chief of the Defence Staff, with other service Chiefs attending as required. There is no doubt that Francis Pym, a newcomer to the Foreign Office and John Nott, who appeared to have little enthusiasm for the conflict, were the weak links in the chain and unable to contribute much compared with their more experienced colleagues in the cabinet. Indeed John Nott's performance at the specially convened emergency sitting of the House of Commons on Saturday 3 April was particularly poor.

Although the 'war cabinet's' decisions were passed direct to Northwood, where the Task Force Commander

(Commander-in-Chief Fleet), Admiral Sir John Fieldhouse, had his headquarters, there was more than one occasion when political goading from Whitehall led to unnecessary and unwelcome pressure being applied direct to military commanders in the South Atlantic. Modern communications, so often the most important factor in war, suddenly became an interfering influence.

There was no doubt that the Government were helped by the support from the majority of the British people, who were equally incensed that Argentinian aggression should not go unpunished. With the strong leadership and determination of Margaret Thatcher, a highly skilled and professional military force, it was clear that Britain meant business from the outset. Whilst political negotiations to secure a peaceful solution continued apace, the Task Force left the United Kingdom fully prepared for any contingency that might arise.

# Task Force Command and Control

It was clear from the outset that the re-occupation of the Falkland Islands would primarily be a maritime operation, and it was therefore inevitable that the Royal Navy took the most prominent part. It was pure coincidence that the current Chief of the Defence Staff was an Admiral of the Fleet, Sir Terence Lewin, who had been First Sea Lord from 1977-79, when he took up his present post as the principal defence adviser to the Government. In late March 1982 he was abroad, attending the NATO Nuclear Planning Group in the USA followed by a meeting of the Five Power Defence Agreement in New Zealand.

Keeping in daily contact with London, he was fully aware of the worsening situation, but Defence Minister John Nott suggested he should not return home early as it might cause unnecessary alarm if he cut short an official visit. Whilst abroad his deputy was Air Chief Marshal Sir Michael Beetham, Chief of the Air Staff, but for some reason he was not invited to the first crisis cabinet meeting on 31 March. It was quite by chance that the First Sea Lord, Admiral Sir Henry Leach was at the House of Commons that evening to call on his own Minister. Leach had been visiting a naval establishment in Portsmouth during the day and on returning to his office, had found a Falklands situation brief on his desk. His fortuitous arrival at the House of Commons coincided with the cabinet meeting and he was called in by the Prime Minister to give his views.

Admiral Leach, who had crossed swords with John Nott over defence matters more than once in the previous two years, undoubtedly feared that the minister might not be too forceful in offering to despatch a Task Force, and he welcomed the opportunity to put the Navy's case personally. His view was that whilst nothing he could do would prevent an Argentine invasion, immediate plans must be made for the re-occupation of the Falklands. No military force could do this without being transported over 8,000 miles with Royal Navy protection. He told the cabinet that a balanced 're-trieval force could sail within days', which would include both his aircraft carriers and 3rd Commando Brigade, whose units were all in the UK at the time. Leach was well versed in naval politics and confidently put forward his case. His forthright advice was an embarrassment to the cautious Nott, and he quietly revelled in being able to score against his 'adversary', particularly when the Prime Minister appeared to hang on his every word. On his return to his office, Leach immediately took the precautionary measure of warning off all major elements that were likely to be required and even ordered some submarines to sail south. This rescinded the pessimistic Nott's earlier assessment that there was 'no requirement' for 3 Commando Brigade, for in the early hours of 2 April, only one day later, they were placed at 72 hours notice to move.

This meeting was probably the most crucial of the emergency as it persuaded the cabinet to authorise the immediate despatch of the Task Force, even though the Foreign Office undoubtedly wished to avoid further provocation in the South Atlantic; but this was over-ruled. Britain's determination to make a show of force resounded around the world, not least in Argentina. Whether the Chief of the Defence Staff would have been quite as forthright in putting his case as his First Sea Lord is a matter for conjecture, but the decision to send the Task Force was taken in his absence, and on his return he put his full weight behind the decision. Admiral Lewin played a vital role in attending and briefing all War Cabinet meetings and his inter-service impartiality, quiet confidence and constructive advice was beyond reproach.

The Chief of the General Staff, General Sir Edwin Bramall, expressed reservations about the hasty actions when the Chiefs of Staff Committee met the following day, as did the Chief of the Air Staff, but it was too late. Both willingly accepted Leach's view and wholeheartedly put the machinery of both the Army and the Royal Air Force into motion. It was clear that the immediate despatch of the Task Force was imperative in case the politicians had a change of heart. All along it was appreciated that a diplomatic solution might be found, but any wavering on the part of the military might be construed as an inability to do the job.

The Command structure for the Task Force was confused. As this was to be primarily a naval campaign the Commander-in-Chief Fleet, Admiral Sir John Fieldhouse was appointed the Task Force Commander (CTF 317). His Headquarters was at Northwood in Middlesex, where his staff carried out their task in the Fleet Operations Room situated in an underground chamber. In addition to commanding the seagoing fleet, Fieldhouse was also Allied Commander-in-Chief Channel and Commander-in-Chief Eastern Atlantic Area, both NATO appointments. Already co-located at Northwood were Vice Admiral Peter Herbert (Flag Officer Submarines) and Air Marshal Sir John Curtiss, command-

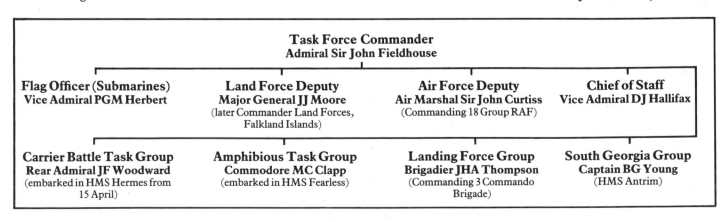

| Task Force Commander<br>Admiral Sir John Fieldhouse | | | |
|---|---|---|---|
| **Flag Officer (Submarines)**<br>Vice Admiral PGM Herbert | **Land Force Deputy**<br>Major General JJ Moore<br>(later Commander Land Forces,<br>Falkland Islands) | **Air Force Deputy**<br>Air Marshal Sir John Curtiss<br>(Commanding 18 Group RAF) | **Chief of Staff**<br>Vice Admiral DJ Hallifax |
| **Carrier Battle Task Group**<br>Rear Admiral JF Woodward<br>(embarked in HMS Hermes from<br>15 April) | **Amphibious Task Group**<br>Commodore MC Clapp<br>(embarked in HMS Fearless) | **Landing Force Group**<br>Brigadier JHA Thompson<br>(Commanding 3 Commando<br>Brigade) | **South Georgia Group**<br>Captain BG Young<br>(HMS Antrim) |

*Brigadier JHA Thomspon CB, OBE, who commanded the 3 Commando Brigade from the initial planning to the final battle for Stanley, being dubbed 'Man of the Match'.*

ing 18 Group Royal Air Force, which controlled all maritime air operations. Curtiss became the Air Deputy to the Task Force Commander and was responsible for all air operations in the South Atlantic.

The decision that 3 Commando Brigade would spearhead the military retrieval force in an amphibious operation meant that the Chief Military Adviser should ideally be a Royal Marines Officer. The Major General Commando Forces, based at Plymouth, who had a fully constituted staff, was the obvious choice. Major General Jeremy Moore should have been relieved in this appointment prior to his imminent retirement in May. However the Commandant General of the Royal Marines had been seriously injured in an IRA bomb attack in December 1981 and Moore, as the senior Royal Marines General Officer had acted in his stead and continued to serve. Moore, with some of his staff, immediately moved to Northwood, initially in an

*Major General Sir Jeremy Moore KCB, OBE, MC★, accompanied by Lieutenant Colonel NF Vaux DSO, talks to WO2 D Greenhough at an inspection of 42 Commando after the campaign.*

advisory capacity as the Land Forces Deputy, and later was appointed the field commander as Commander Land Forces Falkland Islands. On 20 May he flew to Ascension to join 5 Infantry Brigade in the *QE 2* for the journey south.

The naval command became more complex as the campaign progressed. Initially there were five task group commanders, who reported directly to the Task Force Commander (CTF 317); Rear Admiral 'Sandy' Woodward commanded the Carrier Battle Task Group (CTG 317.8); Commodore Mike Clapp the Amphibious Task Group (CTG 317.0); Vice Admiral Peter Herbert the Submarine Task Group; Brigadier Julian Thompson the Landing Force Group (CTG 317.1); and Captain Brian Young in *Antrim* the South Georgia Group (CTU 319.9). All but one were in the South Atlantic and each reported directly to Northwood. This untidy situation meant that Woodward had no direct control over the amphibious group, nor even the South Georgia operation. Only Clapp and Thompson sailed in the same ship, *Fearless*.

The appointment of Woodward over the heads of more senior colleagues, caused some disquiet, but he was already at sea as Flag Officer First Flotilla, in command of Exercise *Springtrain* in the Mediterranean. It was the majority of his ships that formed the spearhead of the Task Force that was ordered south, and he was the natural choice.

One of the consequences of this chain of command was that, while all the information flowed back to Northwood, it was not always easy for the staffs there to disseminate the information, nor appreciate the local conditions prevailing at any time in the South Atlantic. Whilst commanders 'in the field' could communicate with each other direct, their orders came from the United Kingdom. It was thus that Woodward, Clapp and Thompson, all operating in the same area, received orders from the Task Force Commander, which were not always consistent with the ever-changing tactical situation on the spot, and were sometimes resented as interference. Conversely, modern satellite communications gave a swift response to requests from those down south, as was seen in the permission granted to alter the Rules of Engagement to allow *Conqueror* to attack the *General Belgrano*.

More personal command and control was exercised in the planning stages for the recapture of the Islands. Admiral Fieldhouse, Air Marshal Curtiss and Major General Moore flew out to Ascension on 16 April for a planning meeting with Commodore Clapp and Brigadier Thompson on board Admiral Woodward's flagship *Hermes*. Here the Task Force Commander briefed his subordinates on the current political climate, the proposed plans and his overall assessment, while they in turn gave their views. As a result all commanders were fully acquainted with both the latest political situation and, more importantly to them, the main military objectives which were: to establish a sea blockade around the Falklands; to retake South Georgia for

use as a secure base and transit area; to establish air and sea supremacy around the Falklands; and finally to re-possess the Islands.

A fortnight later on 29 April, Moore again flew to Ascension to be briefed aboard *Fearless* by Clapp and Thompson on their proposals for an amphibious landing to re-take the Islands. He returned to Northwood with three alternative plans, discussed in a later chapter, which were ultimately approved by the Chiefs of Staff and presented to the War Cabinet.

When it was decided to send a reinforcement Brigade, it became necessary to appoint a Land Forces Commander of

*Rear Admiral Sir John (Sandy) Woodward, who was Flag Officer First Flotilla, commanded the Carrier Battle Task Group with a brilliant strategic and tactical approach.*

Divisional status. As Major General Moore had been involved from the start in an advisory capacity, he was the obvious choice, even though the force would have five Army battalions out of the eight involved. The staff of the Major General Commando Forces was also immediately available and well versed in combined operations. The Army had no spare Divisional Commander, but Lieutenant

General Richard Trant, GOC South-East District, moved to Northwood as the military adviser. When Moore was appointed as Land Forces Commander on 20 May, the day before the San Carlos landings, Thompson theoretically reverted to commanding 3 Commando Brigade, while Brigadier Tony Wilson commanded the reserve force of 5 Infantry Brigade, still on their way south. However, as Moore was at sea in the *QE 2*, a troopship, and without direct communications with the amphibious force, Thompson remained in command of the land forces until the arrival of the divisional headquarters on 30 May. From then onwards, Moore took command of the Land Forces in the Falkland Islands, co-ordinating and giving orders for the final battles for Stanley, subsequently receiving and signing the instrument of surrender.

During the course of the naval campaign, various Task Units were formed for specific tasks with individual commanders, such as the first group of ships *Brilliant, Glasgow, Coventry, Sheffield* and *Arrow*, under Captain John Coward, to be sent hurriedly south were designated CTU 317.8.2, until the task was completed. Later a group of three Type 42 destroyers and one Type 21 under command of Captain Sam Salt in *Sheffield* were likewise designated CTU 317.8.2.

Ashore the situation was clearer, with 3 Commando Brigade commanding all units until the arrival on 30 May of Headquarters Land Forces Falkland Islands with 5 Infantry Brigade. However there were many grey areas in the realms of control, particularly of naval helicopter and landing craft assets. These remained under the control of Commodore Clapp at sea in *Fearless*, though they were urgently required for military use by the Brigade ashore during the build up and later for operating forward to Teal Inlet in the north and Bluff Cove in the south. The tasking system was untidy and led to conflicting priorities and frustrating shortages of assets particularly when logistic supplies were being built up.

The facility of satellite communications also had an adverse effect from time to time. When the Government were pressing for action to break out from the San Carlos beachhead, mainly for political reasons, Northwood were told in no uncertain terms to get on with it. Thomp-

*Brigadier Julian Thompson (in beret) and Major General Jeremy Moore, both Royal Marines, in conference on the slopes of Mount Kent before the final battle for Stanley.*

son, 8,000 miles away, was summoned to the clear voice link and given direct orders to take Goose Green. His reluctance to move until he had built up sufficient logistic reserves could not be easily understood by those sitting in the bowels of London, and was frustrating to a field commander, who could make a far more detailed and accurate assessment of the local situation.

With such a complex operation, there are bound to be anomalies in command and control, but generally the system worked adequately. Some friction was caused, but this was generally kept within reasonable bounds while everyone got on with the job of winning the war. Speed and secrecy are the essence of military operations, and as the command of all sea, land and air operations remained with the Task Force Commander in Northwood, the Government could be kept fully informed of the progress of the war. Major decision making at War Cabinet level was much easier and though the latter interfered occasionally, they had the added responsibility of placating media pressure and world opinion.

# The Military and the Media

Although the Americans experienced the media on their doorstep during the Vietnam War, this was the first time, with the exception of the Iran Embassy siege and the continuing struggle in Northern Ireland, that the British Forces had faced instant newspaper and television coverage. Their ability to deal with it was probably one of the most controversial aspects of the campaign. It was a no-win situation on both sides.

In time of war the needs of the military and the interests of the press are basically opposite. Included in a paper issued later to the journalists in the task force was *'The essence of successful warfare is secrecy. The essence of successful journalism is publicity.'* This acknowledged that there was liable to be hostility in relations from the outset. After the war the House of Commons Defence Committee identified two basic principles; the right of the public to know, and the government's duty to withhold information in the cause of operational security.

When the conflict broke out, the Ministry of Defence Public Relations Office, situated on the ground floor of Main Building in Whitehall, was immediately besieged by demands from London, provincial and foreign newspapers for representation when the task force sailed. The MOD had no contingency plans for handling the media in such a situation. When the Commander-in-Chief Fleet was asked how many correspondents he would allow to sail, the first answer was none, begrudgingly raised to six then twelve to include *one* television team (combined BBC and ITV sharing the same cameraman). This provoked more difficulties than it solved, particularly as the Royal Navy was adamant that no more spaces could be allocated. Ian MacDonald, temporarily head of DPR, but not himself a PR Specialist, suggested that the press be flown to Ascension Island to join the task force, which would have given a couple of weeks breathing space. However the Navy's strong opposition to more than 10 press travelling forced the Director of the Newspapers Publishers' Association on 4 April to decide which correspondents should be allowed to sail with the Task force and to be at Portsmouth that night. With five places already allotted to TV and another to the Press Association, the four remaining places went by ballot to the Daily Mirror, Daily Telegraph, Daily Express and Daily Mail.

However the intervention of the Prime Minister's Press Secretary, Bernard Ingham and the Minister of Defence John Nott ensured that an adequate and representative group of correspondents, 29 was finally agreed, eventually sailed with the task force, accompanied by three MOD Press Officers. But even so no foreign correspondents were admitted. 15 journalists, now including two full TV teams, sailed in *Hermes* and *Invincible* on 5 April with a further 13 aboard the SS *Canberra* four days later. Others caught up with the groups at Ascension.

The MOD press officers, 'minders' as they came to be known, were unprepared and inexperienced at dealing with the aggressive weight of the Press. They tried vainly to interpret the security rules laid down by the MOD and still keep in tune with the journalists, becoming unwilling censors of their reports. Meanwhile the Press had to rely on extremely limited naval communications and inconsistent censorship to send their stories, not helped by the fact that the Navy were going to war and every moment of air time was precious. Briefings on board were curt and unhelpful, the Minders being aware of the security

*Brian Hanrahan of BBC Television News, had just returned from a sailing holiday when the crisis broke. His quiet manner, accurate reporting and delightful turn of phrase made him, along with Robert Fox of BBC and Michael Nicholson and Jeremy Hands of Independent Television News, household names.*

---

## Media Embarked in the Task Force

*HMS Invincible*

| | |
|---|---|
| Alfred McIlroy | Daily Telegraph |
| Gareth Parry | Guardian |
| Michael Seamark | Daily Star |
| Tony Snow | Sun |
| John Witherow | Times |
| Roger Goodwin | MOD Press Officer |

*HMS Hermes*

| | |
|---|---|
| Brian Hanrahan | BBC Television |
| Bernard Hesketh | BBC Cameraman |
| John Jockell | BBC Sound Recordist |
| Michael Nicholson | Independent Television News |
| Peter Heaps | ITN engineer |
| Peter Archer | Press Association |
| (*later Richard Savill*) | *Press Association*) |
| Martin Cleaver | Press Association photographer |
| Robin Barratt | MOD Press Officer |
| (*later Graham Hammond* | *MOD Press Officer*) |

*SS Canberra*

| | |
|---|---|
| Patrick Bishop | Observer |
| Ian Bruce | Glasgow Herald |
| Leslie Dowd | Reuters |
| Robert Fox | BBC Radio |
| Max Hastings | London Standard |
| Charles Lawrence | Sunday Telegraph |
| Martin Lowe | Wolverhampton Express & Star |
| (*later Derek Hudson* | *Yorkshire Post*) |
| *Robert McGowan | Daily Express |
| Alastair McQueen | Daily Mirror |
| *David Norris | Daily Mail |
| Kim Sabido | Independent Radio News |
| John Shirley | Sunday Times |
| *Tom Smith | Daily Express photographer |
| Jeremy Hands | Independent Television News |
| Robin Hammond | ITN cameraman |
| John Martin | ITN sound recordist |
| Martin Helm | Senior MOD Press Officer |
| Alan George | MOD Press Officer |
| Alan Percival | MOD Press Officer |

*Joined at Ascension Island

implications of saying anything that might be misinterpreted.

Journalists tried devious means to get their messages home, Brian Hanrahan of BBC TV on board *Invincible* uttering the immortal words '*I counted them all out, and I counted them all back*', when describing Sea Harriers on a mission. Meanwhile London editors were thirsty for more, adding their own excruciating headlines such as the Sun's 'GOTCHA!' after the sinking of the *General Belgrano*. The BBC Panorama programme of the 10 May, focussing on opposition to the sending of the Task Force, caused even more furore and was described as 'subversive travesty'. It did nothing but underline the Prime Minister's personal war with the media. One of her chief concerns was to maintain high public morale at home and she was worried at what might appear on our television screens.

In the Task Force life for correspondents was no less difficult. There was little reportable news as the fleet steamed slowly south until tragedy struck. The reporting of the sinking of the *Sheffield* is a prime example of how *not* to handle a situation. The ship was hit about 2pm, confused signals started arriving in London and by 7pm it was clear that a statement would have to be made soon. Only minutes before the BBC Nine o'clock News was due on the air, Mrs Thatcher agreed that some details should be released. In the sombre tones of Ian MacDonald, the announcement shocked

*The slow, measured tones of Ian MacDonald, the MOD's acting Head of Public Relations, seen here with Lieutenant Colonel Tim Donkin Royal Marines, brought the Falklands War daily into everyone's home.*

the nation, but none more so than the relatives of men serving aboard. No information on casualties could possibly be available to those manning the information desks of Services Welfare officers in the ship's home base of Portsmouth, let alone elsewhere. Families were destined to wait anxiously and suffer far more than the men serving in the South Atlantic through media pressure for instant news.

Retired Service Officers appeared regularly on TV and radio discussing possible courses open for the Task and Landing Forces. These were mostly inspired but reasoned guesses, and often hit upon the truth. The media and these officers were accused, mostly unfairly, of giving too much away to the enemy.

There were technical problems in the fleet too. Transmitting television pictures by satellite at sea was exceptionally difficult from a heaving platform. Film had to be shipped to Ascension for onward transmission, later appearing out of date to an eager public. Had direct satellite broadcasts been readily available, the problems of censorship in Whitehall, without an intimate knowledge of the immediate tactical situation, would have been immense. There was a suspicion

among correspondents that technical objections were often used by the Navy as an excuse not to transmit. Radio was easier to control.

After the war considerable weeding had to be done before transmission of TV pictures taken during the campaign could be released. Harrowing scenes of the badly burned and limbless victims were able to be cut. What if they had been broadcast live to an unsuspecting nation in their sitting rooms?

The Government and MOD were accused, often unjustly, that they told only half the truth at press briefings in London. Maybe so, but is it not better to conceal the real secrets of military tactics than to jeopardise the safety of those troops actually taking part? A radio broadcast can be read by the enemy on the ground within minutes of it being transmitted. With modern communications even a newspaper report can find itself on the other side of the world in less than half an hour.

Robert Harris, in his book 'Gotcha! The Media, the Government and the Falklands Crisis', sums up the media war admirably. He concludes '*The instinctive secrecy of the military and the Civil Service; the prostitution and hysteria of sections of the press; the lies, the misinformation, the manipulation of public opinion by the authorities; the political intimidation of broadcasters; the ready connivance of the media at their own distortion all these occur as much in normal peace time in Britain as in war.*'

21

# Chapter One
# The Naval Forces

The most remarkable factor in the whole Falklands campaign was the speed with which the naval Task Force was mounted. From the moment the Argentine scrap metal merchants landed on South Georgia on 19 March, the Royal Navy had been taking a closer look at their contingency plans for the South Atlantic area. On 27 March the British Government had been alerted to the threat of a probable Argentinian invasion. Even before 29 March, two days before Argentina invaded the Falkland Islands, the Commander-in-Chief Fleet at Northwood had been taking precautionary measures based on intelligence reports. On 31 March the First Sea Lord, Admiral Sir Henry Leach, a former gunnery officer whose father had gone down when commanding the *Prince of Wales* in 1941, found himself giving his views personally to the Prime Minister. He claimed he could despatch a Fleet, which included 3rd Commando Brigade, but without the other Services, if necessary, 'within days'. It would then take at least three weeks to reach the Falklands. The following day the Government took the decision to re-take the islands, actually before the Argentinians had landed!

Despite the small size and age of much of the Argentine Fleet, just 1 aircraft carrier, 1 cruiser, 6 destroyers, including two modern Type 42s carrying Sea Dart systems and Exocet launchers, 3 submarines, 3 corvettes, also armed with Exocet, and a number of smaller craft, the threat they posed, over 8,000 miles away, could hardly be ignored. The enemy were within easy reach of their home ports, where they could shelter and resupply in comparative safety.

Like the other services, the Royal Navy had been badly hit by continuous cutbacks in Government defence spending. The 1981 statement, which threatened to reduce the fleet to little more than an anti-submarine force for the North Atlantic, had hit the Royal Navy particularly hard, but fortunately many of the measures had not yet been effected. Admiral Leach had clashed with Defence Minister John Nott more than once over the issue.

The Royal Navy had 2 aircraft carriers, 16 destroyers, 44 frigates and 31 submarines of which about a quarter were either undergoing refits or were in moth-balls. The amphibious force consisted of 2 assault ships and 6 LSLs, the former due to be phased out in the 1980s. *Endurance*, the one ice patrol ship, was on its last commission in the South Atlantic and all future eyes were turned to our NATO commitment.

It is interesting to contrast the 1982 fleet with that of 1956 when the last amphibious operation took place during the Suez crisis. The Royal Navy then had 14 aircraft carriers, 20 cruisers, 68 destroyers, 186 frigates, 54 submarines, 66 landing ships and craft, about half of which were in reserve, and only a small proportion were actually involved, there being large Far East and East Indies Fleets.

The 1982 fleet was based on the carriers *Hermes* and the new *Invincible*, but even these were not expected to be in service beyond 1984. The former was about to be sold to Chile and the latter to Australia, although they would have been replaced by *Illustrious* and *Ark Royal*. Both assault ships were due to be scrapped with the Royal Navy relying on chartered roll-on roll-off ferries for their Royal Marines Commando amphibious force. The total strength of the Royal Navy was 74,000, of whom 8,000 were Royal Marines, organised into a fighting strength of 3rd Commando Brigade of three Commandos (similar in size to Army battalions), two raiding squadrons of landing craft and a Special Boat Squadron.

The Fleet Air Arm had nearly 500 helicopters in a variety of types, divided between anti-submarine, troop carrying and communications aircraft. In addition there were 28 Sea Harriers, the versatile V/STOL jet fighter still untested in battle. These were organised into five squadrons, one of which was a training squadron.

51 warships were deployed on Operation *Corporate* along with over 200 aircraft in 14 Naval Air Squadrons. Despite appalling weather conditions a 90% servicability rate was maintained throughout. At the time there were minor operational commitments in Hong Kong and the Middle East where the Gulf War was interfering with British tankers. There was also a Caribbean guardship operating out of Belize, showing the flag in the West Indies. In the early part of 1982 *Invincible* had conducted its first loading trials with 40 Commando embarked. This proved an invaluable experience in the weeks to come, although the ship was ultimately not to be deployed in the Commando role. *Hermes* had spent much of February exercising with 40 Commando, and indeed the ship reported that over a period of a few days, they carried aboard 29 helicopters, 5 Sea Harriers, 72 vehicles, 70 trailers, a battery of 105 mm guns and a total of 2,511 men for a quick dash exercise. These exercises at least made the crews of each ship think 'amphibious'.

In the Mediterranean, the NATO Exercise 'Springtrain' had involved 16 British destroyers and frigates, most of which were to sail south direct from Gibraltar. The exercise had been commanded by Flag Officer First Flotilla, Rear Admiral JF 'Sandy' Woodward, who, being in the right job at the appropriate time, was immediately appointed Task Force Commander over the heads of some more senior colleagues. Although he had been at a Whitehall desk for the previous three years, he was now at sea and commanding the group of ships that would form the spearhead of the new task force.

Admiral Woodward was a submariner by trade, had commanded the cruiser *Sheffield*, subsequently becoming Direc-

tor of Naval Plans. He was a highly intelligent and forceful officer who did not suffer fools gladly. His background could not have been more appropriate to the job in hand, being brought up in the post-war era of nuclear engineering and advanced computer systems, having an intimate knowledge of anti-submarine warfare whilst he had also been involved in much of the Navy's contingency planning.

As early as 2 April he had been ordered to prepare seven ships to sail south to join the three ships already in the South Atlantic. From 'Springtrain' came the destroyers *Antrim* and *Glamorgan* with their Exocet MM.38s, *Coventry*, *Glasgow* and *Sheffield* with their Sea Dart anti-aircraft missiles and *Brilliant* who could provide point air defence with her Sea Wolf system, along with one general purpose frigate *Arrow*. The older Ikara Leanders were unlikely to be of much use and most were in need of refit or repair, as was *Battleaxe*. The ships paired off with those going south to transfer stores and personnel, an operation completed by last light on 2 April, at the same moment the Argentinians were establishing themselves in Stanley.

*HMS* Plymouth, *patrolling off Chanco Point in Falkland Sound, was attacked by Dagger fighters on 8 June. She was hit by four bombs, none of which exploded, and claimed one aircraft shot down. Standing by is HMS* Avenger.

The main strength of the 1982 Navy lay in its submarine force, which was the only part to be in the throes of growth. Four Polaris submarines, of which only one is on patrol at any time 'somewhere in the world', are the country's main nuclear deterrent. None of these were admitted to be directly deployed in the recapture of the Falklands. However, *Valiant*, four other hunter-killers and one patrol submarine played an important part in keeping the Argentine fleet guessing and safely bottled up in their harbours. The only offensive action was by *Conqueror* when she sunk the *General Belgrano*, while *Onyx* landed SBS patrols in the islands.

Back at home in early April, all available naval ratings were soon employed alongside their Dockyard compatriots in preparing, altering and fitting out warships and STUFT ships for their role. 54 merchant ships were requisitioned and most had to be fitted with Replenishment At Sea (RAS) gear and compatible naval communications for working with the fleet. 15 were fitted with helicopter pads and Harrier facilities were added to container ships. Many ships in refit or reserve were brought forward and civilian shipyards completed three new ships, *Illustrious*, *Liverpool* and *Brazen* ahead of time, although none of them reached the South Atlantic until after the war. Over 30,000 tons of provisions, ammunition and stores and 500,000 tons of fuel were loaded and shipped during the three months of the campaign. Gibraltar dockyard, which had been all but run down, did a magnificent job, alongside those at Portsmouth, Devonport and Rosyth.

Work went on in the naval dockyards and repair yards 24 hours a day, the wartime spirit being rekindled in an effort to beat all records and ensure that the ships and men were properly equipped for the job ahead. The Government's determination to take back the Falklands was mirrored in the sailing of the Royal Navy's Task Force, which amazingly left UK only four days after the Argentines had invaded.

# Submarines

In a war such as that in the South Atlantic, the British submarine basically played a deterrent role. Only one aggressive act was perpetrated, that of the sinking of the *General Belgrano*, though vital intelligence gathering and patrolling were a very positive contribution.

Great Britain possessed three types of submarines, Ballistic Missile submarines (SSBN), Fleet submarines (SSN) and Patrol submarines (SSK), all with a different task within the framework of the Government's defence policy. At the time of the Falklands crisis, Great Britain had four SSBNs, eleven SSNs and about sixteen SSKs. At any one time approximately one third of these would be refitting and another third undergoing minor maintenance or harbour time. It is with the second of these groups, the SSNs, that we are mainly concerned. In addition there was the possible presence of the one Polaris submarine, constantly on patrol somewhere in the world and capable of staying submerged for long periods. Along with the Special Boats Service and Special Air Service operations, the submarine service keeps its secrets well.

*Valiant* (Commander TM Le Marchand) was the first all British nuclear powered submarine and came into service with her sister ship *Dreadnought* in the mid 1960s. She is powered by a small pressurised water-cooled nuclear reactor which produces steam to drive her turbines. She is armed with 21″ torpedoes which can be fired from six forward tubes. The Mark 24 Tigerfish torpedo, which had recently been introduced, is initially wire guided from the submarine, having an active/passive homing device for its final attack. It can run in depths down to 300 feet at nearly 45 knots with a range of 18 miles, seeking out surface or submerged targets. It weighs 3,410 lbs. *Valiant* has a complement of 14 officers and 95 ratings and she is capable of staying submerged for months at a time, having a maximum speed of around 28 knots under water. She has internal ballast tanks, so that the pressure hull takes up the whole girth of the ship making it comparatively roomy. She is self sufficient for fresh water and some oxygen can be produced by electrolysis for additional 'fresh air'.

The Churchill class, of which *Courageous* (Commander RTN Best) and *Conqueror* (Commander CL Wreford-Brown) were part, were newer and improved designs. This class, approximately the same size as *Valiant*, carried only five bow tubes but were faster. The later Swiftsure class of SSNs, which included *Spartan* (Commander JB Taylor) and *Splendid* (Commander RC Lane-Nott), were the result of further improvements in design and performance. They were structurally larger than their predecessors carrying a slightly smaller complement and were capable of longer under water patrols without need of shore support. Amenities were improved which included a distilling plant and laundry, besides newly designed air conditioning and purification plant.

A new anti-ship weapon, the Harpoon UGM-84, was coming into service in 1982 and, during trials two years earlier, *Churchill* had fired this American weapon to great effect. It is launched through the 21″ torpedo tubes by compressed air, and on reaching the surface, a booster rocket ignites causing it to rise and home in on a pre-determined surface target up to 60 miles. For the first time it has given a submarine an over the horizon capability.

The normal task of these SSNs was to seek and destroy enemy submarines and surface ships, but world wide surveillance was included in their clandestine role. Conditions were cramped with the crew knowing that if they were detected and attacked, there was little chance of escape. Submarines normally operate singly but the difficulty of underwater communications where radar and radio waves do not travel well is a major drawback. On the other hand sound travels four times faster than in air though not uniformly, thus making sonar the most important factor in their operating. The correct interpretation of acoustic information is paramount but it depends on such diverse factors as currents, tides, even surface weather and sea life. Atmospheric pressure and the saltiness of the water both have their effects too.

A submariner's job in the cold wastes of the South Atlantic was akin to a blind person, and a particularly high standard of alertness and determination was demanded and maintained.

*Spartan*, *Splendid* and *Conqueror* all arrived in the South Atlantic on 11 April, and while the latter went to South Georgia, the two SSNs patrolled between the Argentine coast and the Falklands.

*HMS* Conqueror, *the Fleet submarine which sank the* General Belgrano *on 2 May, passes HMS* Penelope. *This act effectively bottled up the Argentine Fleet in their home ports. She sailed from Faslane in Scotland on 4 May with Royal Marines of 6 SBS and was on constant patrol throughout the campaign.*

**S 105 HMS Onyx** (*Oberon Class – Patrol Submarine*)
1,610 tons (2,400 tons submerged)
Length: 89.9m
Beam: 8.1m
Draught: 5.5m
Propulsion: 2 × Admiralty Diesel: 2 English Electric motor
Speed: 15 knots (submerged)
Complement: 6 officers, 62 ratings
Armament: 6 × 53cm bow torpedo tubes; 2 × stern tubes
Builders: Cammell Laird
Launched: 18 August 1966
Commissioned: 20 November 1967

*The view through the periscope of an 'O' Class submarine, engaged in exercising with a British Type 42 destroyer. HMS Onyx, which arrived in the TEZ on 31 May, was the only diesel-electric patrol submarine deployed, and besides her deterrent role, landed SBS and SAS teams.*

They were able to impose the Maritime Exclusion Zone which had been established on 12 April. There is little doubt that, had they sighted the Argentine aircraft carrier *25 de Mayo* they would have sunk her. As it was, one of them kept an eye on the approaches to Stanley Harbour.

The third type of submarine *Onyx* (Lieutenant Commander AP Johnson), was the last of her class to be completed, but even so was 15 years old in 1982. Her diesel engines needed surface recharging periodically, though this could be done through the snorkel. Fitted, like her big sisters with 6 forward tubes, she additionally had two stern tubes. These fire the older Mark 8 homing torpedo, which runs at a pre-set depth down to 60 feet at up to 45 knots and weighs 3,375 lbs. Her main task was to operate in coastal waters, land and pick up the SBS and gather information and intelligence, but she was equally capable of hunting and killing both enemy submarines and surface ships. Living and working conditions are cramped compared with the larger fleet submarines, with limited washing facilities for her crew of 6 officers and 62 ratings. There is little room for recreation other than reading and occasional films. After the war, on 21 October, *Onyx* carried out her one overt action when she torpedoed the abandoned Argentinian transport *Bahia Buen Suceso* which had originally landed the scrap metal merchants at Leith and had now been towed into deep water off South Georgia.

During the Falklands campaign it was only acknowledged that a total of six submarines were deployed, though some others were at sea. They provided a constant threat out of all proportion to their numbers to the Argentine Navy and played a silent but vital role in the campaign. It was known that *Splendid* had sailed from Faslane on 1 April and *Spartan* from Gibraltar on the same day. Three days later *Conqueror* sailed from Faslane with No 6 SBS embarked. The four SSNs on station by the end of May made sure that no enemy warship ventured further than 12 miles from their coast, at the same time reporting on merchant shipping movements in the area. The arrival of *Onyx* in the South Atlantic on 31 May gave the SBS and SAS a welcome addition to their clandestine operations. Previously they had been landed from smaller warships, which were more liable to detection by the enemy, but they now had a submarine capable of a more stealthy and probably undetected approach when they were inserted into the hinterland.

A submariner's life is, of necessity, boring with long periods, often weeks, submerged. The Fleet submarines are more spacious than the Patrol submarines, with excellent facilities for recreation, including films, videos, library and even exercise bicycles and rowing machines. Submarines carry about 15 weeks supplies of food which is usually very good and menus varied. This helps the men to maintain an extremely high standard of alertness at all times, besides being able to relax when off duty. It is ironic that for many years the Royal Navy had concentrated on deploying both SSNs and SSKs in the ASW role; during this campaign they found themselves playing a traditional anti-surface warship role. The deterrent patrolling of these submarines kept the Argentine Fleet guessing and mostly bottled up in their home ports after the sinking of the *General Belgrano*, allowing the Royal Navy command of the South Atlantic.

**S 50 HMS Courageous** (*Churchill Class – Fleet Submarines*)
3,500 tons (4,900 tons submerged)
Length: 86.9m
Beam: 10.1m
Draught: 8.2m
Propulsion: 1 × PWR; 2 English Electric steam turbines
Speed: 25 knots (submerged)
Complement: 13 officers, 96 ratings
Builders: Vickers (Barrow)
Launched: 7 March 1970
Commissioned: 16 October 1971

**S 48 HMS Conqueror** (*As above*)
Launched: 18 August 1969
Commissioned: 9 November 1971

**S 105 HMS Spartan** (*Swiftsure Class – Fleet Submarine*)
4,200 tons (4,500 tons submerged)
Length: 82.9m
Beam: 10.1m
Draught: 8.2m
Propulsion: 1 × PWR; 2 General Electric steam turbines
Speed: 30 knots (submerged)
Complement: 12 officers and 85 ratings
Armament: 5 × 53cm bow torpedo tubes
Builders: Vickers (Barrow)
Launched: 7 December 1978
Commissioned: 22 September 1979

**S 106 HMS Splendid** (*As above*)
Launched: 5 October 1979
Commissioned: 21 March 1981

# Aircraft Carriers

At the end of World War 2 the Royal Navy ran down its large aircraft carrier fleet so that at the time of Suez in 1956 it had only fourteen. Although the importance of naval air power had seldom been underestimated, by 1982 the continued stringent cut backs in the Services had reduced the Navy to just three aircraft carriers. No more fixed wing carriers would be built and long range air defence of the Fleet and air strikes on enemy ships would be in the hands of the Royal Air Force. However the need to deploy anti-submarine helicopters saw the introduction of the through deck carrier for V/STOL aircraft, capable of operating the Sea Harrier. These aircraft would provide local air defence around the Fleet and against surface targets, as well as providing ground attack planes in support of land forces, independent of the RAF.

The Fleet Air Arm had taken more than its fair share of these cuts. One carrier was the ancient *Hermes* (Captain LE Middleton), now 22 years old and the other *Invincible* (Captain JJ Black MBE) the first of the modern through deck carriers only 2 years old. The second, *Illustrious* has not yet been completed, while *Ark Royal* was still under construction. It is ironic that the government had proposed to sell *Invincible* to Australia, but this decision was rescinded as a result of the Falklands campaign.

*Hermes* had been transformed from a normal fixed wing carrier in 1971/73 to a Commando carrier as a replacement for *Albion*, retaining her secondary role as an anti-submarine helicopter carrier. But by 1976, after another refit, she changed her role to a CVS (anti-submarine support ship). A further refit in 1980/1 transformed her again, adding a Harrier capabililty, whilst still retaining, in very much a secondary capacity, her ability to carry a Commando Force for short periods at sea. During 1981 she practised her new role, exercising Sea

*HMS* Hermes *was the flagship of Rear Admiral JF 'Sandy' Woodward during the Falklands campaign. Built in 1959 she had been refitted twice since and in 1982 had the dual capability of ASW/ Harrier strike carrier with a secondary role of commando ship.*

Harriers and deploying to the United States for a goodwill trip with 130 marines of 41 Commando embarked. Her public relations visit when the Harriers showed off their paces in front of huge crowds persuaded the United States Marine Corps to buy a large number of these versatile aircraft.

In the early months of 1982, the ship exercised with 40 Commando in her amphibious role, when over 900 commandos embarked for two major landing exercises on the south coast of England. If a longer sea journey was anticipated she had to disembark her Sea Harriers and ASW Sea Kings to make room for the embarked troops and their stores. The ship still retained four LCVPs slung in davits for this role, another bonus for her subsequent employment in the South Atlantic. In early March she carried out anti-submarine exercises in the south western approaches and on 19 March she arrived at Portsmouth for a Dockyard Assisted Maintenance Period.

*Hermes* had a complement of 960 officers and men apart from her embarked squadrons or troops. She had been fitted with a 7° ski-jump ramp, the flight deck having already been angled to 6.5° during an earlier refit. She also had added the American WSC-3 SATCOMM equipment, which was to become crucial

**RO 12 HMS Hermes**
28,700 tons
Length: 227.9m (overall); 198.1m (waterline)
Beam: 34.1m (Flt Deck); 27.4m (waterline)
Draught: 8.8m
Flight Deck angled 6.5° with 7° ski-jump ramp
Propulsion: 2 × Parsons gas turbines
Speed: 28 knots
Complement: 143 Officers, 1027 ratings (excl embarked troops)
Armament: 2 × Sea Cat GWS 22
          4 × LCVP (on davits)
Builders: Vickers (Barrow)
Launched: 16 February 1953;
Commissioned: 18 November 1959

during the subequent war. There was a considerable conflict of ideas in the early stages as to what her role should be, but Northwood decreed that it should be as a Harrier Carrier in order to deploy as many fighters as possible. This led Brigadier Julian Thompson to decide not to use her as his sea-going headquarters.

When the call came, many of *Hermes* crew were on leave, most were accommodated ashore and scaffolding embraced the 'island'. The co-operation of the Dockyard personnel, the rush to bring the ship up to full operational readiness with stores, ammunition and supplies which might normally be expected to take three weeks, was achieved in 72

hours. The Air Group was suddenly expanded and when the ship left Portsmouth on 5 April she had embarked 800 and 899 Naval Air Squadrons of 11 Sea Harriers, 826 NAS (ASW) and 846 NAS (Commando) totalling 18 Sea Kings, as well as A Company of 40 Commando.

Meanwhile *Invincible*, the second carrier, was one of three of a new class of CVS and the first to be designed, ordered and built since World War 2. Originally conceived as a through deck cruiser capable of carrying up to ten medium size helicopters in the anti-submarine role, she was also fitted as a Command and Control ship and her operations room was equipped with Action Data and Automated Weapons System (ADAWS). Along with this went her Type 1006 navigational radar, Type 1022 air warning radar, Type 992Q target indication radar and Marconi ICS-3 communications. With the introduction of the Sea Harrier, ideas on her employment were again changed and in 1975 plans to build a 7° ski-ramp were incorporated, along with her 6° angled deck. She was also equipped with one Sea Dart (GWS 30) missile system with its Type 909 control radar. Her acceptance trials were completed in early 1981 but her sister ship *Illustrious* had not yet been finished, though her builders Swan Hunters of Tyneside made rapid progress to get her accepted by 20 June 1982.

After shaking down in her Harrier and anti-submarine role during 1981 *Invincible* carried out her first exercises with the Royal Marines Commandos. About two thirds of 40 Commando were accommodated on camp beds on the

*The latest British aircraft carrier HMS Invincible leaves Portsmouth on 5 April. During most of the campaign she operated ten Sea Harriers and nine Sea King Mk 5 helicopters, which provided air defence, combat air patrols over the land and anti-submarine protection for the Task Force.*

hangar deck, the other one third being dispersed either in spare bunks, mess decks and even the church and weight training room. This exercise, described as loading trials, went 'smoother than expected' and was another important ingredient that paid dividends in the weeks to come. At least the ship was thinking 'amphibious'.

In February and March *Invincible* had a prolonged ASW exercise with her standard load of nine ASW Sea King Mk 5s and five Sea Harriers. Little did the ship realise that by 4 April 801 NAS would be reinforced to 8 Harriers. There was a shortage of RN fixed wing pilots and although seven fully-navalised RAF

**RO 5 HMS Invincible**
19,810 tons
Length: 206.6m (overall); 192.9m (waterline)
Beam: 31.9m (Flt Deck); 27.5m (waterline)
Draught: 7.3m
Flight Deck angled 6° with 7° ski-jump ramp
Propulsion: 4 × RR Olympus TM 3B gas turbines
Speed: 29 knots
Complement: 131 officers, 869 ratings (excl Air Gp)
Armament: 1 × 2 Sea Dart (GWS 30)
2 × 20mm Phalanx CIWS
2 × 20mm Oerlikon
Builders: Vickers (Barrow)
Launched: 3 May 1977
Commissioned: 11 July 1980

pilots were attached to the two carriers, two joined who were still in the preliminaries of operational training. When she sailed on Monday 5 April *Invincible* not only had her extra complement of aircraft but extra Sea Dart missiles crated on deck. During the campaign she spent 166 days continually at sea and did not return home until relieved by *Illustrious* in August, two months after the end of the war.

*Invincible* had good living accommodation and with a basic complement of 135 officers and 870 senior and junior ratings, she was a good fighting ship. She is powered by four Rolls Royce Olympus gas turbines which can be interconnected to her twin shafts in case of damage. There is no doubt that, had the South Atlantic campaign been prolonged, a third carrier would have been essential. It was quite remarkable that neither ship developed any serious mechanical defect, even more astonishing in view of *Hermes* age. Rear Admiral 'Sandy' Woodward had used *Hermes* as his flagship from the time he transferred from *Glamorgan* in mid-April.

The two Harrier carriers were the most critical factor in winning the war. The Sea Harriers gave the Task Force a decisive air defence capability. The loss of one carrier would have jeopardized the whole campaign. However the continual anti-submarine patrols by their helicopters kept the enemy at bay. Had their Sea Harriers not been able to inflict considerable pressure on the enemy both in the air and in ground attacks, the final outcome might have been delayed with dire consequences.

# Destroyers

Eight destroyers of three different classes were deployed to the South Atlantic during the campaign. The 'County Class' *Antrim* (Captain BG Young) and *Glamorgan* (Captain ME Barrow) and the slightly larger Type 82 *Bristol* (Captain A Grose) were all laid down in the 1960s when the Royal Navy were planning to build more conventional aircraft carriers. These ships were designed to provide area air defence escorts, but like all destroyers they had the additional roles of anti-submarine warfare and bombardment ships.

There were originally to be eight Type 82s, but only *Bristol* was built. In her early days she was used as a Sea Dart trials ship and although commissioned in 1973, she was not accepted for active service until after a major refit in 1976-8. She was then fitted out as a Command and Control ship, and designated flagship for Flag Officer Third Flotilla. As such she was equipped with SCOT (Satellite Communication Onboard Terminal), LINK 11 automated action data communications system for use with the American NTDS or French SENIT systems. The Sea Dart (GWS 30) is a medium range area defence anti-aircraft or anti-missile system firing a 1,210 lbs missile, being guided on to its target by Type 909 radar. Although she could land helicopters, she had no hangar nor repair facilities. In 1980, the American SATCOMM WSC-3 was added, as well as a new navigation system. She was the only ship in the campaign fitted with the Anglo-Australian Ikara anti-submarine torpedo.

The two County Class ships, *Antrim* and *Glamorgan*, also laid down in the 1960s were the first to be designated as Guided Missile Destroyers. Their size effectively made them light cruisers and they were designed round the Sea Slug (GWS 10) and Sea Cat (GWS 22) missile systems. Again they were originally to provide escorts world-wide for the proposed, never to be completed, aircraft carriers and were the first to be fitted with the French Exocet missile in the mid 1970s. The Sea Cat for close air defence proved inadequate in the Falklands as it was not capable of reacting against fast moving aircraft. The Sea Slug system has a longer range for primary air defence up to 30 miles and is guided along a designated beam by the Type 901 radar. Both ships were due to be phased out in 1982/3.

The remaining five destroyers were Type 42, 'Sheffield Class' (ten in all), laid down in the 1970s, also built for area air defence. They were the first ships to be powered with a dual set of engines, the Rolls Royce gas turbine *Tyne* for cruising, and the Rolls Royce *Olympus* for full power, which can be reached in about 30 seconds. Their Sea Dart systems, with a medium level capability, forced attacking Argentine aircraft down to sea level. These ships are highly manoeuvrable, but below decks, the layout leads to very cramped conditions. It was apparent when *Sheffield* (Captain JFT Salt) was hit by an Argentine Exocet missile and also when *Coventry* (Captain D Hart-Dyke) was sunk by bombs that their damage control systems were inadequate.

At the end of March Rear Admiral JF 'Sandy' Woodward, Flag Officer First Flotilla, flying his flag in *Antrim* was engaged in exercises off Gibraltar. Four other destroyers, *Glamorgan*, *Coventry*, *Sheffield* and *Glasgow* (Captain AP Hoddinot OBE) were involved in this exercise and all sailed in the initial Task Force after cross decking and trans-

*HMS* Glamorgan *which led the ships of the Task Force, was the first destroyer to bombard Stanley on 1 May, being bombed in the action. She later covered the Pebble Island raid and was finally hit by a land based Exocet missile on 12 June, which she survived after being set on fire.*

fers of personnel and aircraft in Gibraltar. During the voyage south Admiral Woodward shifted his flag to *Glamorgan*, when

*HMS* Coventry *during a peacetime exercise. While patrolling in the 'missile trap' to the north of the Falklands, she was bombed and sunk by Skyhawks after probably shooting down two with her Sea Dart missiles on 25 May.*

28

*Antrim* was despatched for the retaking of South Georgia.

*Exeter* (Captain HM Balfour LVO) was the next destroyer to be involved. She was on patrol off Belize on 4 May when *Sheffield* was struck by Exocet and a replacement was urgently needed. She was fitted with the more advanced Type 1022 air warning radar system and joined the Task Force on 22 May. Meanwhile, *Cardiff* (Captain MGT Harris) had been on Armilla Patrol in the Persian Gulf and was returning home through the Mediterranean, when she was diverted at Gibraltar on 7 May, sailing south on the 12th. The final destroyer to join the fleet was *Bristol*, who led a group of three Type 21 Frigates reaching Ascension Island on 18 May.

The value of destroyers to the campaign was immense. Apart from providing command and control facilities with SATCOMM, they acted as leaders of detached groups for specific tasks. From 1 May they continually shelled military targets around Stanley airport and other installations. For instance, on 10 May, *Glasgow* in company with *Brilliant*, fired

222 rounds, directed by a Royal Artillery bombardment officer airborne in a Lynx. The ships were quite capable of hitting pin-point targets and were most effective when controlled by forward observers.

Of the eight destroyers taking part in the campaign two were sunk. *Sheffield* was hit by an Exocet missile on 4 May with the loss of 20 officers and men. She was hit amidships in the auxiliary machine room to the forward engine room. Admiral Woodward decided not to sink her when she had been abandoned but to offer her as a decoy target. Later it was decided to tow her to South Georgia but she sunk under tow on 10 May. *Coventry* was bombed and set on fire on 25 May after a sustained period of Argentine air attacks. 19 men were killed and the ship capsized in 15 minutes. Her war had been highly successful to that point, being credited with at least one and possibly three aircraft shot down while her Lynx helicopter had fired the first Sea

*The Type 42 destroyer HMS* Cardiff. *Her Sea Dart missiles (not showing) are fitted just abaft the 4.5" gun turret. This is a third generation surface-to-air missile system for use against fast moving aircraft or incoming missiles. Two of her sister ships* Sheffield *and* Coventry *were both sunk.*

Skua missiles of the war at an Argentine supply ship on 9 May.

Another destroyer *Glasgow* had a remarkably lucky escape on 12 May when an Argentine Skyhawk dropped a 1,000 lb bomb which holed her amidships and went out through the other side without exploding. Despite being holed, losing her two Tyne engines and one Olympus, and with a failure in her propeller shaft, her crew repaired her so successfully in adverse sea conditions that she was in action again within three days.

The part played by the destroyer force was inestimable in terms of air defence and fighter direction. With their bombardment capability, they proved the main work horses of the Task Force.

---

**D 80 HMS Sheffield** (*Type 42*)
4,100 tons
Length: 125m
Beam: 14.3m
Draught: 5.8m
Propulsion: 2 Rolls Royce Tyne Gas Turbines
Speed: 30 knots
Armament: 1 × 4.5in Mk 8 Dual Purpose gun
2 × 20mm Oerlikons
1 × Sea Dart system (GWS 30)
2 × triple ASW torpedo tubes
Aircraft: 1 × Lynx
Builders: Vickers, Barrow
Launched: 10 June 1971
Commissioned: 16 February 1975

**D 108 HMS Cardiff** (*As above*)
Builders: Vickers (Barrow)
Launched: 22 February 1974;
Commissioned: 24 September 1979

**D 89 HMS Exeter** (*As above*)
Builders: Swan Hunter
Launched: 25 April 1978;
Commissioned: 19 September 1980

**D 88 HMS Glasgow** (*As above*)
Builders: Swan Hunter
Launched: 14 April 1976;
Commissioned: 24 May 1979

**D 118 HMS Coventry** (*As above*)
Builders: Cammell Laird
Launched: 21 June 1974;
Commissioned: 10 November 1978

---

**D 18 HMS Antrim** (*County Class*)
6,200 tons
Length: 158.8m
Beam: 16.5m
Draught: 6.3m
Propulsion: 2 Steam turbines; 2 C6 Gas
turbines
Speed: 32.5 knots
Armament: 2 × 4.5in Mk 6 Dual Purpose guns
2 × 20mm Oerlikons
1 × Seaslug 2 system (GWS 10)
2 Seacat systems (GWS 22)
4 × MM 38 Exocet
Aircraft: 1 Wessex 3
Builders: Fairfield (Govan)
Launched: 19 October 1967
Commissioned: 14 June 1970

**D 19 HMS Glamorgan** (*As above*)
Launched: 9 July 1964
Commissioned 11 October 1966

---

**D 23 HMS Bristol** (*Type 82*)
7,100 tons
Length: 154.6m
Beam: 16.8m
Draught: 5.2m
Propulsion: 2 Steam turbines;
2 Rolls Royce Olympus Gas
turbines
Speed: 30 knots
Armament: 1 × 4.5in Mk 8 Dual Purpose gun
4 × 20mm AA guns
1 × Sea Dart system (GWS 30)
1 × Ikara ASW missile system
1 × three-barrelled ASW Mortar
Mk 10
Aircraft: 1 Wasp
Builders: Swan Hunter
Launched: 30 June 1959
Commissioned: 31 March 1973

# Frigates

The Government's White Paper on Defence of 1981 set the Royal Navy's fleet at around 50 destroyers and frigates, and today frigates form the largest single group of warships. However their size and task vary so much that some are even bigger than earlier destroyers, with tonnage ranging from 2,300 to 3,500 tons. With comparatively light hulls their specialist tasks and armament vary considerably.

With the Russians building up their submarine fleet, it had been to Anti-Submarine Warfare (ASW) that the planners had turned in designing the 1970s and 1980s ships, and it was to the frigates they had looked to provide essential anti-submarine defence. With the advent of more advanced missile systems and eyes on Northern European defence, there had been several changes in attitude towards building frigates with conventional 4.5″ guns; guns which could be used either in the bombardment or anti-aircraft role. Indeed new frigates were providing merely missile launching platforms as with the Broadsword Class. The older frigates of the campaign, the Type 12s *Plymouth* (Captain D Pentreath) and *Yarmouth* (Commander A Morton), built nearly 25 years earlier still retained the bombardment role so essential to supporting seaborne landings, as did the later Type 21s of the Amazon class. However the Leanders in varying designs had their turrets removed and were purely anti-aircraft and ASW ships. No Leanders fitted with the ASW Ikara missile were deployed as they were not conidered suitable for the South Atlantic war.

Fifteen frigates were deployed in the South Atlantic and their versatility is shown in their employment. Two were lost to enemy action, *Ardent* (Commander AWJ West) on 21 May and *Antelope* (Commander NJ Tobin) two days later, and several others were damaged, but their value to the military landing force and in protecting the capital ships of the fleet was inestimable. The fact that no damage was done to any of the major aircraft or troop carriers bears witness to their achievement.

Seven of the Type 21s (Amazon Class), built in the mid to late 70s were deployed. These were the first frigates to be built around gas turbine engines, and were of all British design. They use two Rolls Royce Tyne gas turbines for cruising at around 18 knots, but when full power is needed the main Rolls Royce engines can produce 56,000 bhp driving two shafts, developing more than 30 knots. Sensors include the Type 978 navigational radar; Type 992Q providing accurate target information for the ships's fire control system up to 50 miles; and the GWS 24 for Seacat control. As for armament, only five were originally fitted with French Exocet MM 38 missiles, a sixth being added later, but neither *Antelope* nor *Ambuscade* (Commander PJ Mosse) were fitted in 1982. The Exocet is a sea-skimming surface to surface missile with a range of about 45 miles. The bearing and range of the target are fed into its memory before launching, and then the missile skims at 50 ft above the surface reaching 700 mph in under 3 seconds. When nearing its target it locks on with its radar maintaining its low level thus making it difficult to detect. The 365 lbs Hexolite charge is designed to detonate after piercing the outer casing of a ship.

The Amazon class were fitted with the Seacat GWS 24 surface to air missile system. It is a point defence system most effective against low and medium level aircraft up to 6000 yards. It can also be used in the anti-ship role. Its development can be traced back to the late 1950s and it was first trialled in 1962. In the intervening years its performance and operation has been upgraded. The Seacat is guided on to its target by an operator using binoculars, which automatically transmits corrections to the missile. This weighs 150 lbs with a high explosive head and is fired singly. During the campaign the Seacat was severely tested and found wanting in dealing with fast moving fighters and could not cope with their crossing rate. However it was credited with at least two kills.

The Vickers 4.5″ Mark 8 gun was fitted in all ships of this class and provided the main naval gunfire support for the land campaign. It is fully automatic, requiring no-one actually in the turret during firing, providing it has been pre-loaded. Its muzzle break reduces recoil force, saves weight and space, and enables quicker reloading. It can fire a 55 lbs shell up to 12 nautical miles, with close

*HMS Ambuscade, one of seven Amazon Class frigates deployed in the South Atlantic. Her 4.5" gun provided accurate naval gunfire support during 2 Para's final battle for Wireless Ridge.*

proximity fuses, air burst or star-shell. These fuses can be inter-changed within seconds. During the campaign more than 8,000 rounds were fired against military targets in support of the land forces. Most of the fire was controlled by Royal Artillery forward observation teams.

In addition most of this class of frigate carry two triple torpedo tubes (STWS-1) situated amid-ships that can fire the Mk 46 homing torpedo on either side of the ship against submarines. A self defence system used for the first time in the campaign was the Plessey built Corvus Broadband chaff rocket. Metallised strips are dispensed by the rocket as a decoy against a missile's radar seeker, producing a cloud that hides the ship, or alternatively forms a false echo away from the ship which attracts the missile. Normally fired at close range they are instant weapons that need quick reaction from the operations room.

The main anti-submarine weapon system of the ship is the Westland Lynx helicopter, although *Active* (Commander PCB Canter) carried the older Wasp. The

Lynx has twin engines and an all weather performance capable of landing when the deck is rolling to 20°. The helicopter carries the Seaspray surface search radar, enabling it to widen its parent ship's vision over the horizon. It can be fitted either with Sea Skua missiles, Stingray torpedoes or depth charges. Without weapons it can stay airborne for about 2½ hours. Its crew is a pilot, observer and aircrewman and it is capable of carrying up to eight passengers.

The normal crew of the Amazon class is around 170 officers and men and their accommodation is some of the most comfortable in the Fleet. All ships have an aluminium superstructure, mainly designed to save weight, but its low melting point constitutes a considerable fire hazard. Their Type 992Q (target indication) radar proved inadequate when working close to the shore, such as in Falkland Sound, when air targets were indistinguishable from land masses.

The Leanders, *Argonaut* Captain CH Layman LVO), *Minerva* (Commander SHG Johnston) and *Penelope* (Commander PV Rickard) were all over 15 years old and were designed as first generation multi purpose ships. They are similar to the more recent and improved Amazon class carrying three quadruple Seacat surface to air launchers, an anti-submarine

Lynx helicopter, four Exocet launchers which replaced their 4.5" turret during earlier refits, and two triple STWS torpedo tubes, while their only guns are a pair of close range bofors 40 mm. Most of this class carried a small Royal Marines detachment of a SNCO and ten marines. Being only fitted with 2 sets of geared steam turbines meant a slower reaction to full power and less speed and manoeuvrability. They were fitted with the very heavy Type 965 (AKE-1) long range air warning radar, which had been designed nearly 30 years earlier to track sub-sonic bombers. Its shortcomings were very apparent when trying to cope with the

fast modern aircraft. In addition they carried Type 975 surface warning radar and Type 993 medium range information radar.

The Leanders were very seaworthy and manoeuvrable ships with a high freeboard, twin rudders and stabilisers. They were modified at an early stage to use diesel which simplified logistic supply

---

**Type 22** *(Broadsword Class)*
**F 88 HMS BROADSWORD**
3500 tons
Length: 131.2m
Beam: 14.8m
Draught: 4.3m
Propulsion: 2 × Rolls Royce Olympus gas
 turbines
 2 × Rolls Royce Tyne gas turbines
Speed: 30+ knots
Armament: 2 × 40mm Bofors. 4″ MM 38 Exocet
 launchers. 2 × Sea Wolf systems
 (GWS 25). 2 × triple ASW torpedo
 tubes.
Aircraft: 2 Lynx helicopters
Builders: Yarrow, Scotstoun
Launched: 12 May 1976
Commissioned: 4 May 1979

**F 90 HMS BRILLIANT**
 *(As for HMS Broadsword)*
Builders: Yarrow, Scotstoun
Launched: 15 December 1978
Commissioned: 15 May 1981

---

problems. They carry a comparatively large crew of up to 260 in well planned, air conditioned accommodation. In the South Atlantic, this large crew enabled the ships to remain at defence stations for long periods in a fully alerted state, allowing the men sufficient rest and recreation time to keep them at a high state of efficiency.

*Andromeda* (Captain JL Weatherall) was the broad-beamed Leander, similar in design to the others, to be modernised and equipped with the Sea Wolf GWS 25, an advance on the Seacat missile. Mainly designed for use against low and medium level aicraft, the Sea Wolf is capable of hitting missiles in flight and has been known to track and destroy a 4.5″ shell. Its advanced automatic system of combined radar and TV tracking makes it a very expensive piece of equipment.

The Sea Wolf is the most advanced point defence system against both aircraft and missiles. Its Type 967/968 surveillance radar picks up a target and transmits it to one of the six individual launchers. As soon as the fast moving target is in effective range the missile is fired and guided on to it by the Type 910 tracking radar, exploding as it hits or is close by. The missile weighing 175 lbs has a supersonic speed and was once

known to have hit a 4.5″ shell in flight! It has a very fast reaction time and should be capable of picking up and destroying an Exocet in flight. However, even the Sea Wolf had problems, highlighted when *Broadsword* and *Coventry* were attacked by Skyhawks on 25 May. The system did not engage at its best range of 5,000 yds. It appeared to become confused by two targets and although it took only about 3 seconds to switch manually to an alternative mode, the aircraft had successfully completed its attack.

*Broadsword* (Captain WR Canning) and *Brilliant* (Captain JF Coward) were Type 22 frigates of the latest type, the direct successors to the Leanders. At 3,500 tons they are the largest submarine killers, besides being effective surface to surface warships. Indeed *Brilliant* had been in commission for less than a year at the time of the campaign. They were the first to be designed to metric measurements and were the first to be built without a major gun armament. They carried two Lynx helicopters, two Sea Wolf (GWS 25) systems, four Exocet launchers, two triple STWS torpedo tubes, two 40 mm Bofors guns and a Royal Marines detachment.

The Broadsword class carried the new Type 2016 sonar which has a complex monitoring and analysis technique. It can pick out a particular noise, such as a submarine from other clutter and feed it into the Computer Aided Action Information System in the operations room. It all but takes away the decision making from the captain! All are fitted as command and control ships.

*Brilliant* is credited with the first Sea Wolf success when she shot down two Skyhawks in quick succession on 12 May whilst providing point defence for *Glasgow* 20 miles south of Port Stanley. The third missile she fired against a wave-top attack caused the aircraft to take violent evasive action and ditch in the sea. However, in a subsequent attack by four determined Argentine pilots, the

shortcomings of the system were highlighted when the computer, used to saying only 'yes' or 'no', became confused by a multiple attack and packed up. Subsequently, working under considerable pressure, the engineers devised a cure which successfully dealt with future attacks.

*Plymouth* and *Yarmouth* of the Rothesay class were the smallest and oldest of the frigates. The latter was laid down in 1959 and based on the Whitby Class, but modified to include a hangar and Wasp helicopter. They retained a twin mount-

---

**Type 12** (*Rothesay Class*)
**F 101 HMS YARMOUTH**
2380 tons
Length: 112.8m
Beam: 12.5m
Draught: 5.3m
Propulsion: 2 sets geared steam turbines
Speed: 28 knots
Armament: 2 × 4.5" Mk 6 guns.
          2 × 20mm Oerlikon.
          1 Seacat system (GWS 20).
          1 Limbo ASW Mortar Mk 10
Aircraft: 1 Wasp helicopter
Builders: John Brown
Launched: 23 March 1959
Commissioned: 26 March 1960

**F 126 HMS PLYMOUTH** (*As Above*)
Builders: HM Dockyard, Devonport
Launched: 20 July 1959
Commissioned: 11 May 1961

---

ing of 4.5" Mark 6 guns, as well as two 20 mm Oerlikon anti-aircraft guns. Later a Seacat (GWS 20) missile system was fitted and they were the only ships of the fleet to carry the Limbo ASW Mortar Mk 10, which was capable of firing a 450 lbs projectile up to 2,000 yards at a rate of three per minute. The mortar was used in a possible submarine contact on 1 May.

The frigates took the brunt of the sharp end action and their role was ever versatile. Apart from providing point defence against air attacks and an ever watchful anti-submarine surveillance, they landed special forces on the islands from the earliest days, leaving themselves vulnerable to attack. They also became adept at picking up stores and parachutists dropped by long range Hercules aircraft. *Arrow* (Commander P J Bootherstone), was one of the first to sail south and was, along with *Glamorgan* and *Alacrity*, the first to bombard Port Stanley on 1 May. She also took part in one of the last bombardments in support of the land battles for the mountains on 13 June when she fired 103 4.5" shells. Other frigates took their turn and their continual bombardments to harass and confuse the enemy on the ground, did much to destroy the latter's morale. Nearly all the frigates suffered some form of damage except, ironically enough, the oldest ship *Yarmouth*.

*HMS* Andromeda, *a broad beam Batch 3 Leander Class frigate armed with retrofitted Exocet and Sea Wolf. She was* Invincible*'s anti-aircraft 'screen' thoughout the war, being detached occasionally to pick up air dropped supplies.*

When the campaign started, most of the frigates were on the major exercise *Springtrain* in the Mediterranean, and although there was much transfer of stores and personnel between similar ships at Gibraltar, *Broadsword* and *Yarmouth* actually sailed east towards the Suez Canal on 5 April, being recalled shortly afterwards. *Minerva* sailed into Plymouth on 2 April flying her paying off pennant, but was refurbished completely in five weeks. *Falmouth* was about to be sold, but was commissioned in 9 days although never deployed south, while four other ships in reserve in the Standby Squadron *Berwick*, *Zulu*, *Gurkha* and *Tartar* were prepared for service in Devonport and Rosyth.

Other than those sailing direct from Gibraltar or in the initial Task Force from England, most ships spent a few days working up at Portland under the guidance of Flag Officer Sea Training. It was time well spent. Along with the destroyers, the frigates air defence systems were one of the main factors in defeating the Argentine Air Force.

# Amphibious Assault Ships and Landing Ships Logistic

*Fearless* (Captain EJS Larken) and *Intrepid* (Captain PGV Dingemans) were the first and only Landing Platforms (Dock) ever to be designed and built for the Royal Navy. Originally conceived along the lines of similar United States ships, they are among the most versatile in the Fleet, being able to operate landing craft, helicopters and used as a Command ship. They were both laid down in 1962 when Britain's amphibious Commando force had a world wide role and carry a crew of about 580 including 90 Royal Marines. They are fitted with excellent Command and Control communications facilities, can accommodate 700 embarked troops, and can dock down to allow her four LCUs to swim out of the stern. Her four LCVPs are slung from davits on the upper deck. The landing craft are part of the integral Assault Squadron of about 80 RM & RN personnel, which also includes an Amphibious Beach Unit.

The docking area, about 66m × 17m, can be flooded by the ship taking in 3,000 tons of ballast, and troops can embark direct from their mess decks into their landing craft. The flight deck can operate all types of helicopters – up to

*HMS* Fearless, *one of the two assault ships was the hub of the planning for the amphibious landings, where Commodore Mike Clapp (Commodore Amphibious Warfare) and Brigadier Julian Thompson (3 Commando Brigade) set up their Headquarters.*

two Wessex at a time, parking more if necessary – and even Sea Harriers when required. The complement of aircraft varies considerably with their role. With a displacement of 12,120 tons and a speed of 21 knots, they are armed with four Seacat systems for close range air defence and two 40mm Bofors.

Although they were an essential part of Britain's amphibious forces, the stringent financial cut-backs foretold their imminent demise. For nearly a decade one LPD had acted as the Dartmouth Training ship, giving young officers their first taste of sea time, while the other had either been in refit or supporting our amphibious forces on exercise. At the time of the Falklands campaign *Intrepid* had already been paid off and she was being de-stored in Portsmouth prior to being placed in reserve or possible disposal. *Fearless*, also under threat from the scrapyard, had been exercising in North Norway with 42 Commando in February 1982 in her amphibious role, but had reverted to her Training Ship role by March. These two ships were to play a major part in the campaign, and after much hard thinking, the decision to retain them for a few more years at least was one of the outcomes of the conflict.

The plans to replace the LPDs completely with requisitioned civilian Roll-on Roll-off ferries, with which 3rd Commando Brigade had been exercising, was shelved temporarily. It was always

an unsatisfactory situation as far as the Royal Marines were concerned as they were always made to feel passengers in the ferries rather than being an integral part of the Assault Ships.

**Landing Ships Logistic**

During World War 2 there were a variety of Landing Ships, mostly developed along American lines from merchant ships and ferries. There were Landing Ships, Vehicle, Tank, Infantry, Medium, Dock, Fighter Direction, etc. At the end of the war rationalisation took place with a look at the contingencies ahead. At the time of Suez in 1956, the Amphibious Warfare Squadron based in Malta, had but two wartime LSTs though six more were hurriedly brought out of mothballs for the operation. This had proved unsatisfactory, had cost considerable time and money, and needed replacement anyway. But it was six years before a force of six new LSTs was laid down and not till 1964 that the *Sir Launcelot* class were first commissioned.

Even then they were ordered by the Ministry of Transport for use by the Army, being transferred to the Royal

*The stern door of HMS* Fearless *which, after the ship has flooded down, can be opened to allow despatch and docking of LCUs and LCVPs with troops, vehicles and stores. The ship can accommodate 700 embarked troops as well as her crew of 580.*

*HMS* Fearless *leaves South Georgia. With her sister ship,* Intrepid *she carried the bulk of the land forces for the re-occupation of the Falkland Islands. Each carries four LCUs and four LCVPs, is armed with Seacat close air defence systems and has her own helicopters.*

**L 10 HMS Fearless**
12,120 tons (16,950 with dock flooded)
Length: 158.8m
Beam: 24.4m
Draught: 7.0m forward. 9.8m aft.
Propulsion: 2 English Electric steam turbines
Speed: 21 knots
Armament: 2 × 40mm Bofors.
          4 × Seacat systems (GWS 20).
          2 × Rheinmetall AA Guns
          (fitted June)
Aircraft: Up to 4 Sea King helicopters.
Landing Craft: 4 × LCU. 4 × LCVP
Assault Force: RM Commando (650 men) +
          logistic elements
          Commando Light Battery
          (6 + 105mm guns)
          Commando vehicles
Builders: Harland & Wolff
Launched: 19 December 1963;
          Commissioned 25 November 1965

**L 11 HMS Intrepid**
As above except no Rheinmetall guns fitted
Builders: John Brown
Launched: 25 June 1964;
          Commissioned 11 March 1967

**Landing Craft (Utility)**
75 tons (176 tons fully loaded)
Length: 27.5m
Beam: 6.5m
Draught: 1.7m
Propulsion: 2 Paxman diesel engines
Speed: 10 knots
Assault load: 2 Tanks or 140 men or 100 tons
          cargo
Crew: SNCO + 6

Fleet Auxiliary in 1970, by which time there were six, all named after Knights of the Round Table. They were built as multi-purpose vessels to carry troops and heavy vehicles, and employed in peacetime to ferry stores and personnel from their home base at Marchwood, near Southampton, to Antwerp for BAOR and Northern Ireland. They exercised regularly with the Royal Marines Commando Brigade in the Mediterranean and North Norway. Each is fitted as a roll-on roll-off ferry with bow and stern doors. They are manned by 18 officers and about 50 crew, mainly Chinese, and carry a load of up to 400 troops (1,000 for short trips) and 340 tons of stores or vehicles. The LSLs are capable of about 17 knots and are unarmed except for two 40mm Bofors guns. They have two helicopter pads, amidships and aft, from which light helicopters can operate; in addition they carry two Mexeflote powered rafts for ferrying troops, vehicles and stores ashore, which are manned by the Royal Corps of Transport.

In March 1982 four LSLs, *Sir Geraint* (Captain DE Lawrence) and *Sir Galahad* (Captain RJG Roberts) were at Devonport, while *Sir Percivale* (Captain AF Pitt) and *Sir Lancelot* (Captain CA Purtcher Wydenbruck) were at March-

wood. However *Sir Tristram* (Captain GR Green) was in Belize and *Sir Bedivere* (Captain PJ McCarthy) on the Pacific coast at Vancouver. Whilst *Sir Tristram* could be diverted south easily, it was unlikely that *Sir Bedivere* would be available for the landings. In the event the four available ships were quickly loaded with men, stores, vehicles and light aircraft of 3rd Commando Brigade and sailed south on the 6th and 7th April.

*Sir Tristram* joined the Amphibious Task Force at Ascension Island and by 17 April had embarked A Coy of 40 Commando for the passage south. *Sir Bedivere* reached England by mid April, and sailed unaccompanied on 27 April. The other five ships were to play a memorable role in the San Carlos landings, although none of them were actually beached. It had been realised that, after the initial landings, the LSLs would be required to ferry troops and supplies forward and beaching them might have damaged their hulls. An early plan to keep combat supplies aboard the LSLs after the initial landings had to be discarded in view of possible Argentinian air attacks and they were all unloaded on to the beaches in Ajax Bay where the Brigade Maintenance Area was set up.

On 8 June *Sir Galahad* and *Sir Tristram* were bombed, the former being sunk and the latter badly damaged at Bluff Cove when transferring the Welsh Guards and medical supplies. Their temporary replacements in early 1983 were two chartered ro-ro ferries, re-named *Sir Caradoc* and *Sir Lamorak*, but a refitted *Sir Tristram* came back into service in 1985 and a replacement *Sir Galahad* ordered in 1984.

Without this amphibious force of assault ships and LSLs, Operation *Corporate* could not have taken place. Despite their slow speeds, they were the only ships capable of landing a force of some 5,000 men in the initial stages. Their future value, not only in the NATO arena, but in a 'out-of-area' scenario, can be measured in the success they made in the Falklands.

# Hospital Ships and Ambulance Vessels

With a campaign being fought over 8,000 miles from the UK, it was appreciated from the outset that there would be a need for hospital ships for the treatment and evacuation of casualties. The only British warship to have a wartime role as a hospital ship was HM Royal Yacht *Britannia*, nearly 30 years old. She was designed to carry 60 medical personnel and 200 beds in the case of emergency. However a major drawback was her reliance on furnace fuel oil and her employment would have meant a separate and dedicated tanker of her own, a luxury the limited Task Force could not afford.

There were contingency plans, however, for the use of merchantmen as hospital ships and it fell upon the P & O liner SS *Uganda* to fill this role. In early April she was carrying out her normal function as an educational cruise ship in the Mediterranean, and was visiting Alexandria on 10 April when she was requisitioned. On board were 70 teachers and 944 children, as well as 245 cabin passengers. The ship reached Naples on 13 April, where the children and teachers were disembarked, having entered harbour with rousing choruses of 'Rule Britannia'. In their place came an MOD survey team, a consultant surgeon and P & O engineers, who redesigned the interior for her new role. Her master Captain JC Clark, had orders to report to Flag Officer Gibraltar for instructions, which he did three days later.

Work was in hand by the end of that day in the much depleted Gibraltar dockyard, where the 'dockies' worked overtime. They soon stripped the after end of the upper deck to fit a helicopter pad, while between decks, the students' open deck space, verandah and common room were converted into a casualty receiving area, operating theatre and the main ward. Space had to be found for receiving casualties, sorting them into categories, holding rooms, resuscitating rooms, operating theatres and wards. There had to be a dispensary, x-ray facilities, rest rooms, offices, stores and even a mortuary. A burns unit was established along with an intensive care ward.

On the structural side, arrangements had to be made to allow casualties from either the helicopter deck or ship's side to be moved direct to the receiving area

without steep gangways and ladders. This was to be achieved by fitting ramps along which ran hand-operated trolleys with horizontal stretchers. Ultimately there were 94 beds for medium dependency casualties and 20 for intensive care. Larger wards for 20-30 patients were set up in the old schools dormitory accommodation.

Besides the purely medical side of the conversion, came Replenishment at Sea facilities, new satellite communications and a repainting of the ship's side in white with red crosses to replace the normal P & O livery. Fresh water was always likely to be a problem as the ship could not produce enough of her own. Whilst in the South Atlantic she received two reverse osmosis freshwater generators which eased the problem, but water rationing was imposed from the first reception of casualties

The conversion was completed in 65 hours and on 19 April *Uganda* sailed south from Gibraltar, exercising helicopter landings before she was out of sight of land. Being a hospital ship she was not allowed cryptographic facilities under the Geneva Convention. On board she had a medical team of 135 under Surgeon Captain AJ Rintoul RN, which included Queen Alexandra's Royal Naval Nursing Officers and Ratings for the first time at sea, though some officers had been afloat during the Korean war. In addition Naval Party 1830 were embarked as were the Royal Marines Band of Flag Officer 3rd Flotilla, 24 strong, who were quickly trained as helicopter marshals and stretcher bearers.

The first casualties *Uganda* received were on 12 May when those from the stricken *Sheffield* were brought on board. After the landings on 21 May, she moved nearer to the combat zone, despite protests from the Argentinians that her presence endangered her status under the Geneva Convention. On 29 May she moved into Grantham Sound just over a mile from the main shore casualty clearing station at Ajax Bay. During the heaviest fighting she received up to 150 casualties a day, with no differentiation being made between British and Argentinian wounded. In all she received 730 In-Patients, including 150 Argentinians

**HOSPITAL SHIP**

**SS Uganda**
16,907 tons
Built 1952. P & O Passenger liner
Taken up from Trade: 10 April 1982
Modified: 16-19 April
Sailed: 19 April
Returned: 9 August
Emergency modifications by RN Dockyard, Gibraltar
Length: 164.6m
Beam: 21.8m
Propulsion: 2 sets Geared Steam Turbines
Speed: 16 knots

and carried out 554 operations.

Nicknamed NOSH (Naval Oceangoing Surgical Hospital) after the ubiquitous MASH, she reverted to a troop carrying role on the cessation of hostilities and even held a children's party for 92 Falkland Islanders on 12 July, with her Royal Marines band also reverting to their traditional role.

Although the *Uganda* was the main hospital ship employed, the Royal Navy survey ships, *Herald*, *Hecla* and *Hydra* were also painted with Red Crosses as were their unarmed Wasp helicopters. They were to be used as transports between the combat area and the *Uganda* for the evacuation of casualties. *Hecla* was converted for her new role at Gibraltar alongside 'Mother Hen' and the remaining two in Portsmouth Dockyard, sailing as a team between the 20 and 24 July.

An equally important job for these

36

*SS* Uganda, *a P & O educational cruise liner which was converted for use as the hospital ship of the Task Force. During the campaign she dealt with 730 casualties, both British and Argentinian, and carried out 554 operations.*

*HMS* Hydra, *one of three Royal Navy survey ships, which were used as Ambulance Vessels for the transit of casualties. Painted with red crosses for the campaign, they were unarmed and carried no cryptographic facilities.*

ships was to ferry casualties back to Montevideo, British casualties for flights from Peru to the UK, and Argentinian casualties back home. There was some delay in negotiations with Uruguay resulting in suspicion by the Argentine

## AMBULANCE VESSELS

### A 133 HMS Hecla
**(Ocean Survey Craft)**
2,733 tons
Length: 79.3m
Beam: 14.9m
Draught: 4.7m
Propulsion: 3 × Paxman Ventura diesel engines
Speed: 14 knots
Armament: None
Aircraft: 1 × Wasp helicopter
Builders: Yarrow, Blythswood
Launched: 2 December 1964
Commissioned: 9 September 1965

### A 138 HMS Herald
*(Otherwise as Hecla)*
Builders: Robb Caledon
Launched: 4 October 1973
Commissioned: 22 November 1974

### A 144 HMS Hydra
*(As Hecla)*
Builders: Yarrow, Blythwood
Launched: 14 July 1965
Commissioned: 5 May 1966

Government, but on 6 June *Hydra* arrived with the first 51 wounded. These ships also operated in a non-cryptographic role, and on one occasion they were unable to pass on a vital message to Admiral Woodward concerning the bombing of neutral tanker.

The Argentinian naval transport *Bahia Paraiso*, specially designed for working with antarctic survey parties, had taken part in the South Georgia operations and had transported the captured Royal Marines to Bahia Blanca arriving on 13 April. On 8 May she was declared a hospital ship and operated her Lynx helicopters in much the same way as the Royal Navy, working closely with *Uganda* in transferring Argentine casualties. Another Argentine ship which had taken offensive action in the early part of the campaign, *Almirante Irizar*, an ice breaker, was also declared a hospital ship in early June and assisted in the transfer of casualties with the aid of her Puma helicopter.

The importance of hospital ships in such a campaign is paramount, and under the watchful eyes of the International Committee of the Red Cross, both British and Argentine ships worked in close harmony and undoubtedly saved many lives and limbs.

# Royal Fleet Auxiliaries – Tankers

One of the wider variants of maritime warfare lies in the number and types of fuel used by ships. Older ships, such as *Hermes* use Furnace Fuel Oil (FFO), whilst most modern warships use diesel oil (DIESO). Aircraft use Aviation Fuel (AVCAT) and merchant ships differ greatly in their needs, especially where viscosity is concerned. There was also a need for ordinary petrol (MOGAS) once the troops were ashore. Although the Royal Navy had not needed large quantities of such high octane fuel for many years, some RFAs had to be earmarked to carry it, and such will be the case until the military turn over entirely to diesel. It was therefore imperative that, when the various Task Groups were assembled, there was a direct proportion of tankers available to meet their individual needs, and that those needs were carefully monitored and satisfied. In addition fresh water would be needed in large quantities not only by troops ashore, but in many cases by those ships which had limited distilling facilities; *Uganda*, the Task Force hospital ship, was a case in point.

This required considerable logistic planning particularly when the war was being fought over 8,000 miles from home base. Tankers fell into a number of categories and the Royal Fleet Auxiliary were geared to serve the fleet under normal peacetime conditions. Of their three large fleet tankers, the RFA *Olna* and *Olmeda* were deployed south. These are designed to operate up to 10,000 miles and can carry over 20,000 tons of fuel of up to three types. Although they had been in commission for nearly 20 years, they had been subsequently refitted with hangars to house up to four Sea King helicopters, were fully air-conditioned and their hulls were reinforced against ice. They were unarmed except for some improvised machine guns mounted on the superstructure. *Olna* left UK on 10 May, supporting the Bristol Group, ultimately operating in Falkland Sound, carrying out 143 RAS and 70 replenishments in harbour. *Olmeda* sailed with the initial Task Force on 5 April with A Flight of 824 Squadron's helicopters embarked. She supported the Carrier group, before accompanying *Endurance* in the recapture of South Thule. She carried out a total of 185 RAS.

Of a slightly earlier design and being phased out in 1981 were the smaller tankers *Tidepool* and *Tidespring*. Indeed *Tidepool* had been sold to the Chilean Navy and was in the Pacific when the emergency broke out. She was hastily summoned back on 16 April, passed through the Panama Canal and loaded with fuel at Curacoa, before proceeding to Ascension to embark stores and helicopters and thence sail south. *Tidespring* also embarked two heavy lift Wessex V helicopters of 845 Squadron before joining the Antrim group and supporting them during the retaking of South Georgia. By 21 May she had joined the Bristol group, having disembarked some 185 Argentine prisoners at Ascension. These two ships were both used for replenishment in San Carlos Water, these activities being mainly at night. On completion of the campaign *Tidepool* continued her journey to Chile.

Only one of the Rover class of small fleet tankers was deployed. RFA *Blue Rover* leaving UK on 16 April. She supported the South Georgia landings before topping up mainly with AVCAT and MOGAS to supply the military needs ashore in the Falklands. In between her frequent visits into the combat zone of San Carlos, she refuelled herself from requisitioned merchant tankers. Her capacity was about 6,000 tons of fuel and although she had a helicopter pad, she had no hangar.

The Royal Navy have always used large commercial tankers to support them worldwide, which on being chartered are fitted with RAS and limited helicopter facilities. Into such category fall the large Leaf class of around 30,000 tons capable of carrying up to 20,000 tons of fuel, and five of these were deployed. They are of a comparatively recent design, indeed *Bayleaf* was in the hands of the builders when the Task force sailed. *Plumleaf* was in Gibraltar preparing to relieve *Brambleleaf* in the Persian Gulf, *Appleleaf* was diverted to Gibraltar while returning home from Curacoa, while *Pearleaf*, was the only one in home waters on 1 April. She sailed from Portsmouth on 5th and relieved *Blue Rover* on the South Georgia station, later becoming a 'motorway' tanker en route from UK to the South Atlantic. She claimed a world record in a 62 hrs 40 mins RAS with the giant tanker *British Tamar*.

*RFA* Tidepool *(25,930 tons), which had been sold to Chile but recalled for the campaign, replenishes SS* Canberra *in the South Atlantic on 12 May. After the landings she did almost nightly refuelling runs into San Carlos.*

*HMS* Glamorgan (*far side*) *and HMS* Plymouth *refuel from the largest of the requisitioned tankers* Alvega (57,372 tons) *off Ascension Island. From 21 May* Alvega *became the base floating bunker for refuelling warships.*

## FLEET TANKERS

**A 123 RFA Olna**
33,240 tons (full load)
22,350 tons (deadweight)
Length: 197.5m
Beam: 25.6m
Draught: 11.1m
Propulsion: 2 sets Pamatreda geared steam
        turbines
Speed: 19 knots
Armament: Improvised machine guns and rifles
Aircraft: 2 Sea King Mk 2 helicopters
Capacity: 18,400 tons FFO. 1,730 tons diesel oil.
        3,730 tons Avgas
Builders: Hawthorn Leslie
Launched: 28 July 1965
In service: 1 April 1966

**A 124 RFA Olmeda**
(*As for RFA Olna*)
Builders: Swan Hunter
Launched: 19 November 1964
In Service: 18 October 1965

**A 75 RFA Tidespring**
25,930 tons (full load)
18,900 tons (deadweight)
Length: 177.6m
Beam: 26.1m
Draught: 9.8m
Propulsion: 1 set Pamatreda geared steam
        turbines
Speed: 17 knots
Armament: Improvised machine guns and rifles
Aircraft: 2 Wessex Mk 5
Capacity: 17,400 tons FFO. 700 tons diesel oil.
Builders: Hawthorn Leslie
Launched: 3 May 1962
In service: 18 January 1963

**A 76 RFA Tidepool**
(*As Tidespring*)
Builders: Hawthorn Leslie
In Service: 18 October 1963

**A 270 RFA Blue Rover**
11,522 tons (full load)
6,800 tons (deadweight)
Length: 140.5m
Beam: 19.2m
Draught: 7.3m
Propulsion: 2 SEMT-Pielstick diesel engines
Speed: 19 knots
Armament: Improvised
Aircraft: Helicopter deck – no embarked aircraft
Capacity: 6,600 tons FFO. Stores and dry
        provisions
Builders: Swan Hunter
Launched: 11 November 1969
In service: 15 July 1970

*Plumleaf* conducted initial RAS trials with the *Canberra* and *Elk* before they sailed south and then supported the fleet in the TEZ later becoming part of the 'motorway' team. *Bayleaf*, after a rapid completion, had the honour of re-fuelling the *QE II*.

To support all these came fifteen other STUFT tankers ranging from the 25,000 tons support oiler *Anco Charger* to the 57,000 tons base storage tanker *Alvega*. Most of these were hurriedly fitted with RAS facilities and new communications being employed mainly to top up the RFA tankers, but some saw closer action in the Falkland waters. The Canadian Pacific *Fort Toronto* was entirely a water tanker and without her the troops engaged in the land battles could not have survived. She was also on hand to supply the garrison when the cease fire came. Three tankers found themselves in the unaccustomed role of troop carriers. *British Esk* carried 262 survivors of *Sheffield* back to Ascension Island, *British Tay* took aboard 133 survivors of the stricken *Atlantic Conveyor* while *British Avon* brought back the Argentinian naval officer captured on South Georgia, Lt-Cdr Alfredo Astiz to England under escort.

Any campaign fought so far away from base must have very well planned and co-ordinated logistic support, especially in fuel and fresh water. No ship, aircraft or vehicle would have been able to operate, let alone fight, without the help of these 25 tankers, manned by a mixture of Royal Fleet Auxiliary and Merchant seamen, whose bravery and exceptional seamanship were in the highest tradition of our maritime nation.

## SUPPORT OILERS
(*Chartered to Ministry of Defence*)

**A 77 RFA Pearleaf**
25,790 tons (full load)
18,797 tons (deadweight)
Length: 173.2m
Beam: 21.9m
Draught: 9.2m
Propulsion: 1 Rowan-Doxford diesel engine
Speed: 16 knots
Capacity: 1,410 tons fuel
Builders: Blythwood, Scotstoun
Launched: 15 October 1959
In service: 1 February 1960

**A 76 RFA Plumleaf**
26,480 tons (full load)
19,200 tons (deadweight)
Length: 170.7m
Beam: 21.9m
Draught: 9.2m
Propulsion: 1 Rowan-Doxford diesel engine
Speed: 16 knots
Capacity: 684 tons fuel
Builders: Blyth Drydock
Launched: 29 March 1960
In service: 1 August 1960

**A 79 RFA Appleleaf**
40,200 tons (full load)
33,750 tons (deadweight)
Length: 170.7m
Beam: 25.0m
Draught: 11.9m
Propulsion: 2 Crossley-Pielstick diesel engines
Speed: 16 knots
Capacity: 2,498 tons fuel
Builders: Cammell Laird
Launched: 24 July 1975
In service: November 1979

**A 81 RFA Brambleleaf**
(*As for RFA Appleleaf*)
Builders: Cammell Laird
Launched: 22 January 1976
In service: 6 May 1980

**A 109 RFA Bayleaf**
(*As for RFA Appleleaf*)
Builders: Cammell Laird
Launched: 27 October 1981
In service: 26 March 1982

# Royal Fleet Auxiliaries – Supply Ships

The Royal Fleet Auxiliary (motto *Ready For Anything*) supports the needs of the active fleet at sea in peace and war. It is controlled by the Directorate of Supply and Transport (Fuel, Movements and Victualling), which is part of the Royal Navy Supply and Transport Service. The department is directly responsible to the Chief of Fleet Support, a member of the Board of Admiralty and normally a Vice Admiral of the Supply and Secretarial Branch.

Apart from the tankers, covered in the previous section, the RFA has a variety of other functions, the most important of which is the supply of stores, victuals and ammunition. These merchant ships sail under the Blue Ensign (with gold foul anchor) and are owned by the Ministry of Defence. The 3,500 officers and ratings serve under the Merchant Navy Articles of Agreement and many have transferred from independent civilian shipping lines.

Most RFAs are fitted with helicopter pads and most carry their own integrated helicopter support provided by the Royal Navy. They are unarmed ships, though some were equipped with GPMGs and rifles. Twenty-two RFAs, including the six LSLs were deployed in support of Operation Corporate, 90% of the total

fleet. The senior RFA officer afloat was Commodore SC Dunlop, flying his flag in the fleet replenishment ship *Fort Austin*.

From the outset of the campaign, the four largest supply ships *Fort Grange*, *Fort Austin*, *Resource* and *Regent* were at sea with a carefully balanced load of stores and equipment. All are designed to transfer their stores at sea to HM Ships either with Jackstay rigs, by vertical replenishment (VERTREP) by helicopter or to smaller ships alongside. The weight of air-lifted loads is critical especially as most of the helicopters of 772 Naval Air Squadron were the older Wessex Vs. The Forts had two pads while the remainder just one, all situated aft. Stores are usually palettised for easy handling while helicopters lift their loads with rope slings.

*Resource* was the first ship to be involved supporting the carrier group south along with the tanker *Olmeda*. She was one of the first merchant ships to anchor

*The Royal Fleet Auxiliary supply ship Fort Grange (22,750 tons), the newest of four Fleet Replenishment ships to support the Task Force. She was undergoing a long refit when ordered south, carrying aircraft spares, ammunition and food.*

in San Carlos Water on 23 May resupplying the troops ashore during some of the fiercest Argentine air attacks. She remained until 26 May, when she steamed for South Georgia where she embarked much needed refrigerated stores and fresh food from the liner *Saxonia*. She then returned to the Falklands and in all landed over 4,000 pallets in support of ships and troops.

Her sister ship RFA *Regent* primarily supported the amphibious group during the passage south, sailing from UK on 19 April fully stored with two extra Wessex Vs of 848 Squadron embarked, and from Ascension Island on 6 May. She transferred about 3,250 pallets of dry stores and ammunition during the campaign, restocking from the *Saxonia* and *Geestport* in Stromness Bay in South Georgia. The safety of these two stores ships was imperative to the Task Force, losing one might well have delayed the successful outcome.

Meanwhile of the newer Forts, which were mainly armament carriers, *Fort Grange* was undergoing a long refit in Devonport. Day and night work on her meant she was able to sail on 14 May, though her STUFT replenishment ship *Lycaon* actually reached the South Atlantic first. An early chance of action came when she was buzzed by an Argentine C-130 on 31 May, but the aircraft veered off when only 2,000 yards away. Her cargo was mainly aircraft spares, ammunition and food and she joined the battle group on 3 June. Three days later she took aboard all the remaining stores from *Fort Austin* before the latter sailed for home. On 10 June she was back in San Carlos Water transferring stores ashore, leaving later that evening. She remained in the Falklands for two months after the campaign finished as

---

**Helicopter Support Ship**

**K 08 Engadine**
8,690 tons (full load)
Length: 129.3m
Beam: 17.9m
Draught: 6.7m
Propulsion: 1 Diesel engine
Speed: 16 knots
Armament: Improvised – 14 × 7.62mm
machine guns
Aircraft: 4 Wessex V
Builders: Henry Robb
Launched: 15 September 1966;
In Service: 15 December 1967

the garrison support ship.

*Fort Austin* had been in the Persian Gulf for nearly six months when on 29 March, she was sent post haste from Gibraltar to replenish *Endurance* who had only three weeks more supplies aboard and was already heavily committed in the South Atlantic. Although normally unarmed, she had embarked Lynx helicopters, specially fitted for firing the Sea Skua missile, along with

---

### Royal Fleet Auxiliaries (Fleet Replenishment Ships)

**A 385 Fort Grange**
22,890 tons (full load)
Length: 183.8m
Beam: 24.1m
Draught: 14.9m
Propulsion: 1 Diesel engine
Speed: 22 knots
Armament: Improvised
Aircraft: 3 Helicopters, various (Designed for 2 Sea Kings)
Load: 3,500 tons of ammunition, stores and spares
Builders: Scott-Lithgow, Greenock
Launched: 9 December 1976;
    In Service: 6 April 1978

**A 386 Fort Austin**
As for Fort Grange
Launched: 8 March 1978;
    In Service: 11 May 1979

**A 480 Resource**
22,890 tons (full load)
Length: 195.1m
Beam: 23.5m
Draught: 8.0m
Propulsion: 1 set Geared Steam Turbines
Speed: 17 knots
Armament: Improvised
Aircraft: 1 Wessex Mk 5
Load: Ammunition, stores and spares
Builders: Scotts SB, Greenock
Launched: 11 February 1966;
    In Service: 18 May 1967

**A 486 Regent**
As for Resource
Builders: Harland and Wolff, Belfast
Launched: 9 March 1966;
    In Service: 6 June 1967

**A 344 Stromness**
16,792 tons (full load)
Length: 159.8m
Beam: 22.0m
Propulsion: 1 Diesel engine
Speed: 18.5 knots
Armament: Improvised
Aircraft: Helicopter pad – no embarked flight
Builders: Swan Hunter
Launched: 16 September 1966;
    In Service: March 1967

---

*RFA* Resource *(23,000 tons), was in San Carlos Water during some of the fiercest Argentine air attacks. After unloading, she sailed to South Georgia where she re-stocked before returning to the Falklands. She carried one Wessex V.*

special forces for operations to re-take South Georgia. The value of the embarked Lynxes was apparent when she was able to provide anti-submarine support for the *Olmeda*. On D-Day, *Fort Austin* was in Falkland Sound when she was attacked by a Dagger aircraft, which, when only 1,000 yards away, was hit by one of *Broadsword*'s Sea Wolf missiles. Later that day *Fort Austin* claimed to have hit an Argentine Dagger with one of her GPMGs. Three days later she was again near-missed by enemy bombs. Yet another role was in store for the ship when she took aboard 263 survivors of *Coventry* next day, sailing that night. She was the longest serving RFA in the TEZ when she left for home on 6 June, via South Georgia.

Two other supply RFAs had quite different roles. *Engadine* was a helicopter support ship, sailing from UK on 10 May with 270 mixed RN and RAF personnel and carrying a large quantity of aircraft stores and equipment, along with four Wessex Vs and two Sea Kings. She was also buzzed by an enemy Hercules and positively bristled with her defence of 14 GPMGs and LMGs. The arrival of *Engadine* in San Carlos Water brought much needed support for the overworked helicopters controlled by COMAW. Not only was she able to provide second and third line maintenance for the shore based helicopters, but she also provided some recreation facilities for the air and ground crews. She spent nearly 600 hours at flying stations and saw a total of 1,606 deck landings.

The final ship in this group was the RFA *Stromness*, already in reserve in UK. She had been completely destored, but was otherwise ready to sail. It was decided that she should initially be a troop carrier and assault platform and sailed on 8 April with the bulk of 45 Commando and sufficient rations to maintain 7,500 men for a month. She was in the heart of the action on D-Day carrying the second wave of assault troops and was near missed by several bombs during the succeeding days. Sailing for South Georgia, she embarked about 400 men of 5 Infantry Brigade, their stores and ammunition before sailing back to the Falklands on 27 May. She was reunited with 45 Commando after the campaign bringing the unit home as far as Ascension.

These ships of the Royal Fleet Auxiliary were re-supplied by STUFT ships in the TRALA and were committed continuously in the war zone. That none of them was hit was a miracle of planning, superb seamanship and some good fortune. Had they been, the war might well have gone on a little longer.

# Royal Navy Minesweepers, Tugs, etc

At the outset of the campaign the Royal Navy had in commission some 36 mine-hunters, three brand new ones of the 515 ton Hunt class, the remainder being much older and smaller, mostly of the 320 ton Ton class. Conditions in the South Atlantic, coupled with the range, demanded larger vessels not relying on a 'mother ship' and it was decided that five large trawlers, already ear-marked, should be taken up from trade and commissioned as minesweepers with RN crews. These were the only STUFT ships to wear the White Ensign.

The Argentine sea-mine threat was small but real and could have caused problems in selecting a main landing area. In the event, only one enemy mine-laying activity was reported, monitored by one of the patrolling submarines in mid-April off Cape Pembroke at the eastern tip of the Falklands in the approaches to Stanley. This was the only minefield admitted by the Argentinians at the end of hostilities and was partly cleared by the converted minesweepers.

The trawlers taken up as minesweepers were the *Farnella*, *Junella*, *Cordella* and *Northella*, becoming collectively known as the 'Ellas', all were of 1,238 tons (*Junella* 1,615 tons) and capable of long ocean going voyages. Subsequently they were joined by another trawler from Hull, the *Pict*. Plans already existed for their emergency conversion and crews from some of the Royal Navy's Ton class manned them, the new ships becoming HM Auxiliaries as Extra Deep Armed

*The Argentinian oil-rig support vessel* Yehuin *which was used for inter-island supply duties and later in Stanley by the Royal Navy for transfer of troops and stores.*

Team Sweep (EDATS). Their civilian crews volunteered to a man to go south, even suggesting they take their nets with them, but to their regret they were overruled.

They sailed from the UK on 27 April as the 11th Minesweeping Squadron,

---

**Minesweeping Trawlers** – 11th Mine Counter Measures Squadron *Ships Taken Up From Trade and Commissioned*

**HMA Cordella**
1,238 tons
Length: 70.2m
Beam: 12.7m
Propulsion: 1 Diesel engine
Speed: 16.5 knots
Builders: J Marr & Sons, Hull
Launched: 1973; Commissioned 1982

**HMS Farnella**
As Cordella above except launched 1972

**HMS Northella**
As Cordella above

**HMS Junella**
1,615 tons
Length: 66.3m
Beam: 13.1m
Propulsion: 1 Diesel engine
Speed: 15.5 knots
Builders: J Marr & Sons, Hull
Launched: 1975; Commissioned 1982

**HMS Pict**
1,478 tons
Length: 70.1m
Beam: 12.9m
Propulsion: 1 diesel engine
Speed: 13.5 knots
Builders: British United Trawlers, Hull
Launched: 1973; Commissioned 1982

**Offshore Patrol Vessels**

**P 258  HMS Leeds Castle**
1,450 tons
Length: 81.0m
Beam: 11.5m
Draught: 3.4m
Propulsion: 2 Ruston diesel engines
Speed: 20 knots
Armament: 1 × 40mm Bofors gun, 2 GPMGs
Builders: Hall Russell, Aberdeen
Launched: 22 October 1980;
              Commissioned 1982

**P 265  HMS Dumbarton Castle**
As Leeds Castle above

*HMS* Leeds Castle *an offshore patrol boat alongside the base tanker* Alvega *at Ascension.* Leeds Castle *acted as a helicopter refuelling platform during the transfer of troops and stores at South Georgia.*

exercising off Portland before sailing for South Georgia via Ascension. They were quickly used as despatch vessels, transferring men and stores and cross loading between ships anchored there. Some were later used to insert SBS and SAS patrols by night on the Falklands and were available in Falkland Sound during the San Carlos landings should they be needed to sweep mines.

As so often happens to these small ships, their main job started when the war finished and they disposed of 10 of the reported 21 moored mines laid by the Argentinians, before being relieved by the RN's Hunt Class mine hunters.

Two offshore patrol boats, HMS *Leeds Castle* and *Dumbarton Castle* of 1,400 tons, both newly commissioned, were sent as despatch vessels. Initially one became the Ascension guardship, but they were soon plying their way south with essential stores. When the QE 2 was transferring troops in South Georgia, *Leeds Castle* became a floating helicopter refuelling platform.

The first ship to leave UK on 4 April was the Royal Maritime Auxiliary Service

ocean-going tug *Typhoon* of 1,380 tons, soon to be joined by the requisitioned *Salvageman*, *Irishman*, and *Yorkshireman* from the United Towing Company, all fortunately in UK waters at the time of the crisis. The *Typhoon* did sterling but unaccustomed work at South Georgia, being one of the many small ships transferring and cross-loading men and stores of 5 Infantry Brigade. Later she assisted in refloating the Argentine submarine *Santa Fe*.

Meanwhile her civilian compatriots were involved in more tug-like activities, the *Salvageman* going to the help of *Sheffield*, standing by the bombed *Glasgow* and then called to the stricken *Atlantic Conveyor*. *Irishman* was also called to the *Atlantic Conveyor* and two of her crew were decorated for their work aboard the abandoned ship.

The tugs continued their busy pro-

gramme at the end of the war in recovering SBS and SAS patrols dotted throughout the islands and then three of them towed the *Santa Fe* out to sea for disposal. They were then engaged in working on the sunken frigates *Ardent* and *Antelope*. Their work was not completed until long after the war and relief crews were flown out so that they could continue their excellent work. Indeed *Salvageman* did not return to UK until mid-1984.

Another of the unfashionable but essential jobs carried out by the RMAS was that by the Mooring Vessel *Goosander*, which was employed from late May laying buoys and moorings at Ascension.

Of the RFA's 27 ships, all were activated and 22 of them were committed to the Task Force with crews totalling over 2,500 officers and men. The work of them and the RMAS, both of whom provided men for Naval Parties aboard STUFT ships, played a highly essential and efficient part in the success of Operation Corporate. Ten crew members lost their lives including the master of the *Atlantic Conveyor*, Captain Ian North, three officers and six Chinese ratings.

# Royal Naval Parties

Every merchant ship taken up from trade had a Naval Party assigned to it. Most of these were Royal Navy personnel, but for some of the specialised ships, they came from ancilliary services. For instance the Royal Naval Supply and Transport Service provided the Naval Parties for four of the stores ships, while the Royal Fleet Auxiliary provided them for the STUFT tankers. The expertise of the Royal Maritime Auxiliary Service was utilised with the three ocean going tugs and the mooring ship *Wimpey Seahorse*.

These parties varied in size according to the ship and its functions, advising not only on naval communications and procedures but also on the function new to many of the civilian merchant ships of Replenishment At Sea (RAS). All STUFT ships were fitted with compatible communications systems from SATCOM to cryptographic machines. In addition all tankers and supply ships were fitted with RAS gear and many of them helicopter platforms for the first time. The duties of the Naval Parties were not only to advise the master in working with the Royal Navy, but they carried out such tasks as maintaining and operating the new equipment.

Each party had its own engineers, communicators and maintainers to advise the crew and in many cases operate the equipment themselves. In the case of the *Atlantic Conveyor, Atlantic Causeway, Contender Bezant* and *Astronomer*, naval air artificers were embarked to man the newly installed workshop facilities.

There were a number of Royal Naval Reserve officers amongst the crews of the merchant ships whose training gave them a firm grip on the operating procedures of the Royal Navy, one such being Captain W Scott-Masson, the master of the *SS Canberra*. Captain CPO Burne RN as the Senior Naval Officer of NP 1710, found himself dealing with the ever-complaining media as well as the expected duty of advising the master. During the time spent in San Carlos Water, he gave a continuous running commentary on the air attacks over the ship's internal broadcast system; while later in South Georgia he was responsible for the transfer of 5 Infantry Brigade from *QE 2* to *Canberra*.

As will be seen in the accompanying

*Before the Argentinian invasion, the Royal Marines of Naval Party 8901 led a comparatively peaceful life. The detachment, about 35 strong lived at Moody Brook Camp, west of Stanley.*

table, 20 STUFT ships had RN manned Naval Parties, whilst a further 18 had RFA, RMAS or RNS & TS representatives aboard. These Naval Parties, varying in size from over thirty in *Canberra* to two or three in smaller ships, played an integral and important part in the smooth transition of the Merchant Navy to a wartime footing.

The two shore based Naval Parties were completely different in their composition and employment. NP 8901 had served as garrison troops in the Falklands since 1965. Before that Royal Marines detachments from *Protector* had regularly spent time in the islands during their commission in the South Atlantic, and indeed a Royal Marine presence can be

traced back to 1766 when Great Britain established its first settlement on the Falklands. NP 8901 had varied in size over the years but in 1982 it was established at around 35 all ranks. It was sheer coincidence that at the time of the emergency, the new NP 8901 (1982/3) were relieving the old detachment, providing 70 Royal Marines on the islands along with some sailors of a naval survey team. However against the overwhelming odds of the Argentinian invasion they were ordered by Governor and Commander-in-Chief Rex Hunt to surrender after putting up spirited resistance. They were repatriated to the UK by 5 April, but sailed south again a fortnight later forming the nucleus of J Company of 42 Commando.

Meanwhile NP 1222 was formed as a Naval Aircraft Servicing Unit and flew to Ascension Island on 6 April. At its peak NP 1222, with some of its emphasis changed, had 120 men, but was realistic-

## NAVAL PARTIES

### Shore Based

| | |
|---|---|
| 1222 Ascension Island | Royal Naval Aircraft Servicing Unit Capt R McQueen RN |
| 0901 Falklands Garrison | Royal Marines detachment Maj M J Norman RM |

### Embarked

| | |
|---|---|
| 1710 Canberra | Capt CPO Burne RN |
| 1720 Europic Ferry | Cdr AB Gough RN |
| 1810 Stena Seaspread | Capt P Badcock RN |
| 1830 Uganda | Cdr AB Gough RN |
| 1840 Atlantic Conveyor | Capt MG Layard RN |
| 1850 Norland | Cdr CJ Esplin-Jones RN |
| 1870 Iris | Lt Cdr J Bithell RN |
| 1900 Lycaon | Lt Cdr DJ Stiles RN |
| 1950 Nordic Ferry | Lt Cdr M St JDA Thornburn RN |
| 1960 Baltic Ferry | Lt Cdr GB Webb RN |
| 1980 QE 2 | Capt NCH James RN |
| 1990 Atlantic Causeway | Cdr RP Seymour RN |
| 2010 Stena Inspector | Capt PJ Stickland RN |
| 2020 Tor Caledonia | Lt Cdr JG Devine RN |
| 2050 Contender Bezant | Lt Cdr DHN Yates RN |
| 2050 Elk | Cdr AS Ritchie RN |
| 2060 St Edmund | Lt Cdr AM Scott RN |
| 2090 British Enterprise III | Lt Cdr BEM Reynell RN |
| 2100 St Helena | Lt Cdr DN Heelas RN |
| 2140 Astronomer | Lt Cdr R Gainsford RN |

The Royal Maritime Auxiliary Service provided Naval Parties for the following STUFT ships:
Irishman
Yorkshireman
Salvageman
Wimpey Seahorse (NP 2000)

The Royal Fleet Auxiliary provided Naval Parties for the following STUFT ships:
Anco Charger
Balder London
British Avon
British Dart
British Esk
British Tamar
British Tay
British Trent
British Wye
Eburna
Fort Toronto

The Royal Naval Supply and Transport Service supplied Naval Parties for the following STUFT ships:
Avelona Star
Geestport
Laertes
Saxonia.

*Royal Naval air mechanics and artificers of Naval Party 1840 aboard* Atlantic Conveyor. *The forward deck was strengthened to accept Harriers and Chinooks while containers provided protection. All fourteen Harriers were flown off before the ship was sunk.*

ally maintained at 90. Capt Bob McQueen, who had recently been Captain of HMS *Osprey* at the Royal Naval Air Station, Portland, now became the Commander British Forces Support Unit.

Two other specialist Naval Parties were Nos 1 and 3 Fleet Clearance Diving Teams. These are the Royal Navy's bomb disposal experts, more used to working on World War 2 mines washed up on the beaches of Great Britain. FCDT 1, commanded by Lieutenant NA Bruen, successfully dealt with unexploded bombs in *Sir Galahad* and *Sir Lancelot* in San Carlos Water on 24 May, having only arrived in the *Sir Bedivere* earlier that day. Meanwhile FCDT 3, under the command of Lieutenant Commander BF Dutton, had already defused a bomb in *Argonaut* on D-Day, while his second in command Fleet Chief Petty Officer MG Fellowes carried out a ten hours delicate operation on the unexploded bomb in *Antrim*. Amidst the constant Argentinian air raids, these were two cool and calculated acts of bravery suitably rewarded by the DSO and DSC (the first ever to be awarded to the recently restored naval rank of Warrant Officer) respectively. An RAF Explosive Ordnance Demolition Team carried out similar tasks with Chief Technician Hankinson helping with the second bomb in *Argonaut* and Flight Lieutenant A Swan with the unexploded bombs which lodged in the Forward Dressing Station at Ajax Bay on 27 May.

Very often small groups and detachments do not hit the headlines, but each of these was an integral and essential part of the overall team which formed the Task Force and its supporting elements.

# HMS Endurance

One of the Royal Navy's less spectacular but highly productive peacetime tasks is that of specialist surveying and hydrography. For many years the department of the Hydrographer to the Navy has led the world in this field, surveying out the oceans of the world, chart making, and recording oceanographic data. The results benefit both British and foreign merchant fleets as much as their Navies.

The first ship specially designed for the Royal Navy's surveying role was *Vidal*, and indeed it was she, on 18 September 1955 that annexed the Atlantic islet of Rockall for Great Britain, a far sighted operation that ensured Britain's territorial waters for under sea oil exploration in the area. *Vidal* was laid down in 1950 and when she was launched 15 months later she was the first of her type to be equipped with a flight deck and integral helicopter. Before that *Cook* Class survey ships carried out some exploration work, which included Antarctica. The advent of the helicopter enabled survey parties to operate at greater distances from their 'Mother Ship' and for longer periods as it eased the problem of re-supply and emergency evacuation.

Although other warships, notably *Bay* Class frigates were adapted for temporary survey work, it was not until 1964 that a specially designed hydro-oceanographic survey ship was proposed. Before this *Protector*, converted from a net-layer and subsequently designated an Ice Patrol Ship, spent much time from the mid-50s onwards in the South Atlantic and was involved in some Argentinian confrontations. She carried a small detachment of

Royal Marines and acted as Falklands Guard Ship during the summer season. In between transporting her Royal Marines and those of Naval Party 8901, the permanent Falklands garrison, she carried out normal survey work.

*Protector* was finally replaced in 1968 by *Endurance*, which had been built by Krögerwerft of Rensburg, Denmark and completed as the *Anita Dan* in 1956. She was purchased by the Admiralty in 1967 for around £300,000 and converted to become the Falkland Islands guardship and Ice Patrol vessel. She was commissioned on 28 June 1968 and this vessel of 3,600 tons initially had a complement of 13 officers (later up to 20) and 106 ratings, was painted bright red with white upper works for easy recognition and was affectionately known as 'The Red Plum'. A large hangar had been built abaft the funnel, extending her poop deck to create a helicopter landing platform. At the time of the Argentinian invasion she was equipped with 2 Wasp helicopters. She was essentially a peaceful ship with her helicopters painted with day-glo panels and she carried up to 12 members of the British Antarctic Survey team. Her only armament was two 20 mm Oerlikon guns which could be mounted on the bridge superstructure if required.

Her annual programme was to leave UK with her new crew, and Royal Marines detachment of 1 officer and 12, in the autumn each year returning to UK around April. In 1981 the statement on Defence Estimates forecast the imminent disposal of a number of ships, although *Endurance* was not specifically named. However rumours were rife that she would be among those to go and Lord Shackleton raised the matter in the House of Lords. Despite pressure from the Foreign and Commonwealth Office for its retention it was finally announced by Lord Trefgarne, at that time a junior minister in the Department of Trade, that *Endurance* would indeed be paid off in 1982 on her return to UK. It was with this in mind that preparations were being made in the ship for final farewells to the South Atlantic.

Captain Nick Barber was about to complete his second year in command. During this time he had reported an

increasing volume of Argentinian military radio traffic, particularly since Christmas 1981. However those at home, whilst heeding his warnings, had not changed their minds over withdrawing the ship; indeed some even suggested that he was being alarmist in order to save his ship. *Endurance* had paid one of her periodic visits to Chile in January 1982 followed by a four day stay at the Argentinian port of Mar del Plata. Because the seaside harbour was filled with yachts, she was allowed to dock inside the main naval base. Goodwill exchanges were made between the British and Argentinian ships and the genial Capitan de Fragata Horacio Alberto Bicain met Captain Barker at an official reception. They were to meet again a few weeks later when Capitan Bicain surrendered his ship, the submarine *Santa Fe* in South Georgia. From conversations at the time it was apparent that few Argentinian officers knew of the proposed invasion of the Falklands Islands. However when Captain Barker privately met Anglo-Argentinians he became aware of the growing economic problems facing the new Galtieri regime, which was looking for an outlet to take Argentinian minds off the internal troubles, possibly focussing on the Islas Malvinas as a temporary solution.

*Endurance* sailed from Mar del Plata on 22 February, calling at Port Stanley three days later, before setting off south for her final task with the British Antarctic Survey (BAS) team at their base at Rothera. On 16 March she picked up the Joint Services Expedition from South Georgia, said goodbye to Steve Martin the base commander of BAS and headed for her final cruise home, via Port Stanley, Montevideo, Buenos Aires, Barbados and the Azores. But this was not to be.

During the night of 19 March, while the ship was at Stanley, news was received from Martin that a party of Argentinians, supposedly scrap metal merchants, had landed at the old Whaling Station at Leith in South Georgia and raised the Argentinian flag. After consultations with the Governor, Rex Hunt, who informed London, it was decided that these Argentinians should be ordered off the islands. *Endurance* re-embarked her flight, along with the Royal Marines detachment who had been exercising ashore; in addition, the ship embarked a

---

**A 141 HMS Endurance – Ice Patrol Ship**

3,600 tons
Length: 93m
Beam: 14m
Draught: 5.5m
Propulsion: 1 Burmeister & Wain diesel
Speed: 14.5 knots
Complement: 13 officers, 106 ratings (Incl
           1 + 12 RM's), 12 passengers
Armament: 2 × 20mm Oerlikons
Aircraft: 2 × Wasp helicopters
Builders: Krögerwerft (Denmark)
Launched: May 1956 as *Anita Dan*
Commissioned as HMS *Endurance* 28 June 1968

---

*The ice patrol ship HMS* Endurance *which was due to be withdrawn from service in 1982, but subsequently played a vital part in the operations in South Georgia.*

further nine marines of NP 8901 to make up a full platoon and sailed at 0845 on 21 March for South Georgia, 800 miles away. 10 members of her Naval Survey Party remained ashore in the Falkland Islands.

With a maximum steaming speed of only 15 knots, it was to take three days to reach South Georgia, in which time Lieutenant Keith Mills, commanding the Royal Marines detachment and Sergeant Pete Leach, made plans for the recapture of Leith. Observation teams were flown into Jason Peak on 24th by the ship's Wasp helicopter and watch was kept on the Argentinians, who were unloading stores as if they were preparing for a long stay. On 27 March Mills and Leach made a closer recce in appalling weather. *Endurance* shadowed the Argen-

tinian *Bahia Paraiso* during the next few days, and on 31 March Northwood ordered Captain Barker to land the whole Royal Marines detachment at King Edward Point in view of growing intelligence indicating a further Argentinian landing on South Georgia. The military could provide protection for the BAS team, but one platoon covering an island 100 miles in length could be no more than a token force against overwhelming odds.

Meanwhile the ship put to sea whilst her helicopters carried out reconnaissance and surveillance. It was about

1030 on 3 April that the *Bahia Paraiso* informed Mills that 'Following our successful operation in the Malvinas Islands, the ex-Governor has surrendered the islands and their dependencies to Argentina. We suggest you adopt a similar course of action to prevent further loss of life'. An account of the subsequent landings in South Georgia, the spirited resistance by the Royal Marines and the part played by *Endurance* in the subsequent recapture of the islands are included in a later chapter.

There is however no doubt that the permanent presence of *Endurance* in Antarctica, her close liaison with the British Antarctic Survey team, the frequent visits to South America and the intelligence gleaned by Captain Nick Barker played a decisive part in the campaign.

# Queen Elizabeth II

As the *Queen Elizabeth II* passed Bishop's Rock on 3 May on her return from her first visit to Philadelphia to celebrate the 200th anniversary of the city's founding, a BBC World service announcement that the ship was to be requisitioned as a troopship stunned the passengers into disbelief. Captain AJ Hutcheson, although expecting some such statement since the beginning of the Falklands war, had the BBC on his ship-shore telephone within minutes asking for confirmation. But at that particular moment he had none, and it was sad that Cunard had not been able to break the news first. However several hours later when the master was able to confirm the announcement over the ship's broadcast system, it was greeted by prolonged cheering from the British crew.

When the ship docked at two minutes past midnight on 4 May, military and newsmen were waiting for her, and during that day came the shock report that *Sheffield* had been hit by Exocet missiles. It was with great regret that Captain Hutcheson was to pass over command of this great ship to Captain Peter Jackson on one of his final trips before retirement.

The military planners had decided to send 5 Infantry Brigade as reinforcements for 3 Commando Brigade and now needed to transport them south. The *Queen Elizabeth II*, the last of the great ocean liners had been built in 1969 with a gross tonnage of 67,140 tons, the largest passenger liner afloat at the time. Her prestige value was immense and it must have been in everyone's mind that, should she be sunk, Britain's credibility as a maritime nation would be in serious doubt. But transport for 3,000 men had to be found, and she was the only British ship capable of carrying that number over 8,000 miles. As soon as the ship docked, workmen from Vosper Thorneycroft were swarming all over her, removing the luxury fittings and preparing her as a troopship, like her predecessors the *Queen Mary* and *Queen Elizabeth* over 40 years earlier.

As with the *Canberra*, crew members were given the option of leaving the ship, but few did, even though passenger stewards were not needed and crew members under the age of 18 required

their parent's permission. There was a degree of urgency about her modification, but not so much as the earlier STUFT ships which left with the Task Force. There were nine full days for the ship to be altered, loaded, stored and equipped. It is reported that, amongst the military supplies came three million Mars Bars to sustain the troops in the field! Stores for three months were loaded, men working all through the night, while the necessary modifications to fit helicopter pads got underway. These were already under construction by Vospers before the ship arrived home. Much had been learnt by the ship-builders when they had modified the *Canberra* about the fittings required and the task was that much easier. Hundreds of feet of the after decks and verandah windows had to be removed and a double size pad was constructed aft, more suitable for helicopter pilots in the severe weather conditions they might expect later. Another was laid over the swimming pool forward. Under-deck supports were fitted which made some passenger cabins unusable, but as the swimming pools had originally been built to withstand the heavy weight of water, they were ideal.

Communications, which were to prove vital to the Land Force Commander during his voyage south, were fitted and SCOT (Satellite Communications Onboard Tracker) was installed, while a degaussing cable, to reduce the ship's magnetic field, was also fitted. Hardboard sheets were laid along the hundreds of yards of gangways and passages to protect the carpets, while movable fittings such as potted palms, paintings and luxury lamp fittings were taken ashore. Equipment for replenishment of fuel and water at sea was added. Such was the frantic preparation for war.

With more than a week to plan the layout and accommodation, First Officer Phil Rental donned his RNR uniform and became the liaison officer between the Master and Captain NCH 'Jimmy' James RN, adviser and in overall naval charge of the ship, his staff becoming Naval Party 1980. The ship was destined to take the bulk of Headquarters Land Forces Falkland Islands staff, 5 Infantry Brigade HQ, 2nd Bn

**Queen Elizabeth II**
67,140 tons
Naval Party 1980
Launched: 20 September 1967 at John Browns, Glasgow
Taken Up From Trade: 4 May 1988
Modified: 4-12 May
Sailed: 12 May
Returned: 11 June
Emergency modifications by Vosper Thorneycroft at Southampton
Length: 293.5m
Beam: 32.1m
Propulsion: 4 sets geared steam turbines
Speed: 28.5 knots
Aircraft: 2 × Sea King Mk 2 (*UK to South Georgia*)

Scots Guards, 1st Bn Welsh Guards and 1st Bn the 7th Duke of Edinburgh's Own Gurkha Rifles, besides a multitude of support units.

At dawn on 12 May the main body of the first troops arrived, the Welsh Guards, followed later that morning by the Gurkhas and Scots Guards. By mid afternoon the ship's side was lined with over 3,000 waving troops, sad but anxious to make the final painful break from their loved ones and well-wishers on the dockside. Down below, feverish activity ensued as only one of the three boilers was working and that alone would not get the ship very far. However the *QE II* slipped her moorings at 1600 and in bright sunshine, with a band playing 'Old Lang Syne', she moved away from Southampton's Ocean Terminal, which had seen many emotional departures in the past, but none perhaps as momentous as this.

On the journey down Channel the RAS equipment was tested with the RFA *Grey Rover* using troops to haul in the lines. As with *Canberra* the Royal Navy tested her helicopter decks. The voyage south had the air of a cruise except that the passengers had other things on their minds. On 18 May *QE II* docked in Freetown, where she took on fresh water and fuel. No-one was allowed ashore and many troops got their first sight of bum boats bartering alongside. Less than 12 hours later she left Freetown and was not to dock again until reaching Southampton four weeks later.

Whilst off Ascension on 20th, she embarked Major General Jeremy Moore and his 80-strong staff of Land Forces Falkland Islands; then set sail for South Georgia, taking an easterly course, thus

*The* Queen Elizabeth 2, *transfers 5 Infantry Brigade for transhipment to the Falkland Islands, in the shelter of Grytviken Bay, South Georgia.*

keeping out of range of land based Argentinian Air Forces. Blowpipe anti-aircraft missiles were installed on special mountings around the base of the funnel, whilst Browning machine guns were mounted on the bridge wings.

On board the troops enjoyed luxuries they had seldom seen. The Guards messed in the Columbia Restaurant, the Gurkhas in the Tables of the World, while the Penthouse Grill became the Petty Officers and Sergeants Messes. The officers mainly ate in the Queen's Grill. Fresh water was expected to be a problem but the newly installed reverse osmosis systems and four distilling plants proved more than adequate.

From the outset, the Russians had taken a great interest in the ship and occasional spy trawlers were no doubt giving its position away to those who wanted it. Another danger was imminent as the ship sailed further south; the ice belt extended well north of South Georgia, and with thoughts of the *Titanic* in their minds the lookouts were more than ever watchful. With the radar switched off to avoid detection, vigilance was a matter for the 'Mark One Eyeball'.

By 1930 on 27 May *QE II* anchored in the restful but icy waters of Cumberland Bay in South Georgia and cross decking started almost immediately, mostly to *Canberra* which had returned from San Carlos Water. Most of the troops were transferred by boat and trawler, whilst vehicles and stores were airlifted off. Disembarkation continued throughout the 28th, and by mid-afternoon on 29th all was clear. In turn the *QE II* embarked the 629 survivors of the ill fated ships *Coventry, Ardent* and *Antelope*. By late evening she was clear of the ice and running very low on fuel. After 'rassing' with the RFA *Bayleaf* on 1 June she started her long, lonely journey home. Two days later *QE II* was ordered to proceed direct to Southampton and with all good speed she arrived there on 11 June. Her Majesty Queen Elizabeth, The Queen Mother, had asked to meet the ship in the Solent. She embarked in the Royal Yacht *Britannia* and the two ships met off Cowes, where Her Majesty could clearly be seen waving to the men aboard the liner. Signals of greeting were exchanged as the pride of Britain's Merchant Fleet sailed majestically up Southampton Water. She was the first arrival home from the South Atlantic and, with promising news from the battle front splattered across the newspapers, she was greeted with a euphoria not seen in England since World War 2. Crowds lined the approaches and the quayside as shortly after 1100, with the Royal Marines Band playing ashore, she edged her way alongside. At noon families of those injured were allowed on board and as the day wore on, everyone made their way home. Only one of the injured taken aboard in the South Atlantic needed further hospital treatment.

The ship was soon in dry dock, workmen transformed her to her former glory and by 14 August she set sail on her first post-Falklands cruise. Although initially painted with a new pebble-grey hull, this proved unpopular and she soon 'blacked out' to her traditional Cunard colours.

---

**[Embarked Troops]**
*(UK to South Georgia)*

Naval Party 1980
Headquarters Land Forces Falklands Islands
5 Infantry Brigade consisting of:
    4 Field Regiment Royal Artillery (97 Field Battery)
Blowpipe Troop 43 Air Defence Battery
32 Guided Weapons Regiment Royal Artillery
9 Parachute Squadron Royal Engineers
5 Infantry Brigade HQ and Signal Squadron
2nd Bn Scots Guards
1st Bn Welsh Guards
1/7 Duke of Edinburgh's Own Gurkha Rifles
656 Squadron Army Air Corps
407 Troop Royal Corps of Transport
16 Field Ambulance Royal Army Medical Corps
81 Ordnance Company Royal Army Ordnance Corps
10 Field Workshops Royal Electrical and Mechanical Engineers
5 Infantry Brigade Platoon of 160 Provost Company Royal Military Police
8 Field Cash Office Royal Army Pay Corps
81 Intelligence Section
601 Tactical Air Control Party
602 Tactical Air Control Party

# Canberra

One of the most remarkable factors of the early stages of the campaign was the speedy conversion of the SS *Canberra*, flagship of the P & O Fleet to a troopship and its ability to sail within 5 days of the signing of the Order in Council requisitioning it, with more than 3,000 men on board.

At the time of the invasion of the Falklands on 2 April the ship was homeward bound in the Mediterranean with 1,650 passengers from a three months round the world cruise and was due into Southampton on 7th. On the afternoon of 2nd, Captain D J Scott-Masson CBE, RD*, RNR, was informed by signal that it was likely that his ship would be requisitioned. He immediately called a conference of his senior officers and plans were soon underway, to be implemented as soon as the requisition order was received. Captain Scott-Masson was a RNR List 1 Officer which meant that he trained with the Royal Navy during his spare time and was therefore up-to-date with the latest tactical doctrine. His crew were all British, by agreement between the company and the unions.

Military planning teams were flown to Gibraltar, embarked in the *Canberra* and held detailed consultations on the journey home to Southampton where the ship docked on 7 April. As the passengers disembarked they were startled to see a multitude of military and civilian personnel, planners, constructors, advisers and builders, who streamed up the other gangway.

Already plans had been conceived to build two helicopter pads and Vosper Thorneycroft were given the task of fitting them. The choice of where to put the helicopter decks was comparatively easy as the swimming pools were designed to support the weight of at least 70 tons of water, more than enough to withstand a crash landing by a fully laden helicopter. It is reported that the new *Canberra* deck design was hastily scribbled on the back of an envelope. Vospers had already started working on two prefabricated 50-ton structures before Canberra arrived home. The first to be fitted was over the Bonito swimming pool amidships where side screens had to be cut away and aerials re-routed.

The superstructure of most passenger liners is of light aluminium construction and deep trusses were built to run out over the ships side to support the weight of the 50-ton decks. Down below metal shorting posts braced the decks, providing extra strength, for many other heavy stores had to be stowed on the upper decks for a journey of over 8,000 miles through some of the world's most inhospitable seas.

The second helicopter pad was fitted forward of the bridge over the observation deck. Not all the steel was delivered on time and Vospers workmen were still fitting when the ship sailed. Indeed some of them did not leave the ship until it reached Freetown in Sierra Leone on 17 April. No helicopters were able to be flown onto the ship in Southampton, but during the early part of her voyage down Channel, Royal Naval helicopters from RNAS Culdrose tested the new decks. They found the midships area particularly difficult because of gusting winds between the bridge and funnels but useable with less restrictive emergency flying regulations.

Advance parties of the Royal Marines Commandos helped the ship's crew in unloading much of the liner's fittings and furniture. As cranes disembarked *Canberra*'s luxury accoutrements, the same cranes embarked military stores, ammunition and food. Careful planning had already determined the positioning of each item, though some cross-decking was later required. Chacons and containers of military stores arrived on the dockside in a continual stream from depots throughout the country. Replenishment at Sea facilities and improved communications equipment had to be added, turning the ship into a Landing Platform Luxury (Large)! Because of her colour, she was later to be christened 'the Great White Whale'.

At noon on the day following her arrival, the embarked forces began to file aboard. The ship was originally expected to carry 2,000 troops, but this soon rose to 3,000 which included the cream of Britain's mobile forces, 40 and 42 Commandos Royal Marines and 3rd Bn Parachute Regiment, plus numerous ancillaries. Rumour has it that the hardened sea-going Marines plausibly convinced the unsuspecting Paras that the lower accommodation would be better for them as it was less subject to ship's movement. Meanwhile the Marines

Received
- 6 APR 1982
Fleet Manager

DEPARTMENT OF TRADE
PARLIAMENT SQUARE HOUSE
34-36 PARLIAMENT STREET
LONDON SW1A 2ND

Telephone: 01-XX 233-8415

5 April 1982
Our Reference: S T 17/9/017

A Langley Esq
Peninsular and Orient Steam Navigation Company
Passenger Services Division
P & O Building
Leadenhall Street
London
EC3V 4QL

NOTICE OF REQUISITION

The Secretary of State for Trade in exercising the powers conferred upon him by the Requisitioning of Ships Order 1982 hereby requisitions the s.s. "CANBERRA" and requires you to place the said vessel at his disposal forthwith.

The vessel should proceed immediately to Southampton Berth 105.

The Master of the said vessel is being instructed to report to Mr R Brooks, Hogg Robinson(GFA) Ltd, Marchwood as to destination and employment of the said vessel. Please refer any general enquiries to the above address.

A further letter will be sent to you regarding the charter party arrangements which it is proposed to apply to the s.s. "CANBERRA".

Designation of Requisitioning Authority

(S S HOLNESS)
A Senior Principal
Department of Trade

*The Notice of Requisition issued on 5 April by the Department of Trade to the owners of the SS* Canberra, *which followed the Order in Council dated 4 April 1982 in which Her Majesty The Queen, on the advice of Her Privy Council, authorised the Requisition of Ships Order 1982.*

occupied the more luxurious accommodation above them, leaving their rivals in the hot and stuffy berths below. The sight of heavily laden troops, complete with weapons trampling through some of the staterooms made the permanent ship's crew wince even though sheets of hardboard had been laid in places to protect the carpets.

The crew were given the option of leaving the ship before sailing, but few left and 15 women, including an accountant, assistant pursers, telephone operators, stewardesses, a surgeon and nursing sisters finally sailed south. At 8pm on Good Friday, *Canberra* slipped her berth and sailed, fully lit, down the Solent where she was joined by her fellow P & O Ro-Ro ferry *Elk*, whose prime job was transporting the Brigade's war reserve of ammunition, bridging and signalling equipment.

Captain CPO Burne RN became the Senior Naval Officer and adviser to the Master. Colonel Tom Seccombe, an experienced Royal Marines officer, was appointed deputy Brigade Commander and was put in overall command of the embarked troops in *Canberra*. His job as military adviser to Captain Scott-Masson

*The Flagship of the P & O Fleet, SS* Canberra *(44,807 tons), one of the first ships to be requisitioned, became affectionately known as 'The Great White Whale'. She embarked most of 3 Commando Brigade, sailing on 9 April.*

was of inestimable value, and he was also able to keep a wily eye on the three unit Commanding Officers and see fair play in the matter of training areas, times, facilities and so on. He had a small administrative staff and Ministry of Defence Information Officers, who did not always have the strong rapport of the

*During the three months of the conflict SS* Canberra *was the principal troopship, carrying men into San Carlos Water, where she was subject to attention from the Argentinian Air Force, who claimed to have sunk her more than once.*

embarked media.

It was originally thought that *Canberra* would go no further than Ascension Island which she reached on 20 April. During her fortnight there, all troops were landed for military training, stores were unchanged, loads readjusted and replenishments made in all departments. During the second part of the voyage south, more attention was paid to medical facilities aboard, a blood bank with military and civilian crew donors was set up, and emergency training was given so that the civilian crew could take over from military medical orderlies when the latter went ashore. In addition the Royal Marines Band of Commando Forces were trained as stretcher bearers and helicopter marshals. Each evening, and often during the day, they entertained the crew with music, lifting the morale of those on board. Attention was also given to blacking out the ship once it arrived in the operational area. The *Canberra's* Games Deck was converted into an ammunition hold.

During the voyage south, the decks continually pounded to the boots of marching/running troops, determined to keep fighting fit even in the most unnatural conditions. It was nearly quarter of a mile around the Promenade deck of the ship as many a marine and para were to find out. Four times round was completed in about eight minutes fully loaded.

On 19 May, two days before the landings, 40 Commando was cross-decked to *Fearless* and 3 Para to *Intrepid* by landing craft. 42 Commando remained on board as the force reserve. However when the landings began on 21 May, *Canberra*, nakedly exposed to Argentinian attack in her white overcoat, moved into San Carlos Water. Late that day she took aboard some of the first casualties from the stricken *Ardent*, as well as some Argentinian wounded. The Bonito lounge became a 50-bed high dependency ward. By the end of the campaign she had received 174 patients, 82 British, 92 Argentine, none of whom died. The only funeral held aboard was the committal to sea of four Royal Marines aircrew who were killed on D-Day.

Although an Argentinian newspaper of 25 May carried a headline 'Canberra in Flames' she suffered no structural damage. Late on 27th she arrived off Grytviken in South Georgia where 2 Bn Scots

Guards and 1st Bn Welsh Guards were transferred from *Queen Elizabeth 2*, and were landed at San Carlos in misty weather on 2 June, thus avoiding unwelcome Argentinian Air Force attention. On the following day over 100 helicopter loads of stores were landed ashore, before the ship sailed. She did not return to San Carlos until the 15th, the day after the ceasefire, when she picked up 1,121 prisoners-of-war, subsequently on the 17th a further 3,046, whom she discharged at the obscure port of Puerto Madryn two days later. The prisoners were guarded by British troops during the short passage to Argentina where the Red Cross supervised the handover.

The war over, the *Canberra* sailed for San Carlos again, picking up 40 Commando, before embarking 42 Commando at Port Stanley on 25 June, and 45 Commando at Ascension. Thus, with the whole of 3 Commando Brigade aboard, she sailed on her triumphant journey home, being greeted at Southampton on a hot cloudless morning on Sunday 11 July by an unexpectedly euphoric crowd of families, friends and well-wishers.

The task of converting this temporary troopship back to her normal cruise liner status began on 9 August with a three weeks thorough refit and overhaul and on 11 September, she sailed on a 14 days cruise with a mere 1,745 passengers. Royal Navy helicopters saluted her departure and a military band somehow played amidst the streamers that stretched from ship to shore.

# Ships Taken Up From Trade

Contingency plans for every foreseeable emergency are the responsibility of the Operations and Planning Divisions of the Ministry of Defence. It is often difficult, even for the most clairvoyant of planners to predict every chance occurrence. Less than one per cent of such plans are ever realised. However the use of merchant ships in time of crisis was one which had had special attention since the run down of the surface fleet was announced in the Government's White Paper of 1981.

Since 1966 when the withdrawal of our defence forces from the Far East was confirmed, and Britain concentrated its attention to our NATO commitments, the official defence policy had assumed that such an emergency as the Falklands was so unlikely that amphibious type shipping, along with its support, had been run down to a dangerously low point. Exercises had taken place ever since the mid 1970s with civilian Roll-on Roll-off ferries replacing the traditional landing ships within the NATO arena, usually combining two or more nations. 3 Commando Brigade regularly exercised with these ferries, but always for the short distance emergency on the European land continent. These exercises also led to a close understanding between the Ministry of Defence, the Department of Trade and the General Council of British Shipping, who monitored them; and meetings were held regularly.

Out of area operations, away from the NATO scene, were deemed remote and sea voyages of over three days were glossed over. But plans there were, and it was at a special Privy Council meeting on the afternoon of Sunday 4 April that Her Majesty the Queen approved an Order in Council at Windsor Castle and invoked the Requisitioning of Ships Order 1982. The all embracing wording of this order includes

'A Secretary of State or the Minister of Transport or the Lords Commissioners of the Admiralty may requisition for Her Majesty's service any British ship and anything on board such ship wherever it may be.' It goes on to say that the owner of any such ship shall receive such payment for the use of the ship and compensation for loss and damage as shall be decided by arbitration.

By the end of the campaign 49 ships had been taken up, out-numbering the Royal Navy ships involved. Within 48 hours of the Argentinian invasion of the Falklands a TUFT (Taken Up from Trade) meeting was held and the task of identifying the suitability of ships for specific tasks began. Not only was suitability of prime importance but the ease with which conversions and alterations could be made. The Royal Corps of Naval Constructors, based at Bath, had one of the world's most advanced computer design systems. This was able to assess such problems as stability, modification and feasibility. It was a feature of the preparations that everyone worked 24 hours a day, seven days a week, whether at management level or the man in the dockyard welding shop. The wartime spirit was rekindled in a matter of hours.

The prime need was to fit helicopter landing decks, so that stores and personnel could be transferred easily even in the most adverse of sea conditions; many of these pads designed to withstand the weight of the heaviest loaded aircraft (the RAF Chinook) at 46,000 lbs.

The first two ships to be requisitioned on 4 April were the *Canberra*, flagship of the P & O fleet and the *Elk*. Within two days, their tasks having been identified, they had been taken in hand at Southampton. By the middle of April a further 17 ships, from tankers to tugs, troop carriers and even an aircraft ferry, the ill-fated *Atlantic Conveyor*, were in the hands of dockyards as far apart as Gibraltar and Rosyth. Most of these ships were to sail south with the Task Force before 20 April.

There were a number of important considerations in the modifications to be taken into account, particularly regarding stability after the addition of heavy helicopter platforms on the upper decks. The weight of these platforms caused their own problems with extra strengthening being required between decks. In the case of the Royal Mail Ship *St Helena*, being converted into a minehunter support ship, and the cable ship *Iris*, there was insufficient length so a cantilevered flight deck was built out over the stern.

Most merchant ships are built to operate the world's oceans, but some of those requisitioned were only designed for short sea crossings. Their normal

ballast tanks to aid stability had to be modified to accept extra fuel. In turn this created more problems as they could no longer ballast with salt water as their fuel was expended. The ability to survive damage either from the enemy or the elements had to be considered. Warship design takes this into account, but the severe conditions of the South Atlantic winter were an additional hazard for the lighter passenger ships and tankers.

The question of communications posed an enormous problem of its own. The flow of signals traffic under war conditions was much greater than that with which the average merchant ship was used to coping and their operators were not trained to use modern naval cryptography. There was a need to install Ultra High Frequency (UHF) equipment and some ships were also fitted with the Marisat satellite system.

The need for more accommodation was undoubtedly the biggest modifica-

*Some of the 49 merchant ships taken up from trade (STUFT). The* Laertes *(top left) which carried reserve ammunition and stores. Top right is the* MV Elk, *which left UK on 9 April with* Canberra *carrying war maintenance reserve, guns and vehicles. Below* Europic Ferry, Norland, *both troop carriers, and* Atlantic Causeway *in San Carlos Water.*

tion problem, with embarked troops likely to spend long periods at sea, and with it came the need for extra catering and fresh water facilities and storage. Many ships had to transport three times as many personnel, with their weapons, kit and equipment, as they were designed for. The means to refuel at sea provided its own difficulties, while medical facilities had to be added to most ships.

Perhaps the most significant problem was providing a replacement for the lone conventional aircraft carrier *Hermes* should it be damaged. There was nothing

immediately available nor even on the horizon. A perceptive naval captain saw a photograph of the *Atlantic Conveyor*, noted its vast flat deck area and suggested it might act as a temporary aircraft carrier. The ship was duly taken in hand on 16 April at Devonport, modified by having its decks cleared of obstructions and strengthened. Landing aids were fitted, while AVCAT and LOX tanks, aircraft workshop facilities and extra living quarters were added. She initially embarked 4 Chinook and 6 Wessex helicopters before sailing on 25 April and after cross-decking at Ascension Island, she left with a total of 25 aircraft, including Sea Harriers, one of which was at permanent readiness to fly off. Subsequently the *Atlantic Causeway, Contender Bezant* and *Astronomer* were all similarly converted, facilities improving each time with hangars being fitted on the upper decks, fresh water generating plants and refuelling facilities also added.

In a war fought so far from home, adequate medical support had to be provided and hence the P & O liner *Uganda* was diverted from an educational cruise in the Mediterranean, disembarked her passengers at Naples and in 65 hours was converted into a hospital ship at Gibraltar as well as installing ancillary communications and resupply at sea (RAS) facilities. The *Uganda* also embarked the Royal Marines band of Flag Officer 3rd Flotilla, who not only provided much needed musical and morale support, but also acted as helicopter marshals and stretcher bearers. Other ships converted as ambulance ships were the survey vessels HMS *Hydra, Hecla* and *Herald*.

In all 9 ships were taken up as troopships or assault ships, 15 tankers, 2 repair ships, 4 aircraft ferries, 7 stores ships, 5 minehunters with a support ship, 3 tugs, 1 dispatch vessel, 1 hospital ship and 1 mooring vessel, a total of 49 vessels all but 6 of which saw service in the South Atlantic. The ships ranged in size from the 67,140 ton *Queen Elizabeth II* to the 686 ton tug *Irishman*.

The longest conversion of any ship was the minehunter support ship *St Helena* which took 16 days, while many modifications took less than two days. Although there was no pressure on crews to serve in the war, there were very few who took the option of staying behind. Indeed most of the female stewards and nurses remained at their posts and are now proudly entitled to wear the South Atlantic Medal.

During the whole of the campaign and for many months afterwards, these merchant ships supported the Royal Navy, a task which their own Royal Fleet Auxiliary could never have achieved. In all but a very few instances they worked together as a balanced and harmonious force. The last of the STUFT ships arrived home by November although some did another round trip before being converted back to their original form. Only one merchant ship, the *Atlantic Conveyor*, hit by Exocet missiles on 25 May, was sunk, with the loss of twelve lives including that of the master Captain Ian North, who was awarded a posthumous DSC. In addition other Merchant Navy decorations included the Queen's Gallantry Medal to Third Engineer Brian Williams, two Mentions to Despatches, 3 CBE, 4 OBE, 1 MBE, 7 BEM and 1 Queen's Commendation for Brave Conduct.

# Chapter Two
# The Land Forces

The Argentines chose an unexpectedly convenient time of the year to invade the Falklands as far as the available British land forces were concerned. As with the Brunei revolt of 1962, the aggressors chose the day before a weekend when the modern five-day-a-week soldier might be looking forward to some relaxation from his training. Indeed this particular weekend marked the beginning of a fortnight's Easter leave for many servicemen. One could only speculate on the serious problems which might have arisen had they chosen to invade on Christmas Eve or on New Years Eve.

However, it was a time when none of the major British units, not committed to NATO or Northern Ireland, were either abroad or on exercise and hence the whole of the quick reaction force was immediately available. When the Argentines invaded the Falklands on 1st April, and the government had taken the decision to react quickly, there were two main military formations available; 3 Commando Brigade Royal Marines, consisting of 40, 42 and 45 Commandos and the Commando Logistic Regiment plus supporting arms, and 5 Infantry Brigade, the UK's 'out-of-area' formation of 2 and 3 Parachute Battalions and 1/7 Gurkha Rifles, again with supporting arms.

3 Commando Brigade Royal Marines was at its normal seven days notice to move, so that when the call came, they would have been theoretically available on 9 April, a time span that allowed all men to be recalled, stores packed and available for either a sea or air move. The Brigade were Britain's only amphibious force and formed the major part of the UK/Netherlands contribution to the NATO Alliance, with their main tasks concentrated on the northern flank of Europe. Government defence spending cuts, particularly the 1981 White Paper, had curtailed the regular annual Brigade exercise in Norway during the early part of the year, only 42 Commando being deployed. 40 Commando had exercised with both *Hermes* and *Invincible* around the shores of Britain during February and March, while 45 Commando had completed an individual training period in the UK with one company going to Brunei for jungle training. By the middle of March all were concentrated in UK preparing for Easter leave. From their point of view the timing of the Argentine invasion could hardly have been better. In addition the Royal Marines talked the same language as the Royal Navy, and this was to be primarily a naval campaign.

On the other hand, 5 Infantry Brigade had been newly formed in January 1982 and had only worked together on one exercise *Green Lanyard* in Norfolk. It was commanded by Brigadier Tony Wilson, a former Light Infantryman who had won the MC as a Company Commander, and later the OBE in Northern Ireland. It was an untried and untested formation though its three battalions were highly trained as individual units. None of them was committed to NATO or Northern Ireland.

Most of the Army's regular battalions were fully committed either in support of BAOR or in Ulster, and it would not have been easy to withdraw them quickly and despatch them to the South Atlantic. The only battalions that were possibly available were from the Brigade of Guards who were performing London ceremonial duties. This was the limitation in retrospect of dubious value, which successive Governments had set upon the size of British Armed Forces. The other Brigade which could possibly have been used was 1 Infantry Brigade, the Army's ACE Mobile Force (Allied Command Europe), but this was heavily committed to NATO. From this Brigade 1st Bn Queen's Own Highlanders were trained in arctic operations and would certainly be suitable for sending. They were in fact stood by as reserves to fly south if General Moore required them.

From the outset, this was deemed to be a primarily naval affair, and nothing could be more appropriate than to send the Royal Navy's own Commando Force to recapture the islands. However with the reported size of the Argentine occupation force, some 10,000 men, it was tactically unsound to send only the 5,000 marines of 3 Commando Brigade, however well trained, for the task. Military Staff College teaching had always recommended that attackers should outnumber defenders by three to one for a successful enterprise. The troops were just not available.

The British assessment of Argentine Army numbers was basically correct. Under the overall command of Major General Mario Menendez, two Brigades were deployed; III Brigade (Brigadier General Omar Parada) with 4 Regiment covering the western hills around Stanley. 5 Regiment around Port Howard, 8 Regiment at Fox Bay and 12 Regiment based mainly at Goose Green and Darwin, with one Company at Mount Challenger. X Brigade (Brigadier General Oscar Joffre) with 3 Regiment at Stanley, 6 Regiment at the airport and 7 Regiment north west of Stanley, including Mount Longdon and Wireless Ridge. In addition there were 5 Marine Infantry Battalion, which defended Tumbledown and Mount William, and 25 Regiment dispersed around the airport. There were other smaller units and supporting arms. Generally the Argentine units were well equipped and clothed, but the discipline amongst the men, mostly conscripts, was poor. There was a considerable gulf between the officers and their men, which led to poor morale and lack of understanding. Firm leadership, so essential in a campaign fought in extremes of climate with much physical discomfort, was conspicuously lacking. Logistic support for those outside Stanley was not readily forthcoming although there were plenty of supplies stacked at the airport at the end of the war.

Another important consideration that affected the selection of land forces was

the climate and terrain. The Argentinians had circumspectly timed their invasion for the Antarctic autumn. Winter was fast approaching and any British re-occupation would have to contend with the added hazards of a very cold, wet and uncomfortable campaign. With the British determination to re-take the Falklands as quickly as possible, it was important that land troops should be the fittest and toughest available, preferably trained in arctic warfare. The Royal Marines trained in Norway regularly and the Parachute Regiment had some experience on exercises.

It was therefore decided that 3 Commando Brigade should be reinforced by the inclusion firstly of the 3rd Battalion the Parachute Regiment, and subsequently of the 2nd Battalion the Parachute Regiment, giving Brigadier Thompson greater flexibility and more power. Providing he could find an unopposed landing area, he should be able to establish himself and systematically demolish the opposition.

By sending two extra battalions with the initial Amphibious Task Force, 5 In-

*C Company of 3 Para, who had fought the battle for Mount Longdon three days earlier, in joyous mood with their company flag in Stanley on the day of the surrender after they had had a chance to clean up. It was astonishing how many Union Flags appeared immediately the war finished.*

fantry Brigade were left with nothing but 1/7 Gurkha Rifles. 1st Battalion Welsh Guards were ordered to stand by on 4 April and 2nd Battalion Scots Guards on 14 April to join 5 Brigade and the whole formation carried out Exercise *Welsh Falcon* in the Brecon Beacons training area of mid-Wales for a fortnight. This was hardly sufficient to prepare them for what lie ahead, but at least the commanders started to work together in the field and the troops had an opportunity to re-equip and shake down from their ceremonial duties.

The supporting arms for the force were just as important. Both 29 Commando Light Regiment Royal Artillery and 4 Field Regiment were equally pre-

pared for immediate air or sea moves, while Royal Engineers, Royal Signals, RAOC, RCT, REME, Army Air Corps and smaller ancillary Corps played a highly professional role in the campaign. The value of a fully regular army, however small, paid dividends and the immediate availability of an amphibious force and an 'out-of-area' brigade was fully justified.

The Government report after the war admitted '*The specialised training of a substantial proportion of the landing force – such as the commandos – was a particularly significant asset*' and '*the most decisive factors in the land war were the high state of individual training and fitness of the land forces, together with the leadership and initiative displayed particularly by junior officers and NCOs*'. The versatile Royal Marines coupled with the high quality of the Parachute Regiment, could not have served Britain better as an initial strike force. The Guards and Gurkhas, though less prepared for fighting in extremes of climate, proved themselves to be extremely skilled and adaptable soldiers.

# 3rd Commando Brigade, Royal Marines

## Background

The Royal Marines have always been Britain's Sea Soldiers, raised and paid for by the Admiralty and more recently the Navy Department. They trace their ancestry to the Trained Bands of London of 1664, and through many changes have remained soldiers specially trained for service at sea. Before the Second World War they served mainly in the larger ships of the fleet, and these days they still retain small detachments in aircraft carriers, amphibious ships and frigates, as well as *Endurance* which was to play a key role in the campaign.

The concept of a Commando force was born during World War 2, firstly as small raiding parties on enemy held European mainland and subsequently as formed units, specially designed to spearhead seaborne assaults and prepared to tackle hazardous landings such as cliffs and rocky coasts. Fitness, courage and ingenuity were their trademark.

The first Commandos were provided by the Army, but by 1943 the Royal Marines formed nearly half of their numbers. At the end of the war a Parliamentary decision in October 1945 disbanded all Army commandos, and thus gave the Royal Marines an opportunity to take on a role which has since been their lifeblood.

3rd Commando Brigade was formed in November 1943 as 3rd (Special Service) Brigade with Nos 1 & 5 Army Commandos and Nos 42(RM) and 44(RM) Commandos for service in the Far East. With the defeat of the Japanese, the Brigade found itself in Hong Kong and it was there that the new 3rd Commando Brigade Royal Marines was formed with 40, 42 and 45 Commandos. For the next 25 years the Brigade served continuously abroad and saw service in such trouble spots as Palestine, Malaya, Egypt, Cyprus, Aden, Suez, Kuwait, Tanganyika, Brunei and Borneo. Even during the days of National Service the Brigade was primarily a regular force, the Corps taking very few conscripts.

With the withdrawal from the Empire and the establishment of independent rule within the Commonwealth, coupled with retrenchment and cut-backs in the armed forces, the Royal Navy suffering worst of all, 3rd Commando Brigade was withdrawn to the United Kingdom in

*In November 1981 40 Commando carried out 'loading trials' with HMS Invincible off the south coast of England, which helped the ship's crew to 'think amphibious'. Here a stick of C Company embark in a Sea King helicopter, which can take 28 fully armed men.*

*A Royal Marine of 40 Commando, which were originally formed as 'A' Commando in 1942 and took part in the ill-fated Dieppe raid. In 1982 the Commando was based at Seaton Barracks in Plymouth and had a responsibility for 'out-of-area' operations. They had recently served for a year in Londonderry and for six months in Belize. Most marines were arctic warfare trained, and the unit had exercised with both* Hermes *and* Invincible *in the six months prior to the Falklands campaign.*

1971 and given a new role. This was the defence of the Northern and Southern flanks of NATO, besides having an 'out-of-area' capability.

A far cry from the jungles of Malaya and Borneo or the barren mountains of Aden, 45 Commando, based at Arbroath, took on a new, exacting but exciting role as arctic warfare specialists. Every man was taught military skiing and survival in the snow. Meanwhile 40, 42 and the re-formed 41 Commando took their turns at policing and exercising in the rather more hospitable Mediterranean area, besides carrying out annual exercises in such places as Brunei, Canada and West Indies. By the late 1970s 3rd Commando Brigade had an arctic warfare role, but maintained its dual capability. This was illustrated when 42 Commando was sent to Hong Kong in 1979 when illegal immigrants threatened to swamp the colony; and to the New Hebrides, where there was unrest during independence cele-brations the following year.

40 Commandos (41 Commando had once again been disbanded as a result of the government cut back of 1981 after serving in Malta and Cyprus) found themselves as the 'out-of area' Commando and spent a year as garrison troops in Londonderry and six months in Belize, besides exercising all over the world and also on the Northern flank of Europe.

All three Commandos took their turn with army units in peacekeeping duties in Northern Ireland and also as duty 'Spearhead' battalion thus maintaining a continual liaison with army methods and procedures. 3rd Commando Brigade, stationed in Plymouth, regularly exercised its Commandos in amphibious matters and maintained a close contact with the Commodore Amphibious Warfare in the development of new equipment and training.

One of the great advantages Royal Marines have over their army compatriots is that the Corps is a close knit organisation where an individual may serve in more than one Commando, learning the tactics of each, and in a landing craft squadron or serve his time at sea. He is a creature of many habits and skills. With less than 600 officers and 7,000 marines, most of the officers and NCOs know each other, are similarly trained and have a common cap-badge. Assisted by their service at sea and on amphibious exercises, they 'speak the same language' as the Royal Navy and understand their methods. This gave them an enormous advantage over the army particularly during the initial stages of Operation *Corporate.*

The organisation of 3 Commando Brigade is shown in the table. For many years the Brigade relied entirely on army logistic support, but on their return from the Far East in 1971, new thinking and an approach to the Army saw the formation of the Commando Logistic Regiment Royal Marines in 1972 which has an Army officer and a Royal Marines officer alternating as Commanding Officer. In 1982 it was Lieutenant Colonel Ivar Helberg RCT. The regiment differs from similar army ones in its ability to be sea transportable and prepared for immediate service in the arctic or the tropics. It is unique in that all the logistic sub-units are under one command with five squadrons, medical,

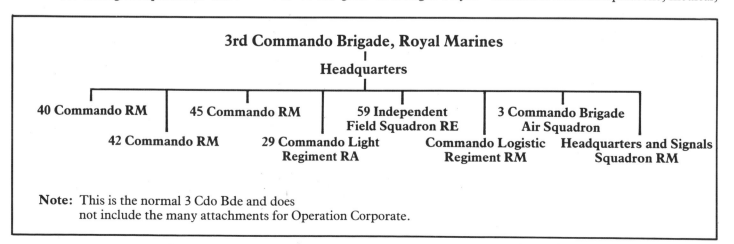

**3rd Commando Brigade, Royal Marines**

**Headquarters**

| 40 Commando RM | 45 Commando RM | 59 Independent Field Squadron RE | 3 Commando Brigade Air Squadron |
|---|---|---|---|
| 42 Commando RM | 29 Commando Light Regiment RA | Commando Logistic Regiment RM | Headquarters and Signals Squadron RM |

**Note:** This is the normal 3 Cdo Bde and does not include the many attachments for Operation Corporate.

transport, ordnance, workshop and headquarters. The personnel are approximately 80% RM, 15% Army and 5% RN medical squadron. It has no BAOR commitment nor does it have to cater for integrated armour support.

In addition 29 Commando Light Regiment Royal Artillery and 59 Independent Squadron Royal Engineers were added to the Brigade in 1971 although both had their origins in Commando support in the Far East earlier. All Army and Royal Navy personnel serving in 3 Commando Brigade are trained on the tough Commando course at Lympstone and earn their green berets under the same conditions as every marine.

The Commando tests include the Tarzan course (5 minutes for recruits; 4½ minutes for young officers); Assault Course (13 minutes; 12.5 minutes for YOs); Endurance course, including 4 miles run back to base and firing on the range (73 minutes; 70 minutes for YOs); 9 mile speed march (90 minutes for all) followed by a troop attack; 30 mile cross country in full order (8 hrs; 7 hrs for YOs) a 30ft rope climb in full kit and a Battle Swimming Test. All these tests are carried out in teams or squads taking the time from the slowest man. This teaches fitness, stamina and above all companionship and dependability. A Royal Marine's initial training takes 30 weeks not including leave, before he starts specialising in one of the many qualifications or trades offered by the Corps.

### Headquarters Commando Forces
After World War 2, Commando training was based at Bickleigh on the south western edge of Dartmoor until 1958 when the Commando School moved to Lympstone between Exeter and Exmouth. It was the responsibility of the Major General Royal Marines, Plymouth Group. When it was announced that 3 Commando Brigade would return to the UK, some redesignation took place in the Royal Marines and MGRM Commando Forces was established at Plymouth on 31 October 1969. This headquarters took over the responsibility for planning and mounting operations and exercises for United Kingdom based Commandos and to organise the deployment of 3 Commando Brigade when it returned.

Its responsibility widened to include advice on training, equipment, amphibious developments and liaison. At the same time the term 'Mountain and Arctic Warfare' was introduced to supersede such terms as cold weather warfare, arctic training, cliff assault and so on. The M & AW Cadre developed from this to train instructors in arctic warfare and survival, long range reconnaisance and cliff climbing techniques. In the Falklands campaign, the Cadre was formed into a small unit and became part of the Brigade Commander's armoury as non-committed reconnaisance and survival specialists. As such they took part in the only day action against Argentine Special Forces at Top Malo House.

When the Falklands campaign erupted, Major General Jeremy Moore was on the point of retiring from the Corps as MGRM Commando Forces. He was a very experienced Commando officer having won the MC in the jungles of Malaya with 40 Commando and later a Bar to the MC with 42 Commando in Brunei. He commanded 42 Commando which saw two tours of Northern Ireland including Operation *Motorman*. He had been MGRM Commando Forces since August 1979 and was fully conversant with all the latest amphibious techniques. He was initially appointed Land Deputy to the Commander-in-Chief Fleet, Admiral Sir John Fieldhouse and moved to his Headquarters at Northwood, Middlesex. He subsequently became Commander Land Forces Falkland Islands and with most of his staff from Commando Forces sailed to the South Atlantic.

### Headquarters 3 Commando Brigade
During 1981 Headquarters 3rd Commando Brigade had exercised in Northern Norway and Holland but in the early part of 1982 only part of the Headquarters deployed to Norway because there had been a squeeze on defence spending. Brigadier Julian Thompson had been the Brigade Commander since January 1981, having previously served in 40 and 42 Commandos in the Near East, 45 Commando in Aden, and 43 Commando at home. He returned to 40 Commando in the Far East, became Brigade Major of 3rd Commando Brigade and subsequently commanded 40 Commando for 2½ years which included a tour in Ulster. He then became Colonel GS on the staff of Headquarters Commando Forces. His knowledge of Commando operations was probably unmatched in the Corps,

*42 Commando were the second Royal Marines Commando to be fully trained in arctic warfare. Since World War 2 action in Burma, the unit had operated in the Far and Middle East, seeing action in Malaya, Egypt, Cyprus, Port Said, Kuwait, Brunei and Borneo. In 1979 they had been sent to Hong Kong when illegal immigrants threatened to swamp the colony and in 1980 to Vanuatu when trouble occurred during independence celebrations. During the Falklands campaign they carried out a classic night flanking assault to take Mount Harriet from the rear.*

except perhaps, by General Moore.

As with any other Brigade it had its own Headquarters and Signal Squadron, which again differs in a few respects from its army counterpart. In addition to the standard communications equipment, it includes an Air Defence Troop, manned entirely by RMs and equipped with Blowpipe surface-to-air missiles. A unique feature is 1st Raiding Squadron Royal Marines, trained and equipped to operate both inflatable and rigid raiding craft, the latter being taken on this occasion. Apart from being manned solely by Royal Marines, they are trained to operate from Forward Operating Bases and capable of camouflaging and concealing their craft in operational areas. 3 Commando Brigade has its own Air Squadron equipped with Gazelle and Scout helicopters, again with a mixture of RMs, Army and a few Royal Navy.

Major General Moore first broke the news by telephoning Brigadier Thompson at 3.15am on Friday 2 April. The Brigade was always at seven days notice to move, but this was reduced to 72 hours from the outset, an unprecedented option. At the time many of the Brigade's key staff officers were in Denmark on a reconnaisance for a forthcoming NATO exercise, while much heavy equipment was on its way back from Norway. He immediately moved his headquarters to Hamoaze House nearby in Devonport, the home of MGRM Commando Forces along with such staff officers who were there. One very surprised officer recalled from leave was Major David Baldwin who had only that week handed over as DAA & QMG to Major Gerry Wells-Cole.

In the first 36 hours, the emphasis was on alerting the three Commandos, finding out what shipping was available, recalling men from early Easter leave and making the initial plans for embarkation for the recovery of the Falkland Islands.

By 9 April, the whole Brigade, enlarged by the inclusion of 3rd Bn The Parachute Regiment and many ancilliary units, was at sea, embarked in

*Royal Marines of J Company, 42 Commando, formerly Naval Party 8901, march into Stanley at the end of hostilities. The twin peaks of Two Sisters can be clearly seen on the horizon.*

a variety of ships, the extent of which had not been seen since World War 2. Brigade Headquarters, along with Commodore Amphibious Warfare, Commodore Mike Clapp and his staff were embarked in *Fearless* and sailed ahead of the Amphibious Task group to meet up with the Task Force Commander at Ascension Island.

## 40 Commando Royal Marines

40 Commando have their origins in the first Royal Marines Commando to be formed in 1942 as 'A' Commando, and saw their first action at Dieppe in August that year. They served with distinction in the Mediterranean theatre from the Sicily landings to Yugoslavia and the Adriatic Islands. After the war they served continually abroad in the Near and Far East until being the last Royal Marines unit to leave Singapore in November 1971. Since then they have been stationed in Devon taking up residence at Seaton Barracks, near Plymouth in January 1972. However they served and exercised overseas regularly, being involved in the withdrawal of British civilians and maintaining the peace during the Turkish invasion of Cyprus in 1974. The Commando did several 4 months roulement tours to Northern Ireland and in 1979-80 spent 12 months as garrison battalion in Ballykelly, near Londonderry.

Their main task was 'out-of-area' operations and they exercised a Company Group regularly in the jungles of Brunei, besides unit amphibious exercises in the West Indies and Europe. In the months leading up to Operation *Corporate* they had carried out amphibious trials aboard *Hermes* which were to prove invaluable during the months ahead. *Hermes* had been a Harrier strike carrier during the previous 12 months and her amphibious expertise was waning. However in February 1982, 40 Commando Group embarked by air and LCVP in Plymouth Sound and carried out two landing exercises on the south coast of England in the next fortnight. The problems of accommodating over 2,000 men for a short stay, along with their vehicles and stores, provided many problems, but the Harriers were able to fly off during most phases of the exercise. It gave many of the younger marines their first taste of sea time with the Royal Navy and stood them in good stead in

the months ahead.

On return from this exercise the Commando embarked on a very different training programme based on adventure training. Once again government restrictions, this time on the use of fuel, forced individual Companies and Troops to indulge in some 23 different activities ranging from climbing in Cornwall, white water canoeing in the Pyrenees, skiing in the French Alps, sub-aqua diving in Cyprus, expert coaching in a variety of more conventional sports and an excursion to Jersey. All these ensured that a high standard of fitness was maintained, and again reinforced the Commando ideals of working as a team and taxing individual initiative.

Lieutenant Colonel Malcolm Hunt who had commanded the unit since September 1981, placed a high priority on fitness, not only taking part in the unit cross country but ensuring that all his officers and men met his high standards. At the time of the crisis, most of 40 Commando were about to return from personal weapon training on Altcar ranges, near Liverpool. The Second-in-Command and the Quartermaster were in Denmark preparing for the forthcoming NATO exercise and everyone was looking forward to Easter leave due to start the following week.

Little did they know that within that week they would have been fully mobilised and embarked in the *Canberra*. Within 48 hours of receiving the call the Commando was concentrated at Seaton Barracks where they prepared for whatever might be ahead, and on Thursday 8 April, the day the British declared a Maritime Exclusion Zone 8,000 miles away, 40 Commando left Plymouth for Southampton.

### 42 Commando Royal Marines

42 Commando trace their origins further back than anyone else and indeed they still carry the broad red cross on yellow of the Lord High Admiral's Regiment of 1664 on their flag. They were formed from 1st Battalion Royal Marines in October 1943 and saw service in the Far East, particularly Burma, in 1944/45. As with the rest of 3 Commando Brigade they served in the Far and Middle East until they were recalled to the United Kingdom in 1954 and reduced to an operational nucleus as a result of another government spending cut. Even then

they sent a large Troop Group (100 men) to Londonderry in 1956, reactivated as a unit for the Suez landings in 1956 and again for the Lebanon crisis in 1958. They were brought up to strength in 1959 and became the first Commando to be embarked in the new concept of the Commando carrier *Bulwark* the following year. Ten years were spent in Singapore, Brunei and Borneo and they were involved in Kuwait (1961) and Aden (1963) before the withdrawal of British Troops from the East when they returned to Bickleigh, still their home near Plymouth.

From here they carried out many roulement tours to Northern Ireland, including Operation *Motorman* and a Company Group was sent to the New Hebrides in 1980 when trouble threatened during the independence celebrations. In the year preceding the Falklands campaign the unit, having been committed as the second arctic-warfare trained unit in the late 70s, had exercised in southern Norway in the

*During the passage south in* Canberra *all troops took the opportunity to test fire weapons. Here a Royal Marine fires the 84mm Carl Gustav light anti-tank weapon, which was primarily used in the sangar-busting role.*

*A Royal Marine of 45 Commando yomping across East Falkland. Carrying well over 100 lbs on his back, he wears normal issue arctic smock and trousers, with snow gaiters and ski-marchboots. To guard against chill wind, he wears his 'headcover' covering his green beret. He carries a standard issue SLR rifle with the forearm covered in sackcloth. The unit, normally stationed at Arbroath, Scotland, was highly trained in arctic warfare.*

spring and Denmark in the summer. In January 1982, due to the moritorium on spending, 42 Commando had been the only major unit to deploy to Norway, where for two months they carried out trials on various equipment from NBC suits to new skis and gaiters culminating in a ten days live exercise.

They returned in mid March to return stores and proceed on three weeks leave. So it was that only a small nucleus of men were on rear party duty on the fateful day. Lieutenant Colonel Nick Vaux, at 46 the oldest of the Commando COs, had only been in command for four months, but again his Commando background was impeccable. As a young Officer he had taken part in the last large scale amphibious assault at Port Said in 1956, had served in the Far and Middle East before becoming a special adviser to the United States Marine Corps and serving in the Operations Division of the MOD. He was due to fly to America on 2 April, but was thwarted by the early morning telephone call which alerted his unit.

Both the Second-in-Command and the Operations Officer were known to be abroad, whilst the 600 men of his unit were on leave. Only one man failed to return to Bickleigh within the specified 72 hours and even he managed to join the *Canberra* before sailing, having been located on the west coast of the USA.

## 45 Commando Royal Marines

45 Commando was formed in August 1943 from the 5th Royal Marines Battalion and saw action on D-Day and subsequently fought across north-west Europe including the crossing of the Rhine. Like the other two Commandos they were involved in Internal Security operations in the Middle and Far East during the late 1940/50s, including carrying out the first ever unit helicopter landing at Port Said in 1956. In 1960 45 Commando was sent to Aden and remained there until the withdrawal in 1967, returning to England. Here they operated continually during unrest in the Colony and also in the mountainous regions of the Radfan. They established their base at Arbroath in Scotland in 1971 and became the first British unit to specialise in cold weather warfare, carrying out annual exercises in Norway.

The Commando Group share their base with Comacchio Group, a Royal Marine unit responsible for the protec-

tion of offshore oil and gas installations, besides the security of naval establishments in the UK.

45 Commando had spent the autumn of 1981 in West Belfast on a particularly harrassing tour, returning in November. After Christmas they had their first break from an arctic exercise for a number of winters, and were reorganising, retraining and as one sage put it 'rediscovering Condor', their base. The severe financial restrictions placed on expenditure made it a quieter period than usual.

Lieutenant Colonel Andrew Whitehead, who had been the CO for exactly a year, was another officer with considerable Commando experience, having served in the Far and Middle East in 42 and 40 Commandos, besides 43 Commando in UK and later 42 Commando again as a Company Commander. He had also been on the NATO planning staff in Oslo for two years. He was another away on a recce in Denmark, along with his Operations Officer, when the recall was started.

The unit had expected to go on two weeks Easter leave later that day and many of them were suspicious when they were telephoned at home in the early hours of the day after April the First. Y Company were somewhere in the Far East on their way back from training in Brunei, Z Company scattered on adventurous training from the South of France to Wales. One officer who was on advanced seasonal leave was in America and another holidaying in the South of France with the daughter of the Governor of the Falkland Islands.

It was to the credit of nearly every member of those recalled that they somehow managed to get back to their base within a few days, many of them within hours. Stories of coaches being stopped on the M1 by the police to locate marines going on leave, railway announcements at Paddington Station and bleary-eyed wives and parents being woken up from their slumbers to break the news to their loved ones, abound. One marine was knocked up by the local bobby and informed 'You've got a recall, son. You're going to war. The Argies have invaded.' It was not until he had said farewell to his local landlord and was on his journey back north that he thought 'What the hell are the Argies doing in Scotland? They must be after the oil!'

# Special Forces

Irregular troops have been used in wars from time immemorial, usually raised specially for a raid or a campaign, but it was not until 1940 that the British put such forces on an official basis, and even then their recruitment, organisation and *modus operandi* were all suspect and often more than irregular.

Special Forces raided enemy coasts in Europe and the Mediterranean during World War 2 forming the basis of the Special Boats Squadron as we know it today, while such specialist parties as the Long Range Desert Group in North Africa were the embryo of today's Special Air Service. Both were primarily the prerogative of the Army, with some skilled assistance from the Royal Navy and the Royal Air Force. In addition, under the misleading title of the Royal Marines Boom Patrol Detachment, swimmer canoeists took part in the celebrated 'Cockleshell Heroes' raid on enemy shipping in Bordeaux in December 1942.

At the end of the war, the Royal Marines took over the SBS role, while the Special Air Service was temporarily disbanded. However the Army immediately carried out a study to evaluate the requirement for small groups of well-trained soldiers who could operate behind enemy lines. Deciding that there was no need for a regular SAS force, recruitment started for 21 SAS in September 1947 as a Territorial Regiment, mostly from the pre-war Artist's Rifles. Later the first regular Regiment 22 SAS was formed and later still, in 1959, another TA Regiment 23 SAS was formed, based in Birmingham.

## Special Boat Squadron

After World War 2, the Special Boat Section was maintained by the Royal Marines at a comparatively low profile for many years. However the technique of beach reconnaissance, underwater swimming, parachuting into the sea and landing from small craft launched from submarines or small coastal craft was kept alive. The very nature of their role as Sea Soldiers meant that special boating and working closely with the Royal Navy's submarine service was second nature to the Royal Marines. The dividing line between SBS and SAS responsi-

bility is a tenuous one, though it is generally assumed to be the high water mark. Whilst both forces demand physical and intellectual stamina, the SBS man, the swimmer canoeist, often mistakenly referred to as a frogman, requires sub aqua swimming and parachuting as part of his qualification. Parachuting into the sea and then swimming to a target is a demanding speciality of its own.

His specialist training is 12 months of hard slogging. Not only does he have to be physically fit and a good swimmer, but he must have an intricate knowledge of signals, explosives, driving, sniping and be an expert map and chart reader. Of those who volunteer for the course, less than half even get through the physical selection stage. Of these a further half will fall by the wayside through injury, lack of temperament or aptitude, whilst more will fail to meet the exceptionally high qualifying standards required, so that it is a very small select bunch that eventually pass through the 'tunnel'.

Like the SAS, the SBS were very actively involved in the Borneo Confrontation of the 1960s, where they carried out clandestine operations in both coastal areas and across the border. For many years during the 1950s and 60s members

*A Royal Marine swimmer-canoeist of the Special Boat Squadron whose prime task was intelligence gathering on the Falklands prior to D-Day. Their long training teaches them to survey and report on beach gradients, texture and the approaches providing information from which operational planners can take decisions. When landing areas were provisionally selected, SBS were tasked to prepare detailed reports, as well as acquiring intelligence on enemy troop movements. The SBS, usually in teams of three or four, were landed by night from frigates and trawlers of the Ellas Squadron, and later by the submarine* Onyx.

*Marines of the SBS are trained to parachute into the sea and swim ashore, or to land in inflatables or two-man canoes launched from conventional submarines. Once in the hinterland their roles are similar to those of the SAS.*

of the SBS trained and operated in Muscat and Oman. In May 1972 two of their number parachuted in mid-Atlantic when the *Queen Elizabeth 2* reported a bomb scare.

Their operations in Northern Ireland are carried out under the same cloak of secrecy as those of the SAS, and their involvement in anti-terrorist exercises in Britain's North Sea oilfields are a continuing part of their job. They have far fewer options for getting to and from their targets at sea. The Royal Marines Reserve also trains swimmer canoeists and keeps a wartime cadre readily available.

In the South Atlantic 2 SBS were involved in the re-capture of South Georgia and 6 SBS were among the first to be landed on the Falklands to carry out their surveillance and reporting role. Indeed 6 SBS arrived at Faslane on 3 April to embark in *Conqueror*, little realising their stay on board would be 22 days. They were more used to conventional submarines, but were strangers in the limited space available in modern nuclear powered ships.

With the remoteness of some of the Falklands settlements and the enormously long coastline, this was a much easier task than against a heavily defended coastline, but the weather conditions made it a daunting prospect. In addition to air insertion by naval helicopters, frigates and trawlers of the 'Ellas' squadron were also used to insert SBS and SAS patrols into the hinterland from 1 May onwards, with the welcome addition of the submarine *Onyx* from the end of May.

When the planners had reduced their options for landing sites down to five, the SBS teams spent much of their time recceing and reporting on the beaches, gradients, hinterland and suitability of the areas, as well as keeping a watchful eye for any build up of Argentine Forces.

## Special Air Service

In the straitened circumstances of the post-1945 Army, there was no justification for the retention of the SAS. It was not until an operational requirement arose for a regular force, the emergency in Malaya, that 22 SAS (initially titled 'Malayan Scouts') were born in 1950. From then onwards, the Regiment has been involved in countless campaigns from Borneo to Aden, Muscat and Oman to Dhofar; since 1976 it has been involved in Northern Ireland and with such media sensitive activities as the Iranian Embassy Siege in 1980.

However their operational activities are far wider than those apparent to the public, but in view of the clandestine nature of their duties, very little is released of their training methods, and that is how they like it, shrouded in a certain mystique. Recruitment for this exclusive Regiment comes from those already serving in the regular army, and occasionally through the Royal Marines. 22 Special Air Service Regiment are based at Stirling Lines, Hereford, to where all potential recruits are sent. Each man must have the special qualities required for the job, fitness, intelligence, reliability, integrity and a high degree of marksmanship, as well as possessing attributes that can only be measured by professional observation. Like their SBS counterparts, and with whom they now work closely, they must be capable of operating in small groups, for long periods under intense stress. Of necessity their work is secretive, maintaining a low profile in all their activities. One suspect mark on their records and they are returned to their parent units without recourse.

22 SAS are organised basically into four Sabre Squadrons, A, B, D and G. In turn each Squadron has four troops, mountain, boat, free-fall and mobility, though this is only a general outline. A Squadron has about 60 men with Captains commanding the Troops. Many of the other ranks forego their army rank when joining the SAS. Since 1976 one Squadron has operated in Northern Ireland while another is always on Stand-by at a moment's notice to fly anywhere in the world. In addition there are Special Project Teams and a Counter Revolutionary Wing. The latter study and teach methods of dealing with hijackings, sieges, bodyguard duties and close quarter battle techniques. Constant use is made in training of the 'Killing House' where the size and layout can be changed to suit any emergency that materialises. Here teams practice before they go into action. Similarly there is a requirement for aircraft 'shells' for anti hi-jacking operations.

*22 Special Air Service provided two Squadrons for Operation Corporate and were involved in continuous patrolling on the Falklands from 1 May, besides taking a leading part in the re-capture of South Georgia. They normally wear standard British Army uniforms in the field, but as their task was mainly reconnaissance and reporting they usually carried light-weight weapons and specialist radios.*

*Anonymity is the byword of the SAS. In the field they usually wear conventional clothing and carry normal infantry weapons, unlike their anti-terrorist role.*

The SAS are armed with the most sophisticated weapons to suit their job. The Heckler and Koch MP5 9mm sub machine gun and Ingram machine pistol being the two most widely known. Stun and tear gas grenades also form part of their armoury. Each man must be proficient in enemy weapons, codes and within limits, languages.

The main task of the Special Forces in the Falklands was that of unobtrusive intelligence gathering, a highly dangerous, always uncomfortable and only occasionally rewarding job. Their brief is not to rush into action, or be involved in the fire fight but to dissolve into the background,

*Two members of the Special Forces, one armed with an M-16 and M-203 grenade launcher, inspect an MB-339 on Stanley airfield.*

leaving not the slightest trace of their presence to the enemy. D and G Squadrons were committed to the Falklands campaign, the former playing a decisive part in the recapture of South Georgia and the attack on Pebble Island, while G Troop were landed along with SBS patrols in many areas of the Falklands themselves. Their expertise in the quick transmission of vital intelligence led to the field commanders being able to assess the situation more accurately before formulating their plans.

## Mountain and Arctic Warfare Cadre, Royal Marines

An unexpected bonus for Brigadier Thompson was his use of the Mountain and Arctic Warfare Cadre, a specialised training unit of the Royal Marines, whose normal parish was northern Norway and Scotland. Formed from the wartime Cliff Climbing Wing, later the Cliff Assault Wing, the Cadre settled into Arbroath in 1970, moving to Plymouth only months before the Falklands campaign started. The instructors were highly skilled in military skiing and arctic survival techniques. They were experts in deep penetration patrolling in adverse conditions, particularly in mountainous terrain. They could hardly have been more suited for the Falklands.

The Cadre normally trained 3 Commando Brigade in winter warfare for their NATO commitment to the Northern Flank. For the previous year Brigadier Thompson had used the Cadre on exercises as a Brigade Reconnaissance Troop, a role which fitted their added expertise in communications. They filled a gap between the areas where the Commando's reconnaissance troops operated and the more remote forward patrols of the SBS and SAS. They became a vital tactical reserve for the Brigade Commander and were to fight the only daylight action against Argentinian special forces during the campaign at Top Malo House.

In March 1982 the Cadre were running a course for Mountain Leaders (Grade 2), and the student marines formed the basis of the operational Cadre with their instructors. As Brigadier Thompson was to say when he visited them during their voyage south *'What do you think of this final exercise that has been organised for you?'* Such was the make-up of the British Special Forces involved in the campaign.

They were dedicated, highly trained and professional marines and soldiers, who through their training were acknowledged to be the cream of the world's specialists in their fields. The training to which all had been subjected was not only hard physically but demanded a mental awareness that included anti-terrorist operations and resistance to interrogation techniques. Their contribution to the success of the war may never be fully known, but they were effective for the very anonymity that surrounds their activities. For once they were exposed to a fully fledged battlefield and, despite the tragic loss of 22 men on 19 May when the very last Sea King helicopter in the cross-decking of SAS from *Hermes* to *Intrepid* crashed into the sea, the Special Forces aquitted themselves in the manner expected of them.

The Falklands was mainly a maritime operation, for which the SBS were suitably trained. It was therefore to the credit of the SAS, who had not worked on a large scale with the Royal Navy

*A four-man team from the Mountain and Arctic Warfare Cadre, who are also specialists in survival techniques and long range reconnaissance, in a river crossing exercise.*

since World War 2, that they adapted so easily to the amphibious scene. The training of both Services in unobtrusive observation in Northern Ireland stood them in good stead, whilst their commitment to the arctic conditions of the Northern Flank of Europe ensured that their clothing, equipment and state of mind were well suited to the Falklands. Neither the SBS nor the SAS had a logistic tail and their demands on clothing and sleeping bag reserves sometimes seemed excessive, but the value of their intelligence gathering was well worth any inconvenience they caused. Flexibility is the keyword of all special forces and their respective mottoes of *'Not By Strength, By Guile'* and *'Who Dares Wins'* were highly appropriate.

# The Blues and Royals

The Blues and Royals were formed on 29 March 1969 by the amalgamation of the Royal Horse Guards (The Blues) with The Royal Dragoons (1st Dragoons). Both these regiments have their origins in 1661 when they were raised by Charles II as Regiments of Horse. Through the ages their titles and roles have changed continuously. Now, along with the Life Guards they form the Household Cavalry, which in addition to being fully operational armoured units, maintain mounted squadrons for public duties.

Even in the early stages of World War 2 they fought as mounted cavalry in the Middle East, but in 1942 they re-mustered with armoured cars. The two regiments retained this role in the immediate post-war years, usually alternating between ceremonial duties in London and tours in the Middle East, Germany or Cyprus.

In 1969 their armoured cars were replaced by Chieftain tanks and they took their place in NATO's North European order of battle. Here they exercised frequently across the plains of Europe, whilst on their home tours they took their place on London ceremonial such as State escorts and the Queen's personal guard. Another major reorganisation took place in 1974 when they were re-equipped with Scorpion and Scimitar light tanks (CVR[T] – Combat Vehicle Reconnaisance [Tracked]). With this move came a new and exciting role, that of armoured reconnaisance, one which proved highly suitable to the Falklands terrain. There were initially doubts about their capability over the bog and rock runs so prevalent in the Falklands, but their general mobility and flexibility proved more than useful.

The Alvis Scorpion is an all-welded aluminium armoured reconnaisance vehicle with an overall combat weight of 17,500 lbs. It is designed to protect the crew from up to 14.5 mm projectiles and 7.62 mm armoured piercing rounds. It has a maximum road speed of 50 mph and a crew of three. The Commander, who also loads the guns, sits on the left in the armoured turret with seven periscopes and a roof mounted sight. On his right is the gunner/radio operator, with two periscopes, a roof mounted sight, and a Rank passive night sight with image intensifier. The driver sits at the front left with a single wide-angle periscope. The Scorpion mounts a 76 mm L23 gun which can fire HE, HESH (High Explosive Squash Head) or Smoke, with a coaxially mounted GPMG. It carries up to 40 rounds, with 3,000 rounds of machine gun ammunition. The Scorpion is powered by a Jaguar 4.2 litre air cooled engine developing 190 bhp, with a seven speed gearbox with a controlled differential steering system. It can carry 93 gallons giving it a maximum road range of 400 miles.

The similarly designed but slightly lighter Scimitar has a 30 mm Rarden cannon capable of firing Armour Piercing Secondary Effects or HE shells, along with a 7.62 mm GPMG. The flat trajectory of the Rarden gun and its 6-shot burst capability gives pin-point accuracy, and it is able to neutralise an identified target very quickly. 165 rounds are normally carried, along with 3,000 rounds of machine gun ammunition. With the two Troops of Blues and Royals was one Samson Armoured Recovery Vehicle. Similarly designed but on a Spartan chassis, it has a variable speed rear winch capable of pulling 11½ tons over 250 yards. The Scorpion, Scimitar and Samson all carry a four-barrelled, electrically operated smoke discharger on either side of the hull.

Their normal tactical use is to stand off about 800 yards to acquire targets often from enemy tracer fire, rather than be jeopardised at close quarters. Soon after the San Carlos landings the Scimitars used their guns effectively in the anti-aircraft role. In addition to their support capability, the Scorpions and Scimitars are experts in route reconnaisance, route clearing and can also be used for evacuation of casualties.

With shipping space at a premium and niggling doubts about their possible role and performance in the boggy terrain, only two troops, Nos 3 (Lieutenant Lord Robin Innes-Ker) & 4 (Lieutenant Mark Coreth) of B Squadron the Blues and Royals were taken, each equipped two Scimitars and two Scorpions, designed to work in pairs. Their Samson recovery vehicle was manned by REME personnel. The inclusion of these mobile gun platforms gave the commanders in the field a greater flexibility and increased firepower, and during the campaign the Scorpions fired an average of 60 rounds apiece and the Scimitars over 100 rounds each.

*A Scorpion light tank, which mounts a 76 mm gun, proved to have a far better cross country performance than expected in the boggy Falklands terrain.*

*A trooper of the Blues and Royals. Only two Troops of B Squadron, comprising two Scorpions and two Scimitars each, plus a Samson recovery vehicle, accompanied the Task Force, because their cross country performance was suspect and there were virtually no motorable roads. In the event, they proved highly manoeuvrable and versatile in the Falklands, and more could have been deployed in close support of infantry attacks. During the San Carlos landings they were carried forward in the landing craft to enable them to fire on to the beaches if required.*

The decision to take the Blues and Royals was taken early on 3 April and only three days later they travelled to Portsmouth and embarked in the *Elk*.

During the passage south to Ascension Island, the role of the light tanks was defined. They would be carried forward in the LCUs of the initial waves, so that their guns could give covering fire over the lowered ramps onto the beaches. This tactic was completely new to the troopers who were more used to firing on land tank ranges than on the unstable and unpredictable platform of a landing craft in a choppy sea. During the cross-decking to *Fearless* new procedures were developed which would give the assaulting troops added firepower.

Their cross country performance in the campaign was better than expected. Whilst escorting the Volvo BV 202E oversnow vehicles, known as 'bandwagons', of Headquarters 3 Commando Brigade across East Falkland they often carried a few troops and some of their equipment, both of which could be ditched easily in the event of an encounter with the enemy. When tasked to re-join 5 Infantry Brigade from Teal Inlet, a journey that was expected to take two days, was completed in 6 hours, thanks to the competence of the experienced drivers. On one occasion a vehicle got badly bogged down only to be released by the powerful Chinook helicopter in

*A news reporter alongside a Scorpion of the Blues and Royals. These light tanks provided much needed mobile fire support for the attacks on Mount Longdon and Wireless Ridge.*

15 minutes, an operation that might normally have taken a couple of days.

The Blues and Royals rejoined 3 Commando Brigade, supporting 2 Para in their attack on Wireless Ridge and 3 Para on Mount Longdon, and later the Scots Guards on Tumbledown. Using their night vision capability they gave covering fire during the attacks on the mountains, providing not only increased firepower, but also a morale boost to the troops. Following the cease fire, they led 2 Para proudly into Stanley, the leading vehicle carrying the Regimental Flag and all four CRVTs were laden with troops.

Although there were initially serious doubts expressed by the planners about their value in the Falklands terrain, their extraordinary cross country performance, their deadly supporting fire, an almost 100% serviceability rate and the expertise of their crews were a major factor. With the shortage of helicopters in support of ground forces, the armoured reconnaisance vehicles provided a welcome additional mobility. It was later agreed that, had there been room in the available shipping, a whole Squadron would have been a considerable bonus.

# Royal Artillery

The Royal Artillery shared with the Royal Navy the role of fire support for the Falklands campaign, each having a rather different but complementary part to play. Without the constant softening up process of bombardment and close support in the land battles, the ground forces would have suffered many more casualties in taking their objectives. The skill and professionalism of Royal Artillery forward observers was never more tested than on this barren island.

The Royal Regiment of Artillery was formed into a permanent force on 26 May 1716, replacing the artillery 'trains' that were raised only when required for a campaign and being disbanded on the cessation of hostilities. Until 1855 they were the responsibility of the Ordnance Board, when they came under control of the War Office. In 1890 another major change saw the formation of the separate branches of Royal Horse Artillery and Royal Field Artillery, and Royal Garrison Artillery, all being reunited again as one Regiment in 1924, the RHA retaining its own title and badge. The Royal Artillery consider their guns as their Colours and do not display battle honours. They share the motto 'Ubique' (Everywhere) with the Royal Engineers.

Prior to 1961, 3 Commando Brigade had no integral artillery support and so 29 Commando Light Regiment, who bore the brunt of the fighting in the Falklands, was formed, seeing its first action in Borneo. Two years later the Amphibious Observation Battery, based at Poole in Dorset, became 95 Commando Light Regiment. On return from the Far East in the early 1970s, 29 Regiment retained three batteries, 8 (Alma), 79 (Kirkee) and 145 (Maiwand) with 148 (Meiktila) Forward Observation Battery replacing 95 Regiment. Every gunner passed the commando course and wore the covetted green beret. The Regiment was equipped with eighteen 105 mm light guns, which could fire a 35 lb shell over 10 miles.

*A Rapier firing post of 12 Air Defence Regiment. Used for the first time in action, this surface to air missile system initially relied on optical tracking, but was later controlled by Blindfire radar.*

Shortage of shipping for their heavy equipment caused a rethink in what 29 Regiment could take south. In place of their 1 tonne gun limbers they took BV 202E oversnow vehicles which were expected to negotiate the boggy terrain better, while observation parties were not allocated vehicles at all. Their equipment would have to be man-packed. It was apparent from the outset that the gunners would have to rely heavily on helicopters, not only to move their guns forward but also for resupply of ammunition. The regiment was split over a variety of ships for the voyage south, *Fearless*, LSLs and the *Canberra* for most of the personnel. Training was limited though most guns managed to practise fire from the ship's decks during the trip. Instruction in target indication was given to the infantry and fitness training took a major role. It was realised that the Falklands rock and peat would limit the depth to which guns might be dug in the boggy terrain, so that earthworks and sangars, with an overhead covering of camouflage nets would be normal.

29 (Corunna) Battery of 4 Field Regiment had been added to the original orbat

commodity which was short. Only one definite kill was credited to the weapon though there were claims (mostly justified) of more than a dozen hits. It undoubtedly had a deterrent effect on enemy pilots and proved far more effective than the cumbersome Argentine Roland system. Most targets were visibly acquired, as enemy aircraft flew at 50 feet

*Camouflaged 105 mm guns of 2 Commando Light Regiment and a Field Regiment Royal Artillery range on to selected targets from below Mount Kent before the attack on Two Sisters.*

*29 Commando Light Regiment Royal Artillery, who train regularly in Norway, were well equipped with arctic clothing. They combined with 4 Field Regiment for the final battles for Stanley and between them they fired over 12,000 rounds of 105 mm ammunition.*

theoretically to support 2 Para, while T (Shah Shujah's Troop) Air Defence Battery of Rapiers and two sections of 43 Air Defence Battery, 32 Guided Weapons Regiment with their Blowpipes also sailed with the amphibious force. All were severely restricted in the number of vehicles and stores they could take. They quickly learnt the complexities of cold weather warfare on light scales from their fellow gunners in 29 Regiment. Most were landed on D-Day and T Battery established 10 Fire Units for immediate anti-aircraft defence, along with the hand held Blowpipes of 43 Battery and 3 Commando Brigade Air Defence Troop.

The Rapier is a surface to air missile, easily transportable and during the campaign proved its versatility and effectiveness. One temporary drawback, which was apparent soon after the landings, was that it needed 24 hours to settle down before being ready for action. It also used more petrol than was anticipated, a

and 500 knots, hugging the undulating hillsides, and the Rapiers had to fire mostly at minimum elevation. The Blowpipe is essentially a lightweight anti-aircraft missile, weighing 42 lbs complete with a range of 3,000 yards, and it was generally manhandled during the campaign. The weapon is optically aimed and has a radio guidance system. It accounted for at least two Skyhawks and undoubtedly several other claims were justified. These two weapons, along with the Royal Navy's larger Sea Dart, Sea Wolf and Sea Cat systems provided substantial defence against the determined Argentine air attacks.

The five Naval Gunfire Support Parties of 148 Battery were involved in almost every action from 1 May onwards, three teams being landed with Special Forces prior to D-Day and two others employed during the retaking of South Georgia. From then on teams were in constant demand, switching from one unit to another, usually moving with the point companies as the battle advanced. They brought accurate and aimed artillery fire to bear on enemy sometimes within 50 yards of attacking troops. For instance during the co-ordinated Brigade attack on 12/13 June, 29 Regiment, having been brought forward by helicopters, were ranged on 47 targets and fired over 3,000 rounds during the battle, a weight supplemented by those fired from supporting warships and a further 70 rounds per gun from the newly arrived 4 Field Regiment. In addition there were four Royal Artillery Naval Gunfire Liaison Officers ashore and the contribution the forward observers made to the success of the war can be measured by six gallantry awards.

The two Field Regiments then supported the final attacks by the Scots Guards and 2 Para, their firing being limited only by the speed with which helicopters could bring ammunition forward. Had more Chinooks been available, which could carry 192 palletted rounds, rather than the Wessex lifting only 24 and the Sea King 48 shells, the build up of stocks would have been that much quicker. There had probably not been such a concentrated British artillery barrage since the war in Korea thirty years earlier. A total of 12,000 rounds were fired during the last six days of the campaign, mostly against an enemy with no armour, using the air burst fuse.

# The Scots Guards

The present Guards Division, since its inception during the 1650s, has had a broad and versatile role. Various battalions were employed as seagoing soldiers during the Dutch Wars, improvised as Camel Regiments in the Sudan campaigns of the 1880s and during World War 2 became mechanised as the Guards Armoured Brigade. Its title has undergone a number of changes. Nevertheless their employment of more recent years has been traditionally ceremonial as well as operational world wide.

Of the three units that were deployed in the Falklands campaign, the Blues and Royals and the Welsh Guards are dealt with separately. Here we are concerned with the Scots Guards, who claim to have been formed from the Royal Regiment of Scotsmen raised for the Irish Rebellion of 1642 under the Marquis of Argyll, but whose official formation was in 1662 as the Third Regiment of Foot Guards. They were known under various titles until 1877 when the present title Scots Guards was adopted. Their battle honours range from the Siege of Namur in July 1695, through the Crimean, Egyptian and Peninsular Wars, to providing three battalions on the Western Front in The Great War. In World War 2 the Scots Guards were involved in numerous actions in North Africa, Italy and Europe.

Although known to the public primarily for their ceremonial duties in London as part of the Household Brigade, the various battalions of the Brigade have taken their turns on active service throughout the declining years of the British Empire. The Scots Guards served in such trouble spots as Malaya during the Emergency of the early 50s and the Borneo campaign of the 60s. They, along with other battalions of the Household Division have taken their turn in Ulster and served with BAOR. At the time of the Falklands crisis there were two battalions in each of the Grenadier Coldstream and Scots Guards whilst the Irish and Welsh Guards retained just one battalion each. Because they were primarily earmarked for service in BAOR and Northern Ireland their equipment, training and thinking was not specifically geared to 'out of area' operations. This was the prerogative of 5 Infantry Brigade and it was certainly not visualised that Guards battalions would form part of that formation. However when both the 2nd and 3rd Bns Parachute Regiment were absorbed into 3 Commando Brigade, two more battalions were immediately required as replacements for what was now only a skeleton Brigade. Ideally units chosen should already be stationed near Aldershot and not have immediate operational commitments. The Ministry of Defence planners looked to the Bri-

*After their fierce battle for Tumbledown, some Scots Guards casualties were ferried direct to the waiting aircraft carriers by Sea King helicopters as part of medical evacuation procedures.*

*The Scots Guards were not normally equipped for cold weather fighting. This guardsman, carrying an SLR fitted with a Trilux night sight, wears a standard DMP windproof smock and quilted trousers which zip up at the bottom to allow boots to be removed. Except when in action, they wore the khaki Foot Guards' beret with bronze cap badge. The Scots Guards met the toughest Argentinian opposition, the 5th Marine Infantry Battalion, during their tough battle for Tumbledown.*

gade of Guards, which always maintained two battalions in London and one in Pirbright.

The 2nd Bn Scots guards were at Chelsea Barracks in London. Although the Welsh Guards were warned to stand by for duty with the Task Force on 4 April the Scots Guards did not receive final confirmation they would be required until 14 April. Both sailed in the *QE 2* on 12 May.

The Scots Guards were due to find two guards for the Queen's Birthday Parade and were involved in London Duties when the call to arms came. It is quite apparent that, when considering which battalions to send, the MOD did not expect 5 Infantry Brigade to be more than a reserve for 3 Commando Brigade but more likely to provide garrison troops on the successful outcome of the campaign. It was certainly not envisaged that they would have to fight across rugged country against some determined opposition.

Whilst the Guards kept up a regular infantry training programme, they were in no way attuned, either mentally or physically, to a full scale battle in hostile terrain. Although they were trained to be air-portable, their more usual role in public duties did not require such an immediate high level of fitness. There was some difficulty, due to shortage of supplies to equip them fully for their new role in a Falklands winter, but they managed to obtain some arctic clothing and equipment, including bergen rucksacks. Knowing they would be almost transportless, the Guards did acquire some elderly over-snow vehicles.

The staff of 5 Brigade realised it was essential to have a tough Brigade exercise with its new battalions, preferably over terrain similar to the Falklands. The Army training area in mid-Wales, the Brecon Beacons, proved to be ideal with its rolling hills, boggy and misty conditions, and a good test for unseasoned troops. Live ammunition could be fired almost at will and an administrative base was nearby. On 21 April, the same day as 3 Commando Brigade were exercising on Ascension, 5 Infantry Brigade, which also included its original battalion of 1/7 Gurkha Rifles, started Exercise *Welsh Falcon*. For the first week the soldiers were put through their paces, with physical fitness being the main priority. Weapon handling followed an important

*Scots Guardsmen dig defensive positions after they had moved forward to the Fitzroy area. Because of the boggy and stony Falklands terrain it was seldom possible to dig more than a foot or so without trenches filling with water, so rock sangars were usually built.*

second with battle procedures close behind. Every man had a chance to fire his and other platoon weapons.

On 3 May the unit returned to its base for final preparations, drew their new kit and snatched a few days leave. The Brigade sailed, mostly in the *QE 2* from Southampton on 12 May, still not really expecting to go to war, but by this time fully aware of the actions already going on in the South Atlantic. HMS *Sheffield* and the *General Belgrano* had been sunk, Port Stanley had been bombarded and South Georgia had been recaptured. Surely it would all be over before they got there.

2nd Bn Scots Guards was commanded by Lieutenant Colonel Mike Scott who had been the Commanding Officer for 6 months when the emergency arose. He had seen service in Kenya, Canada, and Aden, besides twice commanding a company on operational tours in Ulster. The *QE 2* steamed southwards for a fortnight, in which time the men of the

battalions not only enjoyed the luxury of the flagship of the Cunard fleet, but also exercised around the decks as much as space would allow. Weapon training took place in confined spaces as well as on deck and lectures were given on enemy recognition, weapons and capabilities, battle first aid and intelligence. The day they reached the South Georgia area, 24 May, 3 Commando Brigade were consolidating their positions around San Carlos, but they heard of the first Guards Division casualties when five Guardsmen serving with the SAS were killed in a tragic helicopter crash.

Even when the Scots Guards transferred from the *QE 2* to the *Canberra* in the sheltered waters of South Georgia, they did not really expect to be involved in one of the toughest battles of the war on Tumbledown mountain only three weeks later, against the pick of the defending Argentine regulars, their 5th Marine Infantry Regiment.

The transition from ceremonial duties to battle hardened troops had been achieved in a remarkably short space of time. Their fighting spirit and courage could not be faulted and it showed the value of a highly trained and all regular army when pitched against a numerically superior but mainly conscript one.

# The Welsh Guards

The youngest of the Guards Regiments, the Welsh Guards were raised in February 1915, only to find themselves in action a month later on the Western Front. They remained in France till the end of the war enduring some of the hardest battles of the Great War. In the early days of World War 2 they were engaged in the defence of Arras and Boulogne before the withdrawal from Dunkirk. They later saw action in Italy and North West Europe.

During the past 40 years the Welsh Guards have seen service in Palestine, Aden and Cyprus, both during the emergency and later in the UN peace-keeping

*Welsh Guardsmen transferring from the* QE 2, *which had brought them from the UK, to the* Canberra *in the trawlers* Farnella *(below),* Cordella *and* Pict, *in the secure anchorage of South Georgia.*

forces. In addition they have taken their turn in Ulster and served with BAOR. By 1982 they had been reduced to just one battalion, which was stationed at Pirbright in Surrey on the fringes of Aldershot garrison. The Welsh Guards were the first to be warned to stand by for duty with the Task Force on 4 April and they sailed with the remainder of 5 Infantry Brigade in the *QE II* on 12 May.

The Welsh Guards had exercised in Kenya during the winter of 1981/2 and had been *Spearhead* Battalion until mid-March but were now a Public Duties battalion. Apart from these duties they were preparing to Lay Up Their Colours and provide two guards for the Queen's Birthday Parade in June. It was perhaps ironic that, on the day they should have been parading on Horseguards, they were supporting 3 Commando Brigade's night attack on the mountains around Stanley. Despite their imminent departure, which saw the cancellation of

*2nd Battalion Welsh Guards had their morale badly shaken when they were caught by Argentinian Skyhawks disembarking from the LSLs* Sir Galahad *and* Sir Tristram, *but recovered sufficiently to provide the Brigade reserve for the final battles for Tumbledown and Mount William.*

the Laying-Up ceremony, they found time to receive the Freedom of the City of Carmarthen on 30 April and win the Army Rugby Cup for the 11th time.

The Battalion took their place on the 5 Infantry Brigade exercise *Welsh Falcon* in the Brecon Beacons, where they were able to shake down and practise their infantry tactics. Like all troops involved in the campaign they carried the normal range of infantry weapons. Most were armed with the standard 7.62 mm Self Loading Rifle (also known as the FN), which is highly accurate up to 600 yards. Although its magazine holds 20 rounds, the infantryman is taught and encouraged to fire in single, aimed shots. It was not as powerful nor penetrative as the old .303 rifle bullet. During the 1960s the British had decided that a general purpose machine gun (GPMG) should replace both the Bren gun (LMG) and the Vickers medium machine gun, so that all troops could be taught to handle it. This also fired the 7.62 round, but was heavy (24 lbs) and cumbersome for the infantry to carry across country, while it was not really powerful enough for the sustained fire support role, mounted on a tripod, when it had a range up to 1,300 yards.

Infantry support weapons had also changed during the last two decades. The old 2" mortar had been replaced, and the 66 mm light anti-armour weapon introduced. This is basically an expendable weapon, weighing only 5 lbs, firing a 2 lb projectile. It was used with limited effect against Argentine strong-points. The heavier Carl Gustav 84 mm recoilless gun proved far more effective against the well dug in Argentinian positions. Although the Welsh Guards had no chance to employ it as such, other battalions found it a most powerful weapon with its 6½ lb HEAT round breaking up enemy bunkers. The 81 mm mortar, which replaced the 3" mortar, was carried in Support Company by the Mortar Platoon.

Meanwhile 5 Infantry Brigade Headquarters shook down, practised new procedures and trained up the many extra staff that had been hurriedly brought in. During the second week they operated in their new role for the first time and conducted a brigade exercise in which they were actively involved in land fighting in the Falklands. Platoon, company and battalion attacks

*After the surrender, Welsh Guardsmen move wearily down the only road in the Falklands, which leads from Fitzroy to Stanley. The rocky outcrops over which 5 Infantry Brigade had fought are clearly seen.*

preceded a helicopter assault with all 24 Puma helicopters the RAF could provide. To add realism RAF Harriers and Jaguars provided friendly close air support and 'enemy' aircraft. It was to prove invaluable.

It was an impressive exercise, one which with normal peacetime restrictions was inconceivable in its scope and expense. The media, starved of news of the Task Force, reported fully on the exercise and this did not go unnoticed by the Argentinians who were given a measure of Britain's determination. In fact it acted as an unexpected bonus in the propaganda war.

The Welsh Guards returned to Pirbright on 3 May when most, but by no means all, men were able to get away for a few days leave. Enormous quantities of stores arrived, along with some arctic clothing, before the unit moved down to Southampton. The Brigade sailed, mostly in the *QE 2* on 12 May. The Commanding Officer, Lieutenant Colonel John Rickett had assumed command of the 1st Bn Welsh Guards in March 1980 and therefore knew his men particularly well. He had previously seen active service with the South Federation Army in Aden during 1963-64, followed by a tour there with his battalion a year later. He also commanded a

company in Northern Ireland in 1973. He was a highly experienced officer.

Like other troops on board, the Welsh Guards pounded the decks of the great liner to maintain and improve their fitness. With the ship carrying nearly twice its normal complement of passengers training areas were at a premium and one class was reported to have taken place in the Synagogue. The grim realities of the war ahead was brought home when they received the sad news that three Welsh Guards SNCOs, serving with the SAS, had been killed in a helicopter crash.

The Scots and Welsh Guards were transferred from the *QE 2* to the *Canberra* on 24 May, many by the 'Ellas' requisitioned trawlers, which prompted a guardsman to enquire if this was how they were going all the way to the Falklands! The ship reached San Carlos on 2 June and the whole of 5 Infantry Brigade, with its supporting arms, were ferried ashore in landing craft into the Administrative Area.

Even then, many did not really expect to see enemy action, nor contemplate the disaster ahead. It struck the Welsh Guards at Bluff Cove when they were being offloaded from the LSL *Sir Galahad* and Argentine fighters bombed and strafed the ship. Over one fifth of the battalion were casualties in this attack, and two Companies had to be replaced by Royal Marines of 40 Commando for their final engagement to secure Sapper Hill. However their indomitable fighting spirit and courage, even in adversity was indestructible.

# The Parachute Regiment

Although the Parachute Regiment was officially formed on 1 August 1942, the first parachute troops were trained as a result of a memorandum sent by Prime Minister Winston Churchill to General Ismay on 6 June 1940. In it he said *'The following measures should be taken . . . Deployment of parachute troops on a scale equal to 5,000'*. On 22 June he confirmed this in another memorandum *'We ought to have a corps of at least 5,000 parachute troops. Advantage must be taken of the summer to train these forces, who can nonetheless play their part meanwhile as shock troops in home defence'*. However he was later to write 'I regret however that I allowed the scale I had proposed for British parachute troops to be reduced from 5,000 to 500'.

Major John Rock RE was given the task of training the first parachute troops and 370 men, mainly from No 2 Commando, was formed into 11 Special Air Service Battalion in November 1940, later to become 1st Battalion. The 2nd Battalion was formed in September 1941, followed shortly by three other

*Paratroopers gathering in their parachutes during an exercise in the UK. Each man must complete at least eight jumps before qualifying for his 'wings'.*

battalions with the result that the Parachute Regiment came into being. Its famous actions at Arnhem and Nijmegen ensured that, when the war ended, the Regiment, at a wartime maximum of 18 battalions, would remain, albeit reduced to just three battalions.

A reorganisation took place in 1948 and the three battalions formed 16th Parachute Brigade. Acting mostly independently they were involved in many brush fire wars during the 1950s and 60s. Up to 1953 men were volunteers seconded from other regiments, but direct enlistment to the regiment was then introduced. Like the Royal Marines the Parachute Regiment often fought to preserve their identity when more defence cuts were implemented but they managed to survive by taking on the role of normal infantry. 3 Para parachuted into Gamil airfield, 6 miles west of Port Said, to secure the airfield, in November 1956, later to be joined by 2 Para from Cyprus. This was the last time they were used in their airborne role as a unit, though they kept their parachuting expertise alive in numerous exercises.

The Parachute Regiment has provided battalions for operations, mainly in Aden and Borneo during the 1960s. When the situation in Northern Ireland deteriorated in 1971, a battalion was soon despatched, and one has nearly always been part of the security forces there ever since.

## 2nd Battalion

In 1981 2 Para, although part of 8 Field Force, based in Tidworth, were actually serving a 2 years tour of duty in Northern Ireland, from whence they returned in April 1981. Their commanding officer Lieutenant Colonel Herbert ('H') Jones, formerly of the Devon and Dorset Regiment, had joined them a month earlier.

During the summer of 1981 2 Para had taken part in parachute exercises including one on Salisbury Plain when they were joined by 3 Para. *'It was good to be on more than a one battalion exercise'* wrote an officer afterwards. Later that year, one company were helping in the making of a film on the Bruneval raid of January 1942, in which a Company of 2 Para had taken part, while another Company exercised in Kenya in November.

The unit had been to Denmark in September. On 13 December, 8 Field Force became 5 Infantry Brigade and the headquarters moved to Aldershot. The other battalions of the Brigade were 3 Para and 1/7 Gurkha Rifles.

2 Para were due for a tour of Belize starting in April 1982 and their advance party were already in the colony when the warning order putting them at 72 hours notice came on 15 April. Many of the unit were on leave at the time not expecting a call to the South Atlantic, as they were already committed. However they knew that their brothers-in-arms 3 Para had already sailed as part of 3 Commando Brigade. Lieutenant Colonel Jones was indulging himself in his favourite sport of skiing in France when the 'stand by' call came and he had immediately flown home. He was delighted that his unit was to be part of the initial force and under the command of 3 Commando Brigade. He had known Brigadier Thompson since the days they were together in Ulster, one as CO of 40 Commando, Jones as Brigade Major

*To maintain their 'out-of-area' operational expertise, Parachute Battalions periodically train in the Arctic wastes of Norway as well as in the jungle and desert.*

*Whilst on passage to the South Atlantic, weapon training as well as fitness training took place regularly on deck. All men were able to test fire their weapons.*

of 3 Infantry Brigade. His second in command, Major Chris Keeble made all the preliminary arrangements for recalling the unit.

The battalion was organised into three companies of about 100 each, while C Company was designated as a Patrol Company, of a Recce Platoon and a Patrol Platoon. This was larger than the Commando's Recce Troops and proved invaluable in providing information and intelligence. Sniping was an integral part of the battalion's training, but generally their equipment was much like any other infantry battalion. On the call to arms, the battalion was issued with Clansman radios, which their operators worked on during the passage south.

The CO insisted on doubling the number of GPMGs in the Companies and introducing some American M 79 grenade launchers, a decision that was to pay dividends later, despite the extra ammunition it entailed. Appreciating that little

*Two paratroopers with a mounted GPMG, entrenched in a defensive position. Generally the Falklands terrain did not allow digging and sangars of rocks were built above ground.*

transport would be available, the unit concentrated their training on carrying all equipment, food and ammunition on their backs. With the Support Company of machine guns, 81 mm mortars and Milan anti-tank launchers, along with the Assault Pioneer Platoon, experts in demolitions, mining and engineer tasks, the battalion had a formidable armoury.

The advance party was recalled from Belize where the Royal Irish Rangers were ordered to remain as garrison troops, being relieved by 3 Bn Royal Anglian Regiment later. On 26 April 2 Para embarked in the requisitioned *Norland* at Southampton, while much of its equipment went in the *Europic Ferry*. This was to cause some problems later. As the unit were to form part of 3 Commando Brigade a Royal Marines officer, Captain David Constance, was attached as liaison officer and his expertise in flight deck helicopter operations and embarking in landing craft was passed on to the Paras. He was to remain with the unit till the end of the campaign.

Reaching Ascension Island on 6 May, the unit managed to include one landing craft exercise and some field firing before the ship sailed south the following evening. The CO and Intelligence Officer, who had already flown to Ascension, rejoined the unit, which had done some stores cross checking from the *Atlantic Conveyor*.

## 3rd Battalion

Like 2 Para, the 3rd Battalion had also taken its turn serving in Northern Ireland, returning from a four months tour in April 1981. During the summer the unit of 670 all ranks had exercised in Canada as part of Ex *Pond Jump West*, as well as taking part in the two battalion parachute drop on Salisbury Plain. In October the unit completed over 1,500 parachute jumps and individual companies exercised on Dartmoor and at Fremington in Devon. In January 1982, 150 men went to Oman, a familiar training ground to their predecessors, for an exercise so that the battalion was fully prepared for its *Spearhead* duty in late March. It had also joined 5 Infantry Brigade in December, designated for 'out-of area' operations, although *Spearhead* usually meant a quick trip to Ulster.

On 2 April 3 Para, stationed at Tidworth, were ordered to stand by and the following day were put under command

*Paras of 2nd Battalion pass resting comrades on their triumphant march towards Stanley after the surrender. They were the first to reach the capital following up the retreating Argentinian forces after the battle for Wireless Ridge.*

of 3 Commando Brigade. Their Commanding Officer, Lieutenant Colonel Hew Pike, attended the briefing by Brigadier Thompson in Plymouth on 4 April. He was told that the battalion would embark in the *Canberra* four days later with most of their stores going in the *Elk*. Pike had also known his new Brigadier as they had served together as student and directing staff at the Army Staff College, Camberley. The unit did some hasty unpacking for an air move and repacking for a sea move in the next few days. Many of the men had been on weekend leave, but all were recalled within 48 hours, and most were back in barracks long before that, so keen were they to be 'on active service'. They drew Clansman radios and other specialist equipment and embarked at Portsmouth on 8 April. Before doing so the CO addressed the battalion at Tidworth, he

*One of the fiercest battles of the war was 3rd Battalion The Parachute Regiment's fight for Mount Longdon, when Sergeant Ian McKay won a posthumous Victoria Cross for taking out a machine gun post. The Paras wore their own pattern steel helmets with hessian camouflage for the battles, but their red berets were soon prominent in victory. They wore the standard DMS boots which proved a disaster in the cold and wet weather of the Falklands winter.*

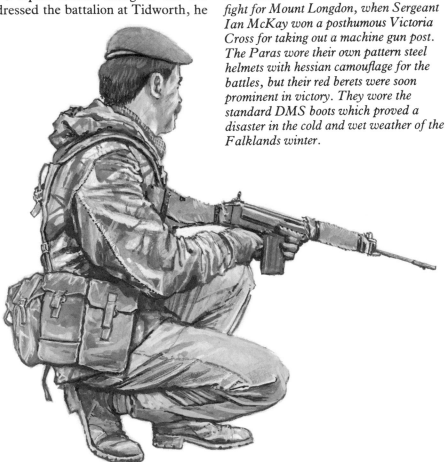

being one of the few who expected they would really go to battle. He said 'There is enormous residual self-confidence in a parachute battalion. People don't worry whether they can do things'.

During their voyage south in company, and friendly competition, with 40 and 42 Commandos, they learnt the ways of seaborne soldiers. They practised new techniques, pounded the decks in an effort to retain their exceptional fitness and learnt the ways of the Clansman radio. At Ascension they were able to take their turn ashore, having a first run in landing craft and assaulting Wideawake Airfield. The anti-tank platoon fired the precious HESH round, 37½ years worth of training ammunition in one day! They continued southwards in *Canberra* cross decking to *Intrepid* on 18 May before the landing in San Carlos.

The men of the Parachute Regiment, with its distinctive red beret and its motto of 'Utrinque Paratus' (*Ready for Anything*), are among the fittest and best trained troops in the world. Their standards are particularly high with each man completing at least eight parachute jumps to qualify for his 'wings'. Their equip-

ment, much like any infanteer, differed in the fibre plastic helmet they wore and parachute smocks, but the DMS boots, which proved one of their biggest drawbacks causing an uncomfortable form of trench-foot, was of standard British Army issue. When 16 Parachute Brigade was disbanded in 1974, many thought it sounded the end for these specialist troops. It was left to individual commanding officers to prove their worth to new Brigade Commanders. It was therefore with some relief that they found themselves under command of the well established 3 Commando Brigade, trained, like themselves for the unusual, rather than the newly formed and inexperienced 5 Infantry Brigade.

Like all troops on the voyage south the Paras concentrated on individual training with weapon skills, battlefield first aid and casualty handling procedures taking priority. They ran round the upper decks to keep themselves fit in their unaccustomed surroundings. With their new radios, the headquarters practised their action drills, knowing that such procedures must be automatic on a battlefield. This concentrated training prepared them for the fierce battles ahead.

*Battle weary but grinning paratroopers raise the Union Flag on their defensive positions overlooking Stanley after they heard news of the surrender.*

# 1/7th Gurkha Rifles

The Brigade of Gurkhas trace their origins back to the Nepalese hillmen who enlisted in the armies of the Honorable East India Company in 1816. The literal meaning of Gurkha was 'defender of cows'. When the Company was abolished in 1858, the Gurkha regiments were absorbed into the British (Indian) Army and fought with great distinction in both World Wars in North Africa and Europe as well as in the Far East. In 1948 four Regiments (2nd, 6th, 7th and 10th) with two battalions each, were selected to constitute the Brigade of Gurkhas, and they continued to serve mainly in the Far East.

With the withdrawal of British troops from east of Suez in the 1970s, one Gurkha Battalion was permanently stationed in England at Church Crookham, near Aldershot, Hampshire. The remainder of the Brigade form the British Garrison in Hong Kong and Brunei. In 1959 the 7th became the Duke of Edinburgh's Own Gurkha Rifles. 1/7 GR arrived in UK in April 1981 becoming part of 5 Infantry Brigade (later 5 Airborne Brigade). As the other two battalions of the Brigade were both from the Parachute Regiment, the Gurkhas were largely left to train by themselves. In 1981 and early 1982 they had companies away in Belize for six months, besides carrying out exercises in Cyprus. On top of this there were Queen's Guard ceremonial duties in London and the British Army Rifle meeting at Bisley which they won.

The Gurkha soldier is a hard, well-trained and highly dedicated individual, generally small and stocky in stature, with an average height of 5′ 4″. His upbringing in the rugged hills of Nepal, north of India gives him a hardiness and endurance second to none. He is physically strong and over the years has trained and fought in most extremes of climates from the cold regions of Nepal to the jungles of Malaya and Borneo. At home in Nepal there are few roads and pack animals in the mountains, and as children they are brought up to carry heavy loads over long distancs. They have a natural eye for fieldcraft and their continual successes at Bisley reflect their weapon prowess.

They are an entirely volunteer force, indeed only one in thirty who apply are finally accepted. 'Hill Selection', which combines physical measuring and assessing potential abilities, is carried out by a touring team of two retired officers who eliminate all but the best candidates. Those chosen then attend a final selection. The Gurkhas have a fierce loyalty and are strict disciplinarians. Their 32 weeks basic training is one of the longest and most demanding in the British army. They then carry out two further months of advanced military training, tactics and an introduction to support weapons. Originally most of their officers came from the British Indian Army, and today they retain a number of British officers. During the 1960s and 1970s the number of Gurkhas commissioned from the ranks increased. By 1982 half their officers were Queen's Gurkha Officers (formally Viceroy Commissioned Officers) normally commissioned after 16-18 years service, while a

*Gurkhas keeping fit while on passage to the South Atlantic in* Queen Elizabeth 2. *More strenuous exercises were undertaken later with full packs, weapons and equipment.*

78

few were commissioned direct from Sandhurst. Many bear identical names, leading to confusion amongst the layman! They share with the Royal Marines the distinction of the wearing of a green beret though of a darker shade than that of the commando.

*'Ayo Gurkhali', the famous battle cry of the Gurkha Rifles, and awareness of their curved kukri fighting knives, instilled terror into the hearts of the Argentine conscripts. Myth has it that the kukri is never drawn without shedding blood. These stocky, tough soldiers from Nepal, who provide six battalions for the British Army, are all volunteers, only one in thirty being accepted for service.*

There had been a 5 Infantry Brigade (as they were now designated) exercise 'Green Lanyard' in Norfolk soon after its formation in January 1982, and when the Brigade were brought to immediate notice to move as first reinforcements for the Falklands, they carried out joint exercises with the Scots and Welsh Guards in the Brecon Beacons area of Wales. They continually practised carrying heavy loads over rough country and polished up their helicopter drills as they were likely to be without vehicles. The Gurkhas were more accustomed to this type of fitness training than their compatriots in 5 Brigade.

Their commanding officer Lieutenant Colonel David Morgan had joined 1/7 GR towards the end of 1981. He was a full career Gurkha officer who had first seen action during the Borneo confrontation. He had recently been Brigade Major of 48 Gurkha Brigade in Hong Kong.

One Company of 1/7 GR was hastily recalled from Belize and embarked only five days after their arrival in UK in the *QE2* at Southampton. Some soldiers were still wearing their jungle boots! The battalion were soon issued with civilian bergen rucksacks, having been bought by Ordnance Services, discarding their 1958 pattern packs as it was clear that they would be quite unsuitable for carrying the loads expected in the Falklands. Otherwise they were dressed in standard British combat clothing and equipment. They were organised as four

*After the collapse of the Argentinian resistance, Gurkhas occupied Stanley airfield, where they found much abandoned equipment including this Rheinmetall 20 mm rapid fire gun.*

rifle companies, one more than the normal British infantry battalion, a support company which included a mortar platoon with eight 84 mm mortars, a recce platoon, and infantry pioneer platoon and an anti-tank platoon. The latter was converted and trained with the MILAN wire guided anti-tank weapon in the fortnight preceding departure. As very few vehicles were to be taken, the Motor Transport Platoon found themselves in the unaccustomed role of a heavy machine-gun platoon, equipped with Browning .50s. With a total of 720 all ranks, they were the largest single unit in the Falklands.

Travelling south in the *QE 2*, they were able to carry out limited physical training, using spaces in rotation with the remainder of the Brigade. Their deployment in the Falklands was less exciting than they would have liked. They cleared the area of Lafonia, using a patrol technique inborn since childhood. Their courageous assault on Mount William with the battle cry 'Ayo Gurkhali' as almost the final coup d'état of the campaign are recounted elsewhere. They were desperately disappointed that most of the Argentine defenders fled before being brought to battle.

Perhaps the Gurkhas most famed weapon is the kukri, a curved fighting knife broadening towards the point, which they all carried. In his youth every boy is brought up to use one for cutting wood, clearing undergrowth and chopping up food. There is no doubt that the knowledge that these tough soldiers had this 'secret weapon', shrouded in its own mystique, was a considerable morale factor in initimidating the Argentine defenders.

# Chapter Three

# The Air Forces

The main role of the Royal Air Force in the 1970s and 80s was concentrated on defence against the Warsaw Pact countries. Since the withdrawal of most British bases from the Far and Middle East, air requirements had been tailored and developed into providing defence of the United Kingdom, support for NATO and the few 'out of area' operations envisaged. During the 1970s the V Bombers gradually handed over their nuclear deterrent role to the Royal Navy's submarines.

The Royal Air Force is divided into three major commands, Strike and Support Commands in UK and Royal Air Force Germany. Other regular commitments include units in Gibraltar, Belize, Hong Kong and Cyprus, each varying considerably in size and constitution. In addition the RAF regiment provides defence for Service air fields and bases, while the Signals branch operates large radar and signals networks world wide. The RAF are also responsible for Military Air Traffic Operations and Meteorology. A modern aircraft needs considerable back-up crews and ground staff. These maintainers, whose jobs are often forgotten, are highly trained technicians. Unobtrusively they prepare, inspect and maintain aircraft to a degree unsurpassed in the world. Along with Squadron aircrew they form part of a close knit team.

Pilot training in the RAF, (the Royal Navy follows a similar pattern) costs about £1.5 million per man, and nearly all are commissioned. About one third of the pilots are recruited direct from University Air Squadrons of which there are 16 throughout the country. Other commissioned aircrew include Navigators, while Air Engineers, Air Electronic Operators and Air Loadmasters may be non-commissioned officers.

A few RAF pilots serve in Royal Naval Air Squadrons, both fixed wing and helicopters, but their strike role with the Fleet Air Arm differs considerably from their training in support of NATO. It is with this background that the two air 'arms' united in conflict against the Argentinians.

In 1982 the Royal Navy had 16 Naval Air Squadrons with over 250 helicopters and 30 Sea Harriers, 28 of which were deployed south. Military aviation was provided by the Army Air Corps and 3 Commando Brigade Air Squadron with their Scout and Gazelle helicopters, which are maintained by REME technicians. These squadrons are discussed in later chapters.

No successful opposed landing could be achieved without air superiority and the commanders could never afford to underestimate the skill and expertise of the Argentine Air Force. From the outset it was clear that the British possession of Ascension Island was to play an important role as a staging post and base. Wideawake airfield, normally used to about 40 movements a month, suddenly found itself with a daily total nearer 400. It has a runway of 10,000 feet, large enough to accommodate the biggest aircraft, but its limited parking space for only 25 aircraft was initially a drawback.

One of the early tasks of the Force Commanders and particularly Air Marshal Sir John Curtiss was to assess the strength and capability of the Argentine Air Force and Naval Aviation Command. Whilst the British were fighting a war 8,000 miles away, the Argentines were only 400 miles from the Falklands and could use mainland bases for launching their attacks. Whilst it was still operating, it was felt that the aircraft carrier *Veintecinco (25) de Mayo*, formerly the light fleet carrier *Venerable* built in 1945, although vulnerable to British submarine attack, was likely to pose a considerable threat. It was known to carry at least 8 Skyhawk fighters, 4 Tracker anti-submarine patrol aircraft and 3 Sea King helicopters. Its limitations were that, in order to launch the Skyhawks, at least 25 knots of wind was required over the deck

and to operate the Super-Etendard, capable of launching the Exocet anti-ship missile, it was stretched to the limit to catapult the 12 ton aircraft.

*25 de Mayo* had supported Operation *Rosario* and was known to be operating around the Falklands. The sinking of the *General Belgrano* on 2 May, forced the Junta to rethink. If they risked their one aircraft carrier further and it was also sunk it would jeopardise their prestige in the world and be a shattering blow to morale at home. As a result the carrier took no further effective part in the campaign.

It was therefore the land based air power that the commanders studied. Exact figures of Argentine aircraft are still not certain, but the most accurate assessment of their attack aircraft was 76 Skyhawks, 24 Daggers, 18 Mirage IIIEAs, 5 Super Etendards and 6 Canberras. In addition they had 114 smaller fighters such as Pucaras, Aermacchi MB-339As and T-34C Mentors, all of which could operate from airfields and airstrips on the Falklands to a range of 300 miles, enough to outnumber the available Sea Harrier force by twelve to one. Many of their aircraft were new, and their pilots were certainly highly trained. It was known that they possessed five Exocet missiles, which had been taken to Rio Grande airfield in Argentina, where the Super-Etendards were based. The Argentines also had a practised air-to-air refuelling capability having two KC-130H Hercules tankers, besides a cargo fleet of seven transport C-130s. Indeed the tankers refuelled 113 fighter and strike sorties during the campaign. Had it not been for the continuous resupply of the garrison by the transport C-130s, the last of the 61 missions arriving in Stanley only the day before the surrender, the war might well have been shorter. The Hercules pilots knew Stanley airport, having occasionally visited there in previous years, the last landing as recently as 6 March with a supposed fractured oil pipe. Just one

Hercules was shot down by a Harrier on 1 June off Pebble Island, but every night during the later stages of the campaign a resupply mission could be heard flying into Stanley.

On the British side, 28 Sea Harriers were immediately available and these were supplemented by 8 RAF Harrier GR3s. It had hardly been conceived by the Air Staff in UK that a conventional bombing raid would ever be carried out over 3,000 miles from an airfield, and the remarkable endurance of the Vulcans and their pilots coupled with the brilliant airmanship of the Victor tanker crews gave the nation a much needed boost. The actual material damage done was small compared with the effort, but it had a high prestige and morale value. Early warning of enemy ships and aircraft by the Task Force was needed, and although the RAF Nimrods flew continuously, mostly from Wideawake, their range of a maximum of 2,000 miles radius until they were converted to inflight refuelling, limited their use when the Task Force were in the TEZ. The

*A Sea Harrier of the Fleet Air Arm and a Harrier GR3 of the RAF in company above HMS* Hermes *in the South Atlantic. Twenty-eight Sea Harriers and 8 GR3s were immediately available in the Task Force. They accounted for 20 enemy fighters in aerial combat without sustaining a single loss.*

longest mission was on 20/21 May when a Nimrod flew 8,453 miles in just under 19 hours, reaching as far as 60 miles from the Argentine coast. However early warning for the fleet was mainly borne on the shoulders of the FAA Sea King helicopters, but there was a large gap in the AEW defences in detecting approaching aircraft at low level in and around the Falklands.

The value of helicopters in an unfriendly environment was never more apparent than in supporting the land fighting. With virtually no roads and with very few oversnow vehicles, most movement was done by air or foot. SBS and SAS patrols were inserted into the Falklands from 1 May, providing essential intelligence. Later where long distances had to be covered to move troops forward, resupply them and evacuate casualties, there were never enough helicopters. The loss of all but one of the large Chinooks in the *Atlantic Conveyor* was a severe blow to the land forces, but the remainder of the smaller helicopters worked overtime, while the troops on the ground suffered more 'yomping' than would otherwise have been needed. However helicopter support in the front line saved many lives through prompt casualty evacuation and was a strong morale factor amongst the battle weary troops.

Flying and safety regulations were often cast aside by the pilots in their desire to support the land forces, and most conservatively put their operating estimate at four times the normal peacetime rates. The logistic problem of keeping even the limited number of aircraft available was phenomenal and the ground crews and support units worked overtime to keep an exceptionally high rate of serviceability.

# Fleet Air Arm Squadrons

The Royal Naval Air Service was founded on 1 July 1914, although the first Inspecting Captain of Aircraft had been appointed as early as 1909, two years before three Royal Naval Officers and one Royal Marines Officer were selected to be first naval pilots. Since then naval aviation has undergone many changes in organisation, personnel and in its aircraft.

Between the Wars there was much controversy as to whether the Fleet Air Arm, as it was then known, should not be absorbed into the comparatively new Royal Air Force, and indeed naval aviators carried a dual rank of both services. The main debate was who should provide air cover for the Fleet, a matter which also came under close scrutiny in the 1960s; indeed in the 1920s, whether air cover for the Fleet was a requirement at all. Until 1937 the responsibility for the Fleet Air Arm was divided between the Royal Navy and the Royal Air Force.

The Second World War was to change that, and since then the Fleet Air Arm has grown, but not without the odd scare. By the end of World War 2 Great Britain had 13 Fleet Carriers and some 24 Escort Carriers; during the Korean War there were always five light fleet aircraft carriers continually involved, and in 1956 at the time of the Suez crisis, the Royal Navy still had 14 aircraft carriers. This incident saw the first operational use of helicopters in large numbers when 45 Commando were landed on the beaches. In fact naval helicopters had first supported troops in the Malayan jungles in 1950 and subsequently in Cyprus. This new form of 'landing craft' had far reaching consequences.

The fixed wing carrier continued to dominate naval air thinking, but in 1959 the first Commando Carrier, *Bulwark* was deployed to the Far East, shortly followed by *Albion*. Between them these two carriers backed 3 Commando Brigade in their peace keeping roles in Kuwait, Brunei, Borneo, Aden and Malaya.

With this growth, the aircraft changed, the number of helicopters increased and their roles divided between troop carrying and anti submarine warfare. On the fixed wing side the angled flight deck which was first incorporated in *Ark Royal* in 1955 made flying that much safer, allowing more modern and faster

*A Sea Harrier pilot dressed in a Mark 10 immersion suit. This fitted loosely over his G-suit and thermal liner, worn by all fighter pilots. He would normally wear a standard NATO type life jacket. Like normal flying suits, this has pads at the knees for writing instructions, besides a number of zip-up pockets for maps, papers, etc. A torch is normally carried.*

jet planes to take off and land. Then came the revolutionary development of the Vertical Take Off and Landing Sea Harrier, requiring a much smaller flight deck. With this came the ski-jump ramp fitted to the new *Invincible* Class of carriers and to *Hermes*. In addition the ASW helicopter began to play an increasingly important role, giving smaller ships a search and kill factor far exceeding the range and scope of its old ASDIC. From 1964 small frigates and destroyers were being fitted with helicopter pads aft, later to include hangar facilities, for the Wasp helicopter. By the late 1960s some Royal Fleet Auxiliary ships were fitted with pads and a Naval Air Squadron formed specially for these ships. During the Falklands campaign STUFT ships, such as the *Atlantic Causeway* were fitted with decks that could withstand the weight and pressure of the Sea Harrier.

Since 1937 front line Royal Naval Air Squadrons have been numbered in the 800 series, while the second line and training squadrons have been in the 700 series. There were occasions during World War 2 and later in the Royal Naval (Volunteer) Reserve when 1700 and 1800 series were used. As with the RAF squadrons, they are normally equipped with only one type of aircraft. The low 800s were Fighter and ASW Squadrons, while the Air Commando Squadrons traditionally started at 845.

In 1982 there were 16 Fleet Air Arm squadrons with about 250 helicopters and 30 Sea Harriers. In addition 3 Commando Brigade Air Squadron of Gazelles and Scouts were based at the Royal Naval Air Station, Yeovilton in Somerset, the home of the Harriers. When the Falklands crisis arose, it was immediately apparent that the size of the Task Force, the distance from the UK and the terrain in the Islands would necessitate every available helicopter travelling south. It meant a rapid re-organisation and expansion to raise more squadrons, and included bringing in a number of RAF pilots to supplement the FAA. There were already 7 fully qualified RAF pilots for the Sea Harriers and two more completed their training on route.

The Sea Kings of 814 Squadron at RNAS Culdrose were transferred to bring existing operational squadrons up to strength and form the basis of 825 Squadron which was embarked in *Atlantic Causeway* and *Queen Elizabeth 2*. The

## FLEET AIR ARM SQUADRON

**737 Naval Air Squadron**
Aircraft: Wessex Mk 3
Embarked: County Class Destroyers,
Antrim and Glamorgan

**800 Naval Air Squadron**
Aircraft: Sea Harriers
Embarked: Hermes

**801 Naval Air Squadron**
Aircraft: Sea Harriers
Embarked: Invincible

**809 Naval Air Squadron**
Aircraft: Sea Harriers
Embarked: Hermes, Invincible
Recommissioned for the Falklands

**815 Naval Air Squadron**
Aircraft: Lynx Mk 2
Embarked: Invincible, Hermes, Type
42 Destroyers, Leander
Class, Type 21 (except
*Active*) and Type 22 Frigates

**820 Naval Air Squadron**
Aircraft: Sea King Mk 5
Embarked: Invincible

**824 Naval Air Squadron**
Aircraft: Sea King HAS Mk 2
Embarked: Fort Grange, Olmeda

**825 Naval Air Squadron**
Aircraft: Sea King HAS Mk 2
Embarked: Atlantic Causeway, Queen
Elizabeth 2
Squadron Recommissioned for the
Falklands

**826 Naval Air Squadron**
Aircraft: Sea King Mk 5
Embarked: Hermes, Fort Austin

**829 Naval Air Squadron**
Aircraft: Wasp
Embarked: Active, Endurance,
Plymouth, Yarmouth,
Survey Ships, Contender
Bezant

**845 Naval Air Squadron**
Aircraft: Wessex Mk 5
Embarked: Invincible, Intrepid, Fort
Austin, Resource,
Tidespring, Tidepool
Also ashore at Ascension Island

**846 Naval Air Squadron**
Aircraft: Sea King Mk 4
Embarked: Hermes, Fearless, Intrepid,
Canberra, Elk Norland

**847 Naval Air Squadron**
Aircraft: Wessex Mk 5
Embarked: Engadine, Atlantic
Causeway
Squadron Recommissioned for the
Falklands

**848 Naval Air Squadron**
Aircraft: Wessex Mk 5
Embarked: Olna, Olwen, Regent,
Atlantic Conveyor
Recommissioned for the Falklands

**899 Naval Air Squadron**
Aircraft: Sea Harriers
Embarked: Hermes, Invincible

*Three Sea Harriers of different Squadrons identified from their tail badges, from top 801 Squadron, 800 Squadron and 899 Squadron. 899 Operational Training Squadron provided its aircraft to bring the others up to strength and re-form 809 Squadron.*

Lynx helicopters of 702 Operational Training Squadron were added to 815 Squadron and dispersed amongst the destroyers and the frigates; 707 Air Commando Training Squadron reformed as 848 Squadron with Wessex Vs; while more Wessex were found to form 847 Squadron in early May which went south in the *Engadine* and *Atlantic Conveyor*, 829 Squadron of Wasps expanded considerably with many helicopters taken from 'store' and were these split amongst many of the smaller and STUFT ships.

As far as Sea Harriers were concerned, the Operational Training Squadron 899 provided some of its aircraft to bring 800 (*Hermes*) and 801 (*Invincible*) up to strength and also form 809 Squadron which was divided between the two aircraft carriers. Twenty eight aircraft were deployed south and their value is shown in 16 enemy aircraft confirmed as shot down with their Sidewinder missiles and four more with their 30mm Aden Cannon, with another three probables.

Between them the Fleet Air Arm Squadrons played an effective part in the air defence of the Task Force, covering the amphibious landings and providing essential troop carrying and casualty evacuation. When air superiority was eventually gained, they gave support to the ground forces who would have been unable to operate successfully without them. In a primarily naval campaign such as this, the retention of a strong professional and dedicated Fleet Air Arm was fully justified.

# The Harriers of the Fleet Air Arm and Royal Air Force

The origins of the Harrier fighter go back to an idea developed by Hawkers in their P 1127, a vertical take off and landing aircraft. It caught the imagination of a naval working party in the early 1960s and indeed the first aircraft carried out trials aboard *Ark Royal* in 1963. Its development was speeded up with the Royal Navy's decision to run down its number of conventional aircraft carriers, and this fixed wing alternative to the normal carrier borne aircraft seemed the ideal solution for the Fleet Air Arm to retain a high performance fighter which could be operated from much smaller ships.

The Royal Air Force were also seeking an aircraft which could operate from forward areas without long runways and the Harrier was their answer. British Aerospace developed the aircraft through the 1960s primarily for the RAF. After prolonged trials the Royal Navy ordered 24 Sea Harriers in 1975, based on the RAF's GR3 which had come into service in 1969, along with one T-4 trainer. Ten more were ordered in 1978. The RAF's Harrier force was ever increasing mostly for service in support of BAOR Germany.

The value of the Harrier was not only its extraordinary take off and landing capability but also its airworthiness and manoeuvrability. By the time of the Falklands crisis, the Navy had 28 operational Sea Harriers, but this was scarcely enough for the needs of a fleet fighting 8,000 miles away, especially if there were to be many losses. No 1 (F) Squadron RAF, based at RAF Wittering, Lincolnshire were therefore alerted on 2 April to the possibility of serving 'at sea'.

Their first task was the modification of the Harrier GR3s, which under the supervision of British Aerospace engineers from Kingston in Surrey, and the Royal Aircraft Establishments at Farnborough and Boscombe Down, was carried out by Wittering Engineering Wing in the remarkably short space of three weeks. First came the modifications to operate from aircraft carriers; secondly was to revise the pilots in air-to-air combat techniques to supplement their normal ground attack role. The main engineering tasks were to add the Sidewinder missile, make complicated changes to the inertial navigational system and to fit I-Band radar transponders to enable aircraft to operate with the Royal Navy. Many minor modifications were also required such as deck lashing rings, nozzle control and nosewheel steering alterations.

The conversion of RAF pilots to fly from aircraft carriers proceeded simultaneously. All flew to the Royal Naval Air Station at Yeovilton in Somerset to practice taking off from the ski-jump ramp there, similar to that fitted in *Hermes* and *Invincible*. In addition they carried out air-to-air combat manoeuvres and studied Argentine aircraft capabilities, tactics and methods. The Squadron Commander, Wing Commander Peter Squire sent two of his officers to Liverpool along with FAA officers to evaluate the feasibility of using a container ship as a seaborne platform for the Harrier. They reported favourably on the few modifications required, mainly in deck strengthening and the removal of some small, items of superstructure. *Atlantic Conveyor* took six GR3s and *Contender Bezant* picked up four at Ascension for the South Atlantic while others were flown to Ascension and thence joined *Hermes* direct in the TEZ.

Eight new Sea Harriers, already in the final stages of construction were hurriedly brought forward to operational standard. Each was fitted with an American device enabling them to drop chaff and infra-red decoy flares. These single seater fighters were primarily for reconnaissance, seeking out shadowing ships and attacking them. Their role was probing and striking, but as the campaign developed they assumed an air defence role and later provided much needed ground support for the troops ashore. They carried two Aden 30mm cannons in addition to their twin AIM-9L Sidewinder missiles. These missiles, each weighing 165 lbs, are infra-red homing devices with a high explosive warhead and a range of about 1,200 yards. In place of their Sidewinders, they can carry three 1,000 lb bombs or up to five BL 755 cluster bombs for low level attack against an area target. The GR3 has slightly different armament and could be adapted to fire two Shrike radar-homing missiles. Later it was decided to convert

*A Sea Harrier hovers over the crowded deck of* Hermes. *Twenty-eight of these single seater fighters were deployed in the two aircraft carriers. A Sidewinder missile is fitted under each wing and the refuelling probe can be seen protruding above the nose.*

the normal 1,000 lb bombs into Paveway laser-guided missiles, and the necessary conversion kits were dropped to the Task Force in the South Atlantic. The Harriers' maximum speed was 690 mph at low altitude and they were all fitted for inflight refuelling.

The Harrier proved far superior to any Argentine aircraft in its performance. Six Sea Harriers were lost, only two by enemy action and none in air-to-air combat. Four GR3s were lost, three being shot down by ground fire and the other crashing during landing. Only four pilots were killed, but some spent some cold and wet moments in the sea before being rescued, Flight Lieutenant Ian Mortimer surviving for 8 hours in his dinghy before being picked up by a Sea King helicopter around midnight. Other Harriers suffered considerably from small arms fire and fragmentation but the sturdy planes stood the damage well.

On the British side Sea Harriers accounted for 28 Argentine aircraft, 23 in aerial combat, while GR3s destroyed four aircraft on the ground. This was proof if needed of the superiority of the

Harrier over the Skyhawks, Mirages and Pucaras. The Sidewinder proved particularly effective, 26 were reported to have been fired, some in pairs at the same target, accounting for 18 enemy aircraft. From subsequent accounts from Argentine pilots the Harriers' small configuration and light colour had made it very difficult to detect and most of those shot down had been taken unawares. Without early warning radar the British pilots had to rely on the 'mark one eyeball' to sight the enemy. Although much has been written about the Harriers' capability to use its VIFF thrust (Vectored In Forward Flight) in combat to enable it to out-manoeuvre the enemy, by slowing suddenly and letting the enemy flash past him, there were no reported incidents during the Falklands campaign. No self respecting pilot would allow an enemy to get on his tail.

The RAF pilots of No 1 Squadron adapted well to their maritime role, 126 sorties were flown by the GR3s, mostly from *Hermes*. There were also seven RAF pilots in 800 and 801 Naval Air Squadrons, two more completing their

*An RAF Harrier GR 3 landing on board* Hermes *in the South Atlantic. They transferred from the ill-fated* Atlantic Conveyor *before she was sunk. They were used mainly in the ground attack role after the landings.*

acquaint training during the voyage south. The serviceability rate of both aircraft was remarkably high considering the antarctic conditions, *Hermes* regularly having 12 aircraft available out of its normal total of 15.

The Argentine Air Force and Naval Air Arm had between them over 140 fighters and fighter-bombers compared with the British total of 34 Harriers, but through the effectiveness of the Royal Navy's destroyers and frigates air-defence screen, coupled with the skill of the small band of fighter pilots, air superiority was achieved over the Falklands within a week of the landings. But it was touch and go during the first few days, and further losses of British aircraft, or the sinking of one of the carriers, would have endangered the successful outcome of regaining the Islands.

# Naval Helicopters

Naval helicopters have three distinct roles, anti-submarine warfare, troop and logistic support, and communication flights. For these roles they have four different aircraft, Sea King, Wessex, Lynx and Wasp and at the outset of the campaign the Fleet Air Arm had nearly 450 helicopters in service and nearly 200 were deployed south.

The Westland Sea King HAS 2, carried aboard some Royal Fleet Auxiliaries was primarily an anti-submarine warfare aircraft, the Royal Navy's primary role in the NATO alliance. The helicopter entered service in December 1976, developed from the HAS 1 which was first deployed in 1969. Secondary roles include Search and Rescue, and over-the-horizon targeting using the MEL ARI 5955 radar with an effective range of 50 miles. The Sea King is also capable of carrying up to 25 passengers. For underwater search the helicopter lowers its Plessey Type 195 sonar up to 150 feet below the sea's surface searching for submarines and has an underwater range in excess of eight miles. In its offensive role it can carry four Mark 46 or Stingray lightweight torpedoes or four Mark 11 depth charges.

Before 1982 the HAS 1 was slowly being replaced by the more advanced HAS 5, which came into service in November 1980, carrying a similar load and armament. It was equipped with the improved Sea Searcher radar which was light weight and operated through 360°, and coupled with LAPADS (lightweight acoustic processing and display system) made it a very high performance weapons

system. The Sea Kings provided the main anti-submarine defence for the aircraft carriers of the Task Force, *Hermes* (826 Squadron) and *Invincible* (820 Squadron) carrying at least nine helicopters each. These helicopters provided round-the-clock ASW protection from the time the Task Force left Ascension. Whilst at Ascension, the Sea Kings joined the massive cross-decking of men, supplies and ammunition, to ensure everything was tactically loaded and stored in the most efficient way for the subsequent landings, such had been the initial rush at Portsmouth, Plymouth and Marchwood (Southampton).

Later, in between their normal screening duties, the Sea Kings were used for search and rescue and for assessing damage to ships like *Sheffield*. The crews achieved an average of 100 flying hours per month during the campaign. HRH The Prince Andrew was one of the pilots in 820 Squadron. On 17 May, because of the additional Harrier GR3s which had been taken aboard *Hermes* from the *Atlantic Conveyor*, four HAS 5 and six crews of 826 Squadron were transferred to the RFA *Fort Austin*. During the journey south, the aircraft were painted in low visibility blue-grey colours and markings to aid concealment. Only two HAS 5s were lost during the campaign, both through malfunctions, but several

*A Wessex HU 5 Commando support helicopter which can carry up to 12 men or an underslung landrover. This aircraft, formerly of 722 Squadron, was transferred to 845 Squadron but remained at Ascension.*

*Royal Naval Squadron ground crew and small flight deck parties continued working night and day aboard* Hermes *and* Invincible *to keep the helicopters flying. They all carry their rank and names on a patch on their back for easy recognition and wear ear defenders to combat the incessant noise. A 95 per cent serviceability rate was maintained during the campaign, surpassing all expectation.*

were buzzed by enemy fighters, when on Falkland Sound sonar duty.

The logistical support Sea King HC 4, developed to support land forces and designed to operate ashore differs from the ASW version, in that the cabin is clear of the dipping sonar and associated equipment of the HAS 5. This allows the carriage of up to 28 fully armed men, 7,500 lbs as an underslung load, enough to lift a fully laden land rover or 105 mm light gun. The premier unit, 846 Squadron, had only returned to Yeovilton in late March 1982 after Exercise *Alloy Express* in northern Norway. It had a complement of 12 helicopters, all painted matt olive drab; of these nine sailed south in *Hermes*, the remainder in *Fearless*. The HC4 had come into service with 846 Squadron in November 1979 and had worked on a number of arctic deployments in support of 3 Commando Brigade with whom they had a particular rapport. One piece of equipment new to them which was to prove its worth during the campaign were Night Vision Goggles, the US Army designed ANVIS, four sets of which were available. Their image intensifying capacity was such that low level night flying was made possible. This enhanced the capability of the HC 4 to insert Special Forces patrols into the Falklands hinterland by night where they could

'contour-fly' at low level. It was one of these Sea Kings, captained by Lieutenant Richard Hutchings RM that flew into Chile on 18 May with an alleged secret mission of SAS, the helicopter being burnt afterwards and the crew surrendering themselves to the authorities – significantly on the eve of the main landings.

During the 10 weeks of the campaign 846 Squadron flew 1,818 sorties with pilots averaging 228 hours each. Much of this was without a co-pilot and 16% was at night. A remarkably high rate of serviceability was maintained by ground crews often working in atrocious conditions ashore. It was the total availability of troop lift helicopters before the final battles for Stanley that gave the Land Force Commander one of his greatest assets.

The other, smaller troop lift helicopters were the twenty two Wessex HU 5s of 845 Squadron which were broken down into A-E Flights of two aircraft each embarked in *Resource*, *Fort Austin*, *Tidespring*, *Tidepool* and *Intrepid*, with four others detached to Ascension. In addition 847 Squadron had 24 Wessex 5s and 848, reformed for Operation *Corporate*, had 12. These were mostly deployed in RFAs but six were lost in the *Atlantic Conveyor*. Two destroyer flights, *Antrim* and *Glamorgan* carried the single engined, anti-submarine version Wessex HAS3s,

parented by 737 Squadron at Portland. The Commando support Wessex 5 can carry 12 fully armed troops or carry an underslung load of a Landrover or 3,500 lbs of stores. By the end of the campaign a total of 56 Wessex 5s had been deployed. They saw action in South Georgia when they inserted an SAS patrol (only to lose two aircraft in recovering them); and a ninth Wessex, an HAS 3, was lost when *Glamorgan* was hit by Exocet on 12 June.

The other two types of naval helicopter were the Lynx and Wasp. The former was embarked in most of the Type 42 destroyers and frigates, while the Wasp was embarked in the older 'Leander' and 'Rothesay' class frigates. The latter's primary role was ASW, with Mk 44/46 lightweight torpedoes, or armed with the Aerospatiale SS 12 wire-guided missile for action against surface targets. The Lynx HAS 2, equipped with Sea Spray radar and the Sea Skua anti-ship missile, has a primary surface search, anti-ship strike and electronic 'barrier' surveillance role. It can also carry up to nine passengers. The smaller and older Wasp HAS 1, which first came into service in 1962, fired the first missiles of the campaign when *Endurance* and *Plymouth's* helicopters attacked the Argentine submarine *Santa Fe* off South Georgia.

This was the first major British naval campaign to be fought since the regular embarkation of the helicopter, although Fleet Air Arm Squadrons had been heavily involved in supporting land forces in Borneo and Aden. Its versatility was undoubtedly proven and its employment covered almost every aspect of the air war from anti-submarine warfare to anti-surface vessel; from search and rescue to logistic support and cross-decking; from casualty evacuation to reconnaisance and command and communications. Helicopter crews and maintainers provided a level of serviceability far greater than could possibly have been expected in the harsh winter conditions of the South Atlantic.

# Military Helicopters

The Scout and Gazelle military helicopters of 3 Commando Brigade Air Squadron and 656 Squadron, Army Air Corps are often described affectionately as 'Teeny Weeny Airways'. As such their part in the success of the campaign should not be overlooked.

The Westland Scout AH 1 had been in service since 1963 and is a rugged battlefield, utility helicopter, which remains in AAC service in Brunei, Hong Kong and the UK. In 3 Commando Brigade Air Squadron, four were fitted with the Aerospatiale SS-11 wire guided missile and two with bulged doors for casualty evacuation, while 656 Squadron had six missile armed Scouts available. The helicopter's main duty was reconnaisance and casualty evacuation. As the Argentines lacked armour, the missile configured Scouts were also used in the sangar-busting role. It was extremely useful in the forward areas for ferrying vital stores and ammunition where larger support-helicopters were too vulnerable. There is no doubt that in the latter stages of the campaign, load limits were often ignored in deference to operational requirements. The Scout normally carried a crew of two, pilot and aircrewman/observer.

The more modern and powerful Westland-built Aerospatiale Gazelle AH 1 had entered British Army service in August 1972 in an air observation role. Generally unarmed, although a few were fitted with Matra 68 mm SNEB rocket pods at Ascension; the weapon proved inappropriate for the campaign. In the South Atlantic its role was primarily as an observation and communications platform, but after the landings, Gazelles were often used for the movement of men and materials, liaison duties, besides ferrying supplies to and evacuating from the forward areas. There were nine Gazelles in 3 Commando Brigade Air Squadron and six in 656 Squadron, Army Air Corps.

When 3 Commando Brigade were put at notice to move on 1 April, the Brigade Air Squadron, normally with nine aircraft based near Plymouth and three at Arbroath in Scotland, recalled its men and prepared to embark in various LSLs. There was a mix of pilots commanded by Major Peter Cameron RM with 25 Royal Marines officers and NCOs, one Royal Navy and five Army personnel, while all the 22 aircrewmen were Royal Marines. They were organised into A, C and M Flights each of three Gazelles and B Flight of six Scouts. On 7 May an advanced detachment of 656 Squadron under Captain John Greenhalgh RCT with three Scouts, which were embarked in the *Europic Ferry* transferred to 3 Cdo Bde as 5 Flight. During the voyage south all flew most days, concentrating on night flying using the new night vision goggles. At Ascension they carried out live firing with guns and rockets.

Most aircraft were cross-decked just prior to D-Day in order to support the landings and provide airborne platforms for artillery and naval gunfire support observers. The first British casualty was Sergeant Andy Evans RM whose Gazelle was shot down by small arms fire when accompanying a Sea King helicopter carrying mortar ammunition and inserting Rapier firing posts. Soon afterwards the Gazelle of Lieutenant Ken Francis RM, on a similar escort mission, was hit by the same group of Argentine soldiers of 5 Infantry Regiment. The two pilots and one aircrewman were killed. During 2 Para's advance on Darwin and Goose Green they initially had two Gazelles in support. When Colonel 'H' Jones was killed two Scouts flew forward under heavy ground fire to evacuate him, one was shot down by two Pucaras with the other miraculously avoiding the fighters. Lieutenant Richard Nunn RM was killed but Sergeant AC Belcher RM was thrown clear when the helicopter crashed. Although 5 Flight supported 2 and 3 Para during the landings, they were re-embarked for the night aboard *Europic Ferry* which promptly sailed, not returning to San Carlos for five days but just in time for 2 Para's attack on Goose Green.

*A Scout helicopter of 656 Squadron Army Air Corps flies low over paratroopers as they advance across East Falkland. These aircraft continually supplied troops in the front line with ammunition and stores, whilst evacuating casualties on their return trips.*

*3 Commando Brigade Air Squadron and 656 Squadron Army Air Corps provided pilots for the Gazelles and Scout helicopters. Aircrew generally wore a mix of clothing for warmth and comfort, but most carried a 9 mm Browning automatic. Apart from communication duties, they were used for limited and essential resupply to the forward areas, and after, the battles, for casualty evacuation.*

Captain Greenhalgh, flying at night in almost blackout conditions and very short of fuel, evacuated a seriously wounded 2 Para officer who would undoubtedly have died; for this he was awarded the DFC.

Meanwhile in UK the remainder of 656 Squadron was put on standby. Although they normally supported 1 Infantry Brigade, the Squadron had worked with 2 Para in East Africa and UK during 1981. 5 Infantry Brigade's integral Air Squadron was the somewhat understrength 658 Squadron, which had had little experience with their new Brigade. Apart from their advance detachment which had left on 25 April, the Squadron had time to bring their aircraft up to operational readiness and also exercise with 5 Infantry Brigade on Brecon Beacons. They embarked their aircraft in *Nordic Ferry* and *Baltic Ferry* with most of the personnel in the *QE 2*, sailing on 12 May. The Squadron landed on the Falklands with 5 Infantry Brigade on 2 June, when the advance detachment reverted to their control.

Like 3 Commando Brigade Air Squadron, 656 Squadron operated continually in the forward areas, tying in casualty evacuation with resupply of ammunition. They covered the area where the heavy troop lift helicopters were unable to venture. Both set up forward arming and refuelling points from where they maintained a high rate of serviceability.

To support and enlarge the troop lift, five medium-lift RAF Chinook HC 1 helicopters of 18 Squadron were em-

*A Westland Gazelle similar to those used in the Falklands. 15 aircraft were deployed, each carrying a crew of two and up to three passengers. Two Royal Marines Gazelles were shot down on D-Day and a further one lost later.*

barked in the ill-fated *Atlantic Conveyor* on 25 April, along with six Wessex 5s of 848 Squadron. When the ship was hit by an Exocet on 25 May, four Chinooks were lost but one was fortuitously away on a training flight. It landed aboard *Hermes* and was the only one available during the campaign. Designed to carry about 45 troops, on one occasion it carried 81 fully armed paratroopers from Goose Green to Fitzroy. On another occasion it carried 64 wounded from the battlefield area to the hospital ship *Uganda*. It was in constant demand particularly for transporting artillery ordnance and ammunition, as it could lift two 105 mm guns at a time. In the two and a half weeks to the surrender it flew 109 hours and lifted over 2,000 men and 550 tons of stores. Following the loss of the *Atlantic Conveyor* six further Chinooks were sent south, three each in the *Contender Bezant* and *Astronomer* reaching the Falklands on 14 and 27 June, subsequently being employed in the massive clear up operations after the cessation of hostilities.

The unheralded work done by the Scouts and Gazelles can be measured by the award of five DFCs and one MC to pilots while a further 14 aircrew were mentioned in despatches. In all six aircrew were killed in action.

# Vulcans and Victors

The Vulcan bomber was first introduced into service in 1957, replacing the Valiant which had carried out the last British high level bombing raids during the Suez Crisis of 1956. In a quarter of a century it had provided a deterrent but had never bombed in anger. A Government Defence White Paper had announced its phasing out during the latter half of 1982 and at RAF Waddington in Lincolnshire preparations were already underway for the disbandment of Nos 44, 50 and 101 Squadrons of Vulcans based there.

The aircraft were slowly deteriorating into disuse, although in February 1982 five aircraft had flown to Nevada for Exercise *Red Flag* and were in a reasonable state of preparedness. Even when the balloon went up on 2 April, the crews did not really expect to go to war 8,000 miles away with only one usable British runway between themselves and the Falklands. Their normal range with a full bombing load was only 4,750 nautical miles and they were fitted and trained in

*British Aerospace (Avro) Vulcan B2s carried out the long-range 'Black Buck' missions, the bombing of Stanley airport, 3,800 miles from their forward base at Ascension Island. Each carried twenty one 1,000 lbs bombs. Five such raids were successfully flown.*

the nuclear rather than the conventional bombing role.

When the Squadron received the order to prepare for operations in the South Atlantic, the Air Engineering Wing at Waddington immediately set to work bringing the air-to-air refuelling systems up to operational standard on ten aircraft. Few had been used in this role over the last decade and the pilots and engineers needed practice once the equipment was fitted. Because the aircraft were due to be scrapped, no new radar or satellite navigation systems had been fitted and so the improved Carousel inertial system, which assisted long distance flying out of the range of land was added. New electronic counter measures equipment was fitted on underwing pylons, specially designed by RAF engineers. This incorporated the Westinghouse AN/ALQ-101 jamming pods.

Conventional bombing equipment which had to be fitted into all the aircraft was designed to take twenty-one 1,000 lb bombs and this was tested during April on the Cape Wrath bombing range. The bombs could be normal or with radar air burst fusing. In the event only the six aircraft which still had both forward and aft redundant Skybolt missile attachments with refrigeration ducts through their wings were converted. Five crews were selected, two from 50 Squadron, one each from 44 and 101 Squadrons with a further crew from the recently dis-

banded 9 Squadron. The aircraft were repainted a dark sea grey on the underside and their squadron insignia removed.

The Vulcan B 2 carried a crew of six, pilot, co-pilot, radar/navigator, navigator/plotter, air engineer and air-to-air refuelling instructor. It was capable of flying at 610 mph at 40,000 feet and besides its bombs, some were later adapted to carry two or four Shrike radiation-homing missiles for use against enemy radar installations. The first two Vulcans flew to Ascension on 29 April requiring two in-flight refuellings before landing at Wideawake airfield. The following day they departed for the first of the 'Black Buck' sorties to Stanley.

There was only one serious emergency in the whole 'Black Buck' missions when, on 3 June, Squadron Leader Neil MacDougall had to fly his Vulcan to Brazil. Having successfully completed his raid on Stanley, he was refuelling from a Victor tanker when the refuelling probe broke. With not enough fuel to return to Ascension, he made a 'Mayday'

## RESUMÉ OF BLACK BUCK MISSIONS

**30 April/1 May – Black Buck 1**
Fl Lt WFM Withers in reserve Vulcan (XM 607) dropped 21 × 1,000 lbs bombs, some of which cratered the runway at Stanley airport.

**3/4 May – Black Buck 2**
Sqn Ldr RJ Reeve (XM 607) dropped 21 × 1,000 lbs bombs, which missed runway but caused damage to military installations.

**7 May – Black Buck 3**
Cancelled for technical reasons

**28/29 May – Black Buck 4**
Sqn Ldr CN McDougall (XM 597) piloting Vulcan loaded with Shrike missiles aborted five hours out due to a Victor's refuelling problem.

**30 May/1 June – Black Buck 5**
Sqn Ldr CN McDougall (XM 597) attacked radar installations with Shrike missiles.

**2/3 June – Black Buck 6**
Same aircraft and crew attacked and destroyed enemy radar. Refuelling probe broke and forced to land in Brazil. Returned to UK 10 June.

**11/12 June – Black Buck 7**
Fl Lt WFM Withers (XM 607) dropped 21 × 1,000 lbs bombs on airport facilities at Stanley.

call and had just sufficient to land at Rio de Janeiro, after ditching all his secret documents in the sea. A superb demonstration of airmanship was required when the aircraft had to touch down first time with insufficient fuel for another circuit of the airfild. Any possibility of a diplomatic row was averted when the Brazilians acted impassively, not even inspecting the Vulcan's secret equipment. The crew were detained but released after a week and flew their aircraft back to UK.

Meanwhile the Victor tankers of 55 and 57 Squadrons, normally based at RAF Marham, Norfolk, were also being prepared though they were in regular service. Some had supported the recent Exercise *Maple Flag* in Canada. During the 1970s twenty-four K 2s had been converted and all but one, which had crashed in 1976, were at Marham. They were already fitted with Carousel or Omega navigational systems. As their first missions were to be long range maritime reconnaisance, cameras were fitted in the noses.

Five Victor tankers arrived at Wideawake on 18 April, four more on the following day. It was a nine hours flight

*A British Aerospace (Handley Page) Victor K2 tanker, about to refuel a Harrier. During the 'Black Buck' missions, eleven Victors were used to refuel one Vulcan bomber in a carefully planned and controlled operation. They carried a crew of five but no armament.*

and each aircraft had itself to be refuelled on route, a considerable logistic problem of its own. Group Captain JSB Price, Station Commander of RAF Marham, arrived as the Senior RAF Officer, Ascension Island. The following day the first Victor mission took off, four aircraft each with 48 tons of fuel, to recce South Georgia 3,850 miles away. Transferring fuel from one aircraft to another at 40,000 feet, they left Squadron Leader John Elliott and his crew, with no defence except their early warning radar to probe the unknown in the South Atlantic and return alone.

By the end of April a further six Victor tankers had arrived in Ascension, and besides backing up the Vulcans, they had the important task of in-flight refuelling of Fleet Air Arm Sea Harriers and the nine RAF Harrier GR3s of No 1(F) Squadron, the latter being fer-

ried out to Ascension between 3 and 6 May via Banjul in the Gambia. Another task was on 1 June when four Victors were required to refuel two Harriers which flew direct from Ascension to *Hermes* inside the TEZ, a similar mission being flown on 8 June. Later they accompanied Phantom FGR 2s of No 29(F) Squadron from RAF Coningsby to Ascension.

In order to mount a 'Black Buck' mission it required at least 15 Victor tankers and 18 air-to-air refuellings just to get one Vulcan, fully laden with bombs from Ascension to Port Stanley and back. This alone required exact timings and execution. In all five 'Black Buck' missions were successfully carried out (Black Buck 3 was cancelled and Black Buck 4 was aborted six hours out) arriving on target on 1, 4 and 31 May, 3 and 12 June. Each took at least 15 hours flying, a remarkable achievement of endurance.

Even the surrender of the Argentinians in mid-June did little to stem the missions carried out by the Victors. Nimrods and Hercules also required air-to-air re-fuelling, and the latter are still making regular trips to the Falklands in 1989.

# Chapter Four

# Supporting Arms

No military force can fight effectively without adequate support. This support can come in many forms, by sea, land and air, or any combination of all three. When the Prime Minister agreed to despatch a Task Force to a remote group of islands over 8,000 miles away, she was well aware that this force would need sustaining and reinforcing out of all proportion to its size. This support would not only be required to back up the ships at sea and the men ashore until the fighting campaign was finished, but also to maintain a large enough physical presence to deter the Argentinians after the reoccupation had been successfully completed.

Previous chapters have dealt with some of the supporting forces, particularly the Ships Taken Up From Trade. Before any force could leave the UK, an enormous amount of logistic planning had to be made to ensure that the right men and the correct ammunition, food and stores were packed as efficiently and tactically as possible in the right ships and aircraft. A large number of contingency plans are constantly being updated by staffs in the Ministry of Defence in order to try to cover every eventuality that might befall a British possession or territory. Such contingencies range from all out war to sabotage on oil rigs, from military aid for natural disasters to internal strikes; indeed any field in which the Services may be called upon to support the freedom of British people or to aid the civil power. Most of these plans are thankfully never needed and hardly touched except to be revised in the light of new circumstances, organisation or equipment. With this in mind, many out-of-area plans existed, including one specifically designed to counter an Argentinian invasion of the Falklands.

The unsung heroes of any campaign are the men behind the men behind the guns. Stores and ammunition depots throughout the UK, although manned mainly by civilian staffs, are geared specially to produce the back-up for the Services at a moment's notice. Thus it was that within 24 hours of receiving the call 3 Commando Brigade's war maintenance reserve, some 4,500 tons of combat supplies, including food, ammunition and stores were on the move from depots the length of the British Isles. At the same time, HM Ships, earmarked for the initial Task Force were also receiving vital supplies to bring them up to a war footing. Meanwhile the Royal Air Force Support Command was gearing itself up to provide the maximum service it could in support of other Services.

This is where the Royal Signals, Royal Army Ordnance Corps, the Royal Corps of Transport, the Royal Electrical and Mechanical Engineers, and the Medical Services come into their own. Other logistic Corps played a smaller but significant role. All are highly trained to support the infantry and armour in a logistic capacity, while the Royal Artillery and Royal Engineers provide immediate support in the battle zone. The extensive use of satellite communications for the first time changed the whole complex of command and control. The voice link between London and the Falklands was generally clear enabling both sides to be kept fully in the picture about the latest situation, although the South Atlantic is not well served by US satellites. This sometimes led to commanders in the South Atlantic being pre-empted into making decisions by their masters in Northwood. Conversely when important governmental or political decisions were required, a prompt answer was always forthcoming.

When Admiral Sir Henry Leach assured the Prime Minister that a Task Force could be sent within days, the whole of the 'behind the scenes' machinery swung into action. HM Dockyards and civilian ship-builders, who immediately set about the conversion of the first of the 49 merchant ships to be requisi-tioned, have been mentioned earlier. In UK some Territorial Army units were used to drive trucks with stores, while British Rail trains were earmarked for transporting stores quickly across the country. On the overseas front, arrangements were immediately made with the USA for the use of Wideawake airfield on Ascension Island, a vital preliminary if Britain was to support a maritime campaign in the South Atlantic. The importance of this British possession off the coast of West Africa cannot be underestimated.

The operational planners worked closely with the supporting arms of all three Services in order to ensure that those who would be in the front line would have adequate reinforcements when the time came. Even after the Task Force had sailed, there was still disbelief that an all out battle would ever take place. However all planning, and indeed actions, had to be directed towards the worst contingency. With vast distances to be covered all ships taken up from trade had to be fitted with Replenishment at Sea facilities, besides compatible communications. These enabled a tanker supply train to be set up between Ascension and the TEZ to resupply and re-store the Task Force. Without this support the campaign could not have been sustained.

Early decisions such as the value of wheeled vehicles as transport across the peaty bog of the Falklands, how many should be taken and whether the BV 202E oversnow vehicles as used in Norway, would be more suitable, had to be taken. Knowledge of the Falklands terrain also influenced the planners to take only two troops of light armoured tanks of the Blues & Royals, a serious mistake as it happened, because their cross country performance proved exceptional. Shipping space was at a premium, so anything that might not be required for the Atlantic winter campaign was immediately discarded.

*A group including Royal Army Medical Corps orderlies after the surrender. Whilst many groups such as Signals, Ordnance Transport and REME, saw little of the fighting, their long hours of devoted work, like those of other supporting arms, was absolutely vital.*

There was a shortage of cold and wet weather clothing and equipment in the UK, although it was already part of 3 Commando Brigade's normal operating scales. Sleeping bags and rucksacks were acquired from civilian firms. There was concern over the amount and types of fuel which would be needed once the amphibious force was ashore. Indeed the Scimitars, Scorpions and Rapier Posts used far more fuel in the cold weather than was initially anticipated, also there was only one military petroleum operator for issuing and quality control included in the original orbat, as those men earmarked for manning the Unit Bulk Refuelling Units in support of 3 Commando Brigade were Territorials and not mobilised.

With the establishment of a forward airhead at Ascension, RAF Support Command were stretched to their limit and both British Airways and Tradewinds Airways provided Boeing 707s. Perhaps a mistake had been made a few years earlier with the phasing out by the RAF of their fleet of Belfast Freighters, as those same aircraft, now belonging to

Heavylift Cargo Airlines, had to be requisitioned to supplement the continuous air lift to Ascension Island. The airfield and port facilities on Ascension provided by the Americans, which included refuelling for the Task Force, was discreet at the outset, but by the end of April their provision of material supplies was more open. The despatch of some of their own KC 135 Tankers to Europe meant that more Victor tankers were available to the RAF. Various missiles, such as the Sidewinder, and Shrike also became more readily available from the USA.

The astonishing work done by the Medical services, mainly the Royal Navy but expertly supported by the Royal Army Medical Corps, ensured that even the most severely wounded survived in

the most appalling weather and operating conditions. The skills of the doctors, anaesthetists and medical staff under battle conditions, coupled with the after care provided in the hospital and other STUFT ships, no doubt saved many lives, and gave those in the field added confidence that they could hardly be in better hands should they be wounded.

The Royal Engineers with their multitude of skills provided essential support not only in UK and Ascension, but in the Falklands both during and after the conflict. Their unheralded work in mine clearance and repairing essential services in Stanley were among the outstanding features of the aftermath. They were ably supported by all Corps of the British Army and the similar organisations of the Royal Navy and Royal Air Force.

Each support element in any campaign is an integral part of the whole team, and the professionalism, skill and enthusiasm with which military and civilians alike went about their individual tasks was typical of the British spirit of togetherness engendered by this limited war.

# Royal Air Force Transport

In any campaign conducted over such long distances, RAF transport planes were bound to play an important role. The VC 10s of No 10 Squadron, based at Brize Norton in Oxfordshire, had been in service since 1966 and its fleet consisted of 13 aircraft. Over the years they had been used initially for air trooping from the Far and Middle East, and into the 70s were still on regular flights carrying British troops to overseas bases.

From the very outset of the campaign they were to be fully employed. The first VC 10 to visit the South Atlantic was flown on 3 April when it picked up Falklands Governor Rex Hunt and the captured Royal Marines of Naval Party 8901 from Montevideo in Uruguay. It arrived back in UK, via Wideawake on 6 April, only to be followed by a similar mission on 21 April to bring back the 22 marines of *Endurance* and the 13 scientists of the British Antarctic Survey team who had been captured in South Georgia. One of the VC 10s was fitted as VIP plane and it took Foreign Secretary Francis Pym to Washington on 23 April for talks with General Alexander Haig,

the American Secretary of State. Other individual missions were flown during the campaign such as those to Fort Bragg in North Carolina on 14 May and another to Wurstmith Air Force Base, Michigan on 5 June.

However the main job of the VC 10 fleet was to ferry men, stores and equipment forward to Ascension for onward transmission by sea to the South Atlantic. Four or five flights a day were normal, most of them staging through Gambia (Banjul) or Senegal (Dakar). On 13 May a VC 10, suitably marked with a large red cross flew 137 Argentine prisoners captured in South Georgia back to Montevideo. Survivors from the *Sheffield* were flown home from Ascension on 27 May in two VC 10s. Later during the campaign they played an important part in ferrying British casualties, who had been taken to Uruguay in the ambulance ships *Herald, Hydra* and *Hecla* back to UK. All aircraft were marked with a red cross and monitored by the International Committee of the Red Cross. Flights continued after the cease fire, one being to take Rex Hunt back to the Falklands on 23 June to assume duties as Civil Commissioner.

The main burden of ferrying was with the 54 Hercules C-130s of 24, 30, 47 (Special Forces) and 70 Squadrons based

*A VC 10 of 10 Squadron, one of thirteen used for ferrying troops and stores to Ascension and bringing casualties home, at RAF Brize Norton.*

*An RAF Sergeant Air Loadmaster kitted out as those who flew in RAF Hercules C-130s. These aircraft dropped vital reinforcements and supplies to the Task Force in the TEZ with round trips from Ascension Island often taking up to 24 hours. Wearing zip-up flying boots and olive green flying suit, this NCO wears a DMP smock and gloves. His headset would be connected to the aircraft's intercom and he would be attached by a harness clip to a strong-point.*

*The workhorses of RAF Support Command, 54 Hercules C-130s were deployed during Operation* Corporate, *many dropping supplies to ships in the TEZ.*

at Lyneham in Wiltshire. Most were C 1s, purchased in the mid 1960s while 12 were the modified C 3s, fifteen feet longer. The first Operation *Corporate* mission was to Gibraltar on 2 April with technical and medical experts, service and civilian, who were to advise on modications to convert STUFT ships for active service. In order to extend their range twin auxiliary tanks were fitted by Lyneham Engineering Wing giving them an extra 3-4 hours in the air. Later two further fuel tanks were added to some aircraft. Marshalls of Cambridge started to install in-flight refuelling probes to enable them to fly non-stop to Ascension. A difficulty was experienced when the

C-130 tried to link up with a Victor tanker whose lowest speed was 20 knots faster than the Hercules maximum. This was resolved by refuelling while descending at 500 feet per minute. Eventually 16 aircraft were modified, the first making its non-stop flight to Wideawake on 14 May. Marshalls also installed Omega precise navigation equipment which was invaluable in air drops in the South Atlantic.

C-130s were busily ferrying troops and equipment from Lyneham forward reaching a peak of 16 missions on 29 April. Each Hercules could carry up to 90 fully armed troops or over 25,000 lbs of freight, including armoured cars and helicopters. When the extended range aircraft had been modified, forward drops to ships of the Task Force became common. For instance, on 7 May after 9 hours in the air, a drop to *Plymouth* had to be cancelled through bad weather, but the following day a mission lasting a total of 17 hours 10 minutes was successful in dropping stores and equipment to *Plymouth* and the tugs *Yorkshiremen* and *Irishmen* and another was made on 11 May to *Fearless*.

24 and 30 Squadrons bore the brunt of the routine ferrying between UK and Ascension while the tactical support role from Wideawake south was carried out by 70 and 47 Squadrons. The latter's Special Forces element flew a remarkable 6,300 miles mission to the TEZ on 16 May when 1,000 lbs of stores and eight parachutists were dropped to *Antelope*. There were at least 30 of these missions, known as 'Cadbury' into the TEZ between 16 May and 14 June, though the longest of 28 hours 4 minutes to supply a Rapier battery near Stanley was made on 18 June after the surrender. The most publicised drop was when Lieutenant Colonel David Chaundler parachuted from 800 feet into the South Atlantic on 1 June alongside *Penelope* to replace 'H' Jones who had been killed in 2 Para's attack on Goose Green. One of the most sought after of these cargoes was the mail drop.

Other air transport used for ferrying to Ascension included Boeing 707s of British Airways and Tradewinds Airways, while former RAF Belfast strategic freighters chartered from Heavylift Cargo Airlines were used extensively until the end of the campaign, proving how short sighted it had been of the Ministry of Defence to dispose of them.

# Signals

Without regular and reliable communications over 8,000 miles away the land forces would have been unable to operate in the Falklands. The Royal Navy and Royal Air Force were accustomed to such long range deployments but the military were not. The advent of satellite communications meant that this would be a war where commanders in the field could talk direct with London, not always an advantage, particularly when the masters tried to influence tactical considerations on the ground. A Royal Signals Satellite Communications Terminal with a Racal SC 2600 installation was included in 3 Commando Brigade's landing force and it set up near the Brigade Maintenance Area at Ajax Bay from where twice daily situation reports were sent. The terminal could only be moved by helicopter and the radio telephone was generally extremely clear.

3 Commando Brigade had a large Signals Squadron manned almost entirely by Royal Marines. They were experts in both naval and army communications and were well drilled in working in the amphibious scene. 566 Rear Link Detachment of 205 Signal Squadron sailed with the Task Force to provide signals links for 3 Para. 5 Infantry Brigade were supported by 205 Signal Squadron, part of 30 Signal Regiment. In all 30 Signal Regiment supplied over 200 men, including those required for service with STUFT ships for maritime rear links. On 8 April a communications centre was flown to Ascension.

The first Royal Signals personnel actually to leave UK, a Tactical Satellite Communications (TSC 502) team, left on 2 April to support Governor Rex Hunt in Stanley. Events overtook this party and after travelling 25,000 miles in 11 weeks at sea, they reached the Falklands the day after the war ended!

The equipment with which the land forces had to operate was mostly of the Clansman family, indeed some infantry units had not previously used it. There are nine different radios in the group, three HF, five VHF and one UHF. All sets share common design features which greatly simplify maintenance. As the war was to be fought mainly by infantry on foot it was the man-portable sets that came into their own. The light-weight PRC 349 (37-46.9 MHz) at 3 lbs with a 1000 yards range was in use at section level, the PRC 350 (30-76 MHz) with its throat microphone at platoon level, while Company Commanders used the PRC 351 with its boom mike, headset and 4' aerial to communicate with their platoon commanders up to 6 miles. Moving upwards, the unit command net used PRC 352, which was a boosted 351, weighing 25 lbs and having a range of 10 miles. All these sets were VHF and worked extremely well.

The HF range, of which only the PRC 320 is man-portable, were also used, their Skywave facility increasing the range from a normal 25 miles to nearly 200 miles in ideal conditions. The older Larkspur A43, the only UHF set, was used for ground to air communications for close air support by the Tactical Air Control Parties. It has a range of 100 miles. Although there were very few available it is known that the SAS used a portable SATCOM radio for voice communications direct with UK in the latter stages of the war. This sophisticated piece of equipment certainly surprised the Argentinians when Colonel Rose used it during the surrender negotiations.

In the field there were no completely secure voice links, but generally communications were very good. There were

*Communications was one of the vital aspects of the war. The Royal Signals and Royal Air Force provided the satellite communications, but 3 Commando Brigade Signals Squadron provided the main links in the field. They took a number of Volvo BV 202E oversnow vehicles, as used in Norway, to transport their heavier equipment, and these proved excellent over the Falklands peaty bogs. The infantry were equipped with the latest Clansman range of wireless sets.*

*A Royal Marines signalman of 3 Commando Brigade Signals Squadron, takes down a message, while still ensconced in the comfort of his sleeping bag.*

a number of voice and teleprinter secure circuits but these were all vehicle borne radios. 3 Commando Brigade had long used heliborne trailer radio stations, the secure circuits they provided being utilised after an objective was taken. Reliance was placed on information being so imminent that the enemy would have little chance to disseminate it, but it was known that Argentine radio operators monitored many of the links. Relay stations were set up as the troops moved forward and step-up facilities provided. One 5 Infantry Brigade relay station on Mount Wickham was so exposed that it found difficulty in functioning.

Within 3 Commando Brigade's Headquarters and Signals Squadron was a large MT Troop, many of them helping to enlarge the Air Defence Troop with their Blowpipe missile launchers, because little transport was taken. The three TACPs (Tactical Air Control Parties), Nos 605, 611 and 612 all controlled strike aircraft on to targets, but had to 'yomp' with their wireless sets across East Falkland. The Regimental Police Troop of 30 marines were initially spread throughout many ships and had the unenviable task of preparing for the 1,400 prisoners taken at Goose Green. Later at Fitzroy, joining with the Royal Military Police of 5 Infantry Brigade, they set up a POW cage in a sheep shearing shed.

Comparatively few vehicles were available but the Volvo BV 202 E, an oversnow vehicle more at home in northern Norway proved an ideal base for radios. 75 were taken, most of the others normally used by 3 Commando Brigade were stockpiled in Norway. They were able to cope with most types of Falklands terrain giving the commanders added mobility. There was no such relief for the man portable sets, as batteries needed more frequent charging than in UK and were an additional heavy load. Whilst standing up to a considerable battering during the campaign, the sets were robust with only their aerials suffering too much damage. Petrol for battery charging was also very short. 5 Infantry Brigade were not so fortunate, only being able to obtain a few old over-snow

vehicles to supplement the limited number of four wheeled drive vehicles taken.

Without good communications no commander can fight a battle successfully. There was a large mix of naval and army radios, satellite communications giving instant access for Northwood to impose their views on the field commanders, which was often recounted Alternately those in the Falklands could ask for immediate reinforcements of

supplies and men. The press communications facilities were inadequate for the task, but there was no room nor manpower to add anything else. Correspondents had to wait their turn, which frustrated their London editors. The most successful press men were those who found co-operative soldiers and sailors willing to send back short messages but only reports that were to the point and factually accurate It was a lesson for both sides.

# Royal Engineers

So often the unsung heroes of a campaign, the Royal Engineers of modern times provide so many skills that they are able to turn their hand to almost anything. Tracing their origins to the early days of the Ordnance Office around 1580, military engineers were recruited as required to support military campaigns. It was not until 1716 that a permanent Corps of Officers was established, being granted the title Royal in 1787. The Royal Sappers and Miners combined with the Artificer Corps to become the Corps of Royal Engineers in 1856. They carry no battle honours, their motto 'Ubique' (Everywhere), like the Royal Artillery, adequately describing their wide role.

The Royal Engineers originally handled military signalling, passing this duty to the Corps of Signals which was formed in 1920. From the early days of ballooning in the 1860s, the Sappers were also responsible for military aviation which was handed over to the Royal Flying Corps in 1912. Since then their role and responsibilities have been tailored to meet modern needs, with their strength reaching a peak of around a quarter of a million sappers during World War 2. Their tasks range from demolitions and mine warfare, bridging and harbour works, repairing airfields and water supply to manning railways and bomb disposal.

Like most of the British Army, the Royal Engineers are primarily trained to support BAOR with four armoured division engineer regiments and an amphibious engineer regiment. In UK there are four field engineer regiments, a Commando Squadron and a Parachute Field Squadron, besides a multitude of specialist and ancilliary detachments. 3 Commando Brigade had their own integrated 59 Independent Commando Field Squadron under command, whilst 2 Troop of 9 Parachute Squadron were included in the initial order of battle, the remainder of the Squadron supporting 5 Infantry Brigade later. All sappers in these Squadrons have earnt their green or red berets.

59 Field Squadron had worked closely with 3 Commando Brigade in Singapore betweeen 1968 and 1971. On their return to UK they converted to become 59 Independent Commando Field Squadron, a formation of about 240 all ranks.

Their training is designed to support the commando brigade world wide, with special skills in mountain and arctic warfare. They pride themselves on being able to take their place as infantrymen in the field if required. When Major Roderick MacDonald took over command of 59 Squadron in 1981 he noted that an operational weakness was a lack of specialist forward engineer reconnaissance troops, and he formed a Recce Troop in February 1982 whose duties also included intelligence gathering. Each Troop in the Squadron can operate independently, having their own transport, stores and signals. Although there was a limitation on the numbers of vehicles, they were able to take their combat engineer tractors with them.

Most of the sappers in the Task Force landed on D-Day, a troop in support of each unit, but their first major action was with 2 Para at Goose Green. The Recce Troop, working in four man groups was responsible for checking bridges for booby traps, dealing with mines and destroying captured enemy equipment. Later when individual troops supported the forward units in the mountains, 1 Troop were left at Ajax Bay to build a pumping and storage system to supply fuel to helicopters. At its peak it dispensed 50,000 gallons a day.

They continued supporting the front line, particularly clearing routes of mines, many of which had been scattered irresponsibly, to start lines before major battles. Indeed it was their expertise that helped to extract the Welsh Guards, who had A & C Companies of 40 Commando under command, from a minefield when they lost their way to form up as reserve for 42 Commando's attack on Mount Harriet.

It had been planned to build a forward air operating base at Port San Carlos but the engineer stores for it,

including runway tracking, fuel systems and tanks were lost in the *Atlantic Conveyor*. Although a helicopter strip had been operating, it was not until the arrival of *Atlantic Causeway* on 1 June with airfield matting and VTOL Harrier pads that 11 Field Engineer Squadron were able to set about building a Harrier strip at Port San Carlos, which came to be known as HMS *Sheathbill*. From here the Combat Air Patrol could operate during the day, saving time and fuel. Further forward 2 Para engineers repaired the bridge at Fitzroy, while water-points were set up there and at Teal Inlet.

At Ascension, the Royal Engineers had already been busy. Early on 17 sappers from 59 Squadron had ripped the upperworks from the *Elk* to enable it to take helicopters. When it was decided to mount the 'Black Buck' missions, there was a tremendous strain on fuel supplies, so the Royal Engineers laid a 4 mile pipeline from the storage farm, which was supplied by tanker ships, to Wideawake airfield, as well as providing extra hardstanding for parked aircraft.

In the battle zone, to back up the combat engineers, each Commando has an Assault Engineer Troop, more highly

*Apart from lifting mines and marking minefields, Royal Engineers were employed in bridging repairs, demolitions, field engineering works and laying airfield tracking and pipelines. 3 Commando Brigade were supported by 59 Independent Commando Squadron, while elements of 33, 36 and 38 Regiments Royal Engineers deployed, along with part of 2 Postal and Courier Regiment.*

*A sapper of 59 Independent Commando Squadron Royal Engineers lifts an Argentinian anti-tank mine. Over 12,000 mines had been laid, many of them indiscriminately.*

trained than an infantry pioneer platoon in field engineering. They were able to provide considerable assistance in the never ending task of mine clearance, particularly after the cease fire. It was only then that the extent of the random scattering of Argentine anti-tank, anti-personnel and beach mines, many of them improvised, became apparent. Aboard ship Staff Sergeant Jim Prescott lost his life when, along with Warrant Officer John Phillips of 49 Explosives Ordance Disposal Squadron, they went to defuse an unexploded bomb in *Antelope*. This team worked closely with the Royal Navy's No 1 Fleet Clearance Diving Team and the RAF's Explosives Ordnance Team.

In a less combative role, but nevertheless in an important morale boosting

*A Harrier GR3 lands on the temporary air strip, nicknamed HMS* Sheathbill, *built by 11 Field Engineer Squadron at Port San Carlos, where the aircraft could be refuelled manually.*

job was No 2 Postal, Courier and Communications Unit, responsible for the vast quantities of mail that arrived in and was despatched from the Falklands.

59 Squadron suffered five killed and seven wounded, while two further Royal Engineers were lost in action. There were still to be a number of serious injuries in the mine-clearing operations which went on long after the cessation of hostilities. An additional problem was the number of unexploded bombs, missiles and shells that littered the battlefields, along with both sophisticated and crudely made Argentinian booby traps. Although Major MacDonald contacted the Argentine chief engineer Lieutenant Colonel Dorago after the cessation of hostilities and asked for maps of the minefields, few were able to be produced and they showed a horrifying picture. For the first few days Argentine soldiers and marines were used to assist in mine clearance on the main tracks.

It appears that the Argentinians laid over 12,000 mines, mainly anti-personnel in four types, many of them being difficult to detect because of their small metallic content. In many ways it seemed that the Royal Engineers part in the campaign was only just beginning.

# Royal Corps of Transport and Royal Army Ordnance Corps

The uninviting terrain of the Falklands made it a campaign where little wheeled transport could move. There were only 12 miles of metalled roads running east from Port Stanley to the airport, and west to Moody Brook camp. The remaining tracks were only practical for lightly loaded four wheel drive vehicles in the summer months. Even cross country movement would be difficult as the unique stone runs precluded all but the sturdiest of tracked vehicles. However the Royal Corps of Transport played a vital if little publicised role.

Two key senior officers came from the RCT; Colonel Ian Baxter was Colonel AQ in Headquarters Commando Forces in Plymouth and as such was responsible for the outloading and embarkation of the reinforced 3 Commando Brigade, subsequently advising 5 Infantry Brigade. He then became Colonel AQ of the Landing Force, responsible for all logistics in the Falklands. The second officer was Lieutenant Colonel Ivar Helberg who commanded the Commando Logistic Regiment Royal Marines, a rotational appointment between the Royal Marines and the RCT, RAOC and REME, which he had held since October 1980.

Coinciding with the call to arms of 3 Commando Brigade, the Transport and Movements Branch of UKLF were alerted for urgent transport assistance. Assault packs of 3 Commando Brigade were reported to be on the move from depots at Kineton, Bicester and Donnington within 25 minutes of receiving the call. The task of getting stores and ammunition to the right port or airport in the right order was a logistic nightmare. During most of the first week of April supplies were moved by road, and to supplement RCT vehicles about 100 civilian 40ft flat bed vehicles were chartered. Territorial Army vehicles and drivers were used to the full over the first weekend. An idea of the extent of the UK movements can be gauged by the use of 350 × 4 tonne trucks, 584 × 8 tonne, 43 × 10 tonne,

200 × 16 tonne and 303 other vehicles which included landrovers and low loaders. 39,108 tons of freight were moved by road alone. From the second week, the RCT used British Rail, 44 special trains being hired.

17 Port Regiment RCT was involved from the outset in providing specialist advice in loading shipping, much of it commercial, and providing detachments on RFA and STUFT ships sailing with the Task Force. The six LSLs were normally based at Marchwood Military Port, near Southampton. The first two LSLs were quickly loaded there, while two more were loaded by the Regiment at Devonport. Each LSL had two detachments of soldiers from 17 Port Regiment; one consisted of Port Operators or stevedores, and the second as crew for the

126 ft powered raft, the Mexeflote which is capable of ferrying 150 tonnes of stores. The Mexeflotes played a vital role in transporting men and supplies ashore at San Carlos, Bluff Cove and Teal Inlet, besides an enormous amount of cross decking at Ascension. It was Sgt Derrick Boultby of the RCT, whose gallantry in rescuing survivors from the stricken LSL *Sir Galahad* with his Mexeflote, and later diving into the freezing water to save a Chinese crew member, which earned him an MM. In all 153 officers and men of 17 Port Regiment sailed with the Task Force.

Just as important was the RCT involvement at airports which was controlled by 29 Transport and Movements Regiment, consisting of 50, 55 and 59 Movement Control Squadrons and 47

*A combat engineer tractor laying a roll of beachway tracking at Ajax Bay. Later they laid airfield matting and VTOL pads above Port San Carlos, which was called HMS Sheathbill, for use by Harriers for refuelling.*

*The Logistic Support given by the various Corps of the Army was essential to the success of the campaign. The Royal Corps of Transport provided crews for the Mexeflotes and detachments on Royal Fleet auxiliaries and STUFT ships. The Royal Army Ordnance Corps supplied the infantry with everything they needed to fight, move and live. This drawing illustrates a member of 160 Provost Company, Royal Military Police, whose duties included documenting and processing most of the 12,000 Argentine prisoners of war.*

*One of the thankless tasks of the Royal Army Ordnance Corps came with the surrender when they had to collect, make safe and often destroy stocks of enemy ammunition.*

Air Despatch Squadron. There were Movement Control Check Points at all ports being used, at RAF Brize Norton and RAF Lyneham, besides in most unit lines. Later a movements section was set up at Ascension. The Air Monitoring Centre at South Cerney in Gloucestershire processed, accommodated and moved troops to airheads, a task which stretched their resources. The Air Despatch Squadron, based at RAF Lyneham, provided two SNCOs for a Special Forces detachment, but their main job was large scale air resupply of the fleet. With two air despatch crews stationed at Ascension, they flew many long sorties to the South Atlantic, some up to 18 hours, to drop urgent supplies to ships of the Task Force. Mail was dropped in converted and waterproofed Exocet spares boxes!

The Royal Army Ordnance Corps support was likewise of vital importance to Operation *Corporate*. Since 1965, when the Royal Corps of Transport was formed, the RAOC took over responsibility for supplying troops with everything they needed to fight, move and subsist. An army can only operate when it has ammunition to do so and the task of estimating requirements, re-stocking and supplying was a vast logistic problem particularly when few vehicles would be available in the Falklands. Like the RCT

their main job was to ensure the correct supplies got to the right ship or aircraft before proceeding south. The loss of the *Atlantic Conveyor* caused much quick re-thinking, but the fact that the infantry were never deprived of the necessities to fight and survive in the field, was mainly due to the tremendous work done, often unobtrusively, by the RAOC. The Ordnance Squadron of the Commando Logistic Regiment and 81 Ordnance Company, who normally supported 5 Infantry Brigade, played their full part in the campaign, as well as many smaller detachments, ranging from laundry and bakery to petrol and ordnance disposal. The Combat Supplies Platoon of 81 Company manned the temporary airstrip at San Carlos, refuelling Harriers, with as many as 120 aircraft movements a day at the peak of the campaign. Later 91 Ordnance Company arrived with 5 Infantry Brigade and subsequently supported them from Goose Green and Fitzroy before the final battles.

Other Army Corps to play their part in the campaign were 10 Forward Workshop of the Royal Electrical and Mechanical Engineers; 6 Field Cash Office Royal Army Pay Corps; 160 Provost Company of the Royal Military Police; 172 Intelligence and Security Section of the Intelligence Corps and elements of the Royal Pioneer Corps. Most of these supporting arms had detachments which were vital to the smooth running of the 'transit base' at Ascension, in addition to providing troops at home and in the Falklands.

# Medical

The Royal Navy bore the brunt of the medical support for the campaign both at sea and ashore. Not only did every warship have a well equipped sick bay, but the converted hospital ship, *Uganda* along with its casualty transports *Hecla*, *Hecate* and *Hydra* were all manned by naval personnel. In addition, the Royal Navy Medical Service provided cover for 3 Commando Brigade in the form of a Commando Medical Squadron, that was part of the Commando Logistic Regiment Royal Marines.

As early as 2 April the Defence Medical Equipment Depot was packing and despatching naval medical war stores to the fleet. Two Surgical Support Teams (SST) from the Royal Naval Hospitals at Haslar and Devonport were alerted, and a high level decision not to take women in the teams meant a quick reassessment and reorganisation. On 4 April Surgeon Commander Rick Jolly, a larger than life character who commanded the Medical Squadron, was despatched to Gibraltar to advise on the medical aspects of converting *Canberra* as a troopship, and possibly later as a hospital ship.

3 Commando Brigade Medical Squadron normally has three medical officers, a Surgeon Commander as OC and two Surgeon Lieutenant Commanders or Lieutenants for Nos 1 and 2 Troop. Two further MOs were drafted in for No 3 Troop, both with previous Commando service. In addition each Royal Marine Commando Unit had its own RN medical officer and staff. When the retaking of South Georgia was mooted, a further medical officer plus two medical assistants (MA) were added for M Company of 42 Commando. In the background three further medical officers, a medical services administrative officer and eight MAs, all commando trained, were earmarked as Battle Casualty replacements. In the rush to deploy there were bound to be misplacements, one such being the Haslar SST embarking in *Hermes*.

With the increased size of 3 Commando Brigade, a Para Clearing Troop (PCT) of 16 Field Ambulance RAMC were later added in support of 2 Para. They joined after 3 Para's mobilization as the Spearhead Unit. Since Kolwezi, 2 Para had had a hostage rescue role and the PCT were the remnants of the old 23 Parachute Field Ambulance, who trace their origins back to Arnhem and Suez. Former 3 Para elements of the PCT were also deployed ashore in the Falklands. 2 Troop, Medical Squadron, whose stores were embarked in the *Canberra* were used to enhance No 3 Surgical Support Team.

The medical support for 5 Infantry Brigade had rather more time to prepare. There was a Regimental Aid Post, which included an RAMC doctor, in each unit, while 16 Field Ambulance, which sailed in the *QE 2*, deployed with an Advanced Dressing Station, three Collecting Sections and a Hygiene Section. An unfortunate grouping came when 1 Collecting Station sailed in *Nordic Ferry* while their stores were in *Baltic Ferry*. They were augmented by the addition of two Field Surgical Teams and a Holding Team from 2 Field Hospital RAMC. After the war, 2 Field Hospital became the Garrison Hospital Falkland Islands.

During the voyage south *Canberra* was prepared as a hospital by Surgeon Captain Roger Wilkes and his team of surgeons, anaesthetists and general practitioners, in conjunction with the ship's medical staff. Medical tutorials were held regularly and films of Vietnam casualties were shown. At a lower level, instructive Northern Ireland slides were shown, advanced first aid lectures and 'practicals' were held for the commandos and paras, while the Royal Marines Band of Commando Forces were given special instruction to train them as stretcher bearers and helicopter marshals. Their subsequent work fully justified this extra role as they practised using the newly installed ramps to bring 'casualties' quickly and safely from the helicopter deck to the operating theatres below, while every evening on board they entertained the embarked troops with varying programmes of music.

If the battles were to be as fierce as some anticipated there might be a shortage of blood. Blood supplies are crucial to the success of battlefield surgery, a lesson not forgotten from World War 2. On board *Canberra* alone 900 half litre bags were willingly donated by the troops as a form of investment on which some were handsomely repaid. This blood was taken a week before the landings – a piece of crucial timing which allowed the lost red cells to be replaced naturally without eating too far into the storage life of four weeks. Another aspect of medical tuition was that of survival in the bleak wastes and freezing tempera-

*Surgeon Lieutenant Commander Phil Shouler, commanding the Plymouth Naval Support Team, operating at the Main Dressing Station at Ajax Bay. Both commando and para medical teams operated in the 'Red and Green Life Machine' named after the colour of their berets.*

tures of the Falklands, the avoidance of trench foot and hypothermia. By the time of the landings on 21 May, all troops on board were thoroughly rehearsed in battlefield first aid, and this teaching paid dividends during the campaign providing immediate first line medical attention.

The original plan was that *Canberra* should remain near enough to the landing area that she could be used as a floating hospital. It was expected that air superiority would have been won allowing the ship to stay. In the event, *Canberra* was ordered by the Task Force Commander to sail before first light on 22 May. It was essential that one FDS was landed before it sailed and Surgeon Commander Jolly had time, along with other logistic elements, in the later stages of D-Day to recce a possible site for a Field Dressing Station ashore, but it was still believed the main medical support would be afloat. He chose the old refrigeration plant at Ajax Bay. With only three hours notice before the ship sailed, medical stores were hurriedly packed and disembarked ashore. With no cranes nor helicopters available in the dark,

*A Scout and Wessex helicopter lift casualties from Goat Ridge after the battle for Tumbledown Mountain. Although under enemy artillery fire, pilots continued to fly resupply missions, taking out the wounded and undoubtedly saving many lives.*

stores had to be broken down into man portable loads as HQ Medical Squadron and No 2 SST landed, where the Para Clearing Troop joined them from the *Norland*. Unfortunately 3 Troop had to be left on board to help run the action medical organisation there.

With both para and commando medics involved, a sign was erected outside the shed 'Welcome to the Red and Green Life Machine' after the colour of their berets. A conscious decision was taken *not* to paint a Red Cross on the roof as the building was surrounded by logistic stores which were undoubtedly a legitimate target. The Ajax Bay complex was a deserted refrigeration plant shaped like a large 'T', showing rotting signs of earlier use as a slaughter-house and packing station. Power was initially provided from a 6kVA generator and although the

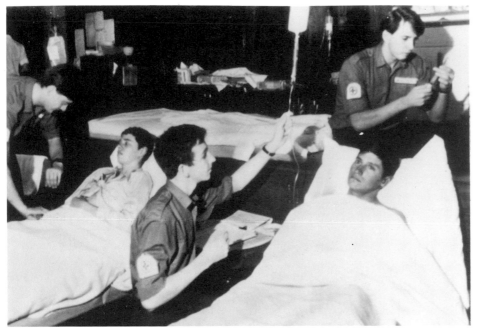

building was knee deep in rubbish, it proved to be reasonably dry and free from vermin. Two operating theatres and a system for the reception of casualties were soon set up. Outside the walls were strengthened by peat blocks. The naval and military teams integrated well because of their shared and fierce affection for their para and commando brethren in the front line.

The first casualties from 3 Para arrived soon after the station was set up followed during the first few days by injured men from the *Coventry*, *Antelope* and *Atlantic Conveyor*. Most were badly burnt, soaked through and shivering with cold. It was noticeable that the Royal Navy anti-flash hood and gloves had stood up well in protecting the sailors. An Argentine Air Force Skyhawk pilot, Teniente Ricardo Lucero, with a compound fracture of the knee was also one of the early customers, and he was to be present during an unwelcome air attack by his compatriots the following day.

On 27 May, disaster nearly overtook the 'Life Machine' when eight parachute retarded bombs were dropped on the Brigade Stores Area, which contained the medical facilities. One bomb, which failed to explode embedded itself in the pipework of the refrigeration machinery and another in the ceiling above. The RAF bomb disposal expert, Flight Lieutenant Alan Swan, explained that these might have delay fuses of up to 33 hours! Other bombs had killed five men and

wounded 27. The ADS was contracted to half its size which only allowed casualties to spend a maximum of 24 hours there, before being evacuated. The hospital ship *Uganda* was by now in a declared Red Cross 'box' about 30 miles off the Falklands.

With 2 Para's attack on Goose Green on 29 May, casualties started to pour back, helicopter pilots flying numerous life saving mercy missions. 47 major operations were carried out, and as a result of the paras' excellent fitness and first class battlefield first aid, every man survived. Indeed this standard of treatment persisted, because not one casualty who passed through the door alive ever left it dead . . . a remarkable record.

There were many killed during the early battles and the dead had to be examined and assessed before burial. The Royal Marines Field Records Office, a unique organisation which had only been trialled the previous year, was now also established at Ajax Bay. It consisted of a nucleus of 1 officer and 5 NCOs, later being augmented by a representative from each major unit. It dealt with casualty reporting, processing of personal effects, death certificates, the registration of graves and control of Battle Casualty Replacements. It more than proved its worth. Casualty evacuation to ships proceeded as soon as patients were fit to travel but Commander Jolly was highly amused at one stage to receive a pompous signal 'requesting him to give 24 hours

notice for helicopters for casualty evacuation'.

The surgeons aboard *Uganda*, many of them new to battle surgery, were at first surprised to receive casualties whose gunshot wounds had been excised, cleaned thoroughly and left opened and unsutured to enhance the healing process.

Meanwhile 5 Infantry Brigade with the remainder of 16 Field Ambulance, were approaching, arriving in *Canberra* on 2 June. 3 Troop at last disembarked. By this time 3 Commando Brigade had yomped forward to the foothills of the mountains ready for the final battles. 42 and 45 Commandos were each reinforced with 1 MO and 1 MA, while 1 MO was attached to 29 Field Regiment. With the occupation of Teal, a forward Brigade Maintenance Area was set up. It became necessary to establish an Advanced Dressing Station there which was set up with an MO, 2 MAs and half the PCT on 3 June, Ajax being redesignated the Main Dressing Station with the remainder of Medical Squadron and No 2 SST. The other half of the PCT reinforced 16 Field Ambulance at another Forward Dressing Station at Fitzroy on 5 June, but many of the new arrivals were caught in the bombing of *Sir Galahad* before they could land, suffering 3 men killed, including the hardworking 2 i/c, Major R Nutbeam. They also lost all their field surgical kit. Over 160 victims of the bombing in Bluff Cove were flown into Ajax, mostly suffering from severe burns, and many of the less serious were moved on by landing craft to *Fearless*, *Intrepid* or *Atlantic Causeway*. There were also casualties from *Plymouth*, which had also been bombed. Even at this stage casevac helicopters were only available on an ad hoc opportunity basis. During the Fitzroy tragedy, helicopters took casualties back to Ajax Bay when they had to refuel, usually as a result of a radio call from their fellow pilots.

On Wednesday 9 June an International Red Cross Inspection Team led by Roland Desmeules arrived at Ajax to report on conditions, particularly the

welfare of prisoners of war. They even asked where they could hire a car to take them to Stanley to report on the Argentine POW facilities! Preparations were now underway for the final push. The Passive Night Goggles used by some pilots enabled almost continuous night flying and saved many lives. By this time all pilots had run out of flying hours.

After the battles for Two Sisters, Mount Harriet and Longdon, 32 major surgical operations were carried out at Ajax, 16 at Teal and 8 at Fitzroy. Two days later, after Tumbledown and Mount William, most casualties were taken to the FDS but some were flown direct to *Uganda*, now slipping daily into Berkeley Sound to receive casualties. There were also over 40 Argentine casualties on West Falkland to deal with after the surrender, many of their injuries being nearly a fortnight old. In Stanley itself the Commu-

nity Centre had been taken over as the Argentinian Field Hospital to supplement the small King Edward VII Memorial Hospital, which was full.

There was no doubt that the British troops were well prepared for battle and their strong motivation led to few reported cases of battlefield shock. However the climate had taken its toll, not as badly as some had predicted. Trench Foot was rife amongst those who had waded ashore at San Carlos, because of poor boots and freezing conditions. The Argentines suffered very badly indeed. Also, despite boiling all water and chlorinating it, there were a fair number of cases of Diarrhoea, known as 'Galtieri's Gallop', which had a debilitating effect.

During the campaign 650 battle casualties were treated and 310 major operations carried out on land. Only three men subsequently died of their

*Casualties are transferred from oversnow vehicles to a Scout helicopter for evacuation to one of the two Forward Dressing Stations set up at Teal Inlet and Fitzroy. Some of the more seriously wounded were evacuated direct to the hospital ship* Uganda *which slipped daily into Berkeley Sound.*

wounds, and no British died whilst still ashore in the medical treatment chain. There is no doubt that the exceptional physical fitness of the land forces played an important role in reducing casualties, but the outstanding professional medical attention given to the wounded in the field, and later in the hospital ships and sick bays of the fleet, saved untold lives. Equally important was the skill and daring of the helicopter pilots who flew in near impossible conditions to evacuate the injured.

# Replenishment at Sea (RAS)

For warships to stay at sea for long periods without recourse to port facilities, the Royal Fleet Auxiliary (RFA) maintain a small fleet of 14 tankers and four fleet replenishment ships. These ships are discussed more fully in the chapters dealing with them. The RFA are acknowledged to be the experts in the world in replenishment whilst underway. There are two basic systems, the RAS(S) for solids and RAS(L) for liquids.

Both systems rely on reasonable weather conditions, a high degree of seamanship and precise navigation. But the skills are not confined to those on the bridge, as the ship's company and RFA crews have to work closely together in ensuring the utmost safety in moving several tons of equipment, any of which, breaking loose, could cause havoc and serious injury. The Royal Navy practise RAS-ing regularly in peacetime, and it has often proved a cheaper and easier method of restocking and refuelling than using foreign ports and paying their harbour dues.

For solids, there are two main methods of resupply at sea. The old and proved method, though sometimes slow and cumbersome, is by derrick and jackstay transfer. This involves the supply ship and the receiving ships steaming along parallel courses at identical speeds at a distance of about 80 feet apart. The supplying ship is always the 'guide', while the other ships keep station on it by minute variations of speed. Firstly lines are fired between the ships with a specially adapted 7.62mm rifle, then wires are hauled between the ships establishing the jackstay along which the stores pass. In the case of HM Ships the necessary fittings were well established, but with the STUFT ships this proved a problem for the constructors.

Each ship had to be individually modified with precise calculations on weight, stress, high points and clearance above the ship's side. The STUFT Ship Department Technical Officer and an RFA Deck Officer from DGNST(N) identified suitable reception points in each ship, which had a nearby winch, although more often than not extra blocks and tackles were needed to round corners and change direction. The necessary shackles, sheaves, slips and pendants were supplied from Naval stores, but when suitable service stocks were exhausted, the equivalent civilian pattern was bought up. Engineers had to inspect and pass every fitment in each ship to ensure compatability and safety.

For 20 years some RFAs have been fitted with helicopter pads and with newer ships they have hangar facilities in addition. Wessex 5s and, in some of the larger ships, heavy lift Sea Kings, capable of underslung loads up to 7,500 lbs,

*The British Telecom Cable Ship* Iris, *which acted as a despatch vessel in the South Atlantic, receives a vertical replenishment from a Sea King helicopter on her specially fitted helipad.*

*The Fleet Replenishment Ship* Fort Grange *(left) replenishes the Cable Ship* Iris *by jackstay transfer. The two ships sail on parallel courses with the receiving ship keeping station about 80 ft from the supplying ship or 'guide'.*

are now used frequently in vertical replenishment (VERTREP). The helicopters come from the specialist support flight of 772 Naval Air Squadron based at Portland and are manned and maintained by the Fleet Air Arm. Most RFAs are fitted with the special lifts to bring bulk supplies from the hold of the flight deck; these are then sorted into loads by size and weight and placed into rope slings and nets.

Most RFA helicopter pads are about 60 feet above sea level, higher than aircraft carrier flight decks. Considerable skill is needed by the pilots, working on additional instructions from the aircrewman, in lifting and dropping loads to avoid obstructions on the ships. Swinging loads from heaving decks are a dangerous hazard.

Ships of the fleet use a variety of different fuels; Furnace Fuel Oil for the older steam driven warships; Dieso for the more modern gas turbine engines;

AVCAT or aviation fuel for aircraft; and lubricating oil of all descriptions. In addition fresh water sometimes has to be supplied and indeed the *Fort Toronto* was taken up from trade specifically as a water carrier. Every STUFT ship had to be fitted with RAS gear for refuelling. Some, like the tanker, only needed simple RAS gear for resupplying fuel to the RFA tankers; others had to be capable of receiving and supplying. In many cases it meant connecting some extra flexible pipe to the normal bunkering position, but this was often a slow method of refuelling. It is reported that the *QE 2* took over 8 hours to take aboard 4,000 tons of fuel in South Georgia.

The RFAs are fitted to resupply fuel abeam and aft. Flexible hose is lifted out by jackstay and coupled with the receiving ship. In group transfers RFAs can supply three ships at the same time though this requires considerable practice, moderate sea conditions and a very high degree of seamanship.

One of the problems facing the merchant ships on board was that of fresh water supply. Ferries that normally ply between the Channel Ports suddenly found themselves carrying a full load of troops for weeks rather than hours.

Others that normally carried a crew of 30 found themselves, like the *Stena Seaspread* embarking over 150 additional naval personnel for the voyage south. The same ship suddenly found herself trying to cope with nearly 500 men from the damaged *Glamorgan* for a short period. Very few merchant ships are equipped with large desalination gear to supplement the fresh water in their storage tanks. The initiative shown by an Inspector of Shipwrights at Devonport in telephoning immediate orders, probably without authority, for reverse osmosis equipment, is typical of the immediate decisions made in the dockyards. It was quickly fitted into most merchant ships, providing them with fresh water in reasonable quantities for washing and laundry as well as drinking.

The success of fighting a mainly maritime campaign at 8,000 miles distance from the UK and 3,800 miles from Ascension on the large scale that developed, needed resupply facilities far beyond the scope of any envisaged. Without these extra RAS facilities fitted, along with wireless equipment, by nonstop working in the Royal Dockyards, the success of the whole campaign would have been jeopardised.

# Ascension Island Operations

Ascension Island lies in the Atlantic Ocean 8° south of the Equator and 1,200 miles off the west coast of Africa. It is a rocky volcanic outcrop about 4,250 miles from UK and 3,800 miles from the Falklands. It had been administered as a British dependency since 1815 when Napoleon was exiled to St Helena, 700 miles to the south-east. The island is about 9 miles across at its widest, completely barren except for the tip of its highest point, Green Mountain (2,700 feet) and has been variously described as a 'huge lump of clinker' and a 'volcanic dustheap'.

A Royal Marines garrison was maintained from 1815 on and off until 1923. Cable and Wireless set up a station there and a BBC relay station opened in 1956. Since then the American NASA has built, under licence, the 10,000 feet runway of Wideawake airfield, named after a species of local wildlife, to support their Satellite Tracking Station. In 1982 the airfield was run by Don Coffey, the Pan-Am Airways manager, who was

*Royal Marines landing craft busily plough between* Canberra *and other ships at Ascension Island where she stayed for just over a fortnight, not only cross-decking stores and equipment, but also ferrying troops ashore for training.*

extremely helpful in affording facilities and offering welcome advice. Britain had always retained the right to use the airfield, and this was implemented with the arrival of the first aircraft, VC 10s, Hercules and charter planes from 4 April onwards, bringing in RN and RAF ground crews, Naval Party 1222, Royal Engineers and others during the ensuing weeks.

The Naval Aircraft Servicing Unit (NP 1222), under Captain Bob McQueen, were part of the British Forces Support Unit, Ascension Island, and were responsible for discipline, welfare, liaison with the residents and the flow of stores through the island. This was helped by a high powered team from the Directorate of Naval Supply and Transport, skilled in the receipt and despatch of naval stores. With the arrival of Vulcans, Victors, Nimrods and other aircraft, the Royal Air Force soon expanded, with the Station Commander of RAF Marham, Group Captain J S B Price taking command. There was little accommodation and unwanted personnel who arrived were promptly despatched back to UK, sometimes on the same aircraft they had flown in on.

The Royal Engineers sent detachments to deal with a multitude of engineer tasks such as to improve the limited

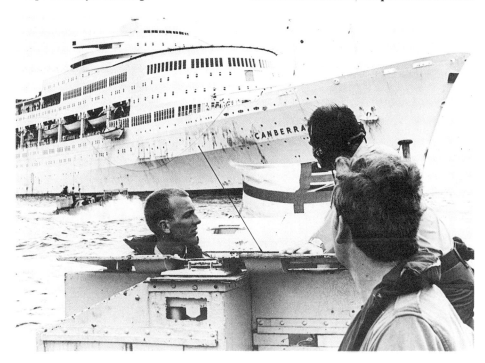

108

*Men of 3 Para live firing on the ranges at Ascension. All units comprising 3 Commando Brigade were allocated as much training time ashore as the limited time and facilities allowed. All weapons were test fired and landing craft drills practised.*

water supply; to help strip the upper-works of *Elk'* to enable the largest heli-copters to land on her upper deck and provide covered stowage for them; and to lay a fuel line from the bulk fuel stor-age 'farm' to the airfield while other Army elements advised in setting up field firing ranges. At its peak Ascension had 120 Royal Navy, 50 Army and 800 RAF per-sonnel working on the island, which doubled the normal population of 1,000, mainly Americans. In turn the residents were restricted by security considera-tions and for a time were banned from making telephone calls to the USA. Their contribution to the success of the opera-tions cannot be overstated and their willingness and friendship was at all times apparent.

The first major assembly of ships at Ascension was on 10 April when the *Antrim* Group, which were tasked to re-take South Georgia, took on board M Company of 42 Commando, 2 SBS and D Squadron SAS, along with two Wessex 5s, which had been flown there from UK. The Group departed the following day. On 14 April *Glamorgan*, with Rear Admiral Sandy Woodward embarked, sailed, and two days later *Hermes* arri-ved, the first of the Task Force direct from Britain. That day over 300 Vertrep (vertical replenishment) sorties were flown and Wideawake had 300 move-ments, the busiest airport in the world

that particular day. Arrivals of Hercu-les, usually six a day, continued and the RAF were indebted to Pan-Am for pro-viding refuelling facilities. Generally the Royal Navy were self-sufficient for fuel and water from their own fleet tankers.

On 17 April, the Amphibious Task Force started to arrive, and cross decking of men and stores immediately got under way readjusting their loads for the plan-ned landing to retake the Falklands. *Hermes, Fearless,* the Landing Ships Logistic and *Canberra* had been hurriedly despatched from UK and were not tacti-cally loaded for an operational landing. A prime decision made at that time was that *Hermes* was not to be used in her LPH role, but as a 'Harrier Carrier'. 3 Com-mando Brigade staff had worked over-time producing loading tables for each ship, but with time so short at Ascension and with the limited number of helicop-ters and landing craft, this was not always possible to the detriment of the landings later.

With the best part of four Battalions or Commandos (2 Para did not arrive in *Norland* until 8 May) wanting to stretch their legs after 11 days at sea, the units were allocated as much training time ashore as possible. During the fortnight at Ascension every man had a chance to check zero his weapon; all heavy wea-pons were fired and the Gazelles, newly fitted with SNEB rockets, were able to fire on the ranges. In addition the Com-mandos re-practised their loading and landing drills with LCUs and LCVPs while 3 Para was acquiring new amphi-bious skills. 2 Para had but one day ashore at Ascension and no chance to practice night loading. Indeed little night training could be done because the larger

*RAF Hercules, Victors and Vulcans parked at Wideawake airfield, which had a 10,000 feet modern runway, built under licence by the US Space Agency. During the campaign, more than 5,000 men and 6,000 tons of freight passed through the airport.*

ships sailed from the anchorage each evening to avoid possible underwater interference from Argentine saboteurs.

Most of the important planning meet-ings were held aboard the Amphibious Force ships whilst at Ascension, Admiral Sir John Fieldhouse and Major General Jeremy Moore flying there on 17 April for discussions with Rear Admiral Woodward, and Moore and his staff on 29 April for talks with Commodore Clapp and Brigadier Thompson on the landing plans.

From then on Ascension became a base for the Victor tankers, Vulcan bom-bers, Nimrods and Hercules. It became a vast ammunition and stores depot for the resupply of the Task and Landing Forces. The shore based helicopters worked overtime and larger planes often flew from Ascension to drop spares to ships in the 'sea train' south. The strain on the island was felt when it launched the 'Black Buck' raids on Stanley, each mission requiring two Vulcans and 11 Victors taking off at one minute intervals.

In its role as staging post, it achieved all it set out to do, not only passing 5,242 passengers through its airfield, along with vast quantities of stores and equip-ment, but also despatching 19,000 bags of mail to the forces in the south. The Falklands could never have been retaken had it not been for this small desolate outpost in the middle of the Atlantic.

# General Logistics

The logistic solution to fighting a military campaign so far from a main base was one of the great achievements of the war. Even after Ascension Island had been built up as a forward supply depot, there were still 3,800 miles to go. The reliance on the Royal and Merchant Navies, and to a lesser extent the Royal Air Force, to maintain more than 100 ships, 300 aircraft and over 10,000 men in action, was a vastly complex problem, which could be never be allowed to take second place to the operational fighting. Without a dedicated and secure supply line, the war could not be brought to a successful conclusion.

When ships were hurriedly loaded at British ports to get the Task Force underway, there was no chance in the few days available to get them tactically loaded for an amphibious assault and therefore it was some relief that the warm comfort of Ascension offered the opportunity to cross-deck and re-stow. The whole operation depended upon having the right men and the right equipment in the correct ships. However much could be achieved at Ascension it could never prevent later cross-decking in the days before the landings, but at least it could minimize it. Most of the Amphibious Task Force spent two weeks on and around the Island, not only training ashore and in carrying out landing rehearsals by helicopters and landing craft, but in transferring essential stores for the possible battle to come. This delay also allowed time for a political solution to be devolved.

Alongside the operational planners, the logistic staff of 3 Commando Brigade worked overtime. All plans were based on the assumption that an amphibious assault landing would take place, though the exact site would not be chosen for some time to come. It was envisaged that all stocks would remain afloat and troops ashore would be resupplied direct from ships by helicopters and smaller craft, such as LCUs and LCVPs. Only first line ammunition and stores would be taken ashore by units with a maximum of two days supplies. Units would leave their echelons on board and the Commando Logistic Regiment would operate from the ships.

3 Commando Brigade was supported by the Commando Logistic Regiment Royal Marines which has five squadrons, Medical, Transport, Ordnance, Workshop and Headquarters. Before leaving England, it had been decided that, as the Falklands lacked motorable roads, only a limited number of vehicles would be taken. It was thought that the Volvo BV 202E oversnow vehicles might be able to cope with the boggy Falklands terrain, but only 75 were taken from UK resources, most of the rest being stockpiled in Norway for 3 Commando Brigade's normal NATO role. With hindsight they should have taken more. The medical aspects are dealt with fully elsewhere, but it was envisaged that *Canberra* would stay in the area of the landings and act as a floating field dressing station.

When air superiority over the amphibious operating area was not achieved, the decision was taken to withdraw many of the larger ships during the night after the landings. This sudden change in plan meant that as many stores as possible had to be taken ashore. It was decided not to beach the LSLs, when an unloading might have taken 40 minutes. Instead LSLs were offloaded by mexeflote, an operation which took at least six hours for each LSL. The Commando Logistic Regiment began setting up a large Brigade Maintenance Area ashore at Ajax Bay, including a vast ammunition dump and a Field Dressing Station close by. The Brigade's supplies were now scattered in 11 different ships, some of which they did not see again until after the conflict. The command and control of all assets in the amphibious operating area were under the command of Commodore Clapp afloat in *Fearless*, but the lack of dedicated helicopters and landing craft to the logistic effort nearly prevented effective re-supply to the five major units ashore.

The Commando Logistic Regiment was not designed nor equipped to support five manoeuvre units, nor did they have stores for them. Later when 5 Infantry Brigade arrived, this same Regiment supplied all eight units over ever-increasing distances with very few vehicles and only occasional helicopters. The loss of the Chinooks in the *Atlantic Conveyor* was an even harder burden to bear. That no unit was ever short of materials with which to live and fight was a miracle of organisation and effort.

Food was all important and arctic rations were taken, but as each 24 hour pack required 8 pints of water to reconstitute its contents, there became a severe shortage of fresh water. These packs are splendid in the arctic where there is plentiful supply of snow to melt down. Considering many men fed on 'compo' (composite rations) for 36 days with very little ill effects was remarkable. Compared with most other terrain there was virtually no fresh vegetation and very little livestock.

Petrol and diesel were in short supply, not only for the vehicles, but also for small landing craft, battery chargers, BV 202Es, the light tanks of the Blues and Royals and the Rapier firing posts whose consumption was greater than anticipated. The only method of holding bulk fuel was in the ten 4-Ton Unit Bulk Refuelling Equipment vehicles of Transport Squadron; each vehicle is capable of holding 3,000 litres. 383 Petroleum Platoon RAOC (V), which formed part of the Logistic Regiment, did not deploy and there was only one qualified petroleum operator who was skilled in issuing and quality control. General Duties marines had to be trained up quickly as petroleum operators.

There were no reported ammunition defects and resupply was maintained as requested by forward units. One shortage was clothing as reserve stocks were not sufficient for five major units. Neither

---

## Commando Logistic Regiment Royal Marines

### Regimental Headquarters

| Headquarters Squadron | Ordnance Squadron | Transport Squadron | Workshop Squadron | Medical Squadron |
|---|---|---|---|---|

---

*After disembarking 3 Commando Brigade for the initial landings,* Canberra *withdrew to the safety of Grytviken harbour in South Georgia, where 5 Infantry Brigade along with their stores were cross-decked from the* Queen Elizabeth 2 *on 27 May.*

*HMS* Leeds Castle, *a despatch vessel more at home patrolling North Sea oil installations, along with* Dumbarton Castle *were based at Ascension. They acted as guardships and ferried stores forward from the airhead to the combat groups.*

the SBS nor SAS had any dedicated logistic support and between them they took half of the reserve stocks of sleeping bags. In addition the Commando Logistic Regiment found itself providing clothing and equipment for survivors from HM Ships which had been sunk, and there was certainly nothing available with which to clothe and shelter the unexpectedly large number of prisoners taken at Goose Green, nor any administration to look after them. This was all taken uncomplainingly under the wing of the Commando Logistic Regiment.

As the advance moved across East Falkland, Forward Administrative Areas were set up at Teal Inlet and Fitzroy, one for each Brigade. These were supplied by the LSLs who plied between San Carlos, re-supply ships at sea and the two forward areas. Commodities were subseqently landed by LCVP and Rigid Raiding Craft. It was on one such re-supply run that LSL *Sir Galahad* and *Sir Tristram* were attacked at Bluff Cove, whilst one of the LCUs from *Fearless*, which was in Choiseul Sound bringing 5 Brigade's vehicles forward from Darwin to Fitzroy, was bombed by Skyhawks and sunk. These landing craft manned by Royal Marines worked almost ceaselessly in resupply in the most hazardous conditions.

The value of the Commando Logistic Regiment was inestimable in such a widespread and complicated operation and this regiment was probably the only one in the British Forces that could have coped with such a diverse combination of air and sea supply methods. That the assets, both helicopters and landing craft, continued to remain in the control of Commodore Amphibious Warfare, rather than being transferred to the operational command of the Brigade ashore, was perhaps a lesson to be learnt. Here was a case where sound and practised operational procedures were able to be expanded and improvised to keep twice as many men as expected fighting fit, was a major triumph.

# Chapter Five
# Strategy and Tactics

To plan and execute a campaign over 8,000 miles from the United Kingdom requires skills not taught at Defence Staff Colleges. Indeed, apart from updating contingency plans periodically, no overt exercises had been carried out which remotely reflected the eventual size and nature of the Falklands campaign. In recent years small relief forces, never more than a battalion, had been flown to such places as the New Hebrides, Belize, Hong Kong and Cyprus when the situation worsened, all places where there was likely to be no more than limited armed insurrection.

The Falklands presented an altogether different problem. Within a month of the Argentine invasion, they had established nearly 10,000 troops, together with associated supporting arms, helicopters, field guns, anti-aircraft batteries and logistic support. Pucara and Mentor fighter aircraft and Tracker anti-submarine planes had arrived in Stanley within the first week of April and by the 29th the Pebble Island grass airstrip on West Falkland had become operational, as well as Goose Green. The latter had been established as BAM Condor with four helicopters and 12 Pucaras, so as to provide dispersal for the fighter aircraft. It also required more than two companies of 12 Regiment to guard it and Darwin Settlement.

In British eyes it was clear that firm bases would be essential for retaking the Falklands. Ascension Island, the British dependency with an American built runway capable of taking any type of aircraft, was situated more or less half way. This would provide an intermediary base, stores and fuel depot, apart from allowing cross-decking and tactical re-loading of embarked stores. But this was still 3,800 miles from Stanley. The lonely South Atlantic lay between them. Neither of the two other British dependencies further south, St Helena and Tristan de Cunha, were suitable as bases; neither could the old British built base at Simonstown in South Africa be used for political reasons.

Although the ships of the Argentine Navy were comparatively old, their three submarines Santa Fe, (formerly the USN Catfish built in 1944), Salta (1974) and San Luis (1974) posed a considerable threat. Their one aircraft carrier Veintecinco (25) De Mayo was originally HMS Venerable built in 1945; and their lone cruiser General Belgrano was originally the pre-war USN Phoenix of 1938. However they did possess two modern Type 42 destroyers Hercules and Santissima Trinidad, along with four second world war American cast-offs. There were three corvettes of 1,300 tons and several patrol craft.

The strategical importance of air power was an equally serious consideration. Five Argentine air bases on the mainland were within striking distance of the Falklands; Rio Grande (Super Etendards, Daggers and later A-4Q Skyhawks) being 440 miles away from Stanley, Rio Gallegos (A-4B Skyhawks) 480 miles, Santa Cruz 475, San Julian (A-4C Skyhawks and Daggers) 455 and Comodoro Rivadavia (C-130s, Boeing 707s, Learjets and Mirages) 605 miles. The Argentines possessed a limited air-to-air refuelling capability from two KC-130H tankers, but only the Super-Etendards and Skyhawks could use them. The Argentine Air Force was known to possess five Exocet AM.39 missiles which could be air launched from Super-Etendards, and were likely to prove the greatest threat to a naval Task Force. The pilots were well trained but had streaks of Latin-American temperament in their performances. If the British lost just one of their aircraft carriers, or a STUFT troop carrier, it might cause the abandonment of the whole campaign to retake the islands. One major advantage that the British did have over the Argentinian Air Force was that its aircraft would be operating initially from aircraft carriers in the TEZ, while most Argentinian aircraft, based on the mainland would be at the limit of their range. This meant that lengthier Air Combat Air Patrols could be maintained by the British, while any enemy air intervention would rely on instant acquisition of targets and attack.

There was one other possible base in the South Atlantic, only 800 miles from the Falklands, South Georgia. Although it had neither accommodation facilities nor an airstrip, it had a fine sheltered natural harbour. From the outset it was clear that any successful campaign would not be possible without its re-possession. Once secured it would provide a safe anchorage for larger ships to transfer troops and supplies from which to reinforce the Falklands. It might also provide a safe haven for damaged ships. The enemy in South Georgia posed less of a problem, there being about 60 Argentine military there. Even before the main Task Force left UK, a special re-occupation force had been earmarked, M Company of 42 Commando with SAS and SBS support.

The biggest problem that the Task Force would face was that of logistic support, and it was here that a strategical plan had to be evolved which had no parallel in recent years. Although there were friendly countries in South America, such as Chile and Brazil, their active participation would be strictly limited and covert. Neither wished to involve themselves in all out war against Argentina, an involvement that might rumble on long after any successful conclusion to the British campaign. In the event they were all but discounted as allies. Freetown in Sierra Leone, was the largest natural port in West Africa, and was user-friendly, the Canberra and Elk being among the first big ships to refuel there on their journey south.

Another strategical consideration was the weather. Winter was approaching, and by the time any Task Force could establish themselves on the Falklands, it

would be very cold, extremely wet and uncomfortable whether at sea or on land. South Atlantic storms might preclude flying from the aircraft carriers, cross decking at sea and even re-supply, especially with the inexperienced STUFT ships. Airborne anti-submarine surveillance might have to be curtailed and defensive air sorties abandoned. This would undoubtedly create added problems for the Carrier Battle Group Commander.

It was also essential that any landing area must have a secure and sheltered anchorage. With available assault troops being numerically inferior to the defenders, the Land Force Commander needed an unopposed landing area to establish his enlarged Brigade. He could not accept unnecessary casualties in the early stages which might delay the successful completion of the campaign. The less time his troops had to suffer the privations and discomforts of an Antarctic winter the better. The marines and paras of his Brigade, tough as they were, would need to acclimatise themselves to some of the worst weather known to fighting man. These factors were an added burden to the strategic

*The Argentine aircraft carrier* Veintecinco (25) de Mayo, *which posed a threat to the Task Force until she withdrew on 4 May to seek shelter in Argentinian coastal waters. She was the former British carrier HMS* Venerable *built in 1945, and carried A-4Q Skyhawks and helicopters.*

considerations.

For strategic and tactical planning, good intelligence is essential. For some time British Intelligence had been reading Argentine communications, but an inadvertent disclosure by a former Labour minister warned the Argentinians of this fact and they immediately changed their codes, causing a crucial delay while counter intelligence broke the cyphers. A lack of good photography either by aerial reconnaissance or satellite photography exacerbated the problem.

While political discussions to settle the dispute amicably were going ahead, in the minds of the Chiefs of Staff, the priorities were quite clear. Firstly came the immediate despatch of a strong naval Task Force; secondly the assembly of a well equipped Amphibious Force; thirdly

the establishment of a strong base at Ascension which would require the full might of Support Command of the Royal Air Force. No weakening of the British commitment to NATO or elsewhere in the world must be apparent and so resources must be found from those not committed.

The next stage, if political negotiations failed, was to gain dominance over the Argentine Navy by the establishment of a blockade around the Falklands; then the winning of air supremacy over the Argentine Air Force; and finally to re-occupy firstly South Georgia and then the Falkland Islands. The biggest aces in Britain's pack were that the Royal Navy was amongst the most efficient and best equipped in the world although short on numbers; the proposed initial landing force of Royal Marines Commandos and the Parachute Regiment could hardly be bettered; and the Royal Air Force, whilst being fully extended, had sufficient experience and expertise to maintain good logistic support. However there was little in reserve if a major vessel was lost. The strategic use of submarines to dominate the South Atlantic might be the trump card.

# Naval Strategy

Having identified the three threats posed by the Argentine forces, sub surface, surface and air, the Royal Naval Task Force which set off from UK and Gibraltar on 5 April had to ensure their priorities were right. The ultimate objective was the re-occupation of the Falkland Islands and the overthrow of the Argentine forces temporarily in occupation. In order to achieve that, they had to ensure that a large enough military force reached the area without serious interference. Though a political settlement was being sought, in their planning they had to dismiss all thoughts of this and concentrate on a purely military solution.

The defensive alliance of NATO had seriously eroded the ability of the Royal Navy to 'go it alone' in an out-of-area conflict. However the Task Force eventually included both its available aircraft carriers, both its amphibious assault ships, all six LSLs, six submarines, eight destroyers, fifteen frigates and various other smaller craft, a total of 51 warships, 171 naval aircraft and 21 ships of the Royal Fleet Auxiliary. It continued to fulfil its commitment to the Standing Naval Force, Atlantic, the Armilla Patrol in the Persian Gulf and maintain a small presence in Hong Kong and the West Indies.

The basic roles of the British Armed Services in 1982 were the defence of the United Kingdom and British dependencies; to provide an independent element of the strategic and theatre nuclear forces committed to the NATO alliance; to provide major land, sea and air contribution to the European mainland and Eastern Atlantic; and to protect maritime trade and off-shore installations. The Royal Navy carried out their part of this commitment by providing the nuclear deterrent of the ballistic missile submarines, a conventional naval defence with surface and sub-surface ships, a Fleet Air Arm based on the Sea Harrier and helicopters, and 3 Commando Brigade's amphibious force.

When the war erupted 8,000 miles away, the naval commanders turned sharply away from the North Atlantic. Very few of their ships and weapons had been tested under battle conditions and the combat capability of the new Sea Harrier was untried. Working on the well established principles of containment of Argentine forces, defence in depth and maintaining the initiative, their first priority was to establish dominance over the Argentine Navy. Conventional submarines were immediately despatched to the South Atlantic, not only to provide a deterrent, but to watch and report on Argentine shipping movements. The next priority was to set up and dominate a total exclusion zone around the Falklands. A 200 mile maritime exclusion zone against Argentine naval ships was announced on 7 April and brought into force on 12th. On 23 April the British affirmed that any threat by Argentine

*The Argentine Navy had three submarines, the World War 2* Santa Fe *and two more modern ones* Salta *and* San Luis. *While they were still at sea they posed a considerable threat particularly to the two aircraft carriers and larger troop carriers. The detection and sinking of the* Santa Fe, *seen disabled in Grytviken Harbour with HMS* Endurance's *Wasp helicopter hovering over her, reduced the threat.*

forces to interfere with the mission of the British Task Force would be met with 'appropriate consequences'. It was not until political negotiations had been nearly exhausted and the Royal Navy had enough ships in the area, that they were able to impose this total exclusion zone on 30 April. This was later extended on 7 May to 12 miles from the Argentine coast, warning that any Argentine warship or military aircraft inside that zone would be treated as hostile. Argentina did not heed the warnings, but the way was still open for political agreement.

In order to transport an Amphibious Task Force to the South Atlantic, protection against enemy attacks by either air or sea by using a convoy system had to be provided. The decision to use STUFT ships including the P & O liner *Canberra* and the roll-on roll-off ferries *Elk* and *Norland* in the initial force created serious problems as they had no form of integral defence against enemy interference. Whatever other losses the Royal Navy might incur, these ships had to reach the Falklands unscathed and

hopefully undetected.

The Task Force Commander, Rear Admiral JF 'Sandy' Woodward's first task was to secure South Georgia and the landing force for this was carried entirely in HM Ships with Royal Fleet Auxiliary support. *Antrim* commanded the group with the frigates *Brilliant* and *Plymouth* ensuring a balanced force with their Sea Cat (close range) and Sea Wolf (point defence) providing air defence and helicopters for anti-submarine protection, with the added twin 4.5″ bombardment capability. Supporting them were the Fleet Replenishment Ship *Fort Austin* and the Fleet Tanker *Tidespring*. Silently patrolling the area was the submarine *Conqueror*.

Woodward's next task was to establish air dominance over the Falklands, without which a successful amphibious landing was hardly feasible. If this could not be achieved absolutely, then he had to maintain the ability to contest the air space. With Argentina 400 miles from the Falklands, any mainland based enemy aircraft would be at the limit of their range and not be able to spend much time over the combat area. His own Sea Harriers

*The Royal Fleet Auxilliary* Blue Rover, *the smallest of the Fleet Oilers, which arrived in San Carlos Water on 1 June, refuels HMS* Exeter. Blue Rover *carried a mixed fuel load which included high octane Mogas for the vehicles and Rapier systems, as well as ammunition.*

would certainly have more air time if they could bring the Argentinians to battle.

It was thought that the surface units of the Argentine Fleet would probably not operate too far from their home bases and seldom east of the Falklands. To eliminate one of their major units, the cruiser or the aircraft carrier, would have a crucial strategic and morale effect. Knowing that the three Argentine submarines would continue to pose a threat, other groups sought them out. It was perhaps fortuitous that the the rather ancient but largest submarine *Santa Fe* was sighted on the surface on 25 April during the re-taking of South Georgia, attacked and disabled.

Other important strategical considerations included the establishment of a secure 'pipe-line' for STUFT ships and requisitioned tankers to voyage south

without interruption. There was also the need to establish a safe area for repairs to ships, self maintenance and transfers of troops and stores, initially known as LOLA (Logistics and Loitering Area), later as TRALA (Tug, Repair and Logistics Area), well to the east of the Falklands and out of range of enemy air activity.

That total domination over the Argentine Fleet was achieved before the amphibious landing, mainly due to the sinking of the *General Belgrano*, was proof that the naval strategy in the South Atlantic was successful. However air dominance was not achieved by D-Day, and there were times when it was touch and go. The superior combat quality of the Sea Harriers and their pilots, coupled with the tenacity and bravery of the crews of the frigates and destroyers were the deciding factors. No ship carrying troops was hit during the voyage south although more than once Argentine propaganda claimed to have sunk the 'Great White Whale', *Canberra*. The Royal Navy achieved their object of landing the amphibious force ashore safely, but not without tremendous losses to themselves.

# Naval Tactics – Total Exclusion Zone

The task of enforcing the Total Exclusion Zone which was imposed by the British on 30 April in an area of 200 miles radius from the Falklands fell to the Commander of the Task Force, Rear Admiral 'Sandy' Woodward. His forces were limited and initially he had only two ships *Brilliant* and *Broadsword* equipped with Sea Wolf which offered some counter to the Argentine air launched Exocet AM.39. Later *Andromeda* joined the force, but that was after *Sheffield* had been sunk.

His main job was to ensure that the amphibious force landed as safely and unhindered as possible, and to achieve this he had to dominate the sea and air space around the Islands. To keep the Argentine Navy bottled up relied heavily on the deterrent effect of his submarines, whose manoeuvrings in the South Atlantic are still a closely guarded secret. To win the battle of the skies he had to make sure his two aircraft carriers *Hermes* and *Invincible* remained unscathed. They were probably the most critical ships in the entire force. Woodward knew that the antiquated Type 965 long range air-search radar fitted in most of his ships was inadequate to give him early warning of air attacks against the fast and highly efficient land based Argentinian Air Force and Naval Air Arm with nearly 200 planes. His 28 Sea Harriers were outnumbered by at least six to one. The air space between the Falklands and Argentina was out of range of the RAF's early warning aircraft, the Nimrod, and he had to rely entirely on his own resources. The aircraft carrier *25 de Mayo* was the biggest potential threat, and although she was equipped with A-4Q Skyhawks, she could not operate the Super Etendards with their Exocets.

He was confident that his anti-submarine search capability was one of the best in the world. Sustaining a continuous search programme by ASW helicopters entailed a time consuming, often boring, patrolling task in very different A/S water conditions. As long as there was one enemy submarine at large, this defensive task had to be carried out. The *San Luis* appears to have carried out four unsuccessful attacks against British warships. The last, against *Alacrity* and *Arrow* on 11 May only being foiled by the torpedo's guidance wire breaking. The torpedo may have hit *Arrow's* decoy torpedo which was being towed astern.

As soon as it was clear that the British intended to re-occupy the islands, Contralmirante JJ Lombardo, the Argentine Fleet Commander formed four Task Groups with his small Navy, which could all operate independently. To the north west was the carrier group, including the two Type 42 destroyers *Hercules* and *Santissima Trinidad*. With them was another group of two Exocet armed old destroyers *Comodoro Py* and *Segui*, while to the north and further east were the three Exocet carrying corvettes *Drummond*, *Granville* and *Guerrico*. With a patrol region to the south between the Isla de los Estados and the Burdwood Bank, the *General Belgrano* with her escorting destroyers, also carrying Exocets, was ready to strike to the Falklands in the north, or perhaps as far as South Georgia no more than two days steaming to the east. Her old but effective 6″ guns could outrange anything the British had. Lombardo's aim was the elimination of at least one of the British aircraft carriers. On 1 May the Argentine Task Groups were all outside the 200 miles TEZ, but approaching it menacingly, particularly in the south.

To counter this Admiral Woodward stood off steady to receive Argentine air attacks which were expected both from the mainland and from the *25 de Mayo*. He kept his carriers to the north east of Stanley. On 2 May a Sea Harrier, piloted by Flight Lieutenant Ian Mortimer, on a silent search patrol 'popped up', switched on his Blue Fox radar and detected the Argentine carrier group. However his warning receiver told him he was being held by an enemy Type 909 Sea Dart tracking radar, which must mean a Type 42 destroyer. He promptly dropped to sea level and reported his find. Generally the British tactics were to station a picket line of Type 42s about 30 miles up threat of the main group, keeping the two Type 22 destroyers with their Sea Wolf as close point defence. The latter came to be known as 'goalkeepers'.

Meanwhile on 1 May Admiral Woodward despatched his first bombardment ships *Glamorgan*, *Alacrity* and *Arrow* to shell military targets in the Stanley area,

*HMS* Conqueror *returns to Faslane, Scotland. Her flag bears crossed torpedos and warship denoting sinking of the* General Belgrano, *and curved dagger indicating successful secret mission of inserting men of the Special Boat Squadron.*

supplementing the extraordinary long range bombing of the Vulcan. This bombardment pattern continued almost nightly. The Argentine Navy were shadowing the British Carrier Force with their Neptune aircraft and planned an air attack on 2 May. A lack of wind upset their plans to launch the heavily laden Skyhawks, which required at least 25 knots wind speed over the decks, from *25 de Mayo*. Indeed the ship never launched an attack before she returned to the shelter of a home port on 4 May.

The main threat to the British that morning came from the *Belgrano* group

in the south. On 2 May *Conqueror* reported that the group was moving eastwards, skirting the TEZ, posing a dire threat to both the British carrier group and also to South Georgia. Should the ship turn north east at nightfall, and close at her full speed of 20 plus knots, she would be in a position to engage the British surface ships with her conventional 6″ guns. With his own carriers manoeuvring to counter the Argentine carrier group, Admiral Woodward was restricted in his ability to match this second threat. His Sea Harriers were fully deployed in the air defence role, and he was left with the *Conqueror* and her 21″ torpedoes. While she was still in contact the submarine could shadow the enemy cruiser group, but it was possible that she might lose them during the night as the Burwood Bank made underwater operations difficult.

Having made up his own mind, Admiral Woodward reported the fact to Northwood and requested an extension of the Rules of Engagement to allow *Conqueror* to eliminate the threat. The War Cabinet approved the attack which was to turn the naval war into Britain's favour and end any serious Argentine surface threat. Five days later the British imposed an exclusion zone on Argentine naval ships beyond 12 miles from their mainland, and their fleet took no further effective part in the war, being ordered to withdraw to the west.

From then on the British naval tactics, designed to support the build up prior to the amphibious landing, were almost entirely concentrated on the air threat, which still posed considerable problems. The sinking of the *Sheffield* on 4 May emphasised the Argentine resolve. Should they sink a carrier, then the strategical balance would be in jeopardy. Almost nightly bombardments of military targets on the Falklands continued unabated, but Argentine air activity was hindered by the weather, and the two submarines *San Luis* and *Salta* were both reported to be back in home ports. The approach of the Amphibious Task Force towards the TEZ posed other problems of defence. On 19 May a major re-shuffle of troops and stores prior to the landings took place about 300 miles to the east north east of Stanley, an uncomfortable experience for those involved in the remoteness of the South Atlantic in winter.

Thus all was set for battle.

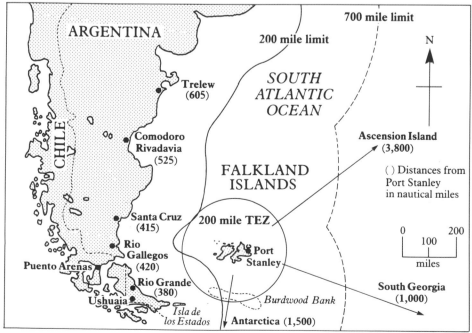

# Naval Tactics in Support of Land Operations

Once the orders for the landings at San Carlos had been agreed by London and signalled on 12 May, Rear Admiral Sandy Woodward turned his attention to supporting the military forces during Operation *Sutton* and the subsequent land operations across East Falkland. His object was to protect the landings from enemy air attack, the naval threat having already been virtually eliminated, and harass military targets ashore, whilst guarding his own major warships and supply lines.

To achieve this he had the Sea Harriers and Harrier GR3s in the two aircraft carriers, in addition to a strong force of naval bombardment ships. All eight destroyers and nine of his frigates had 4.5″ guns, either in twin turrets (Mark 6) or single mountings (Mark 8). The Mark 6 guns could fire a 55 lb shell over 17,500 yards keeping up a sustained rate of 12 rounds a minute. The single Mark 8s, firing a similar shell, had a maximum range of 22,000 yards (12½ miles), at 25 rounds a minute automatic. Some of these ships were deployed almost daily after 1 May in bombarding

military installations around Stanley airport, later directing their attention to other targets. Apart from actual damage, sustained nightly shelling had a considerable morale effect on soldiers, especially amongst the poorly trained conscripts. Much of this fire was controlled and directed by Royal Artillery forward observers, who had been landed with SAS patrols.

The main naval concern during the San Carlos landings was the protection of the STUFT ships *Canberra*, *Norland* and *Europic Ferry*, carrying the bulk of the landing force. Early patrolling to prevent enemy ships leaving or entering Falkland Sound had started in the first week of May. Periodic diversionary bombardments on Port Howard, Fox Bay and Darwin were subsequently carried out, which included dropping of flares by helicopter and forward spotting by night. By 10 May it had been established that the Argentinians had not mined the approaches to Falkland Sound, but navigation between the rocks and reefs was still a hazardous occupation. The following day *Alacrity* sunk the 800 ton

*Isla de los Estados*, ferrying supplies ashore near Port Howard, and made the first passage through the Sound.

These activities, coupled with some off the west coast of West Falkland, and others near Stanley and Bluff Cove helped to keep the Argentinians guessing as to when and where the military landings would occur. Deteriorating weather over the next few days precluded any form of air activity and the Argentine Navy had effectively scuttled off to its home ports. During the whole of the period leading up to D-Day Sea King helicopters were continually flying in and recovering Special Forces patrols by night all over the islands. These were the intelligence gathering teams, and the task of the helicopter pilots was made a little easier by the use of night vision goggles. The major raid by forty five SAS on the airstrip on Pebble Island took

*An* Amazon *class frigate, seven of which were deployed, fires her 4.5″ gun in practice. These ships played a regular part in the almost nightly bombardments of Stanley.*

place on 14 May, supported by naval gunfire from *Glamorgan*. The following day *Alacrity* dropped off two Gemini loads of SBS in Grantham Sound just south of San Carlos

During and after the landings, a new tactic was to be developed, designating areas for missile defence against air attack and others for the Combat Air Patrol of Sea Harriers. At sea a picket line to the west of the Falklands would attempt to give early warning of enemy air approach from the mainland and engage them if possible in what came to be known as the 'missile trap'. The CAP would then be directed to intercept them before they reached the islands. The final line of defence was the close range Sea Wolf of *Brilliant* and *Broadsword* in Falkland Sound, coupled with Sea Cat, and the military's Rapier and Blowpipe missiles over the land.

The effectiveness of this defence to prevent casualties to the landing force was epitomized in that only LSLs *Sir Galahad*, *Sir Bedivere* and *Sir Lancelot* of the amphibious force were hit by bombs, and that was not until D + 3. They all survived these San Carlos attacks. However the Royal Navy suffered deeply, losing *Coventry*, *Ardent* and *Antelope* in

the defence of the landing areas, with *Argonaut* severely disabled. The Argentine pilots insistence on attacking warships rather than amphibious shipping and the STUFT troop carriers was one of the grave tactical errors of the war.

Still maintaining their 'missile trap' at sea and close anti-aircraft support near the shore, the Royal Navy subsequently supported all the major battles until the fall of Stanley. Often, as in the case of *Ardent*, supporting 2 Para at Goose Green, warships remained on station far longer than planned and deemed safe, withdrawing only as dawn broke.

There was an understandable reluctance to expose valuable warships in daylight to possible enemy attacks near the coast, especially as it was known that the Argentines had some shore based Exocet missiles. The fact that *Glamorgan* was hit during the later stages of the war showed the enemy's determination. The LSLs continued to ply almost daily to Teal Inlet and Fitzroy, ferrying forward reinforcements and supplies, particularly those of 5 Infantry Brigade. However the exposure of the LSLs to enemy attack without adequate air defence at Bluff Cove was a sore point amongst those who suffered. Although the Welsh

Guards had been embarked aboard *Fearless* it was not thought prudent by the naval command to hazard such an important ship so close to the enemy. They transferred to *Sir Galahad* which arrived unaccompanied and unexpectedly owing to a breakdown of communications between ships and shore. The tragic results are history.

During the final land battles for the hills overlooking Stanley, a destroyer or frigate would be in direct support of an attacking battalion or commando, being directed by Royal Artillery forward observers, who switched from unit to unit as the attacks developed. This prowess by 148 (Meiktila) Forward Observation Battery was reflected in the number of bravery decorations they received. Without the support of the warships, which had to break away each morning to refuel and re-ammunition, the fight for the hills would not have gone so smoothly. The Royal Navy had certainly played their full part in the land operations by 14 June.

*A Sea King and a Wessex helicopter (with an underslung load) join a Landing Craft (Utility) in ferrying* matériel *ashore from the* Norland *in San Carlos Water.*

# Choosing a Landing Site

As soon as government policy decreed that a landing force should be sent to repossess the Falklands Islands, the planners in 3 Commando Brigade Royal Marines turned their thoughts to possible landing sites. Even before leaving the UK, at a Brigade briefing on 4 April in Plymouth, initial options were being set out; and during the voyage south to Ascension Island, lengthy discussions took place, led by Commodore Mike Clapp and Brigadier Julian Thompson.

A trump card in the British pack was the unpublished book written by Major Ewen Southby-Tailyour when he commanded the Royal Marines of Naval Party 8901 in 1978/79. During his year in the Falklands he compiled a unique pilotage and topographical study of the islands, sailing more than 6,000 miles around the coast. He drew about 60 charts, took hundreds of photographs and made nearly 200 sketches of the coastline, besides painting water colours of the scenery and wild life. He had unbounded enthusiasm for the islands and, apart from those who actually lived there, was probably the greatest authority on them. When, after the war, Southby-Tailyour's book was published, Julian Thompson wrote in the foreword '. . . if I was asked to name one man whose knowledge and expertise was irreplaceable in the planning and conduct of the amphibious operations, I would, without hesitation name Ewen Southby-Tailyour.' Such was the measure of the value of his contribution. Another whose experiences were invaluable was the leader of the recent Joint Services expedition to South Georgia, Lieutenant Bob Veal, a former naval PTI. He was able to describe the bleak and forbidding nature of the terrain around Grytviken and Leith.

The main ingredient in planning any military operation is intelligence of the enemy. Even with two extra Parachute Battalions joining his three Commandos, Thompson knew that the enemy would be numerically superior, probably more than three to one. It was therefore essential that vigorous patrolling of the islands must take place as soon as possible to ascertain not only enemy strengths and dispositions, but also their fighting fitness and weaponry. Whilst maps were reasonably useful, the scarcity of settle-

ments and the barrenness of a terrain lacking normal geographical features like woods and roads, made them of limited value. The greatest shortcoming was that no air photographs were available, a remarkable gap in view of the Falklands being a British dependency. Indeed, no air photographs became available until very late in the campaign and even those were of poor quality and doubtful value. The SBS and SAS, the experts in individual reconnaisance, had a vital role to play before detailed planning for a landing area could be finalised.

With a 3,800 miles sea journey from point of embarkation at Ascension to landing meant that plans had to be sufficiently far advanced before they left the island to ensure tactical loading of all ships.

At the initial conferences aboard *Fearless*, nineteen possible landing points were identified. These were soon whittled down to eight, then five, by the joint staffs of the Commodore Amphibious Warfare and HQ 3 Commando Brigade. The chosen beaches were to become the subject of detailed reconnaisance by Special Boats Squadron patrols. Both naval and military requirements had to be carefully balanced. With such a long

*Major Ewen Southby-Tailyour had spent 1978 in the Falklands when he sailed rounds the islands privately surveying the beaches for a yachtman's guide.*

coastline, it was appreciated that the enemy could not defend it all and an unopposed landing was not only desirable but a practical possiblity. A safe landing on West Falkland would have meant another amphibious crossing of Falkland Sound later and this idea was

*Major Southby-Tailyour (left) with the planning team. From right, Brig Thompson, Major Chester, Major Wells-Cole, Capt Rowe and Lt-Col Holroyd-Smith.*

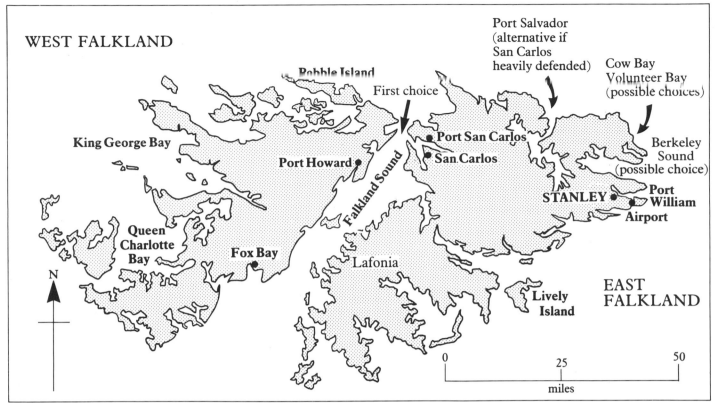

WEST FALKLAND

King George Bay

Pobble Island

First choice

Port Salvador
(alternative if
San Carlos
heavily defended)

Cow Bay
Volunteer Bay
(possible choices)

Port San Carlos
San Carlos

Port Howard

Falkland Sound

Berkeley
Sound
(possible choice)

STANLEY

Port
William

Airport

Queen
Charlotte
Bay

Fox Bay

Lafonia

Lively
Island

EAST
FALKLAND

N

0        25        50

miles

soon discarded. It was also known that the enemy had concentrated their forces around Stanley and its airport with smaller groups at major settlements. Any landing near Stanley would undoubtedly encounter well prepared positions, minefields and wire. With virtually no armoured support this would be suicidal and incur heavy casualties. It might also lead to civilian casualties and damage to property.

A prime naval requirement was to find an anchorage that was sheltered from air attack and particularly from the Exocet missile which needed a sea-skimming line of approach, and also be free of sea mines. In winter, Antarctic winds are strong and unpredictable, seas are variable. It was therefore essential to choose an area which was so sheltered that landings could be made in any direction.

The main military tactical consideration was to capture the high ground to the west of Stanley before any advance could be made on the capital. The enemy would probably expect an attack from the south west of Stanley near Fitzroy, or from Port Harriet, the point at which they had initially landed. Here was the only road leading to the capital, and intelligence reports later proved that was

*When the commanders were choosing a suitable amphibious landing site their priorities were a sheltered anchorage and an undefended, firm beach with good exits. The initial sites were the subject of detailed reconnaissance by the SBS.*

indeed where they had established their main defences.

Two major factors now had to be weighed up; a landing must be out of range of enemy artillery and yet near enough to Stanley to avoid a long approach and logistic resupply before bringing the main enemy forces to battle. Beaches must be able to land LCUs, LCVPs and Mexeflotes and there must be good exits into the hinterland. The beaching of the LSLs was impracticable as they would almost certainly be required again later and structural damage might be incurred; and without complete air domination it was too risky. Any landing area must be easily defendable against possible counter-attacks and large enough to contain five major units, their supporting arms and the mass of ammunition, stores, food, fuel, medical and logistic supplies required to be self supporting.

When Major General Jeremy Moore flew to Ascension on 29 April, Clapp and

Thompson produced operation orders for three alternative landing sites, Cow Bay/Volunteer Bay to the north of Stanley, Berkeley Sound, also north of Stanley and San Carlos Water on the west coast of East Falkland, the privately preferred option. The former two landing sites were only seen possible if intelligence reported that the enemy were unlikely to put up much resistance. Moore took these three options to the Chiefs of Staff in London, who favoured San Carlos. Whilst it was deemed the safest bet for an unopposed landing, it had the drawback of being 50 miles from Stanley with no roads between the two. The nearest major Argentine garrison was at Darwin and Goose Green 20 miles to the south. As they sailed south from Ascension, Thompson and Clapp agreed that should San Carlos be very heavily defended, an alternative might be Port Salvador. This could have been very heavy in casualties. As soon as it was clear that San Carlos was virtually free of enemy, the final planning went ahead.

The Chiefs of Staff signalled their decision on 12 May, but the Operation Order for the landings was already in print! An 'O' Group was summoned on 13th, aboard *Fearless* and Brigadier Thompson gave his orders for the landing.

# Special Operations

The high standard of training and preparedness of both the Royal Marines Special Boat Squadron and the Army's Special Air Service played a crucial part in the planning and retaking of the Falklands. The SBS were highly trained in exercising with the Royal Navy and were fully conversant with their procedures. However the SAS had not worked with the Navy since World War 2 but they quickly made the necessary adjustments to evolve a harmonious working relationship. Apart from their surveillance work, they would also be involved in psychological warfare and deception.

At midday on 26 April, the day that Lt Cdr Alfredo Astiz signed the instrument of surrender aboard *Endurance*, *Conqueror* surfaced nearby and transferred 6 SBS to *Plymouth*. Later that day 2 SBS and D Squadron of SAS embarked in *Brilliant*, having recovered them from Leith Harbour with some difficulty caused by the weather. An SAS trooper was later to remark that the Naval aircrews *'were fantastic during Operation* Paraquat, *they just never gave up.'*

What the commanders needed more than anything else was detailed intelligence on possible landing sites for a seaborne invasion and information about enemy dispositions, strength and degree of alertness. Major Southby-Tailyour's detailed assessment of the Falklands coast certainly limited the areas where beach gradients, tides and hinterland would be suitable for amphibious landings, thus reducing the number of places that needed further reconnaisance by the SBS. Areas of surveillance for Special Forces patrols were also limited by the natural cover and lack of foliage available in the bleak Falklands terrain. By daylight it was essential that patrols hid in scrapes or caves, moving only by night, sometimes covering only 300 yards an hour. It was going to be a slow process if they were to remain undetected, one not fully appreciated by the pundits in London who were pressing for quicker action. Initially Special Forces operations were coordinated by Royal Marines Colonel Richard Preston in *Hermes*. The exact deployment of patrols was decided personally by Brigadier Thompson and Commodore Clapp, with advice from Colonel Mike Rose, commanding 22 SAS who now had two of his Squadrons committed, and Major Jonathan Thompson, commanding the SBS Squadron, who were now aboard *Fearless*.

Detailed operations by the SAS and SBS on the Falklands are unlikely to be released for many years to avoid disclosures of their methods of operation. Most were involved in highly clandestine reconnaisance in small self-sufficient groups. One major attack by the SAS of which there are further details was the successful raid on Pebble Island on 13/14 May. Another was the surprise attack by the Mountain and Arctic Warfare Cadre against Argentine Special Forces in Top Malo House on 31 May, the only major daylight encounter between the two élite groups.

However before that, in the first days of May and a week before the Amphibious Task Group sailed from Ascension, the first patrols of G Squadron were inserted onto the Falklands by Sea King helicopters from *Hermes*. Only four aircraft were fitted with the American Passive Night Vision Goggles enabling the pilots to 'see like daylight' and fly in at sea level to avoid detection. Some landings were 120 miles from the ship but the accuracy of the flying by these naval pilots was unimpeachable. Eight patrols were dropped in those few days from close to Stanley, in the Bluff Cove and Darwin areas, as well as on West Falkland near Port Howard and Fox Bay.

SBS teams were inserted in coastal areas by boats from frigates, some from the trawler *Junella*, to prepare detailed reports on the five options chosen as possible landing sites, particularly around Ajax Bay, already favoured by the commanders for the amphibious landings. It was unfortunate that no conventional submarine was available until 1 June when *Onyx* arrived for the practised method of SBS insertion.

*Panoramic views taken through the periscope of the submarine* Onyx *of West Point Island (below) and Weddell Island on the west coast of West Falkland. From here SBS patrols made their way across the bleak countryside to report on enemy positions.*

Most Special Forces patrols were dropped at least four nights march from their targets and they had to contend with extremely wet, cold and uncomfortable conditions, with little natural cover and not much chance of digging in the boggy peat. Overhead cover made of camouflaged chicken wire afforded little protection against the elements. They lived close to the enemy, were in constant danger particularly when they made their regular wireless transmissions. They would have liked a 'burst' facility whereby long messages can be speeded up and transmitted very quickly. Their rations had to be cked out over longer periods than those for which they were designed and there was little natural vegetation or wildlife to supplement their diet. Some patrols spent more than three weeks completely on their own, sending back vital intelligence daily about the enemy. They got to know his habits, when resupply was likely and the routes taken, his equipment and ammunition, his daily routines building up a remarkably accurate picture of their lives and morale.

The information they did send back was of infinite value to the commanders planning the landings. They reported a larger number of troops than anticipated but generally of poor and inexperienced quality. The enemy were certainly well

*A Royal Marine of the Special Boat Squadron makes his way up the beach. The main task of the SBS was to survey beaches, their gradients and exits into the hinterland, besides reporting on enemy troop movements.*

armed, but did not seem to be well trained, disciplined or led. However there was a spattering of regular units with well seasoned troops whose undoubted ability must not be underestimated.

In his book 'No Picnic' General Thompson says *'The skill and dedication of SBS and SAS patrols was severely tested during the days before D-Day and they did all that was expected of them and more'*.

# Ground Tactics

No military tactics can be formulated without good and accurate intelligence. In the Falklands this was carried out mainly by SBS and SAS patrols inserted into the hinterland from the beginning of May by small ships and helicopters. These teams, usually about four strong, lay up in exposed positions for up to three weeks, reporting on movements, strengths and dispositions. They often had to cover considerable distances on foot in appalling winter weather, with temperatures mostly below freezing and in driving sleet or snow. Exceptionally strong winds could easily blow a heavily laden man over.

The terrain of the country dictated the tactics for both the Argentinians and the British. With most of the population and the little industry concentrated around Port Stanley, this would be the strategic place to defend. Even with 10,000 infantry ashore, it was impossible for the Argentinians to watch every part of the long rambling coastline, nor to defend much more than the main settlements of Stanley, Port Louis, Douglas, Teal Inlet, Darwin, Fitzroy, Port Howard and Fox Bay, plus the major airstrips at Goose Green and Pebble Island. None of these had roads, but merely tracks leading across rolling, rocky and boggy countryside. It was common sense for defenders to concentrate on the tactical features vital to the main targets and deny the attackers their use. Brigadier Thompson saw no reason to doubt the Argentinians would do otherwise.

The Argentinians certainly expected an attack from the south west of Stanley, somewhere near Fitzroy, with the British advancing along the axis of the one motorable road. It was possible that they might land to the north west in the Port Salvador area, but Green Hill, Mount Vernet and Long Island Mount dominated the narrow approach route. To defend Stanley from any advance from the west there were two lines of mountains stretching south from Mount Estancia through Mount Kent to Mount Challenger. Four miles further east, but not as high, was the more easily defendable range from Mount Longdon in the north, through Two Sisters and Goat Ridge to Mount Harriet in the south. The third ridge, and the last defence line before Stanley, contained Tumbledown, Mount William and Sapper Hill. Most of these features were mutually supporting.

Brigadier Thompson knew that, once he had gained a foothold, he would have to tackle these features, and it was essential that he had a secure rear area where reinforcements and supplies could be built up. Ajax Bay, with its sea outlet into Falkland Sound was ideal, although it entailed a long re-supply route to his forward positions. Here in the rocky hills and summits the enemy could establish extremely strong positions which were not easy to identify. Although there would initially be a shortage of troop lift helicopters, the impending arrival of four Chinooks in the *Atlantic Conveyor* would ease the situation.

A complete lack of air photographic cover did nothing to help the situation. In barren countryside such as this, it would mean a prolonged period of night patrolling to assess the enemy's strengths and positions. Indeed, it was the excellent aggressive patrolling of the SAS with naval gunfire support that forced the Argentines to evacuate the westernmost ridge. With the loss of three Chinooks on 25 May there was nothing left for the infantry but to march. After the yomp forward by 45 Commando and 3 Para, 42 Commando were able to fly forward by night to the slopes of Mount Kent and Mount Challenger to establish observation points from where they could observe enemy movements on the next range. The weather often closed visibility down to less than a hundred yards.

From June it was to be the war of the junior leader. For the Commanding Officers to assess and plan their individual attacks, it was necessary to have as much information about the enemy, routes, minefields and obstacles as possible. The distance from their forward positions to their objectives was about 6,000 yards. The ground was open with virtually no cover, boggy and crossed by dangerous stone runs which covered nearly half of the ground. These 'rivers' of large slippery boulders were often 300 yards wide and 1,000 yards long, which made them almost impassable by night. Routes had to be found and marked to avoid them. Both the commandos and the paras were experts at patrolling and their highly professional work during the next few days ensured that the commanders had the best possible intelligence. The Royal Engineers provided the necessary expertise at mine clearing and route marking.

The attack on Goose Green and Darwin, which had been politically pressed from Whitehall, had allowed only one night's patrolling before the attack. This had undoubtedly led to many casualties that could probably have been avoided. Brigadier Thompson was determined that this should not happen again and

*The Argentinian force of more than 12,000 men, about half of them Infantry, were spread around the main settlements, including Fox Bay and Port Howard in West Falkland. In order to open Goose Green as a fighter base, an Infantry regiment and Argentine Air Force personnel were deployed. With a very long coastline it was impracticable to defend all possible British landing sites.*

WEST FALKLAND — EAST FALKLAND

*Pebble Island* **Naval Air Elements** *(120 men)*

*King George Bay*

Port Howard ●
**5 Regt**
**9 Eng Regt(−)**
*(780 men)*

*Ajax Bay*

● Port San Carlos
● San Carlos

*Berkeley Sound*

**STANLEY** ● Port William

*Queen Charlotte Bay*

Fox Bay
**8 Regt**
**9 Eng Coy(−)**
*(890 men)*

Darwin ●

*Lafonia*

*Carlos Water*

**25 Regt**
**601 AA Bn**
Airport

*Lively Island*

**2 Regt**
**12 Regt**
**601 AA Bn(−)**
**Airforce personnel**
*(1,200 men)*

**3 Regt**
**4 Regt**
**6 Regt**
**7 Regt**
**5 Marine Inf Bn**
*(8,400 men)*

N

0  5  10    20
miles

*General Menendez expected the final British attack to come from the south in the region of Port Pleasant and Fitzroy. However he had sufficient forces to maintain strong defensive positions on all the major features to the west of Stanley. He was forced to keep reserves (right) in the east to counter a possible amphibious landing there. The main administrative personnel were at Stanley airfield.*

*From the outset it was clear that individuals would have to carry heavy loads on their backs, up to 140 lbs in some cases. Ammunition, not normally carried on exercises created an extra weight problem. L/Cpl Bone of 42 Commando man-packs a MILAN firing post during trials aboard* Canberra.

would only launch his Brigade attack when *he* was ready. As with the original amphibious landings, diversion attacks were planned to distract the enemy's attention. Fortunately the Brigade Commander had SBS, SAS and the Royal Marines Mountain and Arctic Warfare Cadre available to him as Brigade troops. This was a luxury he exploited to the full. He had no need to deprive Commandos and Battalions of men to deal with small enemy pockets such as those eliminated at Fanning Head and Top Malo House.

With no enemy armour to contend with, 2 Para had found at Goose Green that the 66 mm rocket launcher was excellent at sangar-busting and taking out small pockets of resistance. This information was well digested by the rest of the force and they hoped that the 84 mm Carl Gustav with its heavier warhead and longer range would prove even more effective. However, it was rather heavy and cumbersome, and although carried might have been better dispensed with. Had there been an anti-tank threat, matters would have been different. The larger MILAN, with a 25 lb missile and 3 lb explosive warhead was far too heavy to be readily man-packable. Another weapon which disappointed was the 81 mm mortar. The soft ground often engulfed the base plate making it useless

after a couple of rounds. However, the GPMG, described by many troops as a superb weapon, won most of the firefights. The LMG, modified from the World War 2 Bren Gun, was also carried by the marines and its accuracy and flexibility was commented upon very favourably. It had the added advantage of being lighter and therefore better against aircraft and among the rocks because of its lack of a feed belt. An interesting comment, made by some infantry, was that the clarity of the Falklands air made it difficult to judge distances accurately.

The open ground dictated that all attacks must be by night. Even then tactical use of folds in the ground had to be used where possible as it was known that the Argentines possessed good night vision equipment. A silent approach in the first phase attacks would also catch the enemy unawares, with a heavy artillery concentration expertly directed on the ground ahead as soon as they were spotted, which would neutralise them until the final moments. Every commander had to consider carefully his line of approach, not only to surprise the enemy but to minimise his own casualties. The final assaults would be almost old fashioned by comparison, the infantry, covered by flank supporting fire, finishing the job with bullets and bayonets.

# Air Strategy and Tactics

This was a strange air war. Over 8,000 miles separated the two combatants at the start and the British assessment of the size and capability of the Argentine Air Force (Fuerza Aerea Argentina *or FAA*) and the Naval Air Arm (Comando Aviacion Naval Argentina *or CANA*) was uncertain. Most intelligence efforts had of late been directed towards the Warsaw Pact countries rather than Latin America. The initial assessment was a maximum of 250 enemy fighter and attack aircraft, with a very limited air-to-air refuelling capability, some ancient long range Boeing reconnaisance planes and up to ten Hercules C-130 transports. In addition there were thought to be four large troop carrying helicopters (Bell 212 and Chinook) and a number of small ones. In fact the Argentines possessed rather less serviceable aircraft than anticipated. Certainly the Skyhawks and Mirages posed a long range threat, as did the Super Etendards, the only planes that could carry the Exocet AM.39 missile. Undoubtedly Pucaras, of which the Argentines had over 100, and Aermacchis MB-339s would provide close support from the one airfield and numerous strips on the Falklands.

In order to re-capture the Islands, the British had to achieve air superiority over the combat zone, deny re-supplies to the enemy and protect the Task and Amphibious Forces. Only Stanley provided a sealed and metalled runway long enough (1,360 yards) for large transports and heavily laden fighter bombers to take off. It was fortunate for the British that the distance from the Falklands to the mainland was 400 miles, about the maximum range at which Argentine Skyhawks, Daggers and Mirages could operate without re-fuelling. This meant they would be unable to maintain a Combat Air Patrol (CAP) over the battle area. It always seemed unlikely that the aircraft carrier *25 de Mayo* would pose a serious air threat, nor was there any serious British intention of bombing the Argentine mainland.

As far as aircraft were concerned the Sea Harrier and Harrier GR3 were untried in combat and their numbers were severely limited . . . only 34 were ever available and usually no more than 25 at any one time. Serious losses in combat or by accident would pose an insurmountable problem and the loss of one of the aircraft carriers would probably mean the whole campaign being aborted.

Strategically Ascension Island was required as a forward base and this was built up from 2 April. Even then it was still 3,800 miles from the Falklands; and mounting bombing, reconnaisance and re-supply missions was a daunting prospect of very long flying hours producing comparatively little material damage. The British plan was to try to put Stanley airfield out of action from the moment the TEZ was declared on 30 April. This was done by despatching Vulcans, supported by Victor tankers, on 'Black Buck' bombing raids. Five of these raids were carried out at enormous logistic expense, and although the damage caused was not great, it had a considerable uplifting morale effect at home. The Royal Navy started naval gunfire bombardments of the airfield and installations on 1 May and continued almost nightly till the end of the war. Even so Argentine Hercules continued to use Stanley airfield until the night before the war ended, a remarkable flying achievement. However the continual harrassment did have a harrowing morale effect on the defenders, and also had the effect of limiting the use of the airfield to occasional, long

*Damaged Argentinian Aermacchi MB 339s and Pucaras near Stanley airfield after the war. Stanley can be seen in the background.*

*From D-Day onwards Combat Air Patrols were maintained by Harriers in north, west and south of West Falkland, while HM ships were responsible for air defence within Falkland Sound.*

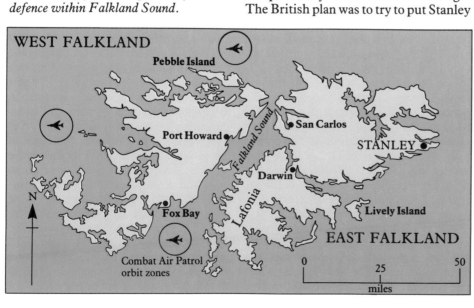

WEST FALKLAND

Pebble Island

Port Howard

San Carlos

STANLEY

Falkland Sound

Darwin

Lafonia

Fox Bay

Lively Island

EAST FALKLAND

N

Combat Air Patrol orbit zones

0     25     50

miles

*The distinctive rotating radome of a Thorn EMI Searchwater radar fitted beneath a Sea King helicopter. It is used for detecting and tracking sea-skimming missiles and low flying aircraft.*

winder missiles proved almost infallible. The fact that no Harrier was shot down in air combat compared with the 23 fighters lost by the Argentines was a major factor in winning the war. Mostly the pilots had to rely on their own eyes to detect an enemy aircraft and never was the VIFF (Thrust Vectored In Forward Flight) used in air combat. From D-1 the Fleet Air Arm were able to maintain a dawn to dusk CAP over the landing zone, subsequently covering the battles as they moved eastwards. They had virtually won air superiority by 25 May controlling the air space above the combat zone except for an occasional hit and run raid. This was achieved from just two aircraft carriers, although later a refuelling strip, nicknamed HMS *Sheathbill* was established above San Carlos Water, enabling Harriers to refuel and maintain lengthier air patrols.

The skill of the helicopter pilots cannot be underestimated. From the early days they flew in Special Forces patrols at low level at night across unknown territory, hugging the rolling hills and depositing their precious cargoes well inland. Their subsequent tactical flying ferrying troops, supplies and ammunition forward, considerably over-stretching their normal flying hours, was a highly skilled piece of professionalism. Their night flying, aided by passive night goggles, saved countless lives in the evacuation of casualties, not only to the advanced dressing stations on land but back to the comfort of the ships at sea.

Tactically, a difficult air war was won with a great deal of planning and a minimum of fuss. The ground crews, both on land and at sea, provided a remarkably high degree of serviceability of aircraft . . . and the aircraft themselves stood up to almost continuous flying. With the advent of sophisticated ground to air missiles, ground attacks made by Harriers in the battle area also had to be carefully planned and identified to avoid time spent over the zone. Too many close support missions were mounted without good prior reconnaisance, which could have proved disastrous against a more determined enemy.

range aircraft and those that had been brought over in April.

The protection of the Task Forces was in the hands of the Fleet Air Arm. The Royal Navy's Type 965 long range surveillance radar fitted in most ships provided limited coverage, but it was almost useless against low flying aircraft. Sea King helicopters, although mainly concerned initially with anti-submarine warfare, were also able to provide some over-the-horizon radar warning. The loss of so many warships during the campaign reflects the lack of an effective airborne early warning system. The RAF Nimrod, a maritime surface surveillance aircraft was fitted with an air-to-air refuelling capability and used its Searchwater radar to good effect. There is no doubt that Special Forces who had been landed on the mainland played a significant part in warning the Fleet that aircraft had left Argentine airfields, but there was no way of indicating their route or targets. Similarly, submarines patrolling nearer inshore probably reported aircraft crossing the coast, but again their information could be no more than a general warning of attack.

The battle in the air proved the turning point of the war. In every way the Sea Harrier was a more adaptable, manoeuvrable and compact aircraft than anything the Argentines possessed. Their Side-

# Tactical Battle for Stanley

Brigadier Julian Thompson had successfully got his 3 Commando Brigade ashore almost without casualties and had won the battle for Goose Green and Darwin. Meanwhile the Royal Navy and Royal Air Force had all but gained supremacy of the seas and skies around the Falklands. By the time Major General Jeremy Moore with his Divisional Headquarters arrived on the Islands on 30 May, two units of 3 Commando Brigade, 45 Commando and 3 Para had yomped forward to Teal Inlet and Douglas Settlement and 42 Commando were preparing to fly forward to Mount Kent. 2 Para still occupied Goose Green while the reluctant 40 Commando remained as the defensive troops around the Brigade Maintenance Area and Forward Dressing Station at Ajax Bay.

Moore knew that the enemy strength still between him and Stanley was about 9,000 men with a further 2,000 Argentinian troops beleaguered on West Falkland, mainly at Fox Bay and Port Howard. Only half of the defending troops were infantry, the majority being poor quality conscripts who were reported to be badly led by their officers and NCOs. There is no doubt that the Argentinians still expected another seaborne landing near Stanley airport to take the capital from the north, south or east and Special Forces patrols probing the area, kept the enemy guessing. General Menendez was therefore forced to keep a strong defensive garrison in the east, leaving only about 3,000 men defending the western approach across the mountains.

These men were in very strong positions, with excellent lines of sight and fields of fire across the barren country. Extensive minefields had been laid, mostly unmarked, and the troops were reasonably well sheltered from the prevailing strong westerly winds. In the rear they had the support of both 155 and 105 mm artillery. Indeed they could have defended these positions from attacks in almost any direction, such was the domination from the rugged peaks and ridges.

*5 Infantry Brigade land at the San Carlos beachhead by LCU, under the watchful eye of a Scots Guards sentry manning a .50 Browning machine gun.*

General Moore and his staff had voyaged from Ascension in *QE 2* and then transferred to *Fearless* for the crossing to San Carlos. Because of a communications misfit in the liner, he had been out of touch with the current situation in the Falklands for more than a week. After careful briefing at all levels, he ordered Brigadier Thompson to continue towards Stanley while 5 Infantry Brigade were arriving in the next few days. Moore refused a request to release

the frustrated 40 Commando from their mundane defensive role while he considered the options open for the final defeat of the enemy. Tasking and command of the SBS and SAS was also taken over immediately by the divisional headquarters.

With the excellent intelligence gleaned from both Special Forces reports and the forward probing by 3 Commando Brigade's patrols, it was clear that the enemy were expecting an attack to come from the Fitzroy area in the south. After London's insistence on early action after the initial landings, which resulted in more casualties at Goose Green than might have been the case in a more carefully considered operation, Moore and Thompson had no intention of being hurried into hasty action. It was essential that the build up of ammunition, stores and reinforcements in the two forward bases at Teal and Fitzroy should be complete before offensive action could take place. The loss of the Chinook helicopters in the *Atlantic Conveyor* had set back any hopes that forward reserves would be adequate by 8 June, Moore's first planned date for the major attacks. The disaster at Fitzroy put the timings back even further. The reluctance of Commodore Clapp to risk his two assault ships *Fearless* and *Intrepid* forward was understandable as it was known the Argentinians had land based mobile Exocets around Stanley, this meant that the LSLs and LCUs bore the brunt of ferrying troops and supplies forward, abetted by the very busy Sea King and Wessex helicopters.

The weather was deteriorating considerably and having a debilitating effect on the troops in the mountains. Inactivity and uncertainty in the severest of cold and icy conditions could also have an effect on their morale and there were some cases of exposure and trench foot. On the plus side, the low cloud had stopped all Argentinian air activity over the battlefield during the first week of June. This had allowed 5 Brigade to come ashore unmolested and now Moore had the task of getting them forward.

Thompson was keen to get his Brigade, which once again had 2 Para under command, into action, but Moore insisted he should wait until he could be effectively supported. There were seven prominent features upon which the Argentinians had based their defences, and these were too much for one concerted brigade attack, even with four units. From the outset both Commanders had agreed that the attacks should be carried out at night, as the enemy had excellent killing grounds across the open terrain leading up to their positions. Thompson's seasoned and highly skilled brigade of marines and paratroopers lent itself to such an operation.

Moore therefore proposed a two phase attack on successive nights. 3 Commando Brigade to take Mount Harriet, Two Sisters and Mount Longdon with units exploiting forward to Wireless

*Scots Guards move out to their forming up position prior to the final mountain battles for Stanley. The Argentinians were expecting the main thrust to come from the south, but the British built up their forces to the west and north.*

Ridge, Tumbledown and Mount William. The following night 5 Infantry Brigade would attack any features which had not already been captured and continue to Sapper Hill to the south west of Stanley.

These attacks would leave him nothing in reserve, just 40 Commando around San Carlos and a company of Gurkhas at Goose Green. If he was forced to deploy these, his rear flank would be unprotected and might encourage the stranded Argentinians on West Falkland to attack across Falkland Sound. The nearest strategic reserves were 1st Battalion Queen's Own Highlanders, standing by in the UK to be flown to Ascension and thence by Hercules to Goose Green.

One of his major plus factors was the support he would receive from the Royal Navy. Rear Admiral Sandy Woodward had promised to make bombardment ships available to individual units for the night attacks and there was still almost the complete force of Sea Harriers and Harrier GR3s for air cover and close support during the day.

There was little room for error in these plans, and any failure might result in the British government being forced to negotiate with the all but beaten Argentinians. However on the battlefield there were no thoughts of defeat. The numerical odds of the opposing forces had narrowed considerably and everyone was mentally and physically prepared. Once the attacks had been launched the order was to keep the momentum rolling; in the event there was a 24 hour delay in the second phase attacks going through, but once they had succeeded, after rather heavier fighting than was expected, the surrender came quickly.

# Chapter Six
# The Falklands Campaign

A small garrison had been maintained on the Falkland Islands for many years, being provided by the Royal Marines as Naval Party 8901. In their normal role this garrison of two officers and about 35 marines spent a one year tour there before returning home. Their main tasks were to provide the Island government with a small force to patrol the vast expanses of the islands, visiting outlying kelpers and their farms, to train the Falkland Islands Defence Force and provide a military presence in this small dependency. It also enabled Royal Marines to train in unfamiliar and open surroundings and carry out a continuous 'hearts and minds' campaign with the local community. Relationships with the locals were generally warm and friendly and many Royal Marines married Falklands girls, some returning to the islands and settling there after their Service time was completed.

Ships like *Endurance* would visit there regularly, giving them a much needed respite from their Antarctic patrolling and providing training facilities for their small embarked detachment of Royal Marines. Antarctic Survey ships, like the RRS *John Biscoe* and RRS *Bransfield* would also visit to refuel and enjoy a few days ashore in convivial company. The Royal Marines looked forward in great anticipation to these visits, giving them opportunities for football, rugby and social encounters. Indeed in October 1981 they played an 'international' against a visiting Polish trawler and, to their chagrin, lost 5-2.

The local government was increasingly aware of the continuing threat from the Argentines, but it had drifted on so long, that they grew to live with it without ever being quite able to ignore it. Somehow no-one really believed a military invasion would happen. But it was the proposed withdrawal of *Endurance* from the area at the end of its final patrol in March 1982, that gave the locals increased cause for concern. They felt the

British Government was abandoning them. The Ministry of Defence was seeking economy measures and although the cost of maintaining *Endurance* was no more than £2 million a year, this cut would not be seen by our NATO allies as affecting our contribution in Europe. Lord Trefgarne had announced the proposed withdrawal in the House of Lords in June 1981, and Argentine enquiries were soon circulating asking if the British intended to withdraw completely from the area.

The new Nationality Bill had also been in the 1981 Government programme and although aimed primarily at restricting the flood of immigration into England of Hong Kong Chinese expected when that colony was handed over to China in 1998, it had deeper effects on Gibraltar and the Falklands. In essence it only allowed automatic right of entry to Britain of those who had at least one grandparent born in Britain. This denied the right to third and fourth generation settlers to emigrate to Britain and was seen in the Falklands with growing concern that Britain was abandoning the colony. There were pleas by Lord Soames and others to make a special case for the Falklanders and similarly placed Gibraltarians. Each case was voted on and whilst Gibraltar won, the Falklands motion was defeated by one vote, putting them in the same category as Hong Kong Chinese. This was almost the last straw and the Governor Rex Hunt and the Royal Marines garrison found difficulty in consoling the 1,800 population that Britain was not abandoning them. This was not lost on the Argentinians who were looking for any excuse to turn their people away from internal strife and to invade the Falklands.

When *Endurance* paid her final visit to Port Stanley, Captain Nick Barker's report on his recent visit to the mainland did nothing to reassure the Islanders, and there was a general state of depression. During the latter part of 1981

Major Gareth Noott and his NP 8901 had endeavoured to defuse the situation. They had exercised near Port Edgar on West Falkland using shepherd's huts as their base. One of the drivers, Marine Tyler, had spent time assisting a leading civilian ornithologist in setting up and storing Steeple Jason, one of the outlying islands. Other patrols had visited outlying farms by sea in the MV *Forrest*, whilst others had trekked overland from their base at Moody Brook Camp on the outskirts of Stanley.

The 'Royal Marine Barracks' at Moody Brook were wooden built but offered reasonable comfort to the marines. It was surely coincidence that the DOE letter giving financial approval for the complete rebuilding of the camp was signed on 1 April 1982! The marines grew their own garden produce, bred their own ducks and geese to supplement their rations and had seven pigs fattening up under their care. In their spare time, some became radio announcers or disc jockeys on the local Falkland Islands Broadcasting Service, while the signals NCO, Sergeant Cruickshank, as an amateur radio 'ham' had in the past 12 months made more than 2,000 contacts in over 60 countries. In October 1981 he was monitoring the progress of round the world yachtsman David Cowper. Thus was the life enjoyed by the Royal Marines detachment, some of whom volunteered for a second or third tour down south.

The commander of the 1978 detachment, Major Ewen Southby-Tailyour, who fell in love with the islands during his tour was to play a key role in the campaign. During his twelve months tour of duty he had charted every creek as well as the shoreline of the coast. He wrote a navigational guide to the islands but could find no publisher until after the campaign. The result of his hobby was to prove invaluable to the planners, as he had an encyclopaedic knowledge of the Falklands and was much in demand at

briefings and for lectures on wildlife during the voyage south.

It so happened that the new NP 8901, under Major Mike Norman had arrivěd in Port Stanley in the *John Biscoe* on 29 March disembarking directly to Moody Brook Camp, the old detachment moving into private accommodation in Stanley in preparation for returning home. Before leaving UK, Norman had been told by the briefers in London that the latest talks between Britain and Argentine had broken down and that 'life might get very uncomfortable in the next six months or so'. However they did not expect a military invasion. Because *Endurance* was sorting out the scrap metal merchants in South Georgia, there was some doubt as to how the new NP 8901 would get from Montevideo to the Falklands. The *John Biscoe* was waiting for them and it was ironic that, as they approached Port Stanley, they were buzzed by a low flying Argentine Hercules, and even waved at it!

On 1 April Rex Hunt (with the appropriate initials RM) summoned the two Royal Marines Majors to tell them that

*Chief Petty Officer Peter Holdgate's famous photograph that sums up the Falklands campaign. Heavily laden Corporal Peter Robinson of 45 Commando 'yomps' through the mud and slush into Stanley after the cease fire. The strong breeze blew the flag off his aerial into a minefield from where he gingerly retrieved it.*

British Government intelligence indicated a large number of Argentine ships were sailing towards the islands, including an aircraft carrier, cruiser, support ships and landing craft. The invasion force could be expected off Cape Pembroke at first light. Norman had taken over operational command from Noott at 0900 that morning. The invasion was expected from the east with the airport as its prime target. Rex Hunt made it quite clear to the marines that shooting was to be avoided in the town of Stanley if at all possible.

Observation Posts were immediately posted in Pembroke lighthouse and on Sapper Hill, while a quick reaction force was held at immediate notice. The total number of men at hand was 85, including

10 naval personnel. *Endurance* had already sailed for South Georgia on 19 March with nine ranks of NP 8901. During the next 24 hours, briefings were held, classified material was destroyed and weapons and ammunition were issued. 23 members of the FIDF volunteered their services, most of them being very young men, and one of them Bill Curtiss immobilisd the directional aircraft beacon.

Moody Brook Camp was evacuated on 1 April when it was apparent that the Islands were about to be invaded the following morning. It was just as well as the first Argentinians made straight for the camp and all but demolished it in a heavy and unprovoked fusilade of fire and grenades around dawn. It is doubtful if any of the marines would have survived. So much for the Argentinians promise to take the islands peacefully. The defending force was organised into an operational Headquarters, six sections of Royal Marines and one of Royal Navy. The aim was to delay the invading force to gain time for negotiations. The scene was set.

# Argentine Landings on the Falklands

When an Argentine Air Force Hercules C-130 made an emergency landing at Port Stanley airport on 11 March 1982, it was not clear whether the emergency was accidental or contrived. It certainly confirmed that the runway could handle heavy transport planes. The incident was reported to London, where it was presumably coupled with the subsequent report of the landing by scrap metal merchants at Leith Harbour on 19 March. This should not have surprised the British as Constantino Davido, who was in charge of the legal dismantling of the Christian Salvensen Company whaling station agreed by a 1979 contract, had sent a letter to the British Embassy in Buenos Aires on 9 March advising them he was sailing with 41 salvage workers for Leith. There had been no objection, although his recce of the area in December 1981 had aroused suspicion with Governor Rex Hunt who had demanded his expulsion.

The Argentines had now put Operation *Alpha*, the stationing of a military presence on South Georgia under the guise of a scientific station similar to that they had already established on South Thule, into motion. The salvage party included a number of naval personnel and had sailed in the Argentine naval ship *Bahia Buen Suceso*, arriving at Leith on 19 March, sailing again on 21st. This action triggered the despatching of *Endurance* from Port Stanley on 20 March with a further 9 Royal Marines added to her permanent detachment of an officer and 12.

At South Georgia on 31 March Captain Nick Barker summoned Lieutenant Keith Mills and ordered him to disembark his detachment to provide a military presence ashore, protect the British Antarctic Survey Team and maintain surveillance over the Argentine scrap metal merchants at Leith. He was also told only to shoot in self-defence and not to endanger life, a confusing mixture. An hour later *Endurance* sailed. At first light next day a four man observation team was sent to Jason Ridge to observe and report on the Leith situation, and later that day they heard a broadcast by Rex Hunt saying an invasion of the Falklands was imminent. At 0600 they heard that landings had been reported.

Mills deployed his men to defensive positions in the knowledge that the Argentine *Bahia Paraiso*, with helicopters and about 40 marines were aboard. The jetty was booby-trapped and home-made mines buried in the sand and pebbles. He ordered the 13 members of BAS to congregate in the church half a mile away from what proved to be the main battle ground at King Edward Point while their leader Steve Martin manned the communications in the radio shack. Just after midday on 2 April the *Bahia Paraiso* appeared in Grytviken Bay but probably because it was blowing a strong gale she soon disappeared and was reported a few hours later in Leith harbour where the corvette *Guerrico* was also seen.

After a night of waiting in which the *Bahia Paraiso* had managed to make radio contact with Mills ordering him to surrender, the weather eased and the enemy closed in. At 1030 on 3 April the two Argentine ships appeared and a helicopter landed eight men about 40 yards from the marines' positions and opened fire. Mills tried delaying tactics by radio

which the Argentines ignored. Further Puma and Alouette helicopters disgorged men, one of the aircraft being hit by small arms fire and crashing on the far side of the bay. Marine Dave Combes engaged and hit the corvette with the second round from his 84mm Carl Gustav and the ship was also engaged with automatic fire. She withdrew and endeavoured to use her heavy armament to shell the marines but the elevation gear was so badly damaged that shots fell well over their target. However Argentine troops, landed from other helicopters, surrounded the small garrison and engaged it from all sides.

Mills, having achieved his aim of making the Argentines use military force and although he had an enemy section

*Argentine Marines of the Buzo Tactico Group and the 2nd Marine Infantry Battalion landed at Mullet Cove and York Bay during the night of 1/2 April. The southern group split into two, making for Moody Brook Camp and Government House.*

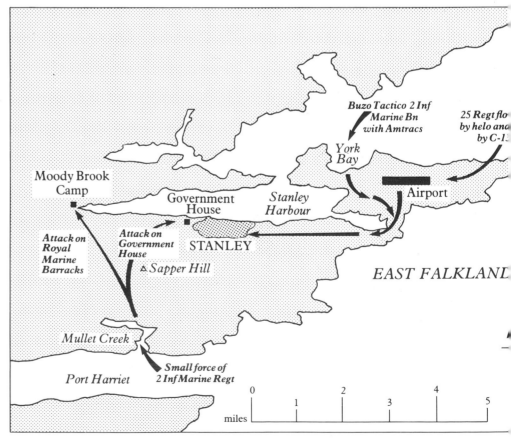

pinned down, realised that his position was hopeless. He already had one NCO badly wounded and there were several Argentine dead. He took the brave decision that surrender was the only way of avoiding further casualties on both sides. Standing up in full view he was greeted by a burst of machine gun fire, but made his position clear. After assurances that his men would be properly treated, he ordered them to lay down their arms. The whole party were subsequently shipped to Porto Belgrano and repatriated through Montevideo, arriving in UK on 20 April.

Meanwhile in the Falklands, Rex Hunt had received a signal from London on 31 March saying that an Argentinian invasion force was approaching Port Stanley, reported to consist of an aircraft carrier, three destroyers, two corvettes, a landing ship and several transports. Indeed they carried not only Argentine Marines of the Buzo Tactico Group but the 2nd Marine Infantry Battalion and

*An Argentine marine lines up captured Royal Marines of Naval Party 8901, after Governor Rex Hunt ordered them to surrender on 2 April to save further casualties. After being repatriated to the UK, these marines formed J Company of 42 Commando and fought in the battle for Mount Harriet.*

an Amphibious Reconnaisance Group. Other supporting arms and infantry reserve battalions were believed to be following.

At 0900 Major Mike Norman took over operational command of the combined Naval Parties 8901 and at 1500 the Governor sent for him and Major Garry Noott telling them an invasion was imminent. Norman's appreciation was that the enemy would probably land on the shelving beaches to the east of Port Stanley with a view to taking the airport first. By 0200 on 2 April he had deployed his Royal Marines, but the area was so vast that his small force might well become isolated if too widely dispersed.

In fact the Argentinians landed south of Port Stanley at Mullet Cove near Port Harriet from the Type 42 destroyer *Santissima Trinidad* soon after midnight and marched the 5 miles via Sapper Hill towards the capital. The invaders presumed the defending marines would still be at Moody Brook Camp and one party made a devastating attack on the building with small arms fire and phosphorous grenades at 0605. The other party made for Government House where they expected to force the Governor to surrender peaceably. In fact they opened fire on Government House about 0615 but their attack was successfully repulsed, the leading officer Capitan Giachino

being the first to be killed in the war. Argentine frogmen had landed at York Bay at 0330 and, reporting it clear, troops had started to come ashore from the LST Cabo San Antonio. From the airport Lieutenant Bill Trollope reported ships to the south and APCs coming over the ridge from York Bay. One was stopped by direct hits with 84mm and 66mm rounds. The British sense of humour even under adverse conditions shone through when a Royal Marine radioed asking what were the priority of three targets. When asked what the targets were he replied 'Target No 1 is an aircraft carrier, target No 2 is a cruiser, target No . . .' at which point the line went dead.

At 0830 it was clear that the enemy had landed in force and were in vastly superior numbers. Hunt and Norman discussed the matter and whilst the latter was eager to break out and take up positions elsewhere, where 'defence would be determined and unrelenting, but would be relatively short lived', the Governor feared that further action might endanger the lives of the civilian population and decided to negotiate a truce. Admiral Carlos Busser, who spoke impeccable English, talked with Governor Rex Hunt, who in turn at 0915 reluctantly ordered the Royal Marines to lay down their arms. The Argentines had suffered 3 killed and 17 wounded whilst the defenders had no casualties.

The Royal Marines were allowed to collect some of their personal belongings when they saw the horrific devastation at Moody Brook, while the Governor donned his full diplomatic regalia and drove to the airport under escort in his London taxi. All the British were flown home via Argentine and Uruguay, landing in England on 5 April, the day that the final six marines of NP 8901, who had been isolated on the other side of the harbour, were captured.

Major Norman and his detachment were to have little rest, for a fortnight later they were on their way south again, twice within a month, to form an extra Company 'J' for 42 Commando and took part in the initial landings at San Carlos and the final mountain battle for Stanley. It was only right that they should have the honour of raising the Falklands flag again over Government House in Stanley after the surrender, only 10½ weeks after they had so ignominiously left.

# Recapture of South Georgia

When the Chiefs of Staff in Northwood surveyed the loss of both the Falklands and South Georgia, their thoughts immediately turned to plans for recovering them. It was apparent that the two groups of islands must be considered as separate tasks and that to capture the Falklands it was essential to have a firm base nearer to the islands than Ascension. Thus it was that South Georgia took on an immediate and unexpected importance. The operation to retake it was codenamed *Paraquet*, but a corruption in an early signal changed the spelling to *Paraquat*, a far more appropriate name being a commercial brand of weed killer.

Before the Task Force had sailed from UK, the troops to retake South Georgia had been earmarked and briefed. Brigadier Thompson's assessment was that, because of the terrain and conditions, only highly trained arctic warfare troops would suffice. As 42 Commando had been the only unit to deploy on winter exercises in Norway earlier that year, it was M Company, under Captain Chris Nunn who were chosen. The 60 or so Argentine military were likely to be either at Grytviken or Leith and that occupation of the high ground overlooking these two would be vitally important. To M Company were added a section of 42 Commando's Reconnaissance Troop, two Naval Gunfire Support Observer parties from 148 Battery, a section of 81mm mortars, a small medical party and No 2 SBS Section. Later D Squadron 22 SAS was added and the total force of about 230 men was commanded by 42 Commando's second-in-command Major Guy Sheridan, a highly experienced mountaineer, who had recently traversed the Himalayas on skis.

The Command structure was untidy from the start. Captain Brian Young, commanding *Antrim* was appointed Commander Task Group and had the large SAS Squadron of around 100 men under his operational control, while Sheridan as the Commander of the Land Forces had Lieutenant Colonel Keith Eve as one of his Royal Artillery Gunfire Officers, besides M Company and attachments. Captain Nick Barker in *Endurance* was the most experienced officer of antarctic conditions, topography and tidal conditions. *Plymouth*, *Brilliant*, the

Fleet Stores Ship *Fort Austin* and the Fleet Oiler *Tidespring* made up the task force. In addition the submarine *Conqueror*, with 6 SBS aboard, was deployed in the area against possible enemy surface intrusion, but South Georgia was out of range of land based aircraft. Although the chain of command worked reasonably well, dissention between commanders was apparent with the decision to land SAS patrols on Fortuna Glacier, a disaster saved only by the courageous and skilful helicopter rescue by Lieutenant Commander Ian Stanley.

On 5/6 April 2 SBS flew to Ascension, with Major Cedric Delves and his D Squadron arriving shortly afterwards. M Company and its support arrived on 7th. *Antrim* left the main task group making best speed for Ascension. *Fort Austin* with some SBS and SAS aboard left Ascension on 9 April while the *Antrim* Group left with the military force the following day, *Tidespring* having embarked two troop-carrying Wessex helicopters of 845 Squadron. Although the force was now assembled and planning to retake South Georgia, final cabinet approval to go ahead was not given until 20 April, pending the outcome of negotiations by the US Secretary of State Alexander Haig. *Conqueror* had been patrolling off shore and had reported nothing untoward.

The plan was to land SBS from *Endurance*, to which they had been transferred, to reconnoitre Grytviken and King Edward Point, while the SAS were given the task of reporting on the Leith and Stromness areas. It was expected that the reconnaissances would take five days and subsequent operations would be finalised from their intelligence. 2 SBS would be landed at Hound Bay to the east and traverse Sorling Valley to Cumberland Bay from where they could approach Grytviken from the south. After giving them their tasks, but against Sheridan's professional advice, the SAS decided to land by helicopter on Fortuna Glacier 5 miles to the west of Leith and out of sight and hearing of the Argentines there, and then to make their approach over the harsh terrain and across Fortuna Bay.

On 17 April Mountain Troop of D Squadron, led by Captain John Hamilton, transferred to *Antrim*, but not before having finding an unexpected bonus aboard *Endurance* when they discovered crates of equipment belonging to the Joint Services Antarctic Expedition. One particular prize was Swedish civilian mountaineering boots with which they replaced their army issue DMS boots. Another bonus was the detailed charts and maps carried onboard.

*The SAS initially landed on Fortuna Glacier and the SBS at Hound Bay to keep surveillance over the Argentinians at Leith and Grytviken. Finally the combined force landed at Hestesletten to the west of Moraine Fjord.*

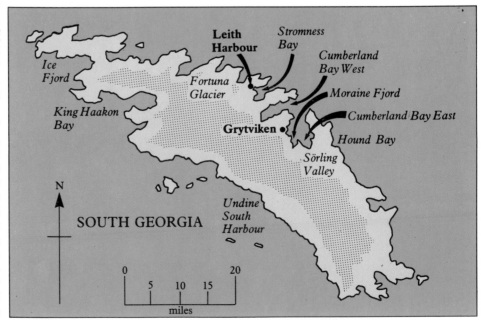

detailed charts and maps carried on-board.

After the word was given by London for the operation to go ahead, *Antrim* and *Tidespring* positioned themselves off Antarctic Bay and the helicopters took off at 1140 on 21 April. The Wessex 3 of *Antrim*'s Flight, piloted by Lieutenant Commander Stanley, was the only one fitted with a computerised flight control system and led the two Wessex 5s over the zig zag route between steep and jagged mountains. Once over the glacier the troop carrying helicopters would have to rely on visual navigation.

The weather was squally and visibility poor but the pilots landed the sixteen SAS troopers safely. For the rest of the day, resting at night, the troopers ploughed onwards making little progress. Next morning the rising gale and deteriorating weather conditions made further progress impossible and Hamilton was reluctantly forced to admit defeat and ask to be lifted off to avoid hypothermia and frostbite. When the Wessex flew in to collect the stranded troopers, the conditions were almost 'white out', the pilots became disorientated and both aircraft crashed, fortunately with no loss of life. Stanley, overloading his own Wessex, lifted off the stranded helicopter crews and SAS troopers safely in two courageous sorties.

Meanwhile 2 SBS encountered the same appalling weather conditions. After being taken ashore by helicopter and marching through Sorling Valley,

the Gemini assault boats dropped to them became so badly holed in the floating ice, the marines could no longer continue their mission and asked to be evacuated and find another route in

With two major setbacks, and a report that the submarine *Santa Fe* was in the area, *Tidespring* with the bulk of M Company aboard withdrew out to sea. On 22 April *Antrim*, made a stealthy approach into Stromness Bay to drop five Geminis with Boat troop SAS who would make their way to Grass Island, a moderate observation point about 2 miles from Leith. But appalling weather again interfered and the Geminis were blown and driven far off course by the strong winds and tides. Three boats eventually reached Grass Island but when they tried to get nearer the next evening, their outboard engines failed and they were blown ashore.

On 25 April Lt-Cdr Stanley sighted and damaged the unsuspecting *Santa Fe* forcing her to remain on the surface. Two more helicopters fitted with AS 12 missiles made further attacks which put the submarine out of action but she just managed to limp into Grytviken harbour.

Major Sheridan, increasingly impatient, now needed to act quickly without the SBS and SAS intelligence he had hoped for. He gathered together all available manpower, M Company Headquarters, the bulk of the company being 200 miles away, the Reconnaissance Section, SBS and SAS who were not committed and the Royal Marines de-

tachments of *Antrim* and *Plymouth*, a total of 75 men. Various plans were discussed and discarded. Keith Eve suggested a naval bombardment, Sheridan a direct hellborne assault, but Captain Young agreed to a compromise to avoid casualties and unnecessary damage to buildings. The first of three separate parties landed on the lower slopes of the Hestesletten at 1430 that afternoon and fanned out towards Grytviken. Meanwhile *Plymouth* and *Antrim* kept up a steady barrage from the east of the Barff peninsular, mostly with air burst shells from their 4.5″ guns slowly creeping towards the enemy positions.

At 1705 Captain Bicain commanding the Argentine force of more than 140 surrendered to Major Delves. The only casualties to either side were an Argentine sailor who lost a leg during the attack on the *Santa Fe* and another who was shot when it appeared he was trying to scuttle the submarine.

The exhausting five days culminated with Captain Young's signal '*Be pleased to inform Her Majesty that the White Ensign flies alongside the Union Flag at Grytviken*'. It was the first step in the recovery of the Falklands Islands.

*King Edward's Point showing the British Antarctic survey settlement with the beached submarine 'Santa Fe' in the foreground and the old whaling station of Grytviken in the background. The Royal Marines fought off the Argentinians at King Edward's Point before surrendering.*

# Naval and Air Attacks on Stanley

The main concentration of Argentine Forces was in Port Stanley and near the all important airfield some two miles east of the town. It was at the latter that any retaliatory action would have to be taken to avoid casualties to the 1,000 civilians who lived in the capital. The airfield was operating a busy schedule with stores and reinforcements arriving almost daily. The next most important military target was at Goose Green where there were thought to be about 500 Argentines and a base for the Pucara fighters.

A Total Exclusion Zone was declared by the British on 30 April heralding probable attacks by air and sea on the Falklands and particularly Stanley. In London plans were already afoot to launch a Vulcan attack during the night of 30 April/1 May. Accompanied by 11 Victor tankers, two Vulcan bombers, each loaded with twenty one 1,000 lb bombs, took off at one minute intervals in pitch darkness and with no navigation lights, from Ascension around midnight on the first 'Black Buck' raid. The primary Vulcan had pressurisation problems and had to return to Wideawake, but Flight Lieutenant Martin Withers and his crew of five pressed on to complete the longest bombing raid in history, nearly 8,000 miles there and back. Two hundred miles from the target the Vulcan dropped to 300 feet to avoid detection, before climbing again to its bombing height of 10,000 feet for the final run in two miles from the target. At 0446 (local), after seven hours in the air and five re-fuellings, all bombs were released in five seconds, the first of the string hitting the runway about half way down and the remainder falling in a line at an oblique angle to the runway. The raid caught the Argentines completely unawares and the Vulcan was only picked up by the Skyguard fire control radar

*British air attacks in the Stanley Airport area with key Argentinian air defences marked. The lower pattern of 1,000 bomb craters, which just straddle the main runway, was caused by the 'Black Buck One' mission. Two more bombing missions were flown and two further 'Black Buck' sorties were aimed to neutralise enemy radar installations by attack with Shrike missiles.*

10 miles out and this was immediately jammed.

The raid probably had more morale effect than actual structural damage as the press splashed their headlines across the world. In order to supplement the success of this raid, twelve Sea Harriers led by Lieutenant Commander Andy Auld were launched from *Hermes* at 0745 for a low level bomb attack on Port Stanley airfield and Goose Green. Dropping a mix of nine air burst and three delayed action 1,000 lb bombs they caused considerable damage and consternation at Stanley, while Lieutenant Commander Rod Frederiksen with three more Sea Harriers caught Goose Green completely unawares destroying at least one Pucara. The Argentinians at last knew the British meant business.

This was not the end of the first day's action as *Glamorgan*, *Alacrity* and *Arrow* steamed towards Stanley for the initial naval bombardment during the afternoon continuing spasmodically until well after dark. They fired 4.5" air burst shells over the airfield before they were themselves attacked by Dagger fighters who slightly damaged both *Glamorgan* and *Alacrity*. The frigates used their Lynx aircraft as spotters, and *Alacrity*'s became the first helicopter to attack a surface ship when she exchanged fire with the patrol boat *Islas Malvinas*, nearly being shot down

*The coastal patrol boat* Islas Malvinas, *which was used for inshore transportation between Stanley and outlying settlements, was attacked and disabled by a Lynx helicopter from* Alacrity *when sheltering near Kidney Island on 1 May.*

in the process.

From 1 May onwards, weather permitting, the Royal Navy shelled Port Stanley airfield regularly until the cease fire. On a typical night, over 100 rounds would be fired harassing the enemy, not only in Stanley, but at Darwin, Fox Bay and Fitzroy. *Glamorgan* made the area its own special task. This continual pounding was a great strain on the morale of the poorly trained Argentine infantry. However, despite the damage, Argentinian supplies continued to fly into Stanley. The nightly Argentine C-130s

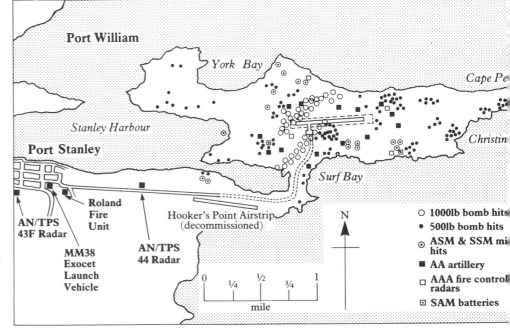

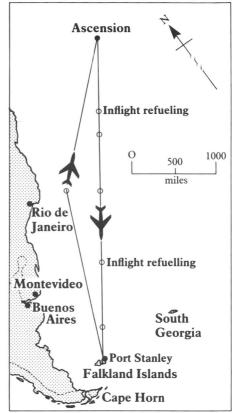

*Stanley airfield after the surrender showing repaired damage to the runway and abandoned Pucara fighters. The Argentines concentrated their main logistic support in the surrounding countryside.*

*Six in-flight refuellings were needed to mount the 'Black Buck One' bombing mission on 1 May. The Vulcan piloted by Flight Lieutenant Withers flew over 7,800 miles, the longest raid ever made.*

developed their own special routine flying in from the mainland without lights and with minimal communications. After landing they would keep their engines running while unloading, taking off within 15 minutes for their return flight. On the runway dummy craters were constructed, and Argentine 155mm guns, which had been flown in on 15 May, occasionally replied to the naval gunfire.

The second 'Black Buck' attack on 3 May successfully dropped its 21 bombs, but none hit the runway and they caused minimal damage. In order to combat enemy radar devices, it was decided to fit the Vulcans with American Shrike radiation-homing missiles and the first of these flew on 'Black Buck 4' (No 3 was aborted) on 29 May. A technical fault caused this also to be aborted five hours out, but 'Black Buck 5' reached the islands on the night of 30 May/1 June. The crew knew where the Argentine radar sites were situated, one near the town not

being attacked to avoid civilian casualties. On a clear night and from 16,000 feet, out of range of anti-aircraft guns, they could see the lights below. With a careful approach Squadron Leader Neil McDougall fired his two missiles and as soon as the crew saw the flash on the ground, the radar signals ceased. It transpired that the Argentine operators had switched off their radar at the last moment and little damage was actually caused.

'Black Buck 6' on 2 May with four Shrikes aboard was nearly thwarted as the Argentines switched off their radar on the aircraft's approach. For 40 minutes McDougall circled the airfield, before making a dummy descent. An enemy radar which was then switched on was identified and hit by two missiles, before the Vulcan had to leave the area. On its way home it broke its refuelling probe and was forced to make an emergency landing in Brazil, where it was impounded until released on 10 June. The final mission '7' on 12 June was similar to the first bombing raid, this time aimed at the airport's facilities and again was highly successful.

Fleet Air Arm attacks against targets around Stanley continued as the weather

permitted and nightly naval bombardments caused much structural damage, *Avenger* later replacing *Arrow* on the gun line. A typical night shoot occurred on 5 June when *Cardiff*, *Active* and *Yarmouth* fired a total of 438 shells on military installations and positions guarding Stanley.

The result of this incessant activity was considerable disruption to the Argentinian supply routes, their forward troops in the mountains being kept very short of logistic support, particularly food. Casualties were surprisingly light, only five Argentinian Air Force ground personnel being killed at Stanley during the whole campaign. It was a slow pulverising war of attrition that wore down the enemy's will as much as his morale. The exceptional skill and professionalism displayed by the Vulcan and Victor pilots caught the public imagination rather more than the unsung daily grind of the pilots at sea in the Task Force, who carried out an equally vital job.

# Sinking of Belgrano and Sheffield

At the end of April the Argentine Naval Fleet commander, Admiral J J Lombardo was considering the options the British had for retaking the Falklands and how best he could counter these actions. A 200 mile Total Exclusion Zone had already been declared and he knew that the approaching British Task Force would outnumber his fleet of one very old aircraft carrier, one even older cruiser, two modern Type 42 destroyers and four old ones, two submarines and three corvettes. All his smaller ships were armed with Exocet M.38s and the *General Belgrano* (Captain H Bonzo) had

*The three Argentine task groups were to pose a pincer threat to the British. HMS* Conqueror *shadowed the* General Belgrano *and torpedoed her 55°18'S, 61°47'W.*

fifteen 6-inch guns, a formidable battery of weapons.

When three British warships were detected off Stanley on 1 May he presumed that an invasion was imminent. His main aim must be to sink the two aircraft carriers. He had already split his limited force into four groups, the carrier group centered around the *25 de Mayo* were some 400 miles north west of the Falklands; the three Corvettes were grouped further to the north; the *General Belgrano* was 300 miles to the south east of the islands escorted by two destroyers and was proceeding eastwards on the edge of the TEZ. A fourth group was further west between the Falklands and South Georgia. The other available asset was the Argentine Air Force but poor liaison between the Navy and Air Force commands meant little co-ordination of attacks on the British Fleet.

On 1 May, unknown to the Argentines, *Conqueror* had been shadowing and reporting the zig-zagging *Belgrano* Group for several hours. The threat posed by this group worried Admiral Woodward and he considered the two options open to the enemy. During the 15 hours of darkness the group could alter course and make 300 miles at full speed towards the British carrier group or alternatively halve the distance between its present position and South Georgia. The *Belgrano*'s guns outranged any he had in his fleet and posed an unacceptable threat to his own Carrier Group, particularly if the weather prevented flying. It was conceivable that the *Belgrano* could shake off the submarine *Conqueror* if it crossed the submerged Burdwood Bank to the south of the Falklands, where the depth was only 150 feet at its shallowest point. This was no place for a fast moving submarine.

Admiral Woodward, himself an experienced submariner, signalled Northwood for permission to change the rules of engagement allowing the submarine to attack the cruiser group. This could only be approved by the war cabinet, who gave their permission, the signal being transmitted at 1330 GMT to the Task Force. It was not until 1730 that Commander CL Wreford-Brown, the captain of HMS *Conqueror*, was fully aware of the changed rules of engage-

ment and made his plans. For two hours he manoeuvred his submarine, coming to periscope depth 5 or 6 times. By 1845 he had reached an ideal position, about 1,500 yards away from the *Belgrano* which was steaming at an economical 10 knots oblivious to the danger. Her position was 35 miles outside the TEZ and close to the Burdwood Bank, the accompanying destroyers on the lee side presumably expecting an attack from the north. At 1857 *Conqueror* fired three Mark 8 torpedoes, two of which hit the port side. The ship should not have sunk under these two torpedoes one of which hit well forward and the other under the after superstructure, but the ship was not at a damage control readiness state and fire quickly spread throughout the ship.

The poor state of readiness in the stricken ship, where many watertight doors had not been closed, undoubtedly led to its sinking with the loss of 321 lives, mostly killed when the torpedoes exploded. The two destroyers *Piedra Buena* and *Bouchard*, instead of picking up survivors, immediately left in pursuit of the submarine, which they faintly detected and depth charged to no effect. When they returned to the scene two hours later there was no sign of the *General Belgrano*. Within ten minutes the ship had listed to 20° and Captain Bonzo gave the order to abandon ship. Over 60 liferafts were launched, some

*HMS* Sheffield, *which was hit by an Exocet missile on 4 May is seen burnt out the day after the Super Etendard attack. This was the first major British loss of the war.*

*The Argentine* General Belgrano *heeling over after being torpedoed by HMS* Conqueror *on 2 May. Although just outside the Total Exclusion Zone, it was assessed that she posed a considerable threat to the Task Force and South Georgia.*

considerably overcrowded with up to thirty men. With the temperature outside the plastic canopies −2°C some sailors froze to death. When darkness fell the wind gusted to 60 knots and 16 ft waves added to their extreme discomfort. Many did not survive the night. It was 48 hours before all the 650 survivors were

*On 4 May the British Task Force was about 100 miles south-east of the Falklands, when it was attacked by Super Etendards. Two Exocet missiles were fired, one of which hit HMS Sheffield.*

picked up. It is perhaps ironic that originally the *General Belgrano* had been the USS *Phoenix*, one of the few ships to survive Japan's attack on Pearl Harbour forty years earlier.

Where the Argentine Navy had now failed, their Air Force took up the challenge. On 1 May they had flown 56 sorties, followed by a further 19 on the day the *Belgrano* was sunk. Admiral Woodward was well aware of the capability, tenacity and skill of the Argentine pilots. He knew that the Argentine Air Force had at least five Exocet AM.39 air launched missiles which could be fired from Super Etendards. He was also conscious that the enemy's main aim was to sink one of his two aircraft carriers. On 4 May an RAF Vulcan had again attacked Port Stanley airfield. His carrier group with both *Hermes* and *Invincible* had run in to within 100 miles of the Falklands. They were protected by three Type 42 destroyers, *Glasgow*, *Coventry* and *Sheffield*, forming a picket line 20-50 miles to the south east. An Argentine Neptune reconnaisance aircraft had reported their position at midday and half an hour later two Super Etendards took off from Rio Grande. They refuelled on the way and turned towards their target. The weather was intermittent with showers and mist at low level but the British picket line was in clear weather below the 1,000 feet cloud base.

The Argentine pilots dropped to sea level, and although there were four Sea Harriers on Combat Air Patrol above, they did not detect the approaching aircraft. *Glasgow* first reported a 'blip' when the attackers were about 25 miles away, warning the other ships. *Sheffield*

switched off her satellite communications equipment and her radar picked up the two Etendards briefly when they climbed to 100 feet to set their Exocets. The range was then only 20 miles and the aircraft were closing at 10 miles a minute. Captain 'Sam' Salt had little time to turn his ship towards the threat and no time to fire chaff rockets as a decoy. A smoke trail six feet above the waves was only detected a minute before the first Exocet struck the *Sheffield* amidships at 1312 tearing the Auxiliary Machine Room apart. Although the warhead did not explode, the missile's fuel ignited, causing blast and smoke while toxic fumes took their toll as flames tore through the stricken ship.

*Arrow* and *Yarmouth* were soon at hand and alongside helping to fight the fires, while Sea King helicopters flew in extra fire fighting and breathing apparatus. By dusk Captain Salt realised that his ship was doomed, ordered it to be abandoned and survivors to be taken off. In all 225 men were saved but 20 officers and men perished, mostly engine room and galley staff. The effect of this loss brought the war forcibly into the homes of the British public with a shock announcement on BBC Television during the nine o'clock news that night. The cabinet had agreed that the name of the ship, the fact that she had been hit by an Argentine missile and was on fire should be mentioned. Naval wives and families at home suffered the agony of not knowing how their loved ones were for nearly 48 hours, while the press and TV crews who had witnessed the rescue of survivors were unable to send back their reports, the first pictures only reaching British screens on 26 May.

When the fires had been extinguished the abandoned *Sheffield* was left floating as bait to try to provoke another Argentine attack, before being taken in tow by *Yarmouth*. In deteriorating weather on the morning of 10 May, the tow having been severed, the ship rolled over and sank.

Two immediate results of this tragedy were to highlight the inadequacy of the Type 965 surveillance radar, and a hurried study by British designers in UK to improve counter-measures against the Exocet. With the sinking of the *Belgrano* and the *Sheffield*, both sides in the conflict were shaken into realising that this was a full scale war.

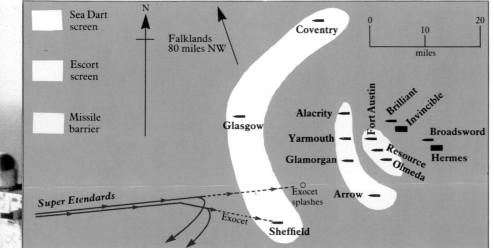

139

# SBS and SAS Operations

As has already been seen members of both the SBS and SAS were heavily involved in the recapture of South Georgia, but there was now an even more important job at hand. That of insertion and surveillance on the Falklands themselves. From 1 May Special Forces patrols had been inserted into the Falklands by helicopter and boats though how many and for how long will probably never be known. Quite rightly a veil of secrecy surrounds many of their operations because their methods, equipment and *modus operandi* should not be aired. However a few of their operations have emerged.

Possibly the first and most secretive of these special forces operations, which can still only be guessed at, was the mission of one of 846 Squadron's Sea King helicopters on 18 May, when it flew from *Invincible* which had steamed close to the Argentine coast that night, and subsequently landed on a sand pit near Punta Arenas in Southern Chile. Here the pilots Lieutenant Richard Hutchings RM and Lieutenant Alan Bennett RN, along with Leading Aircrewman Peter Imrie burnt their helicopter and surrenderd to the Chilean authorities who were friendly to the British. Whether they were heavily laden with SAS troopers destined to 'watch and report' on Argentine aircraft leaving the mainland, or perhaps on a sabotage mission, remains cloaked in obscurity. Some suggest the whole episode was a hoax which alarmed the Argentinians so much that they moved aircraft from some of their airfields in case of interference. It recalls the case of the 'The Man Who Never Was' in World War 2 when a body dressed as Major William Martin, Royal Marines, was washed up on Spanish shores with a false message purporting to give details of the Allied landings in Southern Europe. Whatever the mission, hoax or otherwise, the three gave themselves up on the eve of the British landings amidst a blaze of publicity, and all were subsequently decorated.

While plans were being formulated for the landings in Falkland Sound, the British suspected that a small grass airstrip used by Pucara fighters was being reinforced on Pebble Island, in their rear. On 11 May a recce party from Boat troop of D Squadron landed by canoe on West Falkland, making their way over three nights to observe and they reported 11 aircraft on the airstrip. On 14 May 45 men of D Squadron under Captain John Hamilton were landed by helicopter 5 miles from the spot, marched to the target under cover of *Glamorgan*'s 4.5" barrage and extra illumination from their own 81mm mortars. At 0245 they attacked and destroyed all 11 aircraft, blew up a ton of ammunition and cratered the runway. The Argentinians effected a small counter attack to no avail. *Glamorgan* stayed inshore to cover the withdrawal and *Hermes* helicopters picked up the entire force, the only British casualties being two wounded.

However this success was to be followed by tragedy only 5 days later. During the final cross-decking of troops before D-Day between *Hermes* and *Intrepid* the last Sea King helicopter sortie was possibly hit by an albatross and crashed into the sea. 22 died in this crash including 18 SAS, many of whom had taken part in the South Georgia and Pebble Island operations.

Naval Gunfire Observer Teams, mainly of Royal Artillery, sometimes accompanied SBS and SAS ashore and one such was landed on Fanning Head, overlooking San Carlos, the day before D-Day. These teams always ensured accurate gunfire being brought to bear in support of operations ashore. By this time 3 SBS had joined the Force and it was their favourable reports on San Carlos that enabled the entire force to land unopposed and begin the task of re-occupying the islands. The SBS had set up beach landing lights to guide the leading craft. Meanwhile a large SAS patrol from D Squadron were helicoptered in further south where it was known there was a large Argentine garrison in the Goose Green and Darwin areas. They were supported by *Ardent*. After a 24 hour forced march they put in a diversionary attack against the large garrison there, who thought they were being attacked by a battalion.

After the San Carlos landings, SBS and SAS patrols continued to be deployed to gather further intelligence. Only three days later a large patrol from G Squadron went forward to clear Mount Kent, at 1500 feet the highest point in the range overlooking Port Stanley. Their task was to report on exact dispositions and strengths of the enemy so that Brigadier Thompson could formulate his plans for later operations. They were also able to control naval bombardments and close air support strikes to disrupt the enemy. One SAS patrol of four men reported that the Argentinians moved helicopters each night out of Stanley to a position

*A year after the Falklands War the Royal Marines Mountain and Arctic Warfare Cadre recreated the attack on Top Malo House in the film* Firefight. *Here a member of the fire support group uses an M72 at the start of the attack.*

*The M72s were principally used against Top Malo House which was occupied by Argentine Special Forces threatening the advance on Stanley.*

between Mount Estancia and Mount Kent to avoid damage by naval gunfire. At dawn on 26 May they directed a Harrier GR3 on to the returning helicopters, destroying a Puma and damaging others. When Argentine troops moved off this feature on 28/29 May, leaving it inexplicably unoccupied, it opened the way for 42 Commando to move forward. One other aspect of this group was that

*With the Argentinians driven from the house the assault force, armed with M16 rifles and M79 grenade launchers successfully pressed home the attack.*

they were able to instigate valuable psy-ops ably assisted by Captain Rod Bell, a Royal Marines officer who had been born in Costa Rica and spent much of his early life in Latin America. When he joined, he spoke better Spanish than English. He understood the Argentine temperament well. Around 1 June the SAS had established a line to the Joint Argentine Headquarters in Stanley from Estancia House, close to Mount Kent. After the telephone line had been destroyed by British shelling, another was opened and psy-ops were conducted which tried to undermine the resilience of the Argentine Headquarters. In this they were successful and the SAS had an important role in the final surrender.

Earlier on 24 May *Fearless* had landed a 6 SBS reconnaisance team by rigid raiding craft in the San Salvador area to survey Teal Inlet which was the proposed Commando Brigade forward base. It had a deep water harbour and possible landing beaches which would be used before the final assault on Stanley. Other patrols were inserted on East Falkland by *Glamorgan* and *Ambuscade*, while *Avenger* landed SBS at Volunteer Bay to the north of Stanley on 30 May.

That they and other special forces patrols did so with only one accidental loss of life is truly remarkable. They were in continual close proximity with the enemy for long periods in harsh conditions and mostly with only cold food.

The daylight action at Top Malo

House was of a different nature. The M & AW Cadre were 20 strong, all NCOs and had been used as additional forward patrols since before D-Day. One of them, on a Teal Inlet had reported Argentine Special Forces occupying the high ground overlooking the settlement. In order to eliminate this threat the Cadre were flown in tactically by an overloaded helicopter of 846 Squadron before first light and assaulted the surprised enemy stronghold at bayonet point just after dawn, killing five, wounding seven and capturing the other five.

Although they left the large scale fighting to the major units, the SAS were involved in a number of skirmishes, one such being when a party from G Squadron were providing a diversionary raid for 2 Para's attack on Wireless Ridge. Landing from rigid raiders from 1st Raiding Squadron Royal Marines for a raid on a fuel depot they found themselves caught in an enemy searchlight and suffered some casualties. For once their actions inhibited the major attack and they finally linked up with elements of 2 Para, but their presence so near to Port Stanley undoubtedly had a morale effect on the enemy.

Several members of the SBS managed to infiltrate into the hulk of an old wreck *Lady Elizabeth* in Stanley Harbour from where they could keep watch on the waterfront. They reported that Argentine Officers congregated each night in the Post Office next to the Town Hall. At dawn on 11 June a Wessex from 845 Squadron flew in undetected and fired two AS 12 missiles from about 5,000 yards, one of which missed the target but hit the Police Station opposite. Even though the war had nearly finished on East Falkland, SAS patrols were still active on West Falkland and it was here that the observation post of Captain Gavin Hamilton, who had already seen action in South Georgia and at Pebble Island, was detected by an Argentine patrol and surrounded. In fighting his way out Hamilton was killed but his brave actions allowed his signaller to escape.

That the SAS and Royal Marines should join forces in the final surrender was appropriate. Colonel Mike Rose, who had had an advisory but roving role during the campaign, along with Captain Rod Bell flew into Stanley after the surrender and were instrumental in arranging the peace terms.

# Landings at San Carlos

The assessment of where the initial landings should take place depended on a wide variety of factors. Perhaps the most important consideration was that the attacking force would be numerically inferior to the defenders, a ratio frowned upon by Staff College teaching. That the British were undoubtedly better trained and equipped might narrow that balance slightly but it was paramount that there should be a miniumum of casualties in the early phase of the operation. Other highly important factors were enemy strength and potential by land, sea and air, accessibility of beaches and the ability of the invading troops to fight and move over extremely difficult countryside in the inhospitable weather of a Falklands winter.

The enemy were assessed to have an enlarged Infantry Brigade, commanded by Brigadier General Oscar Jofre, defending Stanley with at least four infantry regiments and a marine infantry unit, supported by artillery of about 30 Italian 105mm pack howitzers. It was also believed they possessed some wheeled 155mm guns with a range of 13 miles, which could be towed or lifted by their two Chinook helicopters. A full complement of supporting arms, including engineers and armoured cars and possibly some amphibious APCs as had been seen when they overran the islands, made this a formidable force. In addition there was an Infantry Regiment of about 500 men at Darwin and Goose Green and a further Brigade on West Falkland. The probable strength of the enemy was assessed at over 11,000, about three times the size of the reinforced 3 Commando Brigade.

As far as the air threat was concerned, the enemy were known to have the Tiger Cat surface to air missile as well as the British Blowpipe and maybe others. From intelligence gleaned they appeared to have about 60 aircraft on the island ranging from Pucara and Aermacchi MB-339 fighters to Chinook, Puma and Iroquois helicopters, besides some transport aircraft. There were 34 airstrips on the Falklands most capable of operating the smaller fighters and of taking helicopters. On the mainland, there were up to 130 aircraft capable of supporting attacks on the Falklands some 400 miles away.

The greatest deficiency in the planners armoury was a lack of air photographs. Without them Brigadier Thompson was severely handicapped. However Major Southby-Tailyour's unpublished notes on the Falklands coastline was of infinite value, giving details of the hinterland as well as the approaches, shore texture and gradients.

The landings in San Carlos Water involved the largest armada of amphibious shipping mustered since Suez. It consisted of the Amphibious Assault Ships *Fearless* and *Intrepid*, five LSLs, the liner *Canberra* and the two ferries *Norland* and *Europic Ferry* to carry the landing force, being supported in Falkland Sound by the destroyer *Antrim* and the frigates *Broadsword*, *Ardent*, *Brilliant*, *Antelope*, *Argonaut*, *Plymouth* and *Yarmouth*. In addition the RFAs *Stromness* and *Fort Austin* were close at hand from which troop carrying Sea Kings could operate. Providing air cover further out to sea were the aircraft carriers *Hermes* and *Invincible* with their escorts. Admiral Woodward had stated as early as 6 May that he could not guarantee air superiority over the landing area and he would not risk either of his aircraft carriers close inshore as the Harriers would be required as defence against the Argentinian air threat.

On 13 May aboard *Fearless*, still 1,000 miles from the Falklands, Brigadier Thompson gave his orders for the landings, Operation *Sutton*. It was based on Major General Moore's directive issued on 12 May which ordered him to secure a bridgehead into which reinforcements could be landed; to push forward as far as maintenance of security allowed and establish moral and physical domination over the enemy. The Operation Order of 47 pages had been given to subordinate commanders 24 hours earlier. The exact date and time of D-Day, H-Hour (when the first landing craft would beach) and L-Hour (when the first wave of helicopters would land) would follow. The timings would be in Zulu time (GMT) four hours ahead of local time.

The following night came the SAS raid on Pebble Island which destroyed all enemy fighter planes there and on 15 May civilians aboard all ships including the Press Corps, were read the Declaration of Active Service, placing them under military discipline. On the next day came reports of a company of Argentinians on Fanning Head overlooking San Carlos Water to the north, and if these were armed with any sort of anti-tank weapon they would pose a threat to the lightly armoured warships and landing craft. A bold plan to land 25 heavily armed SBS with a Naval Gunfire Forward Observer was evolved to neutralise

*A Landing Craft (Utility) (right), a Landing Craft (Vehicle and Personnel) and two Rigid Raiding Craft from the assault ships* Fearless *and* Intrepid *unload near Ajax Bay.*

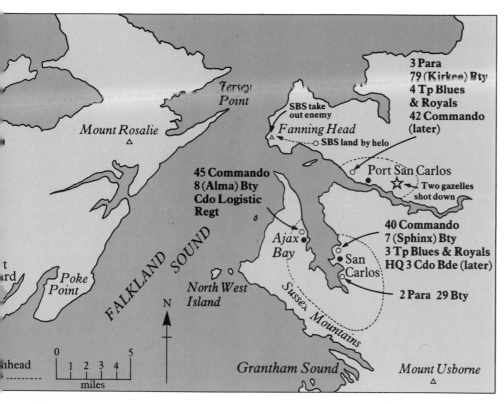

On the map:
- *Jersey Point*
- *Mount Rosalie* △
- **3 Para / 79 (Kirkee) Bty / 4 Tp Blues & Royals / 42 Commando (later)**
- SBS take out enemy
- *Fanning Head*
- SBS land by helo
- Port San Carlos ☆ — Two gazelles shot down
- **45 Commando / 8 (Alma) Bty / Cdo Logistic Regt**
- *Ajax Bay*
- San Carlos
- **40 Commando / 7 (Sphinx) Bty / 3 Tp Blues & Royals / HQ 3 Cdo Bde (later)**
- **2 Para 29 Bty**
- *North West Island*
- FALKLAND SOUND
- *Poke Point*
- *Sussex Mountains*
- N
- 0 1 2 3 4 5 miles
- *Grantham Sound*
- *Mount Usborne* △

*The sheltered landing sites in San Carlos Water, showing 2 Para and 40 Commando near San Carlos, 45 Commando at Ajax Bay and 3 Para at Port San Carlos, where 42 Commando landed later that day. Soon after first light there were 12 vessels in the anchorage.*

them on the night before D-Day and was highly successful. It proved the value of having highly trained specialist troops at the Brigade Commander's fingertips and not committed to the main battle.

On 17 May the main amphibious group caught up with the slower LSLs which had been sent ahead. It was likely that, because of the swell, the cross decking of troops between ships to ensure that group elements married up for the landings would have to be carried out by helicopter rather than landing craft and it would have to be done in daylight. In addition *Canberra*, with the bulk of the Brigade aboard would have to steam on a fixed course with an LPD on either side transferring men singly by jackstay. When dawn broke on 19 May the amphibious force was 300 miles north of the Falklands and the sea had abated slightly enabling a large proportion of the troops to be moved by landing craft. Despite the heaving swell not one man was lost and it was the very last sortie by a Sea

King helicopter that crashed with the tragic loss of 22 men.

H-Hour was fixed for 0230 local time on Friday 21 May. The first warships approached the north of Falkland Sound just after last light on 20 May and the LPDs followed at 2300 anchoring off the entrance to San Carlos Water. The first troops embarked in their landing craft soon after midnight with 40 Commando and 2 Para in the first wave. A small hiccup caused by the Paras having no previous opportunity to practise embarking in the dark delayed H-Hour by 60 minutes. Major Southby-Tailyour travelling in Colonel 'H' Jones LCU led the assault waves down San Carlos Water where they split opposite Ajax Bay with 40 Commando in 4 LCUs and 4 LCVPs landing on Blue Beach One and 2 Para in 4 LCUs on Blue Beach Two. Two LCUs, running into the beach with their bow doors lowered, carried a Scorpion and a Scimitar each of the Blues and Royals ready to give fire support, while another had a Royal Engineer Combat Engineer Tractor.

The craft beached only yards from the waterline some being guided in by torches from the SBS already ashore and the first men touched down, completely unopposed. The marines and paras moved off to dig in on their first objec-

tives, while the landing craft returned for another wave, all being shepherded by *Plymouth* ready to bombard any pockets of resistance, Although the programme was running late, the build up of forces ashore continued unabated, with 3 Para having a small skirmish before occupying Port San Carlos and 45 Commando taking Ajax Bay, a name which was to be synonymous with much heroism later, and the proposed site of the Brigade Maintenance Area.

The first major enemy action was when a Sea King carrying a Rapier firing post and escorted by two Gazelles was fired on by ground forces, the two Gazelles being forced down with the loss of three Royal Marines aircrew, the only casualties of D-Day. The first enemy air attack came at 0855 by a Pucara on the *Canberra* and from then on a continous stream of aircraft from both the mainland and Stanley harrassed the escorting ships and the landing force. The Royal Navy took the brunt of these attacks.

Brigadier Thompson visited his five major units before nightfall, 42 Commando who had been held in reserve afloat during the initial landings were also ashore. It was essential that Thompson's headquarters with all its communications was landed as soon as possible and it was with dismay he received orders that *Canberra*, *Stromness*, *Europic Ferry* and *Norland* must be clear of San Carlos that night. This was the first frustrating intervention from his masters. He had planned to use *Canberra* as a floating field dressing station. In addition the ships carried many unit stores including 90,000 rations, replacement radio batteries and second line ammunition, none of which were seen again until after the campaign was over. The original plan had been to land only each unit's first line of supplies and a maximum of two days War Maintenance Reserve. All other stocks, together with unit echelons and the Commando Logistic Regiments would remain afloat. This unexpected withdrawal of ships caused an enormous change of plan, and had it not been for the extraordinary efforts of the logistic support teams during the night, it could have spelt disaster.

Thus the British force, most of whom had been at sea for more than a month, had successfully gained a first foothold on the Falklands and were poised to consolidate before breaking out.

# Falkland Sound and sinking of HMS Ardent

While the military landings were progressing reasonably smoothly, the Argentine Air Force made it an uncomfortable day for the Royal Navy in Falkland Sound. The northern entrance to the Sound was just over 2 miles wide with high ground up to 750 feet overlooking it from the east at Fanning Head, which also dominated San Carlos Water.

*Ardent* had been the first ship to enter the Sound at 1600 on D–1 with the task of supporting the diversionary SAS raid on Darwin to the south, followed shortly by *Antrim*, who flew off the SBS party which cleared Fanning Head at 1900. *Fearless* came through the narrows at 2245 close in to Jersey Point on West Falkland with *Intrepid* a mile astern. They then docked down to allow their LCUs to float out.

Just after midnight *Brilliant* led in *Canberra*, *Norland* and *Fort Austin* with *Plymouth* in rear. They anchored off San Carlos Water, and at 0100 the silence was shattered when *Antrim*'s guns opened up on Fanning Head in support of the SBS, firing 268 shells in half an hour. The five LSLs sailed into San Carlos Water just ahead of *Canberra*, the most conspicuous ship, which anchored a mile inside Chancho Point.

The landings went ahead and by 0900 there were twelve ships in the narrow confines of San Carlos Water with *Argonaut* guarding the entrance from Falkland Sound. Outside a further five warships patrolled the waters. Soon after first light the Forward Observer with the SAS party saw two Pucaras preparing to take off from Goose Green and called for fire from *Ardent* which succeeded in hitting the runway and destroying an aircraft. However four pairs did take off, one Pucara being shot down by an SAS shoulder-held Stinger missile. The first British casualty was Flight Lieutenant Glover whose Harrier was hit by a British made SAM missile fired by the Argentine Special Forces near Port Howard. He parachuted to safety.

At first light the first Sea Harrier Combat Air Patrol had been over the Sound and a pair of fighters remained within five minutes call for the whole of D-Day. The first aircraft seen by the amphibious force was an MB 339 which slightly damaged *Argonaut* at 0815 before reporting the landings back to Stanley. Soon afterwards an attack by two Pucaras

*A Dagger fighter (Israeli built Mirage 5) flies low over* Sir Bedivere. *On 24 May the ship was hit by a bomb which clipped her crane, passed through a forward bulkhead and exploded in the sea.*

was warded off by *Ardent* with her 4.5in guns and Seacat. 'Air Raid Warning Red' was signalled at 0907 but it was nearly half an hour before three Daggers (Israeli built Mirage fighters) appeared followed by three more, the first fighters to take off from the Argentine mainland. One was brought down but the leader Major Martinez pressed home his attack on *Broadsword* wounding 14 men with cannon fire and damaging the ship's Lynx helicopter. Another aircraft hit *Antrim* with a 1,000 lb bomb causing considerable damage and lodging itself in the seamen's heads without exploding. The next wave again attacked the partially disabled *Antrim* and one Dagger was hit by *Broadsword*'s Seawolf missile only 1,000 yards from *Fort Austin*. Whilst the warships engaged the enemy aircraft with their main armament and missiles, the merchant ships relied on GPMGs mounted on their bridges, which fired with relentless ferocity at any incoming plane.

The warships drew most of the air attacks upon themselves thus allowing disembarkation ashore to proceed almost unhindered. LCUs, LCVPs and Mexeflotes worked overtime in ferrying troops and vital stores ashore, while overhead seven Sea Kings picked up and delivered

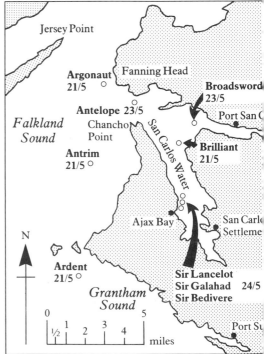

over 220 tons of stores, including 105 mm gun and Rapier firing posts, and 520 men ashore.

After a lull of two hours, in which No 1 Fleet Clearance Team sent a bomb disposal team to *Antrim*, Pucaras again attacked *Ardent* being driven off by her Seacat and later she was the subject of a very low level attack by Capitan Carballo in a Skyhawk who clipped the ship's Type 992 radar antennae.

At 1315 *Brilliant* detected aircraft 100 miles west and sent the CAP to investigate. However six Skyhawks at sea level hugging the coastline suddenly appeared over Falkland Sound and zoomed in on the first ship they saw, *Argonaut* close to Fanning Head straddling the ship with exploding bombs. Another 1,000 lb bomb, which did not explode, pierced the ship's magazine causing a huge fire which swept through the ship, while a second bomb which lodged between the engine and boiler rooms disabled the ship's power and steering gear. But for quick thinking on the part of the Officer of the Watch, Sub-Lieutenant T P Morgan, who lowered an anchor the ship would have run aground. Two men had been killed.

As the Skyhawks sped away to safety, the Harriers contacted and shot down two Daggers with their Sidewinder missiles. At this time, 1345, the air over Falkland Sound was a continuous battlefield and Argentine planes attacked the amphibious anchorage in San Carlos Water for the first time, fortunately leaving the *Canberra* unmolested, possibly mistaking its white paint for a hospital ship. *Antrim*, *Intrepid*, *Broadsword*, *Brilliant* and *Plymouth* all sprang into life with *Brilliant* being hit by cannon shells putting her Operations Room and weapons systems out of action. With so many ships inside the anchorage, *Ardent* found herself steaming northwards unprotected in Grantham Sound having completed her bombardment mission.

The Argentine Naval Air Arm, frustrated that their first Skyhawk mission had been aborted earlier, spotted the lonely frigate. Led by Capitan Philippi, the three aircraft approached at low level from the south, and despite *Ardent*'s spirited defence, pressed home a devastating attack, hitting the ship with three 500 lb Snake-eye retarded bombs, two of which exploded in the hangar. A second wave led by Teniente Rotolo following

HMS *Ardent* which had supported the SAS diversionary raid on Darwin with naval gunfire on 21 May, was hit and set on fire by three 500 lbs Snakeye retarded bombs. She later sunk.

15 minutes later also attacked the crippled ship, hitting her at least twice more, although chaff fired at the aircraft may have avoided further damage. The ship's NAAFI Manager, John Leake, manning a GPMG hit one aircraft's wing, the plane later suffering cannon fire to its undercarriage and being abandoned by its pilot.

Although these Argentine aircraft had not initially been detected, the CAP controlled by *Brilliant* spotted the retreating Skyhawks speeding south at low level. Lieutenant CRW Morrell in the leading Harrier attacked first, shooting down Philippi with his Sidewinder, and in a second attack hit Teniente Arca with cannon fire. Meanwhile his 'pair', Flight Lieutenant J Leeming RAF shot down the third Skyhawk in a copybook attack.

It was some compensation for *Ardent*'s loss of 22 officers and men. *Yarmouth* took off 179 survivors when Commander West ordered his ship to be abandoned and was the last to leave at 1455 when she was well ablaze and listing. She finally sank at 0230 the following morning.

The final air attack of the day came at 1415, when five Skyhawks attacked *Fearless*, *Intrepid*, *Antrim* and *Plymouth*, but no damage was inflicted on either side. The cost for the first day had been heavy. Two frigates, *Ardent* sunk and *Argonaut* crippled, while *Antrim*, *Brilliant* and *Broadsword* had all been hit. In return 12 Argentine aircraft had been destroyed whilst the British air losses had been one Harrier and two helicopters. The aim of the day had been achieved. 3 Commando Brigade, virtually unscathed, were now ashore.

*San Carlos Water, known as 'Bomb Alley', on D-Day with as many as twelve ships including the STUFT ships* Canberra, Europic Ferry *and* Norland.

# Air Operations – Hermes and Invincible

From the day that the Task Force left Ascension Island on 18 April, both *Hermes* and *Invincible* carried out continual air missions in support of the fleet. On leaving UK *Hermes* had 5 Sea Harriers of 800 Squadron, 9 Sea King Vs and 9 Sea King IVs, while *Invincible* had 5 Sea Harriers of 801 Squadron and 9 Sea King Vs. During the passage south and prior to D-Day both ships were to receive reinforcements, the last coming from the ill-fated *Atlantic Conveyor* on 18 and 19 May.

In addition to the fighters, the Sea King Vs of 820 Squadron maintained a continual screen around the carriers in their anti-submarine role. Until 11 May there still remained the threat from one of the two Argentine submarines *Salta* and *San Luis*. It later transpired that, because of torpedo fire control problems, *Salta* carried out no operational patrols. Between them the two carriers kept an average of seven helicopters airborne all

*A Sea Harrier is marshalled on the deck after landing on HMS* Hermes, *while a Sea King helicopter (aft) prepares to take off and another hovers off the port quarter.*

day, with one from each ship searching in the surface role.

By 21 May, although losing one Sea Harrier when Lieutenant Nick Taylor was killed over Goose Green on 4 May and two more when they were lost at sea on 6 May, the strength of the squadrons aboard each ship was more than doubled, particularly with the addition of 6 Harrier GR3s of No 1 Squadron RAF. Along with reinforcements from the newly formed 809 Squadron, which was divided between the two carriers, the two days prior to D-Day were taken up by briefings, familiarisation, interception exercises and deck landing practice. 41 fighter sorties were carried out aboard *Hermes* alone on 20 May, a record for the ship. Generally the Fleet Air Arm's Sea Harriers' task was air defence for the ships in and around San Carlos, being directed by destroyers in the picket line; while the RAF's Harrier GR3s were on call to assist in ground attack for the land forces.

Sea Harriers provided a continuous Combat Air Patrol over Falkland Sound from before dawn on D-Day, the first being launched from *Hermes* at 0635,

until after dusk. However the first air action was when two GR3s attacked the helicopter base near Mount Kent destroying an enemy Chinook and Puma. The second GR3 sortie, not being required to support the ground troops, looked for targets in the Port Howard area and was shot down while taking photographs at low level. The pilot, Flight Lieutenant Jeffrey Glover, ejected safely, and though badly injured was taken prisoner, the only British serviceman to be captured during the re-occupation.

The air defence of the Sound had to be very carefully coordinated. The CAP patrolled the outer layers of defence, while warships, normally a Type 42 with Sea Dart and a Type 22 with Sea Wolf provided the 'missile trap' just outside the Sound. Further inside would be 3 or 4 ships throwing up a wall of fire on the 'gun line', while in what came to be known as 'bomb alley' there were ships with Sea Cat missiles, supplemented by land based Rapier batteries, with the hand launched Blowpipe and machine guns providing the last line of defence. The Sea Harrier radar could detect enemy aircraft at sea but was not too effective inland. Basically three patrol positions were maintained, one each to the north and south of Falkland Sound and a third

over West Falkland.

With their parent carriers about 200 miles away the Harriers could spend only about 20 minutes over the Amphibious Operating Area (AOA). If they became involved in aerial combat or a chase at fullpower, their fuel supply would not last long. They also had to rely on early warning radar information from warships, principally *Brilliant* on the first day, to detect incoming enemy aircraft. The Argentine pilots from the mainland flew at high level (about 17,000 feet) until about 50 miles away and then sped in at wave top, underneath the ship's early warning radar.

The Argentines launched 63 sorties on D-Day in four waves, reasoning that their main chance of success with so little time over the target area was to try to swamp the British missile systems. Only 44 aircraft appear to have reached the islands and of these nine were shot down by Sea Harriers and one by Sea Wolf, while many others were badly damaged,

*A fully armed Sea Harrier takes off from HMS* Hermes, *while Sea King helicopters, with folded blades are parked forward. 1,000lb cluster bombs are ready to be loaded by the flight deck party.*

for the loss of one Harrier GR3. Many of those damaged took no further part in the campaign. A prime factor in their lack of apparent success was that many of their bombs failed to explode on impact, a fault attributed to fuse malfunctions. It was a triumphant day for the British fighters from the two aircraft carriers. Many of the air actions on the first day are described in the preceding chapter.

Two Sea Kings of 826 Squadron, detached for SONAR duties in Falkland Sound reported being fired at, one taking effective evasive action against a Blowpipe missile. There were now four Type 21 frigates in close support *Arrow*, *Alacrity*, *Antelope* and *Ambuscade* providing an anti-aircraft screen.

D+1 was much quieter. The land forces continued their build up ashore almost unmolested, while the Argentine Air Force, licking their wounds and affected by poor mainland weather conditions, made very few sorties. In consequence the dawn CAP from *Hermes*

*Royal Naval Air Engineers at work on a Sea Harrier FRS.1 aboard* HMS Hermes *(in the South Atlantic). Other FRS.1s and Royal Air Force GR.3 wait their turn.*

sighted and attacked the coastal craft *Rio Iguazu* in Choiseul Sound which was ferrying 105mm howitzers from Stanley to Goose Green during the night. The boat was driven ashore, and although the Argentinians recovered the weapons, they were captured three days later. Goose Green became the target for the RAF's GR3s flying from *Hermes* and a low level photographic mission was carried out later in the day.

The first enemy air activity arrived well after lunchtime and even then the Argentines did not come within missile range. However about 1610 two Skyhawks did manage to break through and attack *Brilliant* but without success.

There is no doubt that the Harriers from the aircraft carriers *Hermes* and *Invincible* played a highly significant role in supporting the landing force by disrupting and destroying incoming enemy aircraft. For their part the Argentine Air Force mistakenly concentrated their efforts on the ships of the Royal Navy rather than the amphibious force. The battle for air supremacy virtually changed hands on D-Day, and the Argentines were never able to regain the initiative. The value of the aircraft carrier was proved, but 22 May was only a lull before the next storm.

# Naval Operations and sinking of HMS Antelope

During 22 May the landing force continued to consolidate. Patrols had failed to find any enemy in the vicinity and were probing further afield. More supplies, food and ammunition were ferried ashore from the amphibious ships by Mexeflote and helicopters. T Battery of 12 Air Defence Regiment with their Rapier missiles were now all ashore giving added protection to the ground troops. However there was a sense of uneasy anticipation the following morning after the lull in the Argentine air attacks.

During the night *Plymouth* had left the AOA to recover an SBS team at King George Bay on the west coast of West Falkland, returning before first light, while *Brilliant* and *Yarmouth* intercepted the coaster *Monsunnen* which was forced aground. *Yarmouth* was back in Falkland Sound by dawn but *Brilliant* was ordered to rejoin the carrier group.

Shortly before dawn on D+2, *Antelope* led in the first resupply convoy consisting of *Norland*, *Europic Ferry* and *Stromness*. The carriers continued to supply a CAP and the GR3s took out targets at Dunnose Head and Goose Green. The Lynx helicopters of the frigates now sought their own targets and *Antelope*'s hit the the 10,000 ton cargo vessel *Rio Carcarana* with two Sea Skua missiles near Port King, setting it on fire. Just after midday the Lynx returned to see what damage it had done and found itself the subject of interest of four Skyhawks. It reported back that attacks were imminent and when the first wave of two enemy aircraft attacked *Broadsword*, *Antelope* and *Yarmouth* in the northern reaches of San Carlos Water they were driven off by the anti aircraft barrage. The second pair of Skyhawks, coming in from the north, were more successful, scoring a direct hit on *Antelope* just above the waterline on the starboard side. Once again fortune smiled and the bomb failed to explode, but the Skyhawk, in pulling up from the low level attack, clipped the mainmast, simultaneously being hit by a SAM missile before crashing into the sea. Before the ship could recover, a single Skyhawk appeared on the port beam and deposited another unexploded bomb into *Antelope*. Despite the enormous damage she was still able to move under her own power

*Cloudless skies, ideal for Argentinian air attacks over San Carlos Water, known as 'bomb alley', where HMS* Argonaut *can be seen smouldering, and MV* Norland *had returned on 23 May to unload more stores for the troops ashore.*

and fight. It was remarkable that only one man had been killed.

The next attack came from the west and was not detected until too late. The first aircraft which pinpointed *Yarmouth* failed to release its bombs and the others missed their targets. 10 minutes later at 1320 two Daggers made an unsuccessful pass on the three ships, followed half an hour later by three more Daggers. The last did not press home their attack. All these incoming waves had been detected too late for the CAP Harriers to catch them before they entered the AOA defence zone. However one Dagger was caught on his homeward trip and shot

down with a Sidewinder by Lieutenant Martin Hale in a Sea Harrier of 800 Squadron. This was to be the end of the Argentine aircraft sorties that day. 46 had been planned but only about half reached San Carlos, many not even taking off because of bad weather. Meanwhile Super Etendards, armed with Exocet, had been searching out larger targets at sea, but returned to the mainland on failing to find the British fleet.

Ashore the troops, dug in on the hillsides around San Carlos, had witnessed this remarkable demonstration of Argentinian bravery and the determined defence by the Royal Navy almost as

*A Wessex 5 flies over the stricken HMS* Antelope *on 23 May with HMS* Intrepid *and MV* Norland *standing by. Two unexploded bombs were being defused when one exploded killing Staff Sergeant Jim Prescott, Royal Engineers.*

*Torn apart by a 1000 lbs bomb explosion, HMS* Antelope *had her back broken by a second explosion soon after dawn on 24 May off Ajax Bay, and sank before the eyes of hundreds of troops digging in.*

though they were watching a film. It was described later as uncanny that no aircraft had attempted to attack either ground positions or the amphibious shipping that was feverishly unloading near Ajax Bay.

Late in the afternoon *Antelope* with two unexploded 1,000 lb bombs in her bowels anchored off Ajax Bay and two Royal Engineers bomb disposal experts came aboard. They had already rendered one bomb safe in *Argonaut* and now tackled this new task with cold professionalism and seeming unconcern. Warrant Officer John Phillips and Staff Sergeant Jim Prescott, appreciating the problem here was different, made sure all the crew were safely gathered on the fo'c'sle and flight deck before examining the bomb. With the aid of Lieutenant

Commander RF Goodfellow and Mechanician HB Porter they decided a small defusing charge was required. On going back to inspect the results, the bomb exploded and the two Army men took the brunt of the force. Prescott was killed instantly and Phillips lost an arm. The fire which immediately broke out was fanned by the biting wind and fought by the ship's company. Two LCUs from *Fearless*, busily ferrying stores ashore, immediately came alongside and despite the intense heat and danger of further explosions, one coxwain, Colour Sergeant MJ Francis, ignoring orders, took off survivors when the order to abandon *Antelope* was given at 1820. Smaller Royal Marines landing craft took off Commander Nick Tobin, the last to leave, and ten minutes later an explosion rent the air, possibly the Sea Cat magazine, followed during the night by a series of smaller explosions. At dawn the ship was still afloat and burning, but soon after she exploded for the final time, broke in two and sank with stern and bows still show-

ing. Max Hastings and Simon Jenkins wrote in 'The Battle For The Falklands', *'It was a spectacle that thousands of men ashore and afloat had witnessed from beginning to end. They had never seen a ship sink before. It was an experience that drove into each of them how bitter and how costly the struggle for the Falklands had now become'.*

Out at sea Admiral Woodward was being urged by both naval and military commanders to bring his carriers to within 50 miles of the land so that the CAP could spend more time on station and minimise the risk of further damage from Argentine air attacks. Port Stanley airfield had been bombed by Sea Harriers in a night attack and others strafed the airfield at dawn.

The ships of the fleet had not been idle. During the night LSLs and supply ships were escorted in and out of the AOA, which included refuelling warships from the tanker *Tidepool*. *Arrow* had now replaced *Antelope*, and *Argonaut* had been repaired so that she could sail under her own power.

# Attack on HMS Coventry and Atlantic Conveyor

24 May had seen the first enemy air attacks on the amphibious shipping in San Carlos when LSLs *Sir Galahad*, *Sir Lancelot* and *Sir Bedivere* were all hit by 1,000 lb bombs, none of which exploded but did start fires. The Daggers attacked again later that morning strafing a number of ships and yet another bomb, which hit *Sir Lancelot* did not explode. 3 Daggers were shot down by the CAP and a Rapier missile accounted for a Skyhawk. The loss of ten Daggers of a total of 24 available was a setback from which the Argentines never really recovered, although most of their pilots ejected safely.

Meanwhile in the Task Force, there was apprehension that 25 May, being Argentina's National Day, would herald something special. The Carrier Group was about 80 miles north east of the islands which enabled the CAP to be on station within 20 minutes. In fact the Argentines had planned nothing 'extra' for this day and only 22 sorties were made, with no more than 6 aircraft in any one strike. Although attacks were bravely pressed home on *Coventry* and *Broadsword* in Falkland Sound, the Argentine Air Force was taking a heavy toll with three more Skyhawks accounted for, two by *Coventry*'s Sea Dart, the other by *Yarmouth*'s Sea Cat. Of the last, Teniente Richard Lucero was the first Skyhawk pilot to survive, the previous 15 all having been killed, and he was picked up by a *Fearless* landing craft and taken prisoner.

However in the first wave one 1,000 lb bomb, falling short, came up through *Broadsword* aft and damaged the Lynx helicopter of *Brilliant* which was visiting but yet again the bomb didn't explode. Although the CAP tried to intervene in the next Skyhawk attack, faith in the 'missile zone's' effectiveness kept the Harriers away. The second wave of Teniente Mariano Velasco and Alferez Borge Barrionuevo pressed home their attacks and were fortunate that *Coventry*'s Sea Dart radar control did not acquire them. At 1420 three of their four bombs

*On Argentina's National Day, 25 May, the British Tank Force suffered the double loss of HMS* Coventry, *and* Atlantic Conveyor.

tore *Coventry* apart, exploding in the engine rooms. Within 15 minutes the ship had heeled over. It was remarkable that only 19 men were lost when Captain David Hart-Dyke ordered the ship to be abandoned and 263 survivors were picked up by Sea King and Wessex helicopters as well as *Broadsword*'s boats.

By midday the Carrier Group, now steaming westward and about 60 miles to the north of the islands had been following the attack on *Coventry* with horror. Admiral Woodward was already short of escorts for his big ships as *Antrim* was accompanying *Canberra* and *Norland* to meet up with the *QE2* in South Georgia. His own group was protecting the vitally important *Atlantic Conveyor* on its way with much needed replenishment stores to San Carlos. Most of the aircraft it had brought with it had been flown off to their parent ships including 8 Sea Harriers, 6 GR3s, 1 Wessex 5 replacement and one of its four twin bladed heavy lift Chinook helicopters, urgently needed by 3 Commando Brigade for the move forward towards Stanley.

Ashore in Argentina important decisions had to be made. With two of their precious Exocet AM.39 missiles used, only three were left for the Argentine Naval Air Arm's Super Etendard, and the valuable targets of *Hermes* and *Invincible* were still unscathed. The service of the Neptune maritime reconnaisance

aircraft, which had played an important part in guiding the Super Etendards to the *Sheffield* had been withdrawn from service on 12 May because of age. A mission on 23 May had returned to Rio Grande after 3 hours in the air without finding the Task Force, but information from Stanley on 25th indicated a large target 100 miles north east of the Falklands. Originally planned to take off at 0800 but delayed due to the unavailability of a C-130 tanker aircraft, Capitan Roberto Curilovic and Teniente Julio Barraza left Rio Grande at 1330. After successfully refuelling they dropped to 30 feet above the waves at 150 miles from their target and were surprised to find a positive 'blip' on their first radar sweep, two large ships and one smaller as predicted.

Only 200 yards apart the aircraft fired their Exocets simultaneously at 30 miles range at 1532, immediately breaking off, climbing and turning for home. Another in flight refuelling completed they landed at Rio Grande at 1738 after four hours in the air.

The three ships they had spotted had been *Atlantic Conveyor*, *Ambuscade* and *Sir Tristram*. *Ambuscade* and *Brilliant* had picked up the two Super Etendards and tracked them and all the warships fired their chaff pattern of reflective foil to try to baffle the approaching missiles. This was highly successful in confusing the

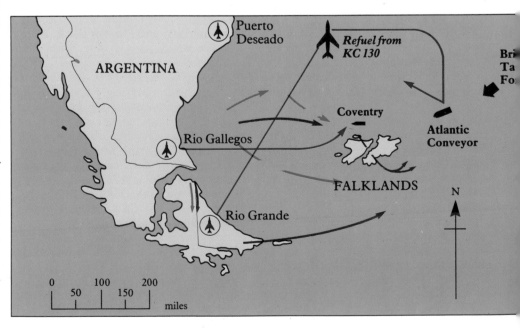

150

HMS Coventry *lists heavily after being attacked by Skyhawks who hit her with three 1,000 lbs bombs, which exploded in her machinery spaces. She sank within 15 minutes with the loss of 19 men.*

missile but it turned and homed in on the one unprotected ship, *Atlantic Conveyor.* At 1538 the missile penetrated the ship's side but miraculously failed to explode. Reports that the second missile also found its target would appear to be erroneous. However the hit quickly caused widespread fires and it was soon obvious the ship was doomed. With so

*Atlantic Conveyor* prepares to fly off a Harrier. In all she transported 8 Sea Harriers, 6 Harrier GR3s, 8 Wessex 5s and 4 Chinooks to the South Atlantic.

many Task Force ships around, assistance was immediately available from Sea King helicopters and although Royal Navy fire fighting teams were put aboard, they could not control the blaze which was spreading towards the hold containing 75 tons of cluster bombs. It was clear that the ship would have to be abandoned and the order was given at 1615.

The Master, Captain Ian North, a colourful seadog of the 'old school', was the last to leave but he sadly disappeared before he could reach a liferaft. Eleven others were lost but 150 were rescued, many of those in the water being for-

*Burning furiously after being hit by an Exocet,* Atlantic Conveyor *stayed afloat for several days but 3 valuable Chinooks and 6 Wessex were lost.*

tunate they were not caught in the ship's propellers. The ship stayed afloat for several days, burning so furiously that none of her stores could be salvaged. On 27 May and despite explosions that had blown the bows from the stricken ship and that she was still smouldering, the tug *Irishman* took her in tow but the line parted after half an hour only to be promptly reconnected. During the night, the tow parted again under severe strain and the *Atlantic Conveyor* sank leaving little trace next morning.

Unknown to Admiral Woodward afloat or Brigadier Thompson ashore, 25 May, which appeared to the British to be a day of utter disaster, turned out to be the turning point of the war. The battle for San Carlos Water had been won and with Argentine Air Force losses so high and their Exocets almost expended, they never again managed to regain air superiority over the battle zone. 45 fixed wing aircraft had been lost either in the air or on the ground while the Royal Navy had lost only three in combat sorties. Only one Exocet M.39 remained. On the deficit side, *Sheffield, Coventry, Ardent, Antelope* and *Atlantic Conveyor* had all been sunk and many other warships were damaged. But the amphibious shipping, which had put 3 Commando Brigade ashore was almost unmarked and no ship was out of action for very long. Why the Argentines concentrated their attacks on the warships in Falkland Sound instead of the landing and supply ships will remain a mystery.

# Attack on Goose Green and Darwin

Ashore, all had not been idle. Reconnaisance teams of D Squadron, 22 SAS, had established positions on Mount Kent during the night of 24 May and a 6 SBS team had been landed near Teal Inlet. On the previous day Brigadier Thompson and Colonel Jones, whose 2 Para were in defensive positions on the Sussex Mountains, had discussed a possible battalion raid on the only Argentine garrison known to be within easy reach at Goose Green and Darwin Settlement. It would be in line with General Moore's directive of establishing domination over the enemy. The settlements were 15 miles away and the only troop lift helicopters available for the whole brigade were six Sea King 4s and five Wessex 5s which meant a strictly limited number of troops could be moved forward. There was no doubt that any major advance would have to be made on foot.

A possible approach by sea down Brenton Loch at night was discounted by Southby-Tailyour as navigationally too risky against an unknown enemy strength. 2 Para had sent out probing patrols southwards and on 24 May occupied the deserted Canterra House 6 miles forward. Jones was keen to get forward as fast as possible. D Company were tasked to push further forward to occupy Camilla Creek House but these plans were thwarted by lack of helicopters and they withdrew to Sussex Mountain.

In London, there was increasing Governmental pressure being levied at Northwood for action, particularly when the losses of *Coventry* and *Atlantic Conveyor* were relayed to a devastated public. With satellite links giving a clear telephone line direct to Ajax Bay, Thompson was ordered unequivocally by the Commander-in-Chief Fleet to remount the Goose Green operation and was made fully aware of the lack of support, except for the Royal Navy, that his brigade could expect. In turn the Brigade Commander ordered Jones to carry out the raid on Goose Green. Latest intelligence indicated at least three companies of infantry, two 105 mm howitzers and a large number of anti-aircraft guns, despite an assurance from the SAS who had carried out the diversionary raid on D-Day that there was no

more than one company. Initially 2 Para would have three 105 guns of 8 (Alma) Commando Battery, which would be flown forward by night, and *Arrow*, with her 4.5 in gun in support up to first light. In the air he would have two Scout helicopters of 3 Commando Brigade Air Squadron.

At dusk on 26 May 'H' Jones led 2 Para off Sussex Mountain and by daylight they had occupied the area around Camilla Creek House. Soon afterwards a pair of Harriers attacked Goose Green, Squadron Leader Bob Iveson being shot down and ejecting after his third run, and around midday the disturbing news was heard loud and clear on the BBC World Service that '*a parachute battalion is poised and ready to assault Darwin and Goose Green*'. The Argentines had been well and truly alerted. Jones was furious.

His plan for the attack was a six-phase night/day assault, quiet at first and noisy later. He wished to protect the lives of the civilian Falklanders as best he could by taking the settlements in daylight. Three Argentine prisoners, taken almost by accident were quickly interrogated by the Spanish speaking Royal Marine Captain Rod Bell, attached for the operation. Another attachment was Lieutenant John Thurman who had intimate knowledge of Goose Green and Darwin from his previous service with Naval Party 8901.

The battalion lay up for most of the day of the 27th in the area of Camilla Creek House pushing out reconnaisance patrols who reported a number of enemy positions. At his O Group Jones had some recently taken air photographs, and there was information on enemy minefields from a captured map. The narrow isthmus near Burntside House leading to the main objectives and lack of air transport

*Lt Col 'H' Jones commanding 2nd Battalion, The Parachute Regiment, won a posthumous Victoria Cross when he led a fearless attack against an enemy machine gun position which was holding up his unit.*

for a flanking attack limited his line of approach to a direct north-south one, easy to defend. Simultaneously 45 Commando and 3 Para were also on the move to the north and east.

A Company moved off on the left flank at 0230 and had their first contact with the enemy who hastily withdrew, twenty minutes later. B Company on the right fought through more enemy positions so that by 0400 the first objectives were taken with D Company in the centre and A Company occupying Coronation Point opposite Darwin settlement. *Arrow* was providing gunfire support controlled by the Forward Observer until dawn,

*A Scout helicopter resupplies the Regimental Aid Post situated in a gorse gulley near Darwin Hill, during the battle for Goose Green. One was shot down by Argentine Pucaras whilst evacuating casualties.*

*Above: some of the 1,300 Argentine prisoners taken during the battle being searched by a paratrooper. The official British figure is that 45 Argentinians were killed while 17 British (15 paras) lay dead.*

*Below: 2 Para were forced to make their attack down the narrow isthmus where the Argentinians had their main defensive positions. No support armour was available, but HMS* Arrow *gave fire support.*

boldly remaining longer in the area than expected.

A Company moving off again at first light met unexpectedly heavy machine gun fire and sustaining many casualties was held up. The CO with his Tac HQ came forward to see what was happening and was clearly frustrated at the lack of progress. At 0930 he decided to take matters into his own hand and fearlessly strode forward on his own to take out an enemy machine-gun position. He was mortally wounded but his supreme gallantry inspired A Company, led by Major Dair Farrar-Hockley, to attack and overrun the enemy. As the two Scout helicopters, who had been busy shuttling ammunition forward and casualties backwards, flew in to evacuate the stricken colonel, they were attacked by Pucaras, one being shot down.

The Second-in-Command Major Chris Keeble flew forward from 2 Para's main headquarters to assume command. Meanwhile both B and D Companies were working round the western flank of Goose Green, fighting every foot of the way against unexpectedly determined opposition. C Company took over from A in the centre and while D Company secured the airstrip, B Company dealt with an enemy reinforcement company flown in from Mount Kent. Skyhawks also hindered their advance, but by 1525 in fading light two Harriers appeared to ward off any further air attacks. By nightfall Darwin had been secured and Goose Green surrounded.

At first light on 29 May two Argentine prisoners were sent into Goose Green with an ultimatum and surrender terms. At 1450 the terms had been agreed and the battle had been won. During the previous night many acts of flying gallantry had taken place evacuating many wounded paras who would otherwise have died in the freezing conditions. The exhausted paras had to spend another very cold night in the open. J Company of 42 Commando arrived as reinforcements but they were not needed. The efficiency and care with which 2 Para had added glories to their Colours may be seen in that not one of the 112 civilians in the settlements had been wounded, but 15 paras lay dead and more than 30 severely wounded. 45 Argentine soldiers had been killed and a further 1,300 were now prisoners. The Staff College 'odds' had been defeated.

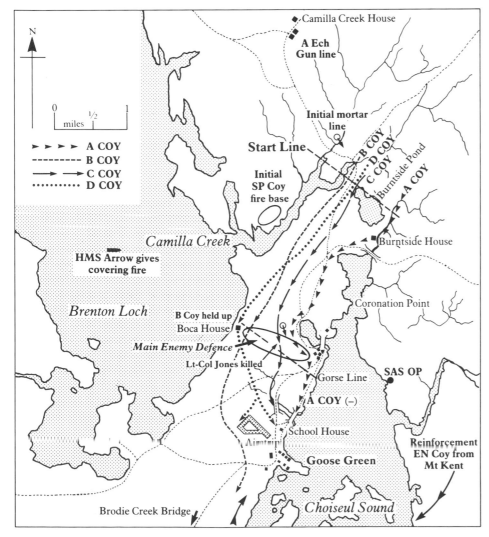

N

0 ½
miles

► ► ► A COY
------- B COY
——→ C COY
········· D COY

Camilla Creek House

A Ech
Gun line

Initial mortar
line

**Start Line**

Initial
SP Coy
fire base

B COY
D COY
C COY
Burntside Pond
A COY

*Camilla Creek*

**HMS Arrow gives
covering fire**

Burntside House

*Brenton Loch*

B Coy held up
Boca House

*Main Enemy Defence*

Coronation Point

Lt-Col Jones killed

**SAS OP**

Gorse Line

A COY (–)

School House

Airstrip

**Goose Green**

Reinforcement
EN Coy from
Mt Kent

Brodie Creek Bridge

*Choiseul Sound*

# Break out from San Carlos

The first days after D-Day had been frustrating to the troops who had landed. Having been cooped up in ships for the best part of a month, they needed to stretch their legs, but few were really prepared for what was to come. 40 Commando had established positions on Verde Ridge in the centre and south of them were 2 Para on the Sussex Mountains; 42 Commando who had initially been the Brigade reserve afloat in *Canberra* landed late on D-Day in the Port San Carlos area when it became clear that London had ordered *Canberra* to leave that night; 45 Commando were dug in on the eastern slopes of the high ground overlooking Ajax Bay; 3 Para having captured Port San Carlos were now occupying the high ground of Settlement Rocks and Windy Gap.

When Brigadier Thompson was being urged 'to get on with it' by Northwood, he formulated plans for the occupation of the high ground overlooking Port Stanley, which the enemy were known to be holding in some strength. The loss of the *Atlantic Conveyor* with the Chinook helicopters and the lack of smaller troop lift helicopters, only six Sea Kings and five Wessex were available for all troop and logistic movement ashore, made it obvious that any major advance would have to be done on foot, and it was 50 miles to Stanley even as the crow flies. One unit might be able to be moved by air, but the remainder would have to 'yomp'. Thompson's logical and tactical thinking, knowing that the enemy was in vastly superior numbers, was to await the arrival of 5 Infantry Brigade and more helicopters; but his masters in London wanted action.

The first move was to occupy Mount Kent with D Squadron SAS and their reconnaisance patrols were flown forward on 24 May to secure a safe landing position, into which 42 Commando with supporting artillery could later land in a helicopter night move. This was completed on the night 30/31 May. SBS patrols had been inserted to report on

*A heavily laden paratrooper, armed with a GPMG, typifies the load and determination of those who yomped across East Falklands. Many loads exceeded 130lbs.*

Teal Inlet and Douglas Settlement was understood to be clear of enemy.

As 2 Para were moving southwards for their attack on Goose Green, 45 Commando left Ajax Bay by LCU for Port San Carlos at first light on 27 May, where they disembarked and started their long yomp eastwards. Each man had at least 120lbs on his back and many more than that. Rucksacks had to be carried as no helicopters were available to bring them forward later. The going on this first 15 miles to New House, two thirds of the way to Douglas Settlement, was undoubtedly the hardest. The peat bog and

rock runs, coupled with scree and tufted grass caused the ankles to turn over and interrupted any marching rhythm. The marines walked in a single file snake, over 550 men in all. Although the weather was reasonable and the country undulating they reached New House about 2200, it rained that night and most woke to find their sleeping bags soaked through, little comfort to an exhausted infantryman. Next morning they reached Douglas, devoid of enemy, and after a short rest they continued on to Teal Inlet a further 15 miles away in a more tactical formation.

Meanwhile 3 Para, who originally planned to follow 45 Commando, had local information that a route to Douglas

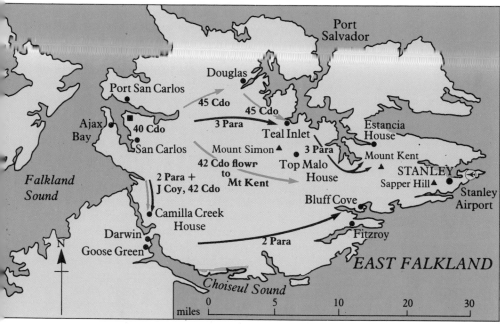

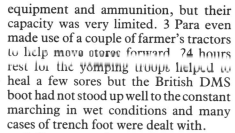

*Whilst 3 Para and 45 Commando yomped across East Falkland, accompanied by the two Troops of Blues and Royals, 42 Commando were helicoptered forward to Mount Kent and 2 Para to Bluff Cove.*

via a track south of Bombilla Hill might be easier. Their experiences on this yomp were similar to those of 45 Commando. Leaving at 1100 on 27 May they marched for a whole 24 hours before reaching their lying up position near the Arroy Pedro river, an astonishing 21 miles. They left a rebroadcast team on Bombilla Hill which gave Brigade Headquarters a secure voice link to their forward troops. At last light they again moved forward and met up with the SBS

team before securing Teal Inlet by 2300.

No 4 Troop, Blues and Royals, who had initially landed with 40 Commando, were due to accompany 45 Commando and 3 Para forward. Lack of diesel caused by the ditching of fuel by *Sir Lancelot* when she discovered an unexploded bomb aboard, meant a delay to their start. However once on their way, the CRV(T)s found the boggy ground surprisingly easy going. They were also used in the role of stores carrier for heavy

*K Coy, 42 Commando on the move near Mount Kent after being flown forward during the night. The SAS had earlier secured this objective, the slopes of which were used as a laying up position before the final attacks.*

equipment and ammunition, but their capacity was very limited. 3 Para even made use of a couple of farmer's tractors to help move stores forward. 24 hours rest for the yomping troops helped to heal a few sores but the British DMS boot had not stood up well to the constant marching in wet conditions and many cases of trench foot were dealt with.

3 Para moved out of Douglas on 30 May for another remarkable march of over 20 miles to Estancia House from where they could see Mount Kent, while 45 Commando also continued their march on 4 June along the same route. It had been planned for 42 Commando with three 105mm guns of 29 Commando Regiment to fly forward to the slopes of Mount Kent, now reported clear of enemy, on the night of 29/30 May, but bad weather delayed them for 24 hours. By first light on 31 May they had occupied the summit of Mount Kent without resistance, and later that day Tactical Brigade Headquarters moved forward to Teal Settlement while their BV202Es with heavier radios motored across the bleak countryside. It was on this day that the Mountain and Arctic Warfare Cadre carried out their successful attack on Top Malo House against Argentine Special Forces.

Major General Jeremy Moore and his HQ Land Forces arrived at San Carlos on 30 May, relieving Thompson of the overall strategy of the campaign and allowing him to concentrate on leading his own Brigade in the final battle for Stanley. He put 2 Para under command of 5 Infantry Brigade and retained 40 Commando in their defensive role around San Carlos Water, much to their dismay.

By 4 June the remainder of 3 Commando Brigade were in position along the Mount Vernet, Mount Kent and Mount Challenger ridge and to Thompson's fury he heard yet another BBC World Service broadcast that announced that Teal Inlet was the headquarters of the attacking force. Although he had ground support, he had no Rapier posts capable of defending the forward areas against unexpected Argentine air attacks, which fortunately never materialised.

There was now only one line of hills to go before occupying Stanley and names like Harriet, Longdon, Two Sisters and Tumbledown were just entering the vocabulary. The pundits in London were happier.

# Disaster at Fitzroy

With 3 Commando Brigade poised for further battle, Brigadier Thompson awaited further orders from Major General Moore's Divisional Headquarters. He had already formulated plans to attack on a broad front, but his waiting brigade were attracting some heavy Argentine artillery fire. Reconnaisance and probing patrols continued unabated, but it was clear that only one brigade, who had already spent three weeks in adverse weather conditions would not be enough to ensure complete victory.

Major General Moore had two options, either to use 5 Brigade to open up a southern route, or to reinforce 3 Commando Brigade and push through from the north and west. With the marines holding all the salient forward features, it was decided to move forward 5 Infantry Brigade, who had been landed at Ajax Bay from the *Norland*, *Canberra* and *Baltic Ferry* by 2 June, on the southern flank. Fog had ensured them a safe distance.

*When 5 Infantry Brigade found that Bluff Cove and Fitzroy settlements were unoccupied they were ferried forward by LSLs and LCUs. On 8 June LSL Sir Galahad and LCU F4 were sunk.*

embarkation. 2 Para, now commanded by Lieutenant Colonel David Chaundler who had been flown out from UK, had been transferred to 5 Brigade, and were tasked with securing Bluff Cove and Fitzroy Settlements. A bizarre telephone call forward from Swan Inlet to the civilian manager at Fitzroy confirmed there were no enemy there and the sole precious Chinook, landing at Goose Green with stores, was seized to ferry the paras forward late on 2 June. 81 men were crammed into the first lift and 75 into the second. Meanwhile 1/7 Gurkhas had set out to march to Goose Green and thence clear Lafonia of any Argentine stragglers, but a similar yomp by the Guards, desperately overladen, was abandoned after 12 hours.

It was now considered safe to ferry troops forward to Bluff Cove. On the night of 5 June in appalling weather 560 men of the Scots Guards were transferred into *Intrepid*'s landing craft near Lively Island, and led by Southby-Tailyour began a seven hour trip to Bluff Cove, where they arrived battered and exhausted at dawn. The ship returned to the shelter of Falkland Sound before first light. That afternoon the Welsh Guards embarked in *Fearless* which was to rendezvous with *Intrepid*'s landing craft off Fitzroy during the night. However

appalling weather meant Southby-Tailyour's craft could not leave Fitzroy and poor communications stopped his signal getting through. *Fearless* waited as long as possible before disembarking two companies of Guardsmen into her own LCUs and withdrawing back to San Carlos with the remainder of the battalion.

It seemed probable that the comings and goings at Fitzroy were being monitored by Argentine observation posts and although air activity had decreased considerably over the past week, the threat was still considerable. Commodore Clapp was told by Northwood that he must not risk either of his amphibious assault ships forward again and the task of reinforcing Fitzroy was to be left to the LSLs manned by RFA crews and with no defensive weapons other than their Bofors. The Task Force commander could not spare frigates for air defence, and the gun ships were supporting the forward troops with night bombardments. *Sir Percivale* at Teal and *Sir Tristram* in the south were providing

*Firefighters try to save the LSL Sir Galahad after she was hit by 500 lbs bombs and set on fire. She had unloaded most of 16 Field Ambulance and a Rapier Battery and was disembarking 350 Welsh Guardsmen.*

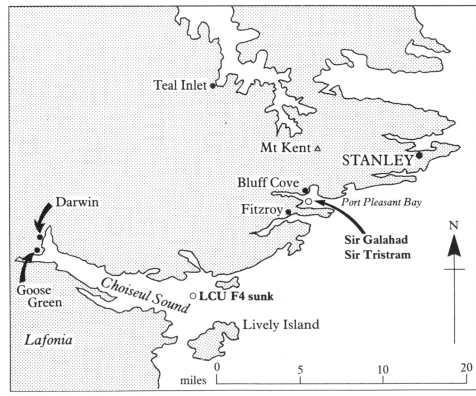

helicopter refuelling platforms as well as ferrying ammunition and stores. On 7 June *Sir Galahad* embarked a Rapier troop, 16 Field Ambulance and the remaining 350 Welsh Guardsmen before sailing at 2200 for Fitzroy.

The morning of 8 June dawned much clearer, an ominous foreboding of the air attacks ahead. *Sir Galahad* arrived unexpectedly off Fitzroy and the available LCUs were already unloading ammuni-

tion into 5 Brigade's stores dumps. Southby-Tailyour offered the Welsh Guards the option of coming ashore but, as their destination was Bluff Cove some 10 miles away, they refused, preferring to wait for the craft to be available to take them direct to Bluff Cove. Just after midday most of 16 Field Ambulance were ferried ashore at Fitzroy and the LCUs then became available for the Guardsmen. The carriers were still providing a CAP over both San Carlos and Fitzroy.

The Argentine pilots of V Air Brigade were eager to get back into the battle after a lull of nearly two weeks during which weather and lack of targets had kept them grounded. At last their OPs reported soft targets in Port Pleasant Bay on the south coast. At 1050 two flights of four Skyhawks took off from Rio Gallegos, but inflight refuelling problems reduced their numbers to 5 aircraft. The first pass over Fitzroy revealed nothing but troops digging in. As they turned they sighted the two LSLs still unloading and prepared to run in from the east, sheltered by light rain squalls. Teniente C Cachon, now leading the group took on *Sir Galahad* with the first three aircraft, his own three 500lb bombs hitting the LSL and setting her on fire. The last two aircraft scored two direct hits on *Sir Tristram* half a mile away.

The damage caused was devastating with the order being given to abandon *Sir Galahad* immediately. The Welsh Guardsmen had been caught disembarking with little warning. Four Sea Kings

*LSL* Sir Galahad *blazes the day after being bombed in Bluff Cove while disembarking her troops. 50 men were killed including 39 Welsh Guardsmen, while 60 were injured, many of them with severe burns.*

and one Wessex were on hand to pick up survivors as well as the landing craft, but the toll was heavy. Remarkable scenes of bravery by the pilots and coxwains were witnessed by all including the press, many vivid and harrowing scenes appearing on British television screens later. In all 50 men were killed including 39 Welsh Guardsmen and nearly 60 wounded, most of them very seriously burnt. A subsequent Skyhawk attack in Choiseul Sound found and sunk LCU F4, which had done such gallant work under CSgt Brian Johnstone, during the San Carlos landings, in the rescue of survivors from *Antelope* and recently in the ferrying of Welsh Guardsmen, with the loss of five marines and sailors.

That day aboard *Fearless* Major General Moore held a 'council of war' with his commanders, which now included Brigadier Tony Wilson, a former Light Infantryman who had won the MC and OBE in Ulster, but whose 5 Infantry Brigade was newly formed and untried. It was there that the cataclysmic news came through of the disaster. With other air attacks on Falkland Sound and troop positions around Bluff Cove, it showed that the Argentine Air Force was back in business.

# Preparation for Battle

The disaster at Fitzroy, although extremely serious, was inflated by the media, many of whom were eye-witnesses of enemy action for the first time, out of all proportion, but it did not delay the execution of the final battles for Stanley. As early as 6 June Brigadier Thompson believed he could carry out a Brigade attack within a few days on Mount Longdon, Mount Harriet and Two Sisters. The cruel weather with its biting winds, sleet and snow was having a debilitating effect on his waiting troops. He was backed by General Moore, who was in turn frustrated by the slow build up of stores and ammunition in the forward areas. This is no way detracts from the supreme efforts of all the logistic services to move supplies forward. For instance, 500 rounds per 105 mm gun were required for supporting the final attacks. Whereas a Chinook helicopter could carry 8 pallets of 192 rounds at a time, the hardworking Sea Kings could manage only 48 rounds and the overworked Wessex Vs, 24 rounds. After the loss of the *Atlantic Conveyor* there was only one Chinook available, and it had many other tasks.

Vigorous patrolling by the units and the SAS had served them well in gaining valuable intelligence on enemy positions and particularly minefields around the features. All Thompson needed was assurance that 5 Infantry Brigade would be ready to support the attack and to keep the momentum rolling once he had broken the Argentine's back. The enemy would soon range their artillery on captured positions, so it was essential to keep going right into Stanley. He asked for 40 Commando, who were still sitting in defensive positions around San Carlos fuming at the bit for action, to join him.

General Moore refused his request, neither could he guarantee support from 5 Brigade, as he now favoured an attack on a narrower front. The Divisional meeting on 8 June aboard *Fearless* broke up with even more imponderables after the news of the Port Pleasant tragedy had come through. With the build up of 5 Brigade around Bluff Cove and Fitzroy the enemy became convinced that the main thrust towards Stanley would come from the south along the axis of the Fitzroy/Stanley road and thus transferred their attention there. This was exactly what the British wanted and when Moore came forward to visit 3 Commando Brigade on 9 June he agreed that the northern and western attack should go ahead. He also agreed to reinforce the Brigade to five units by adding 2 Para and the Welsh Guards, who would have A & C Companies of 40 Commando under command to replace those lost. More helicopters had arrived that day in the *Engadine*.

This was what Thompson had been waiting for and he called an 'O' Group for the following day to give his orders for a night attack probably on the 11th. Units were given the following tasks:

3 Para — Mount Longdon, exploiting forward to Wireless Ridge
45 Cdo — Two Sisters, exploiting to Mount Tumbledown
42 Cdo — Mount Harriet, exploiting through Tumbledown to Mount William if possible

2 Para — Initially in reserve but ready to reinforce the centre line
1 WG — Secure 42 Cdo's start line and standby to support them

In the meantime he needed as much intelligence on enemy dispositions in the dead area between Mount Harriet in the south and Two Sisters in the centre and was able to call on the M & AW Cadre, the Brigade experts in patrolling, to establish a post on Goat Ridge and report. This patrol under Lieutenant Fraser Haddow was highly successful; but there were still no air photographs available.

In support the Brigade would have the 105mm guns of 29 Commando Light Regiment and at sea the heavier guns of *Glamorgan*, *Avenger* and *Yarmouth*.

*With more than a week available for observing and vigorous patrolling, much intelligence was gleaned of enemy positions, minefields and the ground leading to the objectives. Precise field models of the main features were constructed on which all troops were thoroughly briefed.*

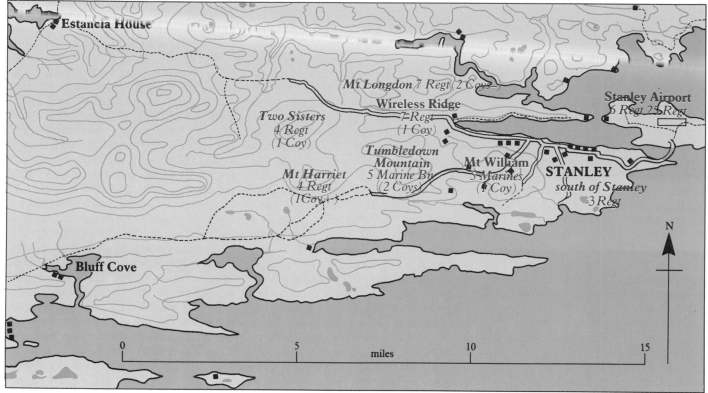

Close air support would be provided by the GR3s now using the San Carlos airstrip HMS *Sheathbill* where they could refuel but not re-arm. There were now many more helicopters available for troop lifts, with 16 Sea Kings of 825 and 826 Squadron, 23 Wessex of 845, 847 and 848 Squadrons as well as the lone RAF Chinook. Supplementing these were Gazelles and Scouts of 3 Commando Brigade Air Squadron. Forward Operating Bases had been established at Teal Inlet for the northern flank and Goose Green in the south.

The main defenders were the Argentine 4th and 7th Infantry Regiments, mostly conscripts with a spattering of regulars, and reportedly, poorly led. However Tumbledown was defended by the regular 5th Marine Regiment. On the whole the Argentines were well equipped, but food was short and morale generally very low. Most had been in the mountains under constant threat for several weeks, being pounded particularly at night, and strafed by Harriers during the day. They were ill-informed even as to their own positions. It was this low morale factor and a lack of training that convinced Moore and Thompson they could deal successfully with numerically overwhelming odds, with only the small military reserve of half of 40 Com-

*Nos 4 and 7 Infantry Regiments provided the main Argentinian defence line on Two Sisters, Wireless Ridge, Mounts Harriet and Longdon, while the crack 5 Marine Battalion held Tumbledown and Mount William. All were supported by 155 mm and 105 mm artillery.*

mando still languishing in defence at San Carlos and a Company of Gurkas at Goose Green.

Air superiority was now in the hands of the British. The Skyhawk attacks of 8 June, in which the Argentine Air Force had lost three of its remaining aircraft to Sea Harrier missiles, were the last to be seen over the Falklands except for a foray by seven aircraft on 13 June which did little damage. The Pucaras, based on Stanley airfield, flew few missions because of unserviceability and the continued attention of the RAF and Fleet Air Arm but three sorties were carried out at dawn on 10 June complementing their own 155mm bombardment artillery against British artillery positions. A similar sortie was carried out at dusk the following day, but neither caused much damage or casualties. There was no sign of the three remaining MB 339s which appeared quite serviceable when captured at the end of the war.

The Royal Navy had continued to sof-

ten up the Argentine defences. *Yarmouth* had bombarded Moody Brook Camp on the nights of the 7th and 8th, and the following night, having re-ammunitioned, she gave Two Sisters, Mounts Harriet, William and Sapper Hill a pounding from her position off Port Pleasant. On 10 June *Arrow* continued the nightly bombardment under the direction of forward spotters. It was known that the enemy had mobile land based Exocets which posed a threat to the bombarding ships. The following morning the two frigates took up the bombardment causing damage to the Stanley road and blowing up an ammunition dump on Mount Harriet. Also on the 11th *Glamorgan* joined in for the night's bombardments and *Yarmouth* relieved *Avenger* on the gun line.

In the air, continuous air raids had been carried out by the Sea Harriers and GR3s against Stanley airfield, 123 missions being flown and 86 tons of bombs delivered. Even a Wessex gunship had attacked the Stanley police station and caused heavy casualties in the military Operations Room located there.

The scene was set for 3 Commando Brigade's attack on the night of 11/12 June, the final encounters between the two armies, and the successful outcome of the war.

# The Battle for Stanley – Mount Longdon

2 Para had flown forward by helicopter from Fitzroy to the Lying Up Position west of Mount Kent during 11 June and as the Brigade attack started soon after dusk they moved up to higher positions from where they could see the battles and be ready to support either 3 Para on Mount Longdon or 45 Commando on Two Sisters. They were pleased to be back in the more confident 3 Commando Brigade after witnessing the Bluff Cove disaster which meant 5 Brigade had to reorganise once more.

Brigadier Thompson had decided on a night attack for several reasons. The enemy were known to be holding all the prominent features covering the western approaches to Stanley and each of these could mutually support the others with enfillading fire. The ground leading up to all these objectives was very open and easily defendable. He was not prepared to underestimate the resolution of the regular elements of the Argentine army, though he knew that many of the conscripts would certainly give up under a determined attack. It was therefore essential to take the three major mountains, Longdon, Two Sisters and Harriet in one co-ordinated brigade attack. He now had the necessary four units, probably the most highly trained and skilled in the British Forces with which to achieve this, and they were experienced in moving and fighting at night.

The terrain of the Falklands was such that very little natural cover was available to assaulting troops and vast distances would have to be covered over open ground which would be swept with machine guns and artillery. Any attack by night would give his men ten hours of darkness to reach their objectives. He knew that moving and fighting over this difficult countryside would be a very slow and painful business. He also decided that the attacks should be silent and devoid of artillery fire that might destroy any element of surprise. An inexperienced enemy would be confused by night fighting, and moon rise about 2015 would help silhouette the main features and guide the attackers. The high calibre of the marines and paras in his brigade were such that night route finding and fighting were second nature to them. He also had considerable artillery (over

11,000 shells) and naval gunfire support (1,400 rounds) in the extremely capable hands of the Royal Artillery's Forward Observers, with close air support from Harriers available from first light. One tactic that had been learnt by 2 Para at Goose Green was that the 66mm anti-tank rocket was highly effective in the sangar busting role.

Lieutenant Colonel Hew Pike had been given the task of securing Mount Longdon on 3 Commando Brigade's north flank with 3 Para. After their yomp across East Falkland from San Carlos, they had occupied the dominating feature of Mount Estancia and the southern slopes of Mount Vernet since 2 June. This gave their observation posts on the high points a clear view of Stanley and even the airport when visibility allowed. From the start it was likely that his battalion would be given Mount Longdon as their objective and with this in mind Pike set up a patrolling programme to glean as much intelligence as possible about the enemy, his positions and strength. Patrol Company took the main share of the reconnaisance work while fighting patrols were sent out from each company. They had some minor clashes with the enemy, and were periodically harassed by artillery. A whole week was a luxury for the planning

and commanders at all levels were able to get a good mental picture of the ground between them and the enemy.

Mount Longdon was a long ragged ridge running east to west. Open ground led up to it on all sides for more than 1,000 yards. Patrols had located minefields on the southern flank and it was likely that the enemy were well ensconced on Wireless Ridge 1,000 yards further east. This left Pike with very little alternative but to attack along the ridge from west to east, which would also avoid any interference with 45 Commando on their right and partially eliminating mutual support from the far end of the ridge.

The first battalion to move off were 3 Para, just after darkness fell, about 1600. They had four hours before the moon rose, to cover their approach to the start line, a small stream running north-south and at right angles to their line of attack. Hew Pike's simple plan of a direct assault along the thin craggy summit of Mount Longdon from the west entailed two companies up. Simple plans are usually the best and so it proved. He knew that the defenders included many of the tough 601 Marine Company, as well as most of 7 Infantry Regiment. Some would be equipped with image

*3 Para attacked the northernmost feature Mount Longdon. They lost 17 killed, including Sergeant Ian McKay (awarded a posthumous Victoria Cross), and 40 wounded.*

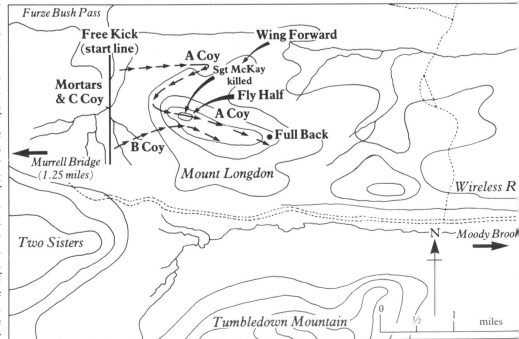

*Two paratroopers relax after the night-long battle for Mount Longdon, when they were able to replace their steel helmets with their red berets.*

intensifying night sights, giving almost a daylight view. Open ground stretching over half a mile in all directions from Longdon was easy to defend and his men had to cross it before reaching the steep slopes of the hill which rose several hundred feet above them. B Company

*An Argentinian foxhole on Mount London is examined after the battle by a Royal Marine. The strong defensive positions were mainly built up as sangars and camouflaged among the rocky outcrops.*

was to spearhead the attack straight along the ridge nicknamed *Fly Half* and take the eastern spur (*Full Back*), while A Company further to the left would take the northern spur (*Wing Forward*). When these positions had been captured, C Company who had remained on the start line with the 81 mm mortars, would fight through to take Wireless Ridge 1000 yds to their front.

The battalion crossed the start line at 2015 just 14 minutes late, a delay caused by unexpected difficulty in fording the Murrell River and a part of 5 Platoon and 6 Platoon who got temporarily separated in the pitch darkness. As the paras moved silently eastwards up the slope, the moon rose and they could clearly see the rugged outcrops on top of Mount Longdon against the lightening sky. In silence they moved for an hour, hearts beating faster as they approached the enemy. The stillness was shattered when an anti-personnel mine was detonated by 4 Platoon, the enemy having their first warning of an impending attack. Shortly afterwards enemy artillery fire began to fall around them. B Company took the western end of Longdon with little fighting, and it was surprising that no enemy OPs were found, but the enemy positions on the lower eastern end, which included a 105 mm gun as well as heavy machine guns, opened up and pinned the leading troops down. Sgt Ian McKay, seeing his platoon commander fall wounded, led

some of 4 Platoon against a heavy machine gun which was holding them up. His inspirational leadership, which cleared the enemy position and silenced the gun, cost him his life along with that of Private Burt, but enabled the Company to continue the advance. Sgt Fuller, gathering the remnants of 4 and 5 Platoons then attempted to take out another machine gun, but he became pinned down and was forced to withdraw. Lieutenant Lee, the Forward Observer was by now bringing down artillery fire on the enemy dug in on the eastern end. B Company Commander, Major M H Argue decided to consolidate for the moment.

A Company had taken a line slightly left of that planned and reaching the crest of the northern spur came under heavy fire from the same enemy positions that were holding up B Company. The enemy were well sited in a classic reverse slope position, and their defensive artillery fire was being well directed. The CO ordered A Company to come through B Company's positions on *Fly Half* and work their way forward with covering artillery, mortar and machine gun fire. A Company, with 1 and 2 Platoons leading, fought their way along the ridge with bullets, bayonets and grenades, edging the enemy out of their trenches and sangars. They reached the eastern end of the feature with the enemy surrendering as they went, while 3 Platoon surged through them to consolidate on the long slope leading towards Wireless Ridge below them.

The battle had lasted nearly 8 hours and dawn was just beginning to break. There was no question of taking Wireless Ridge in daylight, as Tumbledown over to the right which dominated the area had not yet fallen. The exhausted paras dug in on the reverse slopes north west of Longdon against the expected Argentine artillery bombardment. Digging was extremely difficult in the rocky outcrops and sangars were built as protection against the enemy and the elements.

3 Para lost 17 dead and forty wounded, the heaviest casualties of the long night and against the most determined enemy. Now they had 48 hours to survive in the cold and inhospitable mountain during which another four men would be killed by enemy artillery fire being controlled and adjusted by spotters on Tumbledown.

# The Battle for Stanley – Mount Harriet

42 Commando had flown forward to Mount Kent on 31 May and had a full fortnight to patrol forward towards Mount Challenger, Mount Wall, Goat Ridge, and latterly, Mount Harriet. They had to survive the cold and uncomfortable wait longer than other units of 3 Commando Brigade. As early as 3 June it became clear that 42 Commando's likely task would be the capture of Mount Harriet, which was being defended by almost the whole of 4th Infantry Regiment under Lieutenant Colonel Diego Sona. It was active and continuous patrolling that kept the marines' minds off their creature comforts, but it also gave more time for Lieutenant Colonel Nick Vaux, the smallest and just the oldest of the unit commanders, to plan his attack on Mount Harriet. The patrols, one of which set off mines, another which killed six Argentinians in a surprise night attack, provided him with much excellent intelligence. But like other field commanders Vaux deplored the fact that there were no air photographs to help him; however he built up a very good picture of the ground and the related enemy positions from patrol and OP reports, while the gunners calculated crest clearance and distances with absolute accuracy. Deprived of M Company who had been involved in the South Georgia operation, he now had J Company, based on the captured Naval Party 8901 and commanded by Major Mike Norman, as well as K and L Companies.

Mount Harriet overlooked the Goose Green - Stanley track which had been used extensively as a resupply route by the Argentines. It was the most heavily mined of the Brigade's objectives, particularly on the western and southern slopes, the direction from which the enemy expected the main brigade attack. After the war, captured maps showed nine separate minefields; indeed Vaux had personally seen the enemy laying mines. Although Goat Ridge to the north was also 42 Commando's responsibility, it had been designated the unit's left hand boundary with 45 Commando. It would have been too risky to assault from that flank for fear of coming under fire from the next unit in the confusion of darkness. A frontal assault across 2,000 yards of open, heavily mined ground,

even at night, was out of the question. Vaux's plan proved the boldest of the three attacks that night, a long encircling movement to the right flank to take Mount Harriet from the rear. One of his patrols had found a mine-free route. As the enemy were almost certain to have strong-points at each end of Harriet, he planned to attack from the south east with K Company leading. This involved a very long southerly approach march skirting the worst of the minefields, crossing two tracks and around a lake. It crossed the boundary between 3 and 5 Brigades. It was essential that this route was not only thoroughly recced and marked, but that the start line should be secure.

42 Commando were due to cross the start line over 3 miles forward of their assembly area below Mount Challenger, at 2030. To his dismay Vaux was told that the Recce Platoon of the Welsh Guards was to secure this line, a unit from another Brigade with whom he had no direct communications. The success of his daring plan relied on a silent approach to catch the enemy unawares and he feared that the guardsmen, who had not only suffered badly in the recent disaster at Bluff Cove blunting their morale, but were also less experienced at

moving by night over this rugged terrain, might inadvertently alert the enemy. As it happened the 42 Commando leading patrol and the Welsh Guards platoon missed each other in the dark which delayed the attack an hour, long enough for the moon to rise and make them more vulnerable.

Earlier J Company had occupied and set up their mortars on Mount Wall, nicknamed *Tara* after one of the CO's daughters (the other main objectives were Mount Harriet – *Zoya* after his wife and Goat Ridge – *Katrina* after his other daughter). K Company left the assembly area at 1730 with L Company an hour behind them. In contrast to the attacks on Longdon and Two Sisters which were silent, Vaux had designed a deception plan involving a pre-assault artillery barrage on Mount Harriet which had been approved by brigade headquarters. Although this had the effect of alerting the defenders, the Argentines might presume the attack would come from the west from where J Company were firing their mortars and machine guns. The noise of the two northern attacks could

*42 Commando's bold plan for taking Mount Harriet from the rear involved a long approach march skirting a lake and minefields to the south. Surprise was achieved by the direction of attack.*

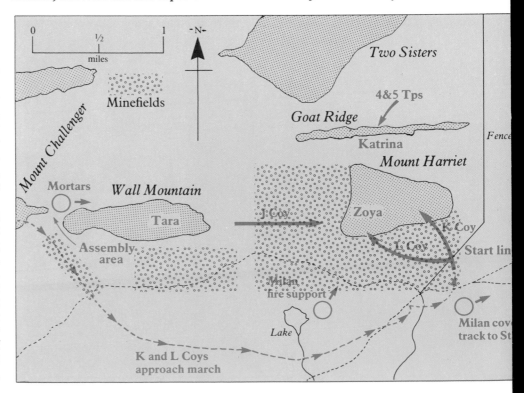

*A painting by Peter Archer, commissioned by the officers of the unit, depicting 42 Commando's audacious assault on Mount Harriet.*

be clearly heard as the marines formed up.

Crossing the start line to the south east of *Zoya* at 2200, Captain Peter Babbington led his K Company 700 yards up the slopes before they engaged the enemy only 100 yards to their front. Taken by surprise from the rear, the enemy still put up a spirited resistance, but one particular position was taken out almost single handed by Corporal Steve Newland who, despite being wounded in both legs, tossed a couple of grenades into the enemy positions before charging in with his sub machine gun. The posi-

*Lt-Col Nick Vaux, the Commanding Officer, shares a joke with members of a fighting patrol from L Company on Mount Challenger.*

tion was finally taken out by Corporal Chris Ward with a round from a 66 mm light anti-tank weapon. K Company secured the eastern end of Harriet while L Company commanded by Captain David Wheen, had the unenviable task of taking the western end which was now fully alerted to the direction of attack. They had to cover 600 yards and calling for MILAN fire to silence the machine gun positions the marines surged forward engulfing the defenders and capturing a large number of enemy on the feature.

One horrifying incident which was etched on the minds of the CO and his headquarters on *Tara* was when *Glamorgan* which had been giving them some excellent fire support was suddenly hit by a land based Exocet missile. The helpless watchers actually saw the missile seeking its way at an ever increasing speed towards the destroyer and hit it with a devastating explosion.

With Harriet captured, the CO and J Company came up to join the leading companies warily treading through the minefields and the next objective was Goat Ridge half a mile to the north. K Company swarmed across towards it, not seeming to feel the weariness of the past two weeks. The enemy had fled into the night. Before first light *Katrina* was theirs, as were 300 dishevelled and deflated prisoners. Enemy artillery began to fall around the marines as they dug and built their new defensive positions. The attack had taken longer than expected and there was no time to exploit forwards to their next objective of Mount William.

42 Commando had lost but two JNCOs killed in action and 17 men wounded, including their attached Argyll and Sutherland officer, Lieutenant Ian Stafford. The audacity of the attack and the brilliance of its execution had proved the value of highly trained, fit troops in the most appalling conditions. The Falklands winter was now at its height.

The night of 11/12 June had been an overwhelming success for 3 Commando Brigade. They had beaten a numerically superior enemy and had only one more barrier to cross, one that would be left to their own 2 Para and 2nd Bn Scots Guards of 5 Infantry Brigade. During the daylight hours, Argentine 155 mm and 105 mm peppered the brigade's positions and the scene was being set for the final denouement.

# The Battle for Stanley – Two Sisters

45 Commando in the centre, whose objective was the highest point, the twin peaks of Two Sisters at 1,000 feet, were ordered to cross the start line an hour after 3 Para. The objective was just over a mile long from west to east with five rocky ridges giving it an extremely sharp and rugged spine. From the valley there was a steep climb of 300 feet over treacherous rock runs and difficult scree. It made progress painfully slow even for the ultra-fit marines, many of whom were natives of Scotland, where the Commando was normally based. The enemy was a Company of 4 Regiment, mainly conscripts, but well dug in and supported by mortars and heavy machine guns.

Colonel Andrew Whitehead, not underestimating the time the attack would take, planned a two phase assault with X Company taking the ridge, nicknamed *Long Toenail*, slightly to the southwest of the main features, and then giving covering fire to the main advance from the northwest from the area of Murrell Bridge. He would also be in a position to cover Goat Ridge, the inter-unit boundary with 42 Commando to the south, with supporting fire and deny it to the enemy. Z Company would take the western peak of Two Sisters with Y Company following through them to take the eastern feature (*Summer Days*). The initial attack would be silent but *Glamorgan* and *Yarmouth*, artillery and the unit's own 81 mm mortars were all available on call.

He had been well briefed by Sergeant Wassell of Lieutenant Haddow's patrol which had established themselves near the eastern end of Goat Ridge on the night of 8/9 June. With six marines of the M & AW Cadre providing rear and flank protection, Haddow and Wassell had sat all day back to back watching the Argentinians, oblivious to their presence, on the well used track that ran between Two Sisters and Tumbledown only 50 yards away. They plotted enemy positions and pin-pointed an important command-detonated mine position on the eastern peak of Two Sisters. The value of the intelligence gained by this highly skilled reconnaissance party caused two Commanding Officers to modify their plans slightly to avoid casualties. The patrol returned safely without being seen by the enemy.

As there was about 4 miles for Y and Z Companies to cover to their start line, much of it in dead ground and with no predicted air threat, Whitehead decided they should move by daylight to a forward lying up position with the cover of Mount Kent shielding them. It would shorten the distance they had to move in the dark. This foresight was justified when later X Company, heavily laden, not only with their own kit, but with Milan firing posts and missiles, an extra 35 lbs per man, found their night move to the start line much slower going than planned, taking six hours rather than the planned three. The Company Commander even broke radio silence lest his CO was anxious about his lack of progress.

To the north 45 Commando could see and hear 3 Para's bloody battle on Mount Longdon, as Y and Z Companies moved to their start line arriving a few minutes ahead of schedule. Whitehead decided not to wait for the delayed X Company's attack, which had started about 2300, to finish. After taking the first pinnacle without too much trouble X Company met spirited machine gun opposition on their exploitation for-

*An 81 mm mortar team dug in on the wet and windy rear slopes of Mount Kent watch a Wessex helicopter bring in much needed supplies. Such mortar teams supported the combined brigade attack on 11/12 June.*

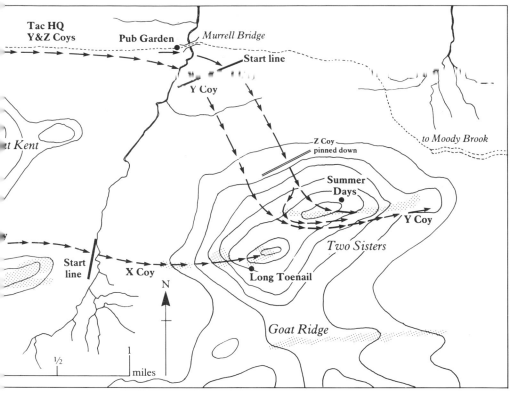

weapon sight to intensify the night image, located a number of enemy positions. Y Company had also gone to ground further right and when enemy fire was opened at them they were both in dead ground. Following up a preplanned artillery stomp on the position, Dytor, with shouts of 'Zulu, Zulu' led his Troop forward with an air of bold defiance and aggressiveness over-running the enemy despite much skirmishing and hand to hand fighting.

Meanwhile Y Company had to hold back lest they became involved in Z Company's battle and were heavily mortared by the enemy, two officers being among the wounded. The .50 heavy machine guns continued to rake their positions, but by skillful battlecraft and determined leadership the attackers began to make progress. Whitehead, well up with his leading troops, ordered Y Company to swing right and advance between the twin peaks, which they did on the southern side of the thin ridge. Although enemy resistance was still fierce, controlled use of the considerable firepower available enabled them to maintain momentum and take the eastern peak of Two Sisters. Immediately enemy artillery fire rained down on them.

Julian Thompson in his book 'No Picnic' was to write of this battle, '*the combination of good control, fitness and the proper use of fire power had enabled them (sic 45 Commando) to take this formidable position with light casualties. Their Commanding Officer's calm voice on the radio had been like a tonic to all who heard him.*' Whitehead immediately prepared for the next phase of the attack against Tumbledown, but because, at 0430, there were only two hours to go before daylight, no naval gunfire support would be available during the day and the fact that 42 Commando had not yet secured Goat Ridge between them and Mount Harriet, the brigade commander called a halt for the night.

The battle had been long and fierce, the firefight lasting over 2½ hours, and 45 Commando had suffered their fair share of casualties, four killed and eleven wounded. They had taken the highest point in the mountains capturing 44 Argentines; the remainder had fled leaving ten dead behind them. As dawn broke, those on the ridge could just see Stanley Harbour in the hazy distance. They were nearly there.

ward. As 1 Troop, and then 3 Troop moved along the ridge, the CSM with seven LMGs and three 66 mm LAWs moved on a parallel course about 200 yards down the ridge ready to give immediate close supporting fire as required. The enemy were well sited in mutually covering defensive positions and determined attempts to take them by both 1 and 3 Troops were initially held up. However following up Lieutenant Christian Caroe with 2 Troop fought his way through the rocky boulders to the top, only to be driven off by Argentine artillery DF tasks.

Soon after midnight Whitehead ordered Phase Two to begin. Y and Z Companies moved off, the slight delay in crossing the start line fortunately causing them to miss a heavy enemy artillery 'stomp' through which they would have passed. Z Company on the left had nearly threequarters of a mile of steady up hill climb to their objective which was now outlined in the moonrise. Going to ground, apparently unobserved, 8 Troop Commander Lieutenant Clive Dytor, crawled forward and using his individual

*One of the twin peaks of Two Sisters is clearly visible in the distance as marines of 45 Commando make their way forward towards Sapper Hill.*

# The Battle for Stanley – Other Operations

Whilst the land battle was in full swing on the night of 11/12 June, there was plenty of activity to support them. At sea *Glamorgan* and *Yarmouth* fired some 428 rounds of 4.5 in HE shells at the enemy dug in on Two Sisters, Tumbledown and Mount Harriet, with *Avenger* supporting 3 Para on Mount Longdon. Their Naval Gunfire Forward Observers from 148 Commando Battery Royal Artillery controlled the fire from positions with the leading troops of 3 Commando Brigade, as well as fire from 29 Commando Regiment.

It was known that the Argentines had some land based Exocet MM.38 surface to surface missiles mounted on trailers in the Port Stanley area with an improvised computer firing system, and these posed a dire threat to bombarding warships at sea. These Exocets had been removed from the Argentine corvette *Guerrico*, which had earlier taken part in the South Georgia operation, but which had now been withdrawn from service. A missile was launched on the night of 27 May and locked on to *Avenger* but passed over the ship. On the night of 11 June this mobile Exocet had been set up on the track from Stanley, behind Mount Harriet. *Glamorgan* was about 18 miles south west of Harriet and retiring after completing her gunfire support role when at 0235 she was struck. *Avenger* had reported seeing a missile and it was picked up by *Glamor-*

*A land based Exocet MM 40 missile mounted on a lorry chassis in peace-time. A similar MM 38 hit HMS* Glamorgan *when she was giving supporting fire to the ground forces.*

*gan* which promptly turned to present the smallest target and fired a Sea Cat which deflected it slightly. The Exocet hit the edge of the port upper deck and exploded in the hangar and galley areas. Thirteen men lost their lives, a further fourteen were wounded, and fires were started which were eventually extinguished. Despite the damage the ship's speed never fell below 10 knots and although she had an 8° list, all her armament remained operational.

To the north *Arrow* had joined the gunline bombarding Stanley airfield, the racecourse and Sapper Hill with 238 shells. The RAF were not to be left out as the final Vulcan 'Black Buck' raid of the campaign dropped twenty-one 1,000 lbs bombs on the airfield facilities about 0445.

As the land battle casualties mounted it was essential in the freezing conditions to evacuate them as fast as possible, either to the Forward Dressing Stations at Teal and Fitzroy or further back to the Main Dressing Station at Ajax. As soon as it was possible the helicopters designated for casualty evacuation were working overtime. The speed and efficiency with which they performed their task undoubtedly saved many lives. On 12 June 16 surgical operations were carried out at Teal, eight at Fitzroy and 32 major operations were performed at Ajax. It was ironic to think that many of those badly wounded at Bluff Cove and even more guardsmen dug in on the mountains preparing for the next phase of the battle would, under normal circumstances, have been on the Queen's Birthday Parade on Horseguards that day.

Orders for the final attacks to take the last hills before Stanley were given that day. These were planned for the night of 12/13 June. This time it was to be 5 Infantry Brigade's turn. Brigadier Tony Wilson quite rightly asked for a 24 hours postponement to enable his troops to familiarise themselves with the ground and this was granted. His plan to take the final Argentine defence line was for the Scots Guards to attack Mount Tumbledown in the centre of the front, while 1/7 Gurkhas secured Mount William to the south with the Welsh Guards following through to occupy Sapper Hill.

It was obvious to Brigadier Thompson that the occupation of Wireless Ridge to the north of Stanley Harbour was essential to the mutual success of Tumbledown and he ordered his reserve battalion, 2 Para, who were eager to get back into the battle under their new CO Lieutenant Colonel David Chaundler to prepare for a simultaneous attack. In addition two diversions were to be

*Heavily laden and battle weary Scots Guardsmen move off after the battle. Thirty guardsmen had made a successful diversionary attack to the south of Tumbeldown.*

made, one to the south of Tumbledown by thirty Scots Guardsmen under HQ Company Commander Major the Hon

Richard Bethell, a former SAS officer, and a second raid by the SAS landed from rigid raiding craft of the Royal Marines Raiding Squadron to harass the enemy east of Wireless Ridge.

During the day 3 Commando Brigade Headquarters was unexpectedly strafed by seven Skyhawks in two waves led by Captain Varela in his unique grey painted fighter. They each dropped a parachute-retarded 500lb bomb, the last landing only 50 yards from the Headquarters, causing damage to three light helicopters and splintering the sides of the briefing tent. Two hours later and it might have caught all the commanding officers assembled for the Brigade 'O' Group. It would not seem to have been a pre-planned attack on the headquarters by this group of inexperienced pilots, but a general mission to destroy any troop positions seen. It was the last air attack of the war and nearly the first Skyhawk mission to make an air to air kill when the last aircraft damaged a Sea King of 846 Squadron with its cannon. Eight Skyhawks, in addition to eight Daggers, had been shot down by Sea Harriers in aerial combat during the campaign

*The view the Scots Guards would have had when assaulting Tumbledown had it been daylight, showing how easy it was for the Argentinians to defend amid the rocky outcrops.*

emphasising the latter's superiority.

5 Infantry Brigade now prepared themselves for the task ahead. During the 13 June, in beautiful sunshine reminiscent of an English spring day, the Scots Guards moved into their assembly area and spent the remaining daylight hours studying the ground ahead of them, Tumbledown, where they were to earn another famous battle honour in the next 24 hours. 1/7 Gurkhas were also eager to press ahead, their task being to exploit forward to Mount William as soon as Tumbledown had fallen. Behind them came the composite Welsh Guards/ 40 Commando battalion. All was set for the final denouement. That evening the waiting troops heard on the BBC World Service that the Argentines were suffering on another field. In the preliminary rounds of the World Cup in Spain, Belgium had beaten them 1-0. What a disastrous week for them!

# The Final Battles – Wireless Ridge

The attack by 2 Para on Wireless Ridge on the north shore of Stanley Harbour was planned to coincide with the Scots Guards attack on Tumbledown on the night of 13/14 June. 2 Para had been raring to go after their inaction since Goose Green nearly three weeks earlier. Their new CO Lieutenant Colonel David Chaundler had unusually joined his unit, parachuting into the sea on 1 June from a Hercules, being picked up promptly by *Penelope*, and later delivered to his battalion. He had been a student of Brigadier Thompson at the Army Staff College Camberley and they 'spoke the same language'. It is never an easy task to take command of a unit that had already proved itself in battle, but there was no doubt the battalion were eager to settle some more scores with the enemy.

Wireless Ridge, actually two ridges, runs about a mile east south east of Mount Longdon, now securely in the hands of 3 Para, and 250 feet below it. It dominated the track leading from Moody Brook Camp to Teal and further south the eastern slopes of Tumbledown. It was undulating rather than steep sided.

In support 2 Para were to have a troop of the Blues and Royals, besides *Ambuscade* and two batteries (7 and 8 Btys) of 105 mm guns and sixteen 81 mm mortars of 2 and 3 Para combined. Chaundler's original plan to assault left flanking from the north had to be modified in view of new unit boundaries imposed and additional information that the enemy still held two prominent knolls to the north east of his projected line of advance. However he still favoured the northern route. Like 42 Commando's attack on Mount Harriet, his was to be a noisy attack with a pre-planned bombardment, which would also help divert defending eyes away from the tougher target of Tumbledown. The 2 Para attack would now be in four phases.

The battalion had reached their assembly area near Furze Bush Pass on 12 June. At 2145 the following day, D Company after a 30 minutes preliminary naval and artillery bombardment, crossed the start line with Scorpions and Scimitars of the Blues and Royals giving added fire and moral support. The enemy fled at their approach. Shortly afterwards with A Company on the left and B Company on the right, 2 Para advanced under heavy enemy shell fire from the persistent 155 mm guns. Their objective was the northern spur of Wireless Ridge, nicknamed *Apple Pie* and their fire support, controlled by the indomitable Captain Willie MacCracken, who had already supported 3 Para on Longdon, devasting. Expected minefields were traversed without casualties on the rough slope up to the flat ridge, where deep ponds added another hazard in the dark. What little opposition there was was soon mopped up but enemy shelling on their position intensified. There was no doubt that the lessons learnt at Goose Green were beginning to pay dividends, particularly the use of the 66 and 84 mm rockets in the block-busting role.

*One of the final battles of the war showing 2 Para's three phase left flanking attack on Wireless Ridge, supported by 4 Troop of the Blues and Royals with their Scorpions and Scimitars. In addition HMS Ambuscade provided fire support with their 4.5" gun.*

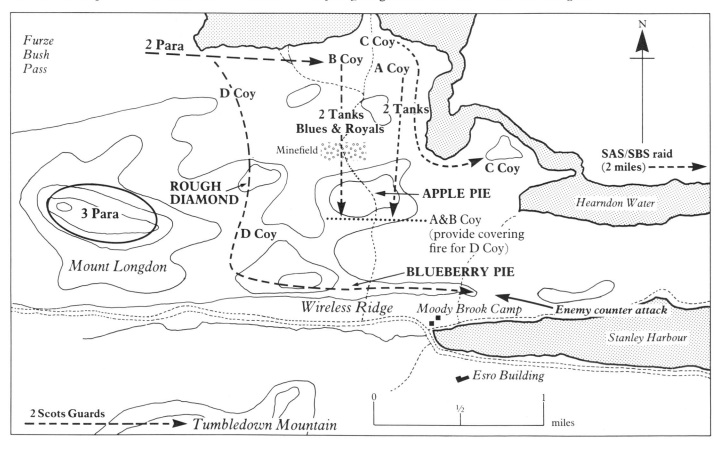

It was now C Company's turn to advance and accompanied by the morale boosting Blues and Royals they swung further left to check out reported enemy positions there. Once again the Argentines of 7th Infantry Regiment had retired hurriedly. The final phase was now in the hands of D Company, moving up from their recently taken ground to secure Wireless Ridge. They could hear the noise of the Scots Guards' battle away to their right. The western end of the ridge was reached with more difficulty than expected before they began to wheel left along the line of the rocky outcrops. Withering covering fire, not only from the heavier artillery but also from the machine guns of A and B Companies on *Apple Pie*, softened up the enemy. An unfortunate short round killed one of the paras in the leading 11 Platoon but they pressed on, fighting their way from bunker to bunker. Eventually as they approached the eastern end of the ridge, they discovered the enemy had cleared

*2 Para were the only unit to fight two full scale battles. Exhausted paratroopers are seen resting after their stiff fight for Wireless Ridge.*

off, leaving D Company to reorganise and await the expected artillery retaliation.

For almost the first time during the campaign, a counter attack was launched by the Argentines soon after dawn broke. Although D Company had run low on ammunition and the gunners were down to single figure rounds per gun, the attack was easily repelled and as the light came up the bedraggled enemy could be observed making their way down the road that led to Stanley.

There had only been one hitch in 2 Para's otherwise text book attack and that was not of their making. The SAS patrol, which had landed further east, had unexpectedly been illuminated by searchlight during their diversionary raid on 2 Para's left flank and sustained some

serious casualties. Captain John Greenhalgh RCT of 656 Squadron AAC, who had distinguished himself when evacuating casualties during the Goose Green action, once more flew his helicopter on numerous mercy missions, and later in the day he changed his role to fire SS-11 missiles at enemy reinforcements to the rear of Sapper Hill.

The supporting frigates had, as usual, withdrawn before first light, but not before ensuring the success of both the Tumbledown and Wireless Ridge attacks. Between them *Yarmouth*, *Avenger* and *Ambuscade* had fired 628 rounds that night to soften up the enemy and help destroy his morale. The heavier transport helicopters had been for ever busy bringing up supplies and ammunition to the forward troops. The paras holding the two forward positions seemed to gain unexpected strength in the knowledge that the end was near and were now keen to get into Stanley and finish it off.

# The Final Battles – Tumbledown

13 June was a busy day. The sun shone brightly which somehow lifted the morale of those troops who were to make the final attacks that night. Although they were certain the end of the war was near, few would have forecast that Argentine resistance would fold completely the next day.

The bombarding ships had left the area well before daylight to refuel and re-arm. *Arrow* completed her final shoots softening up the area of Sapper Hill and Moody Brook. She had fired 902 rounds during her month long vigil in the TEZ.

Argentine C-130s had continued to fly in reinforcements right up to the end, one of the last being a replacement 155mm gun for that destroyed by a GR3 Harrier which had scored a direct hit on a mounting near Moody Brook. A team from the International Committee of the Red Cross also arrived in Stanley that day. Later an Argentine Air Force Canberra, escorted by Mirages, was brought down by a Sea Dart missile from *Cardiff* after releasing her bombs harmlessly. The last attack on a ship would appear to have been that against *Penelope* who had come up on to the gunline.

The Scots Guards were led to their start line below Goat Ridge by Lieutenant Haddow who had carried out his lonely vigil there only five days before. Lieutenant Colonel Mike Scott was well aware that the tough 5th Argentine Marine Battalion were his main opposition, probably two companies with another supporting them from Mount William to the south east. His plan was to take the mile long ridge in three phases from west to east, one Company moving through another as each took their objective. To the south he would mount a major diversion force of his Recce Platoon accompanied by 4 Scimitars and Scorpions along the track towards Stanley.

G Company crossed the start line at 2100 on a cold clear night and occupied their first objective two miles away on the western ridge of Tumbledown without trouble. Only then did the Argentine snipers with their night sights start picking them off. The enemy were waiting for them as they had the previous night and the battle was on.

The Left Flank Company under Major John Kiszely skirting to the south of G Company met determined opposition as they came up the slope towards the dominant central feature, with heavy machine guns temporarily pinning them down. Even the trusted 66 and 84mm rockets did not seem to be effective against the well dug in Argentine regulars. The Royal Artillery Forward Observer called for fire from *Active* who that night fired 220 rounds onto Tumbledown including eight starshell which illuminated the area like daylight. In addition 105mm howitzers joined in support, but the Scots Guards were held up for a couple of hours.

At 0230 Major Kiszely, impatient to get on, led 15 Platoon forward and the citation for his MC reads '*Under fire and with complete disregard for his own safety, he led his men up a gully towards the enemy. Despite men falling wounded around him he continued his charge, throwing grenades as he went. Arriving on the enemy position, he killed two enemy with his rifle and a third with his bayonet . . . His was the culminating action in the Battalion successfully seizing its objective*'. The cost had been heavy, only seven men actually reaching the crest and of those only four were

*The Scots Guards' frontal assault on Tumbledown Mountain, which was held by the regular Argentine 5th Marine Battalion. They had fire support from 3 Troop, the Blues and Royals and HMS Active.*

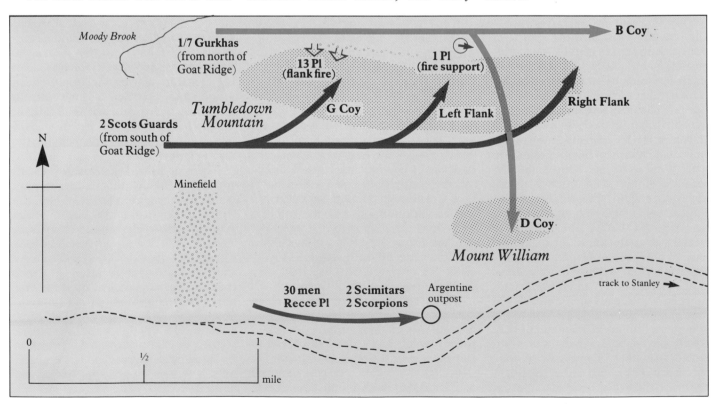

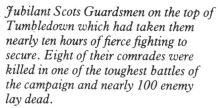

*Jubilant Scots Guardsmen on the top of Tumbledown which had taken them nearly ten hours of fierce fighting to secure. Eight of their comrades were killed in one of the toughest battles of the campaign and nearly 100 enemy lay dead.*

*An Argentinian view from the top of Tumbledown looking west from where the Scots Guards launched their successful attack. The 5th Marine Regiment were well dug in, in well constructed sangars amongst the rocky outcrops with excellent fields of fire, and had to be winkled out one section at a time.*

unscathed.

As the Guardsmen fought their way along the craggy Tumbledown ridge, they had to winkle the Argentine marines out one by one. Major Simon Price commanding Right Flank Company then took on phase three. He carried out a right flanking movement to try to dislodge the last enemy on a small knoll before daylight. At 0600 the guardsmen edged their way slowly up the rocky hill fighting through with bullets and phosphorous grenades. The enemy were well dug in behind carefully sighted sangars as befits regular troops. Lieutenant Robert Lawrence was severely wounded leading his platoon against intense fire from a machine gun position in one of the final attacks of the war.

By 0800 Tumbledown was theirs after one of the bloodiest battles of the campaign. Eight Scots Guardsmen had been killed and 33 wounded in the eleven hour battle, but the enemy toll was far higher with some estimates as high as 100 dead and 30 captured.

As dawn broke, the extent of the enemy defences could be seen. The battlefield was littered with dead and wounded, their equipment scattered everywhere. The Scots Guards reorganised and from their positions the FOOs could at last direct fire on to Stanley which lay before them.

Helicopters scuttled to and fro evacuating casualties, both British and Argentine. It was only then that other tales of bravery came to light. During the latter part of the battle of Tumbledown, Captain Sam Drennan, a former Scots Guards NCO, flew his Scout helicopter forward to the battalion's front line to evacuate the very seriously wounded, many of whom would not have survived the night. In all he lifted sixteen wounded under extremely hazardous conditions, well aware that one shot or shell might end his life.

With the Wireless Ridge battle successful on the left, the last bastions of Argentine resistance were crumbling but Tumbledown had been one of the hardest nuts to crack.

Even before the Scots Guards had taken Tumbledown, the 1/7 Gurkha Rifles were on the move. They were champing to get into the fight with their reputation undoubtedly spreading fear into the conscript Argentines. The decision was taken to maintain the momen-

tum by attacking Mount William in daylight. Led by Royal Marines Sergeant Wassell, they marched round the north of Tumbledown, skirting a minefield as they went, being covered by the Scots Guards. As they approached Mount William half a mile to the south east, they charged up the hill with their battle cry of 'Ayo Gurkhali' and they saw dispirited Argentine soldiers running down the reverse slope towards Stanley. The Gurkhas occupied the summit without a fight, much to their disappointment.

The Welsh Guards following, with only one of their own fighting companies still intact, continued towards Sapper Hill. They had had a nerve racked night waiting as reserve for the Scots Guards attack on Tumbledown, being subjected to desultory shelling. With the Argentines withdrawing rapidly, Lieutenant Colonel Johnny Ricketts was able to call on helicopters to lift forward A and C Companies of 40 Commando, who were under command, to the slopes of Sapper Hill. The scene was set for the final surrender. June 14 had been a long day.

# Stanley Falls – Defeat of General Menendez

General Mario Menendez, the Governor and Commander of the Argentine troops in the Falklands, suffered from continual interference from his superiors on the mainland as much as his opposite numbers did from Northwood. He had had no visits from top Argentine Military Commanders since General Galtieri's visit on 22 April when the Commander of the Joint Operations Centre in Comodoro Rivadavia, General Diego Garcia, stayed on till the 24th. Since then he had relied on the telephone to talk and be talked at by his masters.

In Argentina, there was no appreciation of the desperate situation which the Commander in the field found himself. Ever since the San Carlos landings they had been urging him to counter-attack the British 'invaders' without giving him encouragement, the men or the logistic support. They had little feeling for the conditions under which the Argentinians, mostly conscripts, were living and fighting, nor the strains and frustrations felt by Menendez. On 26 May, Garcia, probably encouraged by the Junta, rang Menendez ordering him to launch a counter attack against San Carlos. The views of the hierarchy were that the Navy and Air Forces had made their sacrifices and it was now time for action by the army. This showed the complete lack of comprehension of the reality of the situation by those far away from the actual battle zone.

Even up to the last minute, when Argentine positions in the mountains were being overrun, Galtieri was fanatically urging counter attacks, despite Menendez' gloomy reports. From 10 to 13 June for all practical purposes contact was cut off with the mainland as the Pope was visiting Argentina. The euphoria of this visit seemed to motivate Galtieri into even more frenzied miscalculations and predilections. On 13th he ordered Menendez to make a stand around Stanley, as though the capital was easy to defend without control of the surrounding mountains and hills. The Governor asked for more reinforcements and was told that the two Hercules which had arrived recently with stores were surely enough. There was no conception in Rio of the futility of the military situation.

Menendez had already accepted his fate when Two Sisters and Mount Harriet were lost. He would do his best with the limited resources he had, but however much his will to succeed, he knew the end was near. 'Hold out for what?' was for ever in his thoughts. Even the spirited counter attacks launched by 6 Regiment and the 5th Marines had not much conviction in them. By 0830 on 14th his army was pouring back into Port Stanley with little heart left for a fight. An hour later in a telephone call to General Garcia he explained the hopeless situation and asked them to find a political solution to end the fighting without losing too much face. When he spoke to Galtieri a little later he asked if the President could again look into the possibility of accepting Resolution 502. After saying that this was impossible Galtieri suggested that as the British were undoubtedly a spent force after their attacks, the struggle could continue. The conversa-

*Major General Jeremy Moore, Commander of the Land Forces Falkland Islands, holds a copy of the surrender document which he and Major General Mario Menendez signed on 14 June 1982. The only word that Moore conceded should be struck out was the word 'unconditional' before surrender.*

172

tion finished with abruptness when Capitan Melbourne Hussey, an Argentine Naval officer, informed Menendez that he had received a communication from the British which offered surrender.

Menendez relief was plainly clear as, until that moment, he had little idea how to end the fighting. He signalled General Garcia who authorized him to accept it with a proviso from the President that any surrender was not to include anything that might be construed as a 'political compromise' for his country, and certainly not Resolution 502.

On the British side General Moore's staff had for several days been endeavouring to contact the beleaguered garrison with a view to negotiating surrender terms. They had used the Falkland Islands medical radio link which was still open to the hospital in Stanley. Dr. Alison Bleaney, the islands' deputy medical officer, who had worked continually to help the islanders during the occupation, was the catalyst to help set up the surrender negotiations. Captain Rod Bell, who throughout the campaign had employed his language skills mainly in interroga-

tion, now became the chief interpreter. With Lieutenant Colonel Mike Rose, CO of 22 SAS, they flew into Stanley by Gazelle helicopter, a large white sheet draped under the fuselage. When it became clear that the Argentinians would agree to negotiate, British troops were ordered to fire only in self defence. The time was 1105.

They landed a short distance from the secretariat and had to scramble through a few wire fences before meeting Capitan Hussey. As they passed the hospital they met and thanked Alison Bleaney for her intermediary work and she informed them that the only three civilian casualties of the campaign had been killed by a naval bombardment three days earlier.

The conference room was already laid

*Marines of K Company, 42 Commando, patrol through an abandoned and battle scarred part of Stanley waterfront after the surrender. The Argentine prisoners were quickly moved out of the town and assembled at the airport, from where they were repatriated by sea as quickly as possible.*

out neatly as Rose and Bell took their places. The negotiations lasted 90 minutes with Colonel Rose using his portable satellite radio channel with London to keep them informed, while Bell's link was with General Moore. On the Argentine side Menendez was in direct contact with President Galtieri. When terms had been agreed by both sides, they informed General Moore who was delayed flying in from *Fearless* by a snow storm. However a Sea King of 820 Squadron brought him ashore at 1800 and with both commanders saluting but not shaking hands they discussed the final details of the surrender document. The Argentines, still conscious of the morale effect caused by photographs of Astiz signing the surrender of South Georgia, requested that no press should be present. The only alteration that Moore conceded was that the word 'unconditional' should be struck out before surrender. It was signed by General Menendez and General Moore as at 2359Z (2059 local) and witnessed by Colonel Brian Pennicott. The saddened figure of Menendez was allowed to break the news to his troops at the airport, before he was evacuated to *Fearless* the following morning.

Appropriately having been the only unit to fight two major battles, 2 Para had already marched into Stanley at 1330 that afternoon, Major Dair Farrar-Hockley leading A Company, now with red berets replacing their steel helmets. The following morning J Company of 42 Commando, most of them from the original NP 8901 hoisted the same flag over Government House that they had so ignominiously taken down just 74 days earlier.

Major General Moore was able to make the following signal:

'HQ LFFI Port Stanley. In Port Stanley at 9 o'clock pm Falklands Islands time tonight the 14th June 1982, Maj Gen Menendez surrendered to me all the Argentine Armed Forces in East and West Falkland, together with their impediments. Arrangements are in hand to assemble the men for return to Argentina, to gather in their arms and equipment, and to mark and make safe their munitions. The Falkland Islands are once more under the Government desired by their inhabitants. God Save The Queen.

Signed J J Moore'.

# Return of Argentine Prisoners

It is easier to start a war than to finish it. When the armistice finally came on the evening of 14 June 1982, the realisation on both sides had a remarkably deflating effect on both victors and vanquished. Four weeks of extreme physical endurance in one of the worst climates in the world, below freezing temperatures, incessant sleet and snow flurries, with virtually no natural cover to give the slightest protection from the biting cold and wet winds that swept the bleak countryside, saps the strength far more than the close proximity of the enemy.

During a battle, the adrenalin flows, excitement and tension increase, the discomforts of the climate are temporarily forgotten and an inner fire keeps the mind and body active. It is only after a battle that the realities of the elements bite hard, the anti-climatic period. The British and Argentinians alike had endured the same conditions with remarkable tenacity and patience. The last few days of fighting had undermined the resistance of the defenders, while the attackers had found an extra untapped reserve of willpower which kept them going. With the cease fire, both sides

*Argentine prisoners stream down Mount Kent, where they had been taken after 42 Commando had captured them on Mount Harriet on the night of 11/12 June.*

were physically and mentally exhausted and like most soldiers, craved for some creature comforts.

As the Royal Marines and Paratroopers made their way into Stanley to seek whatever shelter they could for the night, they passed thousands of dejected and exhausted Argentines sitting disconsolately by the roadside. Many were wounded, most had thrown away their arms. A century earlier Ullyses S. Grant, the American General had written about a defeated enemy '*My own feelings, which had been quite jubilant, were sad and depressing. I felt like anything rather than rejoicing at the downfall of a foe who had fought so long and gallantly*'. Such were the feelings of many of the men who marched into Stanley in the next few days. It was a sight never to be forgotten.

Although the Secretary of State for Defence announced to Parliament that 11,400 prisoners had been taken, the total number documented was 12,978, a number far exceeding the attackers of the Land Forces. Many were in very poor physical condition, suffering privation and shortage of food as well as physical infirmities. About 8,000 prisoners were immediately moved out of Stanley to the airport area, where they could be more easily watched. There they had to improvise shelter as best they could. Their poor condition was in part due to the lack of concern by their own

officers and NCOs. There were reasonably large stocks of Argentine food still in containers which had not been distributed to forward troops and these were soon made available. Some clothing was also spared and there was a genuine concern among the British Command of more deaths and that disease might spread in this unhealthy climate. It was essential to repatriate all prisoners as quickly as possible.

When the first prisoners were taken at Goose Green, the 1,300 far outnumbered anything visualised. There was no organisation to deal with them, no bed-

*The Argentine* Almirante Irizar, *which had taken part in the initial Argentinian landings in April, finished the war as a hospital ship, repatriating prisoners home.*

*Some of the 12,978 Argentine prisoners arrive back in Puerto Madryn, after being taken there by SS* Canberra, Norland *and Argentine hospital ships.*

ding nor tentage and no provision for feeding them. The greatest barrier to interrogating and administering them was language, as there were very few Spanish speakers in the Force. This lack of interpreters was apparent throughout the campaign.

Matters had improved slightly by the fall of Stanley. From the start, prisoners were processed and documented. By dusk on the first day 1,121 had been accepted by *Canberra* anchored in San Carlos Water, being guarded by the Royal Marines Band, Welsh Guardsmen and RAF personnel. By 1300 on 16th she had anchored to the east of the Falklands off Port William where she was to embark more prisoners. By the time she sailed the following day she had 4,167 aboard. All had been stripped and searched, labelled with P & O tags, and carefully documented. The search had revealed hidden weapons and ammunition, tokens of war. For those who had defended the bleak hills surrounding Stanley only two nights before, they could hardly have expected to return home in a luxury liner, one which they had been told had been sunk during the war.

Many wounded were taken on board the *Bahia Paraiso*, now fitted as a hospital ship, and also the *Uganda* in Falkland Sound. However it was the duty of the Junta to repatriate their own men and they agreed, after successful Red Cross negotiations, to allow *Canberra* to proceed direct to Puerto Madryn, an obscure port in Argentina. She entered the harbour at 1000 on 19 June escorted by the Argentine destroyers *Santissima Trinidad* and *Comodoro Py*. Here they were signed for while the Red Cross supervised the transfer certifying that all was in order. Wearily the prisoners loaded into buses and lorries. Three hours after docking, *Canberra* quietly slipped out of harbour to return to the Falklands and pick up the men of 3 Commando Brigade for a far different homecoming.

On 17 June *Norland* arrived at Port William where she embarked a further 2,047 prisoners, following the same course as her fellow P & O ship, arriving at Puerto Madryn on 21st. She also returned to Stanley with the more happy task of taking aboard the two Parachute battalions for their voyage home. It is ironic that the defeated arrived home nearly three weeks ahead of the majority of the victors. Most of the remaining prisoners were repatriated by the *Bahia Paraiso* and *Almirante Irizar*, both of which had been involved in the Falklands invasion of early April.

There was still one prisoner to think about, the only Britain to be captured, Flight Lieutenant Jeffrey Glover who had been shot down on 21 May. He had been taken to the military hospital in Comodoro Rivadavia with a broken arm and on recovery was flown home on 8 July.

Apart from prisoners, there was the unenviable task of clearing up the piles of abandoned stores, weapons and equipment left behind by the defeated army. The main concern was the hundreds of plastic anti-personnel mines that had been scattered without record. These had to be dealt with in slow time along with those laid in the hills, during the months ahead. Not only were they a hazard to humans but they would jeopardise the sheep which roamed the Falklands battlefields. On the airfield nine damaged Pucaras and an Aeromacchi were strewn, ammunition dumps and stores lying everywhere. It was a depressing site. The filtration plant which supplied Stanley with water had been destroyed in the bombardment. All these needed to be dealt with.

The final Argentine prisoners to be repatriated, about 300 Special Category ones, including General Menendez, had been held in the *St Edmund* and were landed at Puerto Madryn on 30 June. The war was over, but the rehabilitation had only just begun.

# Return of the Task Force

It was ironic that the defeated Argentinian Army, over 12,000 of whom had been taken prisoner, should arrive in their homeland long before the victorious forces of Britain. However their unpretentious, quiet arrival at Puerto Madryn was in sharp contrast to the euphoric welcome that awaited the British Task Force at the sea ports and airfields around England.

Some ships, like the *Queen Elizabeth 2*, reached the United Kingdom even before the final battles had been won 8,000 miles away. Indeed the great Cunarder docked in Southampton at midday on 11 June with some 629 survivors from the *Ardent*, *Antelope* and *Coventry*. The more seriously injured had been given first class cabins, where they received excellent medical care and attention. HM Queen Elizabeth, The Queen Mother, aboard the Royal Yacht greeted the ship in the Solent. The seafront at Cowes in the Isle of Wight was lined with expectant crowds waiting to catch a glimpse of the majestic liner. All the way up Southampton Water cheering groups of people had gathered since dawn and there were thousands, mostly families of those on board, to greet them as the ship came alongside. That night, 8,000 miles away, 3 Commando Brigade began their last, gruelling attacks on the mountains around Stanley.

Other servicemen, many of them the more seriously injured, had been flown home from Ascension, receiving a quieter, but nonetheless, enthusiastic welcome from their anxious families and waiting RAF personnel. The Welfare Services had worked day and night to ensure that as many next of kin as possible were there to greet their loved ones.

Meanwhile, down in the Falklands, there was still the task of clearing up the more remote areas and especially West Falkland. 40 Commando, which had impatiently remained in defensive positions around San Carlos and Ajax Bay, while their fellow marines were fighting the Battle for Stanley, were tasked with taking the surrender of the Argentinian garrison at Port Howard, where they found 850 pitiful and neglected men of the 5th Regiment, whose officers included Second Lieutenant Menendez, the son of the Argentine Commander. Fox Bay was cleared by a naval landing party

from *Avenger*, and helicopter and landing craft patrols searched the islands for Argentinians who were only too eager to surrender.

Elsewhere, there remained the re-occupation of Thule, the remote island 450 miles south-east of South Georgia. 81 Royal Marines of M Company, 42 Commando, embarked in a small Task Unit, comprising *Endurance* (Captain Nick Barker was to be involved to the end), *Yarmouth*, the RFA *Olmeda* and the tug *Salvageman*. On 18 June they landed on the barren island and took possession of the Argentinian Scientific and Meteorological Base which had been set up illegally there in 1976. 10 Argentinians were taken off and the Union Flag hoisted.

Meanwhile there was still much work to be done by the Task Force. The repatriation of Argentine prisoners in the *Canberra* and *Norland* had taken priority. It meant they and *Europic Ferry* were not available to embark the marines and paras until 25 June. At sea the Royal Navy had to maintain vigilance over the TEZ in case of any reaction from the defeated Argentinians. Although no major invasion was visualised, the latin temperament might lead a determined pilot on a suicide mission or infiltrators might try to land on the islands. Despite the official end to hostilities, the Services had to keep as regular watch as they had done during the previous two months.

The commanders agreed that the whole of 3 Commando Brigade, which still included the two Parachute Regiments, should be repatriated as quickly as possible. 5 Infantry Brigade were already there and further reinforcements started to arrive as soon as the war had ended on 14 June. Although the surrender had been signed there could be no let up in the security and alertnesss of those on the Islands. 5 Brigade were to be the immediate garrison troops, although many, particularly the Scots Guards, had fought a major battle in the final days before the capitulation. The logistic services worked overtime to improve accommodation, to repair the water supply system, build up food and clothing stocks, and generally restore life in Stanley to as near normal as was possible after such an upheaval. Already the

Islanders realised that life was never going to be the same. The small Royal Marines garrison which had once looked after their security, had already been replaced by a vast military machine that would disrupt their lives into the forseeable future.

Former Governor Rex Hunt immediately returned to the Falkland Islands, taking over again as the senior Government Officer from Harold Rowlands, the Financial Secretary who had remained during the occupation. His new title was the Civil Commissioner, with powers equating to that of his former appointment as Governor, but without being Commander-in-Chief. The Military Commissioner was now his defence adviser. He set about the re-habilitation and establishment of a new and enhanced civil administration. For the moment the military were in total control, the victorious Major General Jeremy Moore, his job completed, was relieved by the

*HRH The Prince of Wales with officers aboard* Canberra. *From top Lt Col Malcolm Hunt (40 Cdo), Lt Col Nick Vaux (42 Cdo) and Lt Col Mike Holroyd Smith (29 Cdo Lt Regt RA) (saluting).*

*'The Great White Whale', SS* Canberra, *carrying most of 3 Commando Brigade, steams triumphantly up Southampton Water amidst a fleet of welcoming little boats.*

Army's Major General David Thorne. While wartime conditions still existed there was a lax economy in the use of food, fuel, transport and stores. The Daily Telegraph Correspondent Major General Edward Fursdon, who visited the Islands shortly after the war, reported that the islanders hitched helicopter rides regularly and felt that *'the constant military assistance was not only the 'norm', but theirs by right'*. A Military Commission Command Secretary was immediately appointed, Jack Morgan, who had a stringent brief to control spending and

get things back to normal as far as spending was concerned. He was a senior civil servant working for the Ministry of Defence, and by its very nature, his job was not to prove a popular one either with the military or civil administrations, but it was vital to get the Islands back on a sound financial footing.

Rex Hunt established a Civil/Military Committee, which met once a week to sort out and report on the problems emanating from the aftermath of the war. The military had the equipment, men and means to help restore the island to a peacetime environment and were welcomed into the homes of the Falklanders with unfailing hospitality. For many months public buildings were taken over by the military, while the hospital and other facilities were shared.

HM Ships were slowly relieved in the South Atlantic and made their way individually home. It gave the crews, especially those in ships which had suffered death and severe damage, time to come to terms with the horrors they had been through and contemplate the new life ahead of them. The time lapse between leaving the Falklands and arriving home allowed reports to be written, lessons to be assessed and wounds, physical and mental to be healed. Wars do not stop routine correspondence and regular returns to be made; these had to be caught up on during the voyage home, so that when the ship did arrive, men could immediately go on leave for the rest and recuperation they sorely needed.

One of the first warships to arrive home was *Glasgow*, which had been badly

*The last action of the campaign when M Company, 42 Commando re-occupied the remote outpost of South Thule, where Argentina had set up an illegal Scientific Base.*

*Falklands Governor Rex Hunt passes No 166 Troop for duty at the Commando Training Centre Royal Marines, during his temporary exile. He returned as Civil Commissioner on cessation of hostilities.*

damaged by a bomb passing through both sides of her hull without exploding. Her warm welcome at Portsmouth on 21 June was an occasion which was to be repeated many times during the next few months. The first warship into Devonport was *Alacrity* on the 25th.

On that day, the burnt out hulk of *Sir Galahad* was towed out to sea where the submarine *Onyx* scuttled her with a torpedo. The other badly damaged LSL *Sir Tristram* was refloated and towed into Stanley, to be brought home two years later. Other ships to be disposed of at sea were the badly damaged Argentine auxiliary *Bahia Buen Suceso* and the crippled submarine *Santa Fe*.

Rear Admiral 'Sandy' Woodward, now flying his flag in *Bristol* was relieved by Rear Admiral Derek Reffell on 1 July and three weeks later the TEZ was reduced to 150 miles and retitled Falkland Islands Protection Zone. By this time the victorious troops were well on their way home, relaxing in the tropical sunshine as they sailed towards Ascension Island. It had been sensibly decided that the Royal Marines and Parachute Regiment should be split for the return, so that each could be welcomed into the bosom of their own families.

2 and 3 Para embarked in the *Norland*, in which they celebrated Airborne Forces Day on 4 July, with their heavy equipment travelling in *Europic Ferry*, and sailed for Ascension on 25 June. The Chief of the Defence Staff, General Sir Edwin Bramall was amongst those who greeted them there. From Wideawake airfield they flew home by RAF VC 10s to a tumultuous welcome at Brize Norton. The Prince of Wales, as Colonel-in-Chief of the Parachute Regiment, along with Admiral Sir John Fieldhouse and many other senior officers, greeted the men who had fought so gallantly at Goose Green, Mount Longdon and Wireless Ridge. But it was the families, who had watched their loved ones depart only three months before who gave them the biggest welcome. Forty men of the two battalions had been killed in action and would never return.

As each HM Ship arrived at her home port, there was a deafening, but warm reception from families and holiday-makers alike as they lined Southsea seafront or Plymouth Hoe. On Saturday 11 July, all roads leading into Portsmouth were jammed with traffic as *Glamorgan* made her triumphant entry into the harbour. But the most spectacular reception, covered fully by the media, was on the following day for the 'Great White Whale' herself, carrying nearly 2,000 marines of 3 Commando Brigade. The morning dawned fine but hazy as *Canberra* crept slowly round the Isle of

Wight. Prince Charles, this time in Royal Naval uniform, along with Admiral Sir John Fieldhouse and the Commandant General Royal Marines, General Sir Steuart Pringle, along with a large press corps, helicoptered aboard the ship in the early hours of the morning. Small and large boats, later fire tenders, escorted the pride of the P & O Line up the Solent and into Southampton Water after 94 days at sea.

There is something special about a great ship, still scarred by rust and war paint returning from a war, that evoked memories of campaigns gone by. The weather could hardly have been fairer as the marines lined the decks draping hurriedly painted banners over the side, bearing such slogans as 'Lock Up Your Daughters – The Bootnecks Are Back', all the while listening to the Royal Marines Band playing on the forward flight deck. There were tears as well as cheers as many of the young veterans, each containing his own emotions, watched their temporary 'home' slowly glide into Southampton. The sheer scale of the welcome took them by surprise. It was a supreme example of emotional patriotism. A fly past by helicopters saluted the ship and thousands of bal-

loons were released into the air. As each man disembarked he was presented with a rose and fought his way to his family through the multitude on the quayside. Other proud Britains around the country watched it all live on television. The marines embarked in their vehicles for their bases, and as they drove westwards through southern England, the Sunday crowds cheered them all the way.

If this welcome has been singled out, it is because it attracted the biggest crowds, but scenes like this, during the beautiful summer days of July and August 1982, were oft repeated during the ensuing weeks by warships, RFAs and STUFT ships alike. Devonport was to give its own welcome to *Brilliant* on 13 July, followed by her sister ship *Broadsword* ten days later. *Fearless* and *Intrepid* arrived back on 14 July and a week later the flagship of the task force

*HMS* Cardiff, *which had frequently bombarded installations at Stanley airport and later become* Canberra's *escort, returns to Portsmouth on 28 July.*

*Hermes* sailed majestically into Portsmouth, Prime Minister Margaret Thatcher and Admiral of the Fleet Sir Terence Lewin having helicoptered out to her off Spithead. Each arrival, however large or small, was very special to her own crew and their close families.

Meanwhile there was much work behind the scenes in the UK. The Welfare services were working overtime to comfort and succour the bereaved. The South Atlantic Fund was set up and attracted over £11 million. A committee was established to administer this fund in the fairest possible way. Despite some outspoken media expressing dissatisfac-

tion when they presumed to have discovered an isolated injustice, all wounded, bereaved and suffering, many with mental illnesses, were handsomely compensated. The large sums they received, in addition to their pensions, far exceeded anything paid to servicemen in past wars and campaigns. It must be remembered that they were all disabled doing the job they joined for.

Service hospitals, and those such as the specialist spinal unit at Stoke Mandeville, carried the burden of after care and rehabilitation. Each case was treated with the individual touch that is so essential for recovery. 777 men had been wounded, some very seriously indeed, and in many cases it has taken years for them to recover; but one Royal Marine who had lost a foot on an enemy mine was on patrol in Ulster in a very different type of 'active service' only six months later.

# The Aftermath

A war, however long or short, brings with it considerable post-emergency problems. Some are comparatively short lived, but most are likely to be very long term, some are personal, some geographical and some physical; others are political and military. Each one needs careful assessment to see whether there is, indeed, a problem at all.

The effects of the war on the small, compact and seemingly isolated British dependency, 8,000 miles from its motherland, are probably the most lasting. Life can never be the same again. Before the Argentinians invaded 1,800 Falklanders lived a quiet, unobtrusive life, with the same sort of climate and conditions as those who live on the remote islands of the Outer Hebrides. Most were farmers or fishermen living in small settlements throughout the islands. Suddenly their friendly garrison has been increased from just 35 Royal Marines to an occupation force of several thousands. Their airstrip, capable of receiving only short range transport aircraft has now been replaced by the busy Mount Pleasant airport, opened by HRH The Prince Andrew on 12 May 1985, and situated half way between Stanley and Goose Green. It has a modern runway where the largest and most sophisticated aircraft can land, with 120 buildings for stores, offices and accommodation. During the peak of its construction, it employed 2,000 men. The Falklands seas, once the domain of small-time fishermen, has now become a hive of international industry.

Although the occupying garrison is billetted away from the main town of Stanley, all sea traffic to and from the islands must pass through the port. This has enhanced their trade and commerce. As soon as the war finished speculators were descending on this new and enlarged colony to reap what pickings they could, by 1989 many had left, some disillusioned, others having made their not insignificant 'pile'. After seven years, life is settling down to normal, but in the background there is still a strong feeling among the locals that Britain might well abandon them again after a few years. A change of government in the UK and a change of policy might tend to see matters in a different light. Already a new and determined regime in Argentina is looking eagerly for signs that British resolve to retain the absolute sovereignty over the Falklands might be weakening. Indeed the Argentinians have still not officially declared a cessation of hostilities. There can be no letting up.

The present case for retaining sovereignty over the islands is strong. There is a new global awareness of the strategical importance of the mineral resources in Antarctica, and the territorial waters surrounding the Falklands are rich. The greedy uncertainty of successive callous and unpredictable Argentinian governments offer little comfort to the Falklanders who are firm in their resolve to maintain the status quo. Possibly stronger still is the determination to punish Argentina for a blatant breach of international law when they invaded in 1982; and to ensure that it does not happen again. The Falklanders are of a strong and determined stock, not easily shaken in their resolve to fight for freedom. However much they resent the presence of British troops on their islands, they know that needs must. They also resent the conditions of the 1981 Nationality Act, equating their status with that of the Hong Kong Chinese, whereby third and fourth generations have no right of residence in the UK. However the newly instituted Falkland Islands Development Corporation set up in 1988, aims to increase employment opportunities, improve community relations and develop the natural resources of the islands.

The residual military problems are perhaps clearer. The immediate requirement in 1982 was to identify and clear the thousands of Argentinian mines, many of which had been scattered indiscriminately. Clear areas were slowly declared, though it was impossible to ensure that all was entirely safe. Huge stocks of Argentinian clothing, equipment and ammunition had to be disposed of, and new roads were built. With a large garrison to maintain, comforts were added, which also affected the civilian population. A taped television service now operates, and direct dialling telephone facilities with the UK have been introduced.

The skill and quality of the British servicemen is unquestioned; the size of its armed force is. Their speed of reaction to this emergency remains one of the extraordinary features of the war.

Its equipment was severely tested during the campaign, and generally found to be excellent. The Harrier with its Sidewinder missiles, proved unmatched by the more antiquated Argentine fighters; the Royal Navy's missile systems were generally found adequate though sadly lacking in the most important aspect of early airborne warning radar and identification of low level aircraft; the Exocet missile's spectacular success was due entirely to this lack of warning, and could well be neutralised in a future

*Lt HRH The Prince Andrew, who served in 820 Sqn, unveils the Mount Pleasant plaque watched by Michael Heseltine and Sir Rex and Lady Hunt.*

have a large new training area; giving scope for exercises that can be realistic and less restrictive than at home. They can also be longer and with more continuity as the close proximity of families is no longer a problem. Whilst NATO field conditions cannot be simulated, survival and fitness can be exploited to the full. It is an area in which the Royal Navy and Royal Air Force, in particular, have a continuing operational role.

The war also highlighted the need for dedicated amphibious shipping. Although civilian ferries were taken up and sailed into unfamiliar waters, it was the six LSLs which bore the brunt of the action and supplied the added expertise so essential to maritime operations. The medical services learnt its lessons too, but the dedication of doctors and medical staff, the skilful surgery and after care was beyond reproach. The shortage of helicopters in close support of ground operations was no more apparent than when the commandos and the paras 'yomped' across East Falkland, but later partially rectified when casualty evacuation was at a premium.

The residual problems at home were of a different and perhaps more lasting nature. 777 British servicemen were wounded in the campaign and each needed his own special care and attention. Financially each one was secure, receiving carefully resolved gratuities from the South Atlantic Fund, which reached the staggering height of £11 million. However the mental and physical scars will take time to heal. Various complaints have been made, mainly through the media of television films and books; one certainly depicting the Services as mean and uncaring; another that recovery and rehabilitation can be as near complete as possible with sufficient will-power and determination. The Welfare Services were initially hampered by media reports of disasters being broadcast before they received casualty lists. This new problem to the British of having instant media coverage will be with us for ever.

But what of the cost? Was it worth it? These are questions which only time will answer. In terms of sacrifice, 255 British and 750 Argentinians lost their lives. The calculated decision to send a British Task Force to protect sovereign rights and the freedom of the individual against unprovoked aggression was undoubtedly fully justified.

conflict. Warship design came in for considerable criticism, particularly in its lack of fire resistant qualities; while at the other end of the scale, the infantry's DMS boot was virtually useless in the wet and cold of an Antarctic winter.

Much has been written about the cost of maintaining a large garrison in the Falklands; but it must be remembered that there has been no expansion in the size of the British armed forces since 1982; all these men would have been serving elsewhere, being fed and accommodated. What it has highlighted is the limited ability of Britain to fight and sustain a campaign outside the European theatre; and the enormous logistic support required to keep such an occupation force, which costs a great deal of taxpayer's money.

On the plus side, all three Services

# MAJOR HONOURS AND AWARDS

## Army

**VC (Posthumous)**
Lieutenant Colonel H Jones OBE, 2 Para
Sergeant IJ McKay, 3 Para

**DSO**
Major CNG Delves, Devon & Dorsets
Major CPB Keeble, Para
Lieutenant Colonel HWR Pike MBE, Para
Lieutenant Colonel MIE Scott, Scots Gds

**DSC**
Warrant Officer 2 JH Phillips, RE

**MC (Posthumous)**
Captain GJ Hamilton, Green Howards

**MC**
Major MH Argue, Para
Captain TW Burls, Para
Major DA Collett, Para
Lieutenant CS Conner, Para
Major JH Crosland, Para
Major CD Farrar-Hockley, Para
Major JP Kiszeley, Scots Gds
Lieutenant RAD Lawrence, Scots Gds
Captain WA McCracken, RA
Captain AJG Wight, Welsh Gds

**DFC**
Captain SM Drennan, AAC
Captain JG Greenhalgh, RCT

**DCM (Posthumous)**
Private S Illingworth, Para
Guardsman JBC Reynolds, Scots Gds

**DCM**
Corporal D Abols, Para
Staff Sergeant B Faulkner, Para
Sergeant JC Meredith, Para
Warrant Officer 2 W Nicol, Scots Gds
Sergeant JS Pettinger, Para

**CGM (Posthumous)**
Staff Sergeant J Prescott, RE

**MM (Posthumous)**
Private RJdeM Absolon, Para
Lance Corporal GD Bingley, Para

**MM**
Corporal IP Bailey, Para
Lance Corporal SA Bardsley, Para
Sergeant TI Barrett, Para
Lance Corporal MWL Bentley, Para
Sergeant DS Boultby, RCT
Corporal T Brookes, R Signals
Corporal TJ Camp, Para
Private SG Carter, Para
Guardsman SM Chapman, Welsh Gds
Corporal JA Foran, RE
Sergeant D Fuller, Para
Private BJ Grayling, Para
Corporal TW Harley, Para
Bombardier EM Holt, RA
Sergeant RW Jackson, Scots Gds
Lance Corporal DJ Loveridge, Welsh Guards
Sergeant JG Mather, SAS
Sergeant PHR Naya, RAMC
Warrant Officer 2 BT Neck, Welsh Gds
Guardsman AS Pengelly, Scots Gds
Lance Corporal LJL Standish, Para
Sergeant RH Wrega, RE

**CBE**
Colonel IS Baxter (late RCT)
Colonel JD Bidmead (late RCT)
Colonel DBH Colley (late RCT)
Colonel BC MacDermott (late RAMC)

**OBE**
Lieutenant Colonel AE Berry, RGJ
Lieutenant Colonel IJ Hellberg, RCT
Lieutenant Colonel MJ Holdroyd-Smith, RA
Major PJ Hubert, Queen's
Lieutenant Colonel WSP McGregor, RAMC
Lieutenant Colonel DP de C Morgan, 7GR
Lieutenant Colonel JF Rickett, Welsh Gds
Lieutenant Colonel (QM) PJ Saunders, RE
Lieutenant Colonel R Welsh, RAMC

**MBE**
Major EL Barrett, RCT
Major CG Batty, RAMC
Major CM Davies, RE
Warrant Officer 1 (RSM) AJ Davies, Welsh Gds
Major JA East, RAMC
Warrant Officer, 1 L Ellson, Welsh Gds
Major AR Gale, R Signals
Major C Griffiths, RAMC
Major (QM) GM Groom, RCT
Warrant Officer 1 T Haig, RE
Major L Hollingworth, RAOC
Captain TG McCabe, RAMC
Warrant Officer 1 MJ McHale, RAMC
Captain R Marshall, Int Corps
Captain (QMP) NE Menzies, Para
Lieutenant FJ Moody, Scots Gds
Warrant Officer 2 D Moore, RCT
Warrant Officer 1 RG Randall, RE
Major (OEO) JM Ridding, RAOC
Major RJ Stuart, R Signals
Warrant Officer 2 PM Williams RCT
Major TJ Wilton, RA
Major GJ Yeoman, RCT
Warrant Officer 2 RC Yeomans, R Signals

**MBE (Civil)
(Army Sponsored)**
Mr AM Cleaver, Corr PA
Mr JRR Fox, BBC Rep

**BEM**
Staff Sergeant WF Blyth, RCT
Staff Sergeant EG Bradbury, RE
Sergeant RJ Brown, RE
Staff Sergeant MJ Dent, RE
Staff Sergeant J Fenwick, REME
Staff Sergeant RL Griffiths, R Signals
Corporal NJ Hall, RE
Sergeant D Harvey, RAOC
Staff Sergeant CL Henderson, ACC
Corporal GJ Herrington, RPC
Staff Sergeant JD Holmes, RAOC
Corporal WH Hopkins, RAOC
Private DJ Hunt, ACC
Sergeant DR Pasfield, RE
Staff Sergeant P Rayner, RE
Warrant Officer 2 M Reid, RAMC
Staff Sergeant CG Taylor, REME
Sergeant A. Worthington, RE

## Royal Navy and Royal Marines

**KCB**
Major General JJ Moore OBE MC
Rear Admiral JF Woodward

**CB**
Commodore MC Clapp
Brigadier JHA Thompson OBE ADC
Rear Admiral AJ Whetstone

**DSO**
Captain ME Barrow
Captain JJ Black MBE
Captain WR Canning
Captain JF Coward
Captain PGV Dingemans
Commodore SC Dunlop CBE RFA
Lieutenant Commander BF Dutton QGM
Captain CH Layman MVO
Captain ESJ Larken
Captain LE Middleton ADC
Captain D Pentreath
Captain PJG Roberts RFA
Lieutenant Commander I Stanley
Lieutenant Colonel NF Vaux RM
Lieutenant Colonel AF Whitehead RM
Commander CL Wreford-Brown
Captain BG Young

**DSC (Posthumous)**
Lieutenant Commander GWJ Batt
Captain I North, Merchant Navy
Lieutenant Commander JM Sephton
Lieutenant Commander JS Woodhead

## DSC
Lieutenant Commander AD Auld
Lieutenant ARC Bennett
Lieutenant Commander MD Booth
Commander PJ Bootherstone
Lieutenant NA Bruen
Lieutenant Commander HS Clark
Commander CJS Craig
Lieutenant Commander JA Ellerbeck
Fleet Chief Petty Officer MG Fellows BEM
Captain GR Green RFA
Lieutenant R Hutchings RM
Captain DE Lawrence RFA
Lieutenant Commander HJ Lomas
Lieutenant KP Mills RM
Sub Lieutenant PT Morgan
Commander A Morton
Lieutenant NJ North
Captain AF Pitt RFA
Lieutenant Commander NW Thomas
Lieutenant SR Thomas
Lieutenant Commander SC Thornewill
Commander NJ Tobin
Commander ND Ward AFC
Commander AWJ West

## MC
Captain PM Babbington RM
Major CP Cameron RM
Lieutenant CI Dytor RM
Lieutenant C Fox RM
Lieutenant DJ Stewart RM

## DFC (Posthumous)
Lieutenant RJ Nunn RM

## DFC
Captain JP Niblett RM

## AFC
Lieutenant Commander DJS Squier
Lieutenant Commander RJS Wykes-Sneyd

## DCM
Corporal J Burdett RM

## George Medal (Posthumous)
2nd Engineer Officer PA Henry RFA

## George Medal
Able Seaman JE Dillon

## Queen's Gallantry Medal (Posthumous)
Colour Sergeant D Johnston RM

## Queen's Gallantry Medal
Chief Engineer Officer CKA Adams RFA
Lieutenant JK Boughton
Marine Engineer Artificer K Enticknapp
3rd Officer A Gudgeon RFA
Petty Officer Medical Assistant GA Meager
Lieutenant PJ Sheldon
3rd Engineer BR Williams Merchant Navy

## DSM (Posthumous)
Petty Officer Marine Engineering Mechanic DR Briggs
Corporal MD Love RM

## DSM
Colour Sergeant MJ Francis RM
Leading Aircrewman PB Imrie
Sergeant PJ Leach RM
Petty Officer JS Leake
Sergeant WJ Leslie RM
Petty Officer GJR Libby
Chief Marine Engineering Mechanic MD Townsend
Chief Petty Officer GM Trotter
Chief Petty Officer Aircrewman MJ Tupper
Leading Seaman JD Warren

## MM
Corporal AR Bishop RM
Sergeant M Collins RM
Sergeant T Collings RM
Corporal M Eccles RM
Corporal D Hunt RM
Marine GW Marshall RM
Corporal SC Newland RM
Corporal H Siddall RM
Corporal CNH Ward RM
Sergeant JD Wassell RM

## DFM
Sergeant WC O'Brien RM

## Queen's Commendation For Brave Conduct
Marine PA Cruden RM
Petty Officer B Czarnecki Merchant Navy
Chief Marine Engineering Mechanic AF Fazackerley
Weapon Engineering Mechanic 1 JR Jesson
Petty Officer Weapon Engineering Mechanic GR Lowden
2nd Officer I Povey RFA
Chief Weapon Engineering Mechanic W Rumsey
Radio Operator 1 DF Sullivan
Marine Engineering Mechanic 1 TA Sutton
Colour Sergeant DA Watkins RM

## GBE
Admiral Sir John Fieldhouse GCB

## KBE
Vice Admiral DJ Hallifax

## CBE
Captain P Badcock
Captain NJ Barker
Captain CPO Burne
Captain RH Fox
Captain J Garnier MVO
Captain MHG Layard
Captain R MacQueen
Captain IJR Tod
Captain JP Wrigley

## OBE
Commander TA Allen
Commander LSJ Barry
Commander P Birch
Major RJ Bruce RM
Major JS Chester RM
Commander M Cudmore
Captain JV Dickinson RFA
Commander FB Goodson
Commander TL Hickson
Surgeon Commander RT Jolly
Commander CJ Esplin-Jones
Captain JS Kelly
Commander DAH Kerr
Commander ML Ladd
Captain PJ McCarthy RFA
Commander PJ McGregor
Major DJ Minords RM
Commander AW Netherclift
Captain AJ Oglesby
Captain PG Overbury RFA
Commander GS Pearson
Captain CA Purtcher-Wydenbruck RFA
Captain S Redmond RFA
Commander AS Ritchie
The Rev AM Ross
Commander RA Rowley
Commander JT Sanders
Commander RJ Sandford
Major JMG Sheridan RM
Commander DW Shrubb
Major SF Southby-Tailyour RM
Major JJ Thompson RM
Commander CW Williams
Commander GAC Woods

## MBE
Lieutenant SJ Branch-Evans
Lieutenant Commander MJD Brougham
Lieutenant Commander RV Caesley
Lieutenant RS Collins
Lieutenant AD Dummer
Lieutenant Commander CJ Edwards
Fleet Chief Radio Supervisor DJ Eggers
Lieutenant Commander R Goodenough
Lieutenant Commander M Goodman
Lieutenant Commander RW Hamilton
Captain HCF Howard RM
Lieutenant Commander GM Irvine
Lieutenant Commander PJ James RNR
Fleet Chief Writer CG Lamb
Fleet Chief Petty Officer MJ Legg
Lieutenant Commander JH Loudon
Lieutenant Commander HA Mayers
Lieutenant Commander IS McKenzie
Lieutenant Commander JM Milne
Fleet Chief Marine Engineering Artificer PW Muller
Fleet Chief Petty Officer RJ Nicholls
Lieutenant DCW O'Connell
Lieutenant Commander LD Poole
Lieutenant B Purnell
Captain MJ Sharland RM
Surgeon Lieutenant Commander PJ Shouler
Lieutenant DF Smith
Captain D Sparks RM
Lieutenant Commander JNO Williams
Lieutenant Commander DJR Wilmot-Smith

## BEM
Petty Officer Medical Assistant K Adams
Air Engineering Mechanic 1 JL Bailey
Chief Air Engineering Mechanic NR Barwick
Marine Engineering Artificer 1 TJ Bennetto
Chief Air Engineering Artificer 1 DM Childs
Master-at-Arms AF Coles

Chief Marine Engineering
Mechanic GS Cox
Chief Air Engineering Mechanic
WD Eaton
Air Engineering Artificer 1
SJ Goodall
Chief Air Engineering Artificer
DJ Heritier
Chief Petty Officer LB Hewitt
Chief Petty Officer Caterer
JA Jackson
Air Engineering Artificer 1
DE Jones
Air Engineering Artificer 1
RAJ Mason
Medical Technician 1
S McKinlay
Chief Petty Officer Cook
MG Mercer
Leading Wren Stores
Accountant J Mitton WRNS
Chief Wren Education Assistant
A Monkton WRNS
Air Engineering Assistant 2
AJ Smith
Chief Petty Officer OG Stockham
Air Engineering Artificer 1
RJE Strong
Chief Air Engineering Mechanic
1 TL Temple
Leading Wren Dental Hygienist
V. Tunis WRNS
Leading Stores Accountant
GJ Walsh
Petty Officer JJT Waterfield
Petty Officer EL Wells
Air Engineering Mechanic 1
DJ Williams
Sergeant B Winter RM

## Royal Air Force

**CB**
Air Vice Marshal GA
Chesworth OBE, DFC
Air Vice Marshal KW Hayr
CBE, AFC
**DSC**
Flight Lieutenant DHS Morgan

**DFC**
Wing Commander PI Squire
AFC
Squadron Leader RU
Langworthy AFC
Squadron Leader CN McDougall
Squadron Leader JJ Pook
Flight Lieutenant WFM
Withers

**AFC**
Wing Commander D Emmerson
Squadron Leader R Tuxford

Flight Lieutenant HC
Burgoyne
Squadron Leader AM Roberts

**QGM**
Flight Lieutenant AJ Swan
Flight Sergeant BW Jopling

**Queen's Commendation for
Brave Conduct**
Junior Technician A Thorne
Senior Aircraftsman KJ
Soppett-Moss

**Queen's Commendation for
Valuable Service in the Air**
Squadron Leader TN Allen
Squadron Leader AF Banfield
Squadron Leader GR Barrell
Flight Lieutenant ME Beer
Flight Lieutenant JA Brown
Flight Lieutenant JD
Cunningham
Flight Lieutenant JN Keable
Flight Lieutenant MM
MacLeod
Flight Lieutenant GD Rees
Flight Lieutenant RL Rowley
Flight Sergeant SE Sloan
Flight Lieutenant PA Standing
Squadron Leader MD Todd
Squadron Leader EF Wallis
MBE

**KBE**
Air Marshal Sir John Curtiss
KCB

**CBE**
Group Captain CE Evans
Group Captain AFC Hunter
Group Captain P King OBE
Group Captain JSB Price ADC

**OBE**
Wing Commander AJC Bagnall
Wing Commander DL Baugh
Wing Commander P Fry MBE
Squadron Leader BS Morris
AFC
Wing Commander JK Sim AFC
Wing Commander AP Slinger
Wing Commander CJ Sturt
Wing Commander BJ Weaver

**MBE**
Warrant Officer DP Barker
Flight Lieutenant EM Clinton
WRAF
Flight Lieutenant J Dungate
AFM
Squadron Leader CG Jefford
Squadron Leader WF Lloyd
Flight Lieutenant BT Mason
Flight Lieutenant A Neale
Squadron Leader DM Niven

Flight Lieutenant PA Room
Squadron Leader T Sitch
Master Air Loadmaster AD
Smith
Squadron Leader EJ Stokes

**BEM**
Flight Sergeant JH Bell
Sergeant JM Coleman
Flight Sergeant K Kenny
Chief Technician TJ Kinsella
Sergeant P Tuxford
Chief Technician RK Vernon
Sergeant JC Vickers
Corporal DJ Vivian

## Civil List

**Life Peer**
Admiral of the Fleet Sir Terence
Lewin GCB, MVO, DSC

**Knight Batchelor**
RM Hunt CMG

**CB**
KJ Pritchard

**CMG**
DH Anderson

**OBE**
Captain DA Ellerby
I McL Fairfield
Miss JM Hutchinson
RT Jackling
Captain DJ Scott-Masson
Captain JP Morton
NH Nicholls
EJ Risness
WB Slater
JRC Thomas

**OBE**
PD Adams
RG Algar
The Rev H Bagnall
MJ Beynon
Mrs AA Bleaney
Mrs MJ Bourne
R Butcher
DW Chalmers
Captain WJC Clarke
Captain A Fulton
RO Gates
AJ Glagsow
EJ Harvey
SS Holness
VE Horsfield
C Hulse
Miss MM Jones
D Lewis
AFC Moss
JP Raby
Captain DM Rundle

Captain MJ Slack
The Rt Rev Mgr DM Spraggon
RS Tee
P Varnish
R Watson
R Weatherburn
JA Weldon

**MBE**
Mrs VE Bennett
Mrs JH Bolto
CM Boyne
DL Breen
RA Brown
TJ Carey
ED Carr
AFC Collins
AJ Coleman
PMJ Cook
FJ Cooper
DJ Cormick
RA Drew
Miss P Durling
S Earnshaw
Miss MG Elphinstone
Miss RM Eldson
JA French
BA Gorringe
EM Goss
MJS Hatton
Miss SM Hill
GWT Hodge
W Hunter
RD Lawrence
RGJ Lloyd
D McAlpin
WR McQueen
D Monument
TR Morse
Mrs VA Mothershaw
Mrs DBM Murray
Mrs PM Nutbeem
Squadron Leader TJ Palmer
RAF (Retd)
Miss EM Patten
TJ Peck CPM
D Place
JT Price
JF Quirk
P Robinson
JRP Rodigan
KW Shackleton
MS Shears
Captain D Sims
Miss A Slaymaker
Squadron Leader JM Smith
RAF (Retd)
RL Start
Mrs A E Thorne
J Turner
PJ Watts
RS Whitley

**BEM**
AJ Aldred
M Ashworth

| | | | |
|---|---|---|---|
| G Bales | JA Goldie | P McEwan | V Steen |
| Mrs II Bardsley | LS Harris | M McKay | LK Suen |
| R? D...tt | RJ Hatch | P Miller | DV Threadgold |
| DP Betts | J ........ | ?G M...an | Miss KL Timberlake |
| RS Blanchard | J Johnston | AJG Nisbett | H T... |
| MH Boyes | JF Jones | Mrs HB Perry | FJ Tough |
| Mrs MD Buckett | B Oram-Jones | PR Peterson | Mrs E Vidal |
| T Dobbyns | BJ Joshua | RA Rabjohn | Miss BV Williams |
| EC Emery | SM Kang | DRT Rozee | CW Wilson |
| Luis Estella | GJ Lane | EW Sampson | CJ Winder |
| JS Fairfield | AJ Leonard | V Seoglautze | |
| RJ Ford | JA Lynch | DA Smerdon | |

---

## CASUALTIES

Private AJ Absolon MM, 3 Para

Petty Officer Air Engineering Mechanic MJ Adcock, HMS Glamorgan

Air Engineering Mechanic 1 AU Anslow, 845 Sqn, Atlantic Conveyor

Marine Engineering Mechanic 1 FO Armes, HMS Coventry

Able Seaman DK Armstrong, HMS Ardent

Corporal RE Armstrong, Special Air Service

Sergeant JL Arthy, Special Air Service

Warrant Officer 1 M Atkinson, Special Air Service

Staff Sergeant JI Baker, R Signals

Lieutenant Commander DI Balfour, HMS Sheffield

Lieutenant Commander RW Banfield, HMS Ardent

Able Seaman AR Barr, HMS Ardent

Lieutenant JA Barry, 2 Para

Lieutenant Commander GWJ Batt DSC, 800 Sqn, HMS Hermes

Corporal WJ Begley, Special Air Service

Lance Corporal G Bingley MM, 2 Para

Able Seaman IM Boldy, HMS Argonaut

Petty Officer Marine Engineering Mechanic DR Briggs DSM, HMS Sheffield

Petty Officer Engineering Mechanic P Brouard, HMS Ardent

Private G Bull, 3 Para

Lance Corporal BC Bullers, Army Catering Corps

Sergeant PA Bunker, Special Air Service

Lance Corporal A Burke, Welsh Gds

Doreen Burns, Falkland Islands civilian

Corporal RA Burns, Special Air Service

Private SJ Burt, 3 Para

Chief Weapons Engineering Artificer JDL Caddy, HMS Coventry

Marine PD Callan, 45 Commando

Marine Engineering Artificer 1 PB Callus, HMS Coventry

Lance Sergeant JR Carlyle, Welsh Gds

Petty Officer Aircrewman KS Casey, 846 Sqn, HMS Hermes

Electrical Fitter Leung Chau, RFA Sir Galahad

Bosun Yu Sik Chee, RFA Sir Tristram

Lance Corporal SJ Cockton, Army Air Corps

Private AM Connett, Army Catering Corps

Catering Assistant D Cope, HMS Sheffield

Lance Corporal A Cork, 2 Para

Private JD Crow, 3 Para

Sergeant PP Currass, Special Air Service

Lieutenant WA Curtis, 801 Sqn, HMS Invincible

Guardsman IA Dale, Welsh Gds

Sergeant SAI Davidson, Special Air Service

Marine C Davison, Commando Logistic Regiment

Petty Officer Catering Accountant S Dawson, HMS Coventry

Guardsman DJ Denholm, Scots Gds

Captain C Dent, 2 Para

Private SJ Dixon, 2 Para

Bosun JB Dobson, Atlantic Conveyor

Weapons Engineering Mechanic 1 JR Dobson, HMS Coventry

Private MS Dodsworth, 3 Para

Cook RJS Dunkerley, HMS Ardent

Guardsman MJ Dunphy, Welsh Gds

Cook B Easton, HMS Glamorgan

Guardsman P Edwards, Welsh Gds

Weapons Engineering Artificer 1 AC Eggington, HMS Sheffield

Sergeant C Elley, Welsh Gds

Sub Lieutenant C Emly, HMS Sheffield

Sergeant R Enefer RM, 45 Commando

Sergeant AP Evans RM, 3 Commando Brigade Air Squadron

Corporal K Evans RM, 45 Commando

Lieutenant Commander JE Eyton-Jones, 801 Sqn, HMS Invincible

Petty Officer Cook R Fagan, HMS Sheffield

Butcher Sung Yuk Fai, RFA Sir Galahad

Lance Corporal IR Farrell, RAMC

Colour Sergeant GPM Findlay, 2 Para

Corporal PR Fitton, 45 Commando

Chief Petty Officer Writer E Flanagan, Atlantic Conveyor

Private MW Fletcher, 2 Para

Leading Cook MP Foote, HMS Ardent

Marine Engineering Mechanic 1 SH Ford, HMS Ardent

Major ML Forge, R Signals

Mechanic F Foulkes, Atlantic Conveyor

Petty Officer MG Fowler, HMS Coventry

Lieutenant RD Francis RM, 3 Commando Brigade Air Sqadron

Warrant Officer 2 L Gallagher, Special Air Service

Sapper PK Ghandi RE, 59 Indep Cdo Sqn RE

Guardsman M Gibby, Welsh Gds

Lance Corporal BP Giffin RM, 3 Commando Brigade Air Squadron

Cook NA Goodall, HMS Sheffield

Mary Goodwin, Falkland Islands civilian

Guardsman GC Grace, Welsh Gds

Guardsman P Green, Welsh Gds

Private AD Greenwood, 3 Para

Staff Sergeant CA Griffin, Army Air Corps

Marine RD Griffin, HMS Fearless

Guardsman GM Griffiths, Welsh Gds

Private N Grose, 3 Para

3rd Engineering Officer CF Hailwood, RFA Sir Galahad

Weapons Engineering Mechanic 1 IP Hall, HMS Coventry

Captain GJ Hamilton MC, Special Air Service

Steward S Hanson, HMS Ardent

Corporal D Hardman, 2 Para

Sergeant WC Hatton, Special Air Service

Steward DRS Hawkins, Atlantic Conveyor

Flight Lieutenant RG Hawkins, Royal Air Force

Able Seaman SK Hayward, HMS Ardent

Lieutenant RR Heath, HMS Coventry

Private PJ Hedicker, 3 Para

Air Engineering Mechanic 1 M Henderson, HMS Glamorgan

2nd Engineering Officer PA Henry GM, RFA Sir Galahad

Able Seaman S Heyes, HMS Ardent

Lance Corporal PD Higgs, 3 Para

Air Engineering Mechanic 1 BP Hinge, HMS Glamorgan

Private M Holman-Smith, 2 Para

Radio Officer R Hoole RFA, Atlantic Conveyor

Corporal S Hope, 3 Para

Guardsman DN Hughes, Welsh Gds

Mechanic J Hughes, Atlantic Conveyor

Sergeant WJ Hughes, Special Air Service

Sergeant IN Hunt RM, Special Boat Squadron

Private S Illingworth DCM, 2 Para

Marine Engineering Artificer AS James, HMS Fearless

Guardsman B Jasper, Welsh Gds

Private TR Jenkins, 3 Para

Colour Sergeant BR Johnston QGM, RM, HMS Fearless

Sergeant B Jones, Special Air Service

Private MA Jones, Army Catering Corps

Sapper CA Jones RE, 59 Indep Cdo Sqn RE

Private CE Jones, 3 Para

Lieutenant Colonel H Jones VC, OBE, 2 Para

Seaman Yeung Swi Kami, RFA Sir Tristram

Guardsman A Keeble, Welsh Gds

Lance Sergeant K Keoghane

Lai Chi Keung, HMS Sheffield

Leading Marine Engineering Mechanic AJ Knowles, HMS Sheffield

Laundryman Kyo Ben Kwo, HMS Coventry

Private SI Laing, 3 Para

Weapons Engineering Mechanic 1 SJ Lawson, HMS Ardent

Chief Air Engineering Mechanician D Lee, HMS Glamorgan

Sergeant RA Leeming RM, 45 Commando

Marine Engineering Mechanic 2 AR Leighton, HMS Ardent

Lance Corporal PN Lightfoot, Special Air Service

Corporal MD Love DSM, RM, 846 Sqn, HMS Hermes

Lance Corporal CK Lovett, 3 Para

Marine SG MacAndrews, 40 Commando

Air Engineering Mechanician 1 A McAuley, HMS Ardent

Air Engineering Artificer 2 KI McCallum, HMS Glamorgan

Corporal KJ McCarthy, 3 Para

Corporal DF McCormack, R Signals

Corporal MV McHugh, Special Air Service

Corporal AG McIlvenny RE, 9 Para Sqn

Sergeant IJ McKay VC, 3 Para

Marine PB McKay, 45 Commando

Corporal SPF McLaughlin, 3 Para

Marine CG MacPherson, 45 Commando

Cook BG Malcolm, HMS Glamorgan

Guardsman D Malcomson, Scots Gds

Guardsman MJ Marks, Welsh Gds

Leading Cook T Marshall, HMS Sheffield

Private T Mechan, 2 Para

Corporal M Melia RE, 59 Indep Cdo Sqn RE

Private RW Middlewick, Army Catering Corps

Leading Marine Engineering Mechanic D Miller, HMS Fearless

Lance Sergeant C Mitchell, Scots Gds

Guardsman C Mordecai, Welsh Gds

3rd Engineering Officer AJ Morris, RFA Sir Galahad

Leading Seaman MS Mullen, HMS Ardent

Lance Corporal JH Murdoch, 3 Para

Lieutenant B Murphy, HMS Ardent

Leading Physical Training Instructor GT Nelson, HMS Ardent

Lance Corporal SJ Newbury, Welsh Gds

Corporal J Newton, Special Air Service

Guardsman GD Nicholson, Welsh Gds

Petty Officer Weapons Engineering Mechanic AR Norman, HMS Sheffield

Captain (Ship's Master) IH North DSC, Atlantic Conveyor

Marine MJ Nowak, 45 Commando

Lieutenant RJ Nunn DFC RM, 3 Commando Brigade Air Squadron

Major R Nutbeem, RAMC

Staff Sergeant P O'Connor, Special Air Service

Cook DE Osborne, HMS Sheffield

Weapons Engineering Mechanic 1 DJA Ozbirn, HMS Coventry

Petty Officer Weapons Engineering Mechanic AK Palmer, HMS Ardent

Private DA Parr, 2 Para

Guardsman CC Parsons, Welsh Gds

Lance Corporal JB Pashley RE, 9 Para Sqn

Marine Engineering Mechanic 2 TW Perkins, HMS Glamorgan

Guardsman EJ Phillips, Welsh Gds

Marine K Phillips, 45 Commando

Guardsman GW Poole, Welsh Gds

Seaman Ng Por, Atlantic Conveyor

Staff Sergeant J Prescott CGM RE, 49 Sqn RE

Corporal SN Prior, 2 Para

Leading Air Engineering Mechanic D Pryce, 845 Sqn, Atlantic Conveyor

Guardsman JBC Reynolds DCM, Scots Gds

Cook JR Roberts, HMS Ardent

Lieutenant Commander GS Robinson-Moltke, HMS Coventry

Craftsman MW Rollins, REME

Sergeant RJ Rotherham RM, HMS Fearless

Guardsman NA Rowberry, Welsh Gds

Marine AJ Rundle, HMS Fearless

Leading Cook M Sambles, HMS Glamorgan

Lance Corporal DE Scott, 3 Para

Private IP Scrivens, 3 Para

Lieutenant Commander JH Sephton DSC, HMS Ardent

Craftsman A Shaw REME, 3 Para

Seaman Chan Chi Shing, Atlantic Conveyor

Leading Cook AE Sillence, HMS Glamorgan

Sergeant J Simeon, Scots Gds

Private F Slough, 2 Para

Corporal J Smith RM, 42 Commando

Lance Corporal NR Smith, 2 Para

Corporal IF Spencer RM, 45 Commando

Steward MR Stephens, HMS Antelope

Leading Radio Operator BJ Still, HMS Coventry

Guardsman AG Stirling, Scots Gds

Marine Engineering Artificer 2 GLJ Stockwell, HMS Coventry

Lance Corporal AR Streatfield, REME

Weapons Engineering Artificer 1 DA Strickland, HMS Coventry

Steward JD Stroud, HMS Glamorgan

Seaman MJ Stuart, HMS Argonaut

Weapons Electrical Artificer 1 KRF Sullivan, HMS Sheffield

Corporal PS Sullivan, 2 Para

Able Seaman AD Sutherland, HMS Coventry

Cook AC Swallow, HMS Sheffield

Lance Corporal PA Sweet, Welsh Gds

Corporal SJG Sykes, Special Air Service

Guardsman R Tanbini, Scots Gds

Sapper WD Tarbard RE, 9 Para Sqn

Lieutenant N Taylor, 800 Sqn, HMS Hermes

Lance Corporal CC Thomas, Welsh Gds

Guardsman CK Thomas, Welsh Gds

Lance Corporal NDM Thomas, Welsh Gds

Guardsman RG Thomas, Welsh Gds

Chief Weapons Mechanician M Till, HMS Sheffield

Lieutenant DHR Tinker, HMS Glamorgan

Marine Engineering Mechanic 2 S Tonkin, HMS Coventry

Cook I Turnbull, HMS Coventry

Corporal AB Uren RM, 45 Commando

Petty Officer Aircrewman CP Vickers, HMS Glamorgan

Mechanic EN Vickers, Atlantic Conveyor

Guardsman A Walker, Welsh Gds

Weapons Engineering Mechanic 2 BJ Wallis, HMS Sheffield

Corporal ET Walpole, Special

Air Service
Lance Corporal CF Ward, Welsh Gds
Corporal LG Watts RM, ~~...~~
Guardsman GF Weaver, Welsh Gds
Leading Cook AK Wellstead, HMS Sheffield
Master-at-Arms B Welsh,

HMS Sheffield
Private PA West, 3 Para
Weapons Engineering Artificer 2 PP White, HMS Coventry
~~Leading Marine Engineering~~
Mechanic SJ White, HMS Ardent
Leading Marine Engineering Mechanic G Whitford,
Warrant Officer 2 D Wight,

Scots Gds
Sergeant M Wigley, Welsh Gds
Guardsman DR Williams, Welsh Gds
~~Marine Engineering Mechanic~~ GS Williams, HMS Ardent
Weapons Engineering Artificer IR Williams, HMS Coventry
Cook KJ Williams, HMS Sheffield

Marine D Wilson, 45 Commando
Corporal S Wilson RE, 9 Para Sqn
Sue Witney, Falkland Islands Civilian
Captain DA Wood, 2 Para
Lieutenant Commander JS Woodhead DSC, HMS Sheffield

## Summary of Fatal Casualties

|  | Offrs | Men | Civs | Total |
|---|---|---|---|---|
| Royal Navy | 13 | 72 | 2 | 87 |
| Royal Marines | 2 | 24 | — | 26 |
| Army | 7 | 115 | — | 122 |
| Royal Air Force | 1 | — | — | 1 |
| Royal Fleet Auxiliary | 3 | 4 | — | 7 |
| Merchant Navy | 2 | 7 | — | 9 |
| Civilians | — | — | 3 | 3 |
| Total | 28 | 222 | 5 | 255 |

## CHRONOLOGY

**Fri 19 March** – Scrap metal merchants land at the disused whaling station at Leith and raise the Argentinian flag.

**Sun 21 March** – *Endurance* at (Port Stanley) re-embarked her flight, RM detachment and 9 ranks NP 8901 and sailed for South Georgia.

**Mon 22 March** – *Bahia Buen Suceso* departs Leith Harbour leaving behind 48 scrap metal merchants.

**Tue 23 March** – NP 8901 provide overnight security at Stanley airport.

**Wed 24 March** – *Endurance* lands Royal Marines party to watch Argentinian activities at Leith.

**Thu 25 March** – *Bahia Paraiso* lands Argentinian marines at Leith.

**Sat 27 March** – NP 8901 provide first light cover at Stanley airport.

**Mon 29 March** – New NP 8901 arrives Stanley. Junta approve final plans for invasion.

**Wed 31 March** – *Endurance* disembarks her RM detachment at Grytviken.

**Thur 1 April** – Operational command of RM Detachment passes to new NP 8901. Both detachments deploy to defensive positions around Stanley. SBS ordered to mobilise. *Splendid* departs Faslane.

**Fri 2 April** – Argentine troops invade Falklands. Governor Rex Hunt orders surrender. All troops including Governor and wife flown to Comodoro Rivadavia. UN adopt Resolution 502 ordering Argentine withdrawal. 3 Cdo Bde alerted. Task Force prepare.

**Sat 3 April** – Emergency Parliamentary sitting. Argentines overrun 22 marines at

Grytviken, South Georgia. Captured NP 8901 flown to Montevideo (Uruguay).

**Sun 4 April** – UN condemns Argentine aggression. Rear Adm Woodward transfers flag from *Antrim* to *Glamorgan*. Brig Thompson briefs COs in Plymouth. *Conqueror* departs Faslane with 6 SBS.

**Mon 5 April** – Foreign Secretary, Lord Carton resigns. Succeeded by Francis Pym. Task Force sails from Portsmouth with HQ 3 Cdo Bde and elements of 40 & 42 Cdos. Final 6 marines of NP 8901 surrender. NP 8901 arrive Brize Norton. First Nimrods reach Ascension.

**Tue 6 April** – NP 1222 arrive Ascension.

**Wed 7 April** – *Antrim*, *Plymouth* and *RFA Tidespring* refuel from Fort Austin. Reagan approves Haig peace mission.

**Thu 8 April** – *Broadsword* & *Yarmouth* sail from Gibraltar. Haig arrives UK.

**Fri 9 April** – (Good Friday.) *Canberra* sails from Portsmouth with 40 & 42 Cdos and 3 Para.

**Sat 10 April** – Antrim Group arrive Ascension. Haig arrives Buenos Aires.

**Sun 11 April** – M Coy Gp of 42 Cdo embark *Antrim* at Ascension. Group sails.

**Mon 12 April** – Britain declares 200 miles Maritime Exclusion Zone. 809 NAS formed. Haig returns to London.

**Tue 13 April** – Organisation of American States appeals to both sides.

**Wed 14 April** – *Brilliant* Group leaves Ascension. Rear Adm Woodward leaves Ascension in *Glamorgan* plus *Alacrity*, *Broadsword* and *Yarmouth*. Haig briefs Reagan in Washington.

**Thu 15 April** – Haig returns to Buenos Aires.

**Fri 16 April** – Task Force sails from Ascen-

sion. *Hermes* arrives Ascension. Adm Woodard flies to *Fearless* for talks with Comdr Clapp and Brig Thompson. *Invincible* leaves Ascension. Wideawake airfield busiest in world that day.

**Sat 17 April** – *Fearless*, *RFA Stromness* and two LSLs arrive Ascension. C-in-C Fleet (Adm Fieldhouse) and Maj Gen Moore fly to Ascension to brief Rear Admiral Woodward, Comdr Clapp, and Brig Thompson on board *Hermes*. A Coy (40 Cdo) transfer to LSL *Sir Tristram*.

**Sun 18 April** – *Hermes*, *Invincible*, *Broadsword*, *Glamorgan*, *Yarmouth*, *Alacrity* and *RFAs Olmeda* and *Resource* sail from Ascension. 6 Victor tankers arrive Ascension. *25 de Mayo* returns to port.

**Mon 19 April** – NP 8901 leave UK by air. 848 NAS formed.

**Tue 20 April** – Government gives the go-ahead for Op Paraquat. *Canberra* and *Elk* arrive Ascension. Marines captured in South Georgia and 13 members of British Antarctic Survey team arrive UK.

**Wed 21 April** – *Antrim's* Wessex recces and drops SBS and SAS on S Georgia. Sea Harrier intercepts snooping Boeing 707.

**Thu 22 April** – SAS retrieved from Fortuna Glacier. Two helicopters (Wessex) crash. Francis Pym to Washington.

**Fri 23 April** – All ships change to Zulu time Argentine submarine *Santa Fe* sunk. M Coy (42 Cdo) land on South Georgia. PO B Casey first casualty – killed in Sea King crash – 846 Sqn.

**Sat 24 April** – *Atlantic Conveyor* completes fitting of helicopter decks at Devonport.

**Sun 25 April** – *Intrepid*, *Atlantic Conveyor*, *Europic Ferry* leave UK. LSL *Sir Bedivere* arrives UK from Vancouver. Nimrods sight Rio de la Plata near Ascension. Carrier group meets up with *Sheffield* group.

**Mon 26 April** – Lt Cdr Astiz signs surrender document in South Georgia. RFA *Blue Rover* arrives Ascension. Meeting of Organisation of American States in Washington.

**Tue 27 April** – War cabinet approves Operation *Sutton*. *Norland* and *Sir Bedivere* sail from UK. Heavy gales prevent flying and replenishment in South Atlantic.

**Wed 28 April** – Britain announce Total Exclusion Zone to include aircraft and ships of all nations. SS *Uganda* arrives Ascension.

**Thu 29 April** – SS *Uganda* leaves Ascension. Maj Gen Moore files to Ascension to brief Comdr Clapp and Brig Thompson in *Fearless*.

**Fri 30 April** – Reagan declares support for Britain. Britain enforces 200 miles Total Exclusion Zone. Main Task Group reach TEZ. 2 Vulcan bombers and 11 Victor tankers take off from Ascension (Black Buck 1). 8 Sea Harriers fly to Ascension.

**Sat 1 May** – Gen Haig's peace mission fails. Maj Gen Moore appointed land deputy to C-in-C Fleet. RAF Vulcan bomber craters Stanley airport runway. Sea Harriers bomb and rocket Stanley airfield and Goose Green. Shoot down 1 Mirage and 1 Canberra. Naval bombardments of installations around Stanley airport commence. *Arrow* slightly damaged. SBS and SAS patrols landed on Falklands. *RMS Queen Elizabeth II* requisitioned.

**Sun 2 May** – *General Belgrano* sunk by submarine *Conqueror*. Russian spy trawler seen off Ascension. BAS Survey team and two lady photographers leave in *Antrim* and *RFA Tidespring* for Ascension. Francis Pym in Washington.

**Mon 3 May** – Helicopters from *Glasgow* and *Coventry* sight and sink patrol vessel *Alferez Sobral*.

**Tue 4 May** – Sea Harrier shot down over Goose Green. Black Buck 2 Vulcan attack on Stanley. *Sheffield* hit by Exocet missile.

**Wed 5 May** – 8 RAF Harriers of No. 1 Sqn arrive Ascension.

**Thu 6 May** – 2 Sea Harriers lost in fog. *Argonaut* group sail Ascension. 2 Para arrive Ascension. No 3 Wing RAF assume control in Ascension.

**Fri 7 May** – Secretary General of UN, launches peace initiative. *Norland* arrives Ascension as main body of Amphibious Task Group leave.

**Sat 8 May** – Extended TEZ enforced. First long range air drops to Task Force in South Atlantic.

**Sun 9 May** – Argentine 'spy' trawler *Narwhal* strafed by Sea Harriers, then boarded and sunk. Argentine helicopter shot down. *Sir Bedivere* leaves Ascension.

**Mon 10 May** – *Sheffield* sinks under tow.

First Nimrods of 206 Sqn RAF support Task Force. Marconi radio station established on Ascension. *Bristol* group leaves UK.

**Tue 11 May** – Argentine supply ship *Isla de los Estados* sunk by *Alacrity* in Falkland Sound. Argentine Puma shot down.

**Wed 12 May** – *QE 2* sails from Southampton with 5 Inf Bde. *Glasgow* holed by Argentine aircraft. 4 Argentine Skyhawks shot down. Sea King ditches. *Cardiff* (from Persian Gulf) leaves Gibraltar. Nimrod sights Argentine Boeing 707. *Uganda* receives first casualties. 3 Cdo Bde Operation Order for landings issued.

**Thu 13 May** – Brig Thompson holds 'O' Group in *Fearless*. 5 Minesweeping trawlers leave Ascension.

**Fri 14 May** – SAS raid Pebble Island and destroy all aircraft. 'Active Service' declared. British Ambassadors to USA and UN return to London for talks.

**Sat 15 May** – SBS land in Grantham Sound.

**Sun 16 May** – British Ambassadors return to USA.

**Wed 19 May** – Cabinet approval given for landings. Amphibious force carries out cross decking. Sea King of 846 Sqn with SAS on board crashes during cross decking.

**Thu 20 May** – Sea King from *Invincible* lands in Chile where crew surrender and are repatriated.

**Fri 21 May** – San Carlos landings by 3 Commando Brigade. Diversionary attack on Goose Green. *Ardent* sunk. 16 Argentine aircraft shot down.

**Sat 22 May** – 3 Commando Brigade established ashore with BMA at Ajax Bay.

**Sun 23 May** – *Antelope* sunk after bomb explosion. 7 Argentine aircraft shot down.

**Mon 24 May** – *Sir Lancelot*, *Sir Galahad* and *Sir Tristram* bombed in San Carlos Water. 4 Argentine aircraft shot down.

**Tue 25 May** – *Coventry* and *Atlantic Conveyor* sunk by Exocets. UN Security Council debate ends. 3 Argentine aircraft shot down.

**Wed 26 May** – 2 Para start advance on Goose Green. UN adopts Resolution 505.

**Thu 27 May** – 45 Cdo and 3 Para start yomp from San Carlos. Large SAS patrol flies to Mount Kent. *QE 2*, *Canberra* and *Norland* rendezvous in South Georgia. 5 Brigade starts cross decking.

**Fri 28 May** – 2 Para battle for Goose Green and Darwin.

**Sat 29 May** – Argentinians surrender at Goose Green. Over 1,300 prisoners taken. *Atlantic Conveyor* sinks under tow.

**Sun 30 May** – Maj Gen Moore arrives in Falklands. Argentine air attacks resumed on Task Force but Exocets missed. 2 Skyhawks shot down.

**Mon 31 May** – 42 Cdo fly forward to Mount Kent. Mountain and Arctic Warfare Cadre attack Argentine Special Forces at Top

Malo House. UN Secretary General presents new peace plan. 45 Cdo reach Teal Inlet. 3 Para reach Douglas Settlement.

**Tue 1 June** – Black Buck 5 attacks radar installations at Stanley airport. 5 Brigade begins disembarking at San Carlos. *Sir Percivale* arrives at Teal Inlet where 3 Cdo Bde forward base established. 42 & 45 Cdos and 3 Para commence patrolling programme in mountains around Stanley.

**Wed 2 June** – 2 Para fly to Bluff Cove. Surrender leaflets dropped on Stanley.

**Thu 3 June** – Black Buck 6 raid on Stanley airfield. Vulcan lands in Brazil after refuelling problems. Versailles summit opens. Reagan five point plan given to Britain.

**Sat 5 June** – Scots Guards embark for Fitzroy in *Sir Tristram*.

**Sun 6 June** – Welsh Guards embark for Fitzroy in *Fearless* but ship withheld. Scots Guards land at Fitzroy, where 5 Bde forward base established.

**Mon 7 June** – UN Secretary General announces peace plan.

**Tue 8 June** – *Sir Galahad* and *Sir Tristram* bombed at Bluff Cove. 51 killed, mostly Welsh Guards. LCU F4 sunk in Choiseul Sound – six dead. *Plymouth* damaged by UXB. 3 Argentine Skyhawks shot down. Maj Gen Moore calls O Group and finalises plans for attacks.

**Fri 11 June** – Battle for Stanley begins. 42 Cdo attack Mount Harriet; 45 Cdo, Two Sisters; 3 Para, Mount Longdon.

**Sat 12 June** – All attacks successful by dawn. *Glamorgan* hit by land based Exocet. Black Buck 7 bombing raid on Stanley installations.

**Sun 13 June** – 2 Para attack Wireless Ridge; Scots Guards, Tumbledown; 1/7 Gurkhas, Mount William.

**Mon 14 June** – All objectives taken. All Argentine forces surrender.

# SELECTED BIBLIOGRAPHY/ACKNOWLEDGEMENTS

Adams, Valerie **The Media and the Falklands Campaign** (Macmillan Press – 1986)
Arthur, Max **Above All Courage** (Sidgwick & Jackson – 1985)
Beaver, Paul **Encyclopaedia of the Modern Royal Navy** (Patrick Stevens – 1985)
Bishop, Patrick & Witherow, John **The Winter War** (Quartet Books – 1982)
Brereton, JH **A Guide to the Regiments and Corps of the British Army** (Bodley Head – 1985)
Briasco, Jesus Romero & Huertas, Salvador Mafe **Falklands, Witness of Battles** (Frederico Domenech, Spain – 1985)
Brown, David **The Royal Navy and the Falklands War** (Leo Cooper – 1987)
Burden, Rodney (with Michael Draper, Douglas Rough, Colin Smith & David Wilton) **Falklands – The Air War** (Arms & Armour – 1986)
Couhat, Jean Labayle **Combat Fleets of the World** (Arms and Armour – 1984)
Cardoso, Oscar and others **Falklands – The Secret Plot** (Preston Editions – 1987)
Dyson, Lt-Cdr Tony **HMS Hermes – 1959-84** (Maritime Books – 1984)
Ethell, Jeffrey & Price, Alfred **Air War South Atlantic** (Sidgwick & Jackson – 1983)
Foss, Christopher F **Jane's Light Armoured Tanks and Armoured Cars** (Jane's – 1984)
Freedman, Lawrence **Britain & The Falklands War** (Blackwell – 1988)
Frost, Maj-Gen John **2 Para Falklands** (Buchan & Enright – 1983)
Gunston, Bill **Modern Fighting Aircraft** (Salamander Books – 1984)
Hasting, Max & Jenkins, Simon **The Battle For The Falklands** (Michael Joseph – 1983)
Hanrahan, Brian & Fox, Robert **I Counted Them All Out and I Counted Them All Back** (BBC – 1982)
Harris, Robert **Gotcha! The Media, The Government and the Falklands Crisis** (Faber – 1983)
Hill, JR **The Royal Navy Today and Tomorrow** (Ian Allen – 1981)
Jolly, Rick **The Red and Green Life Machine** (Century Publishing – 1983)
Middlebrook, Martin **Operation Corporate** (Viking – 1985)
Miller, William & Hutchings, David F **Transatlantic Liners at War** (David & Charles – 1985)
Perkins, Roger **Operation Paraquat** (Picton Publishing – 1986)
Thompson, Julian **No Picnic** (Leo Cooper – 1986)
Tucci, Sandro **Gurkhas** (Hamish Hamilton – 1986)
Seymour, William **British Special Forces** (Sidgwick & Jackson – 1986)
Southby-Tailyour, Ewen **Falkland Islands Shores** (Conway Maritime Press – 1985)
Strawson, John **History of the SAS Regiment** (Secker & Warburg – 1984)
Underwood, Geoffrey **Our Falklands War** (Maritime Books – 1983)
Vaux, Nick **March to the South Atlantic** (Buchan & Enright – 1986)
Villar, Capt Roger **Merchant Ships at War** (Conway Maritime Press – 1984)

## Other Publications

Marshall Cavendish **The Falklands War** (14 weekly parts)
**Falklands Task Force Portfolio** (Maritime Books – 1982)
**Canberra – The Great White Whale Goes To War**
**Falklands Armoury** (Blandford – 1985)
**Battle for the Falklands (1) Land Forces (2) Naval Forces (3) Air Forces** (Osprey – 1982)
**P & O In The Falklands** (A Pictorial Record) (P & O – 1982)
**The Falklands Campaign – The Lessons** (HMSO – 1982)
**The Falklands Conflict – Sir James Capel** – US Naval Institute – 1982

## Regimental Journals of

The Guards, The Royal Marines, The Parachute Regiment, The Royal Artillery, The Royal Engineers, The RAOC, The Royal Signals, The RCT.

The author would like to thank the following who provided help during the writing of this book: Major General JHA Thompson CB, OBE (for permission to quote from 'No Picnic'), Rear Admiral JR Hill (Naval Review), Paul Beaver (Jane's Publishing), John Harding (Army Historical Branch), Colonel RA Hooper MA, Lieutenant Colonel GJ O'N Wells Cole OBE, RM, Surgeon Commander RT Jolly OBE, RN, Captain JW Edington RM, Captain QE Oates 7GR, Matthew Little (RM Museum), Captain AG Newing (The Globe & Laurel), Major HW Schofield MBE (Guards Magazine), Major DM Cuthbertson-Smith Para (Pegasus), Major JD Braisby RA (Gunner), Major JT Hancock RE (The Sapper), Lieutenant Colonel KEP Andrews MBE (The Wire), Lieutenant Colonel MHG Young (RCT Review), CE Webb (RAOC Museum) and the many participants who provided snippets of information. He would also like to acknowledge those authors listed in the bibliography for providing much background and technical information.

The publishers and researchers gratefully acknowledge the following for their help with illustrations:
W Bain: p180-181. BBC TV: p27, 87. British Aerospace: p45, 83, 84, 85, 90, 91, 99(b), 146, 147, 151(b1). Camera Press: p66, 102. Express Newspapers: p77, 104, 105, 153, 174-175. Fleet Photographic Unit: p23, 36-37, 42-43, 52-53, 60, 108, 114, 115, 119, 122, 123(b), 131, 135, 136, 137, 142, 144, 145, 146-147, 148, 149, 151(t), 151(br), 154, 156, 157, 175, 179. Imperial War Museum: p47, 55, 67, 97, 100, 106, 107, 109, 128, 172. MOD (RN & RAF): p11, 24-26, 28-35, 39-41, 49, 59, 68-69, 76-77, 81, 88, 94, 95, 111, 117, 118, 126-127, 138, 140, 141, 155, 169. Parachute Regiment: p7, 64(b), 74, 75, 108-109, 152, 161. P&O: p37, 38, 50, 51, 177. Photographers Int: p64(t). Rex Features: p13, 14, 15, 18. Royal Army Ordnance Corps: p100. Royal Marines: Front cover, p17, 19, 44, 63, 65, 99(t), 103, 120, 123(t), 125, 129, 131, 163, 164, 165, 173, 174, 178(1). Scots Guards: p70, 71, 166-167, 171. Soldier Magazine: p20, 78, 79, 93, 158, 176. Frank Spooner pictures: p12, 21, 133, 139, 178(r). Welsh Guards: p72, 73. Westland Helicopters: p89, 127.